MW01690483

DAILY PRAYER 2025

Sunday Year C ✦ Weekday Year I

A book of prayer for each day of the liturgical year

Kathryn Ball-Boruff ✦ Nora Bradbury-Hael
Ben Caduff ✦ Rebecca Calderone ✦ Kathy Coffey
Rosina B. F. Hendrickson ✦ Corinna Laughlin
Sara McGinnis Lee ✦ Christine Ondrla
Gloria Purvis ✦ Jonathan F. Sullivan

LTP

Nihil Obstat
Deacon David Keene, PHD
Chancellor
Archdiocese of Chicago
January 18, 2024

Imprimatur
Most Rev. Robert G. Casey
Vicar General
Archdiocese of Chicago
January 18, 2024

The *Nihil Obstat* and *Imprimatur* are declarations that the material is free from doctrinal or moral error, and thus is granted permission to publish in accordance with c. 827. No legal responsibility is assumed by the grant of this permission. No implication is contained herein that those who have granted the *Nihil Obstat* and *Imprimatur* agree with the content, opinions, or statements expressed.

Daily Prayer is based in part on the pattern established in *Children's Daily Prayer*, by Elizabeth McMahon Jeep. This book was edited by Danielle A. Noe. Michael E. Novak was the production editor, Anna Manhart was the designer, and Mark Hollopeter was the production artist. The reflection for December 30, 2024 is by Bernadette Gasslein. The reflection and intercessions for November 19, 2025 were written by Daniella Zsupan-Jerome.

Printed in the United States of America

ISBN: 978-1-61671-758-2

DP25

Contents

Introduction

> Rejoice always.
> Pray without ceasing.
> In all circumstances give thanks,
> for this is the will of God for you
> in Christ Jesus.
>
> *1 Thessalonians 5:16–18*

Welcome to *Daily Prayer 2025,* Sunday Year C and Weekday Year I. This well-loved prayer book provides a familiar order of prayer for each day of the liturgical year, from the First Sunday of Advent, December 1, 2024, through November 29, 2025, the final day of the liturgical year.

Selected readings from the daily Mass are provided, and the prayer texts and reflections are connected to the liturgical time, solemnities, feasts of the Lord, and the memorials of the saints.

The Order of Prayer

Daily Prayer 2025 follows a simple, and familiar, order of prayer:

- Sign of the Cross and Opening Verse
- Psalm
- Scripture Reading
- Reflection
- Intercessions
- Lord's Prayer
- Closing Prayer
- Sign of the Cross and Closing Verse

This order remains consistent for each day of the liturgical year, allowing its repetition to become part of your daily rhythm and routine.

The prayers on these pages, intimately connected to the liturgical time, will inspire and bring you to a deeper appreciation for the Word that is proclaimed and for Eucharist that is shared in the liturgical life of the Church.

Daily Prayer 2025 is organized by liturgical time, and the Psalter is located at the back of the book (beginning on page 365). Everything you need is conveniently contained in this resource. Refer to the table of contents for easy reference.

Daily Heading

Daily Prayer 2025 is easy to use. A heading is provided for each day of prayer so you will always know where you are and what you should pray. The heading includes the date and the name of the liturgical observance. Typically, optional memorials are not celebrated in *Daily Prayer 2025*; if celebrated, however, the optional memorial will be noted in the heading. The liturgical observances are those according to the norms prescribed by the Secretariat of Divine Worship.

Opening and Closing Versicle with Sign of the Cross

The order of prayer begins and ends each day with the sign of the cross and a versicle, or opening/closing verse. While saying the opening verse aloud (or quietly) make the sign of the cross. These versicles are taken from the refrains proper to the responsorial psalms from the Mass; antiphons from *The Liturgy of the Hours* and *The Roman Missal*; verses from the acclamation before the Gospel (*Lectionary for Mass*); and lines from Scripture, especially the psalms.

Psalmody

The psalms are an important part of Catholic prayer. As poetic readings from sacred Scripture, the psalms reflect upon God's saving work in various ways: praise, thanksgiving, and lamentation. The psalms in *Daily Prayer 2025* have been selected for their liturgical significance.

Reading

Each day of prayer includes a reading from the daily Mass. This enables further reflection upon the Word of God proclaimed during the Eucharistic celebration (Mass)—the source and summit of our faith. On some days, excerpts, not the full text, from the Scripture passage have been selected. It is noted when the Scripture reading is taken from the observed memorial or commons instead of the seasonal weekday.

Reflection

Each day also includes a short reflection for meditation. These reflections guide the reader to a deeper relationship with God, neighbor, and self. Often, an author may pose a question or two that can help guide your prayer throughout the day.

Intercessions

The intercessions are the prayer of the baptized who, through Christ, voice their concerns to God regarding the Church, the world, the oppressed, local needs, and other concerns. Thus, the prayers in this book connect the individual and small faith groups to the universal Church and those most in need of God's love and mercy. Although specific prayers are provided in this resource, others may be added.

The Lord's Prayer

Jesus taught us how to pray. It is fitting to follow the universal prayer with the Lord's Prayer, for it encapsulates the humility and reverence we give to our God—and neighbor—while asking for God's mercy and forgiveness.

Closing Prayer

The closing prayer follows the form of the traditional collect. This prayer "is usually addressed to God the Father, through Christ, in the Holy Spirit" (*General Instruction of the Roman Missal*, 54). Essentially, this prayer "collects" our daily prayer, the prayers found in this book, and those of our hearts and minds, those as individuals or groups, into one Trinitarian prayer, concluding with our assent of faith in the response "Amen."

Using This Book

This resource may be used by individuals, families, or prayer groups; on retreats; to begin meetings or catechetical sessions, formational and youth ministry events; or as prayer with the aged, sick, and homebound. The prayers may be used at any time during the day, and given this book's convenient size, it is easily transported to meet various prayer needs and situations.

The order of prayer may be prayed silently or, especially for groups, prayed aloud. If used for prayer gatherings, it might be helpful to designate someone to open the prayer, lead the universal prayer, begin the Lord's Prayer, and conclude the prayer. Select an additional volunteer to proclaim the reading. Allow the faithful to read the psalm together either as an entire group or divide the stanzas among the faithful with alternating recitation. When used individually you may wish to change the tense of the prayers from plural to singular.

The psalms begin on page 365. You will see page number references to the specific psalm for each day. For ease of use, you might want to look at the page number before beginning prayer, especially with groups. Mark the page with a bookmark so that you can flip easily to the page during prayer.

Feel free to adapt these prayers for specific needs—intercessions (or petitions) may be added, music may begin and conclude the service, and the psalm response to the universal prayer and the Lord's Prayer may be chanted or sung.

About the Authors

KATHRYN BALL-BORUFF is a writer and catechist who lives in South Bend, Indiana, with her husband and three children. With more than a decade of professional ministry experience, she currently serves the upper elementary children at Good Shepherd Montessori School. Her work has appeared in *Pastoral Liturgy*, *The Journal of the National Association of the Catechesis of the Good Shepherd*, and *Church Life: A Journal for the New Evangelization*. Katie holds undergraduate and graduate degrees in theology from the University of Notre Dame and has completed Catechesis of the Good Shepherd formation in Levels I, II, and III.

NORA BRADBURY-HAEL is a Catholic youth and young adult minister and the author of *The Twentysomething Handbook*. She coauthored *The Freshman Survival Guide*, has been a development editor for St. Mary's Press, and a contributing editor for BustedHalo.com. She's also written *Sunday Prayer for Teens* and *God's Word Your World*, both from LTP. Nora is active in interfaith work in her hometown of Rochester, New York.

BEN CADUFF lives in Minnesota with his wife and two children. He has master of divinity and master of arts in systematic theology degrees from Saint John's School of Theology and Seminary in Collegeville, Minnesota. He has worked in professional ministry for seventeen years and is currently the managing director of Parish Ministries at Our Lady of Lourdes Parish in Minneapolis, Minnesota.

REBECCA CALDERONE studied religion at Cornell College before continuing her education at St. John's School of Theology and Seminary where she received a master of divinity degree in 2014. Rebecca is a board-certified chaplain through the National Association of Catholic Chaplains. She works with CentraCare Health in Minnesota as the director for Catholic Mission and Spiritual Care for the St. Cloud Hospital and St. Benedict's Senior Community. Rebecca met her husband while studying at the School of Theology and they have two young children. She enjoys spending time on the lakes of Northern Minnesota and many outdoor recreational activities.

KATHY COFFEY is the author of thirteen award-winning books and many articles in Catholic periodicals. She taught for fifteen years at the University of Colorado, Denver, and Regis Jesuit University. A mother of four and grandmother of four, she lives in Denver, Colorado.

ROSINA B. F. HENDRICKSON is the training and events coordinator at Liturgy Training Publications and the coordinator of family faith formation at St. Thomas the Apostle Church in Chicago. She has served in parish and diocesan faith formation ministry in the Dioceses of Davenport, Sacramento, Dallas, and the Archdiocese of Mobile.

CORINNA LAUGHLIN is the pastoral assistant for liturgy at St. James Cathedral in Seattle, Washington, and liturgy consultant for the Archdiocese of Seattle. She has written extensively on the liturgy for many publishers and holds a doctorate in English from the University of Washington.

SARA MCGINNIS LEE is a mission integration leader in Catholic healthcare with deep respect for the sacred encounter between clinician and patient. She loves creating formation experiences for groups that inspire a sense of calling, community, and shared purpose. She and her husband have two young adult sons.

CHRISTINE ONDRLA is retired after twenty-three years as director of Religious Education at Ascension Parish, Oak Park, Illinois. She has a theology degree from Loyola University, Chicago, and a master's in religious education from Loyola's Pastoral Institute. A contributor to many pastoral resources, she is the recipient of the Excellence in Religious Education award from the NCEA. She lives in Oak Park with her husband.

GLORIA PURVIS is an author, commentator, and the host and executive producer of *The Gloria Purvis Podcast*. Through her media presence, she has been a strong Catholic voice for life issues, religious liberty, and racial justice. She has appeared in numerous media outlets and hosts *Morning Glory*, an international radio show. She is a Pastoral Fellow at the McGrath Institute for Church Life at Notre Dame University and recently received honorary doctorates in humane letters from the University of Portland and from Saint Martin's University.

JONATHAN F. SULLIVAN directs the Office of Catechesis for the Diocese of Lafayette-in-Indiana. A Kansas native, he holds an MA from Aquinas Institute of Theology. In his spare time he enjoys reading, building things, and playing tabletop games. He and his wife have ten children.

About the Artist

KIM SMOLIK, EDD, is an artist, international nonprofit executive, speaker, educator, leadership coach, and social justice advocate. She received her doctorate in education from the University of St. Thomas in Minneapolis, Minnesota. Kim has served as the chief executive of two worldwide Catholic nonprofits, Leadership Roundtable and Franciscan Mission Service, through which she has regularly contributed to national and international thought on leadership in the Catholic Church. She has extensive cross-cultural expertise, having taught high school and college in Cuba, Guatemala, Ecuador, and Mexico. She has worked in and traveled to over sixty-five countries. Kim's spiritual life and formation in the Franciscan tradition, extensive international experience, and deep love of nature are the sources of inspiration for her art.

About the Art

The cover of *Daily Prayer 2025* depicts two honeybees and a lily in full bloom. These elements of the natural world invite us to contemplate various aspects of our faith.

- Bees are integral to our lives because they pollinate the food we eat; they help sustain life and the flourishing of creation. A healthy beehive requires cooperation and sacrifice. This cooperative work helps the community flourish: honey overflows, the hive is cleaned and maintained, the young are nurtured. The bee's life is a symbol of the Christian community. We are called to cooperate with Christ's mission and one another using our gifts actively and creatively for building up the kingdom. Like bees, we diligently attend to the needs of the world, "pollinating" it with the Good News of salvation. St. John Chrysostom says bees are honored more than other animals because they labor on behalf of others, which is what the paschal mystery calls each baptized person to do as well.
- The lily is a familiar symbol, especially at Easter Time, when its sweet fragrance fills the church. Like a trumpet, it announces Christ's resurrection and the promise of new life. Lilies symbolize purity and innocence, which is why St. Joseph, the most chaste spouse, is often depicted with a lily and why this beautiful flower is a symbol for the Blessed Virgin Mary. In the Old Testament, we learn of the Lily of the Valley in Song of Songs 2:1–2, 16 and it's even the name of the tune assigned for Psalm 45, Song for a Royal Wedding.

✙ In you, I have trusted;
let me not be put to shame.

Psalm 72

page 376

Reading

Luke 21:25–28

[Jesus said to his disciples:] "There will be signs in the sun, the moon, and the stars, and on earth nations will be in dismay, perplexed by the roaring of the sea and the waves. People will die of fright in anticipation of what is coming upon the world, for the powers of the heavens will be shaken. And then they will see the Son of Man coming in a cloud with power and great glory. But when these signs begin to happen, stand erect and raise your heads because your redemption is at hand."

Reflection

Jesus rightly warns us to be on guard. He sees clearly that life is full of evil. To really live as he did requires tremendous courage, clear-sightedness, and strength. Christianity isn't all cozy potlucks, inspiring choirs, and lovely liturgies! Jesus never denies harsh reality, but he always offers hope. He knows that we'll often hit bottom, but even there he won't betray us. His love extends into the deepest pit and the worst tragedy.

Prayers

others may be added

Trusting in God's presence we offer these prayers

℟. Hear us, O God.

- That as the days grow colder, we may reach out to serve those in greater need than ourselves, we pray: ℟.
- That as we enter this season, we may have courage to turn inward and accept what we find, we pray: ℟.
- That our eyes may be open to signs around us of the coming of Christ, we pray: ℟.
- That all who have died may know the eternal light of the One who called us into being, we pray: ℟.

As we wait for the Blessed Hope,
the Christ, to return, let us pray
in the words he gave us.

Our Father . . .

Redeeming God,
you never abandon us,
and your love gives us strength
to face the challenges of this world.
Help us to trust in the journey
that is before us as we await
the coming of your Son.
Who lives and reigns for ever and ever.
Amen.

✙ In you, I have trusted;
let me not be put to shame.

Monday, December 2, 2024

✠ Behold, our Savior will come;
you need no longer fear.

Psalm 24

page 367

Reading

Matthew 8:5–11

When Jesus entered Capernaum, a centurion approached him and appealed to him, saying, "Lord, my servant is lying at home paralyzed, suffering dreadfully." He said to him, "I will come and cure him." The centurion said in reply, "Lord, I am not worthy to have you enter under my roof; only say the word and my servant will be healed. For I too am a man subject to authority, with soldiers subject to me. And I say to one, 'Go,' and he goes; and to another, 'Come here,' and he comes; and to my slave, 'Do this,' and he does it." When Jesus heard this, he was amazed and said to those following him, "Amen, I say to you, in no one in Israel have I found such faith. I say to you, many will come from the east and the west, and will recline with Abraham, Isaac, and Jacob at the banquet in the Kingdom of heaven."

Reflection

Before receiving the Eucharist, we repeat these words of the centurion: "Lord, I am not worthy." It is true that we, on our own, are not worthy to have Christ enter into our homes and our lives. It is through our response of faith that we are brought into communion with him. Each day we are challenged to open our heart to recognize him in the people we meet and the situations of our life. Through our encounters with others, we encounter the living Christ. May our lives reflect the faith of the centurion, confident that God's word has the power to heal and transform us.

Prayers

others may be added

Placing our hope in the God who hears our every need, we offer these prayers:

℟. **Healing God, hear our prayer.**

- For residents of long-term and congregate care facilities, that their needs and voices be heard, we pray: ℟.
- For wisdom and strength to heal our own inner wounds, we pray: ℟.
- For the health and safety of our local communities and the world, we pray: ℟.
- For caregivers and all who work in a helping profession, we pray: ℟.

As we wait for the Blessed Hope,
the Christ, to return, let us pray
in the words he gave us.

Our Father . . .

God of love,
you guide us as advocates to those
in need.
Give us strength to respond to
the needs of others in love.
Through Christ our Lord.
Amen.

✠ Behold, our Savior will come;
you need no longer fear.

✚ I will praise you, Lord,
among the nations.

Psalm 33

page 369

Reading

Isaiah 11:1–3

On that day, / A shoot shall sprout from the stump of Jesse, / and from his roots a bud shall blossom. / The Spirit of the LORD shall rest upon him: / a Spirit of wisdom and of understanding, / A Spirit of counsel and of strength, / a Spirit of knowledge and of fear of the LORD, / and his delight shall be the fear of the LORD. / Not by appearance shall he judge, / nor by hearsay shall he decide . . .

Reflection

In this beautiful prophecy from Isaiah, we are given a glimpse into the characteristics of the Messiah, of the one for whom we are waiting during this Advent season. The Spirit of the Lord showers wisdom, understanding, counsel, strength, knowledge, and fear of the Lord upon him. The Spirit pours these same gifts out upon us when we are baptized, and they are strengthened in us at confirmation. As we embrace these gifts in our own lives, we are aligning our hearts and minds with the Messiah, the one who has shown us the path to our Father in heaven.

Prayers

others may be added

In times of joy and suffering, we trust that our God is always with us and listening. And so we offer these prayers.

℟. Loving God, hear us.

- For strength to remain faithful to our spiritual practices, we pray: ℟.
- For all to grow in their respect for human life, we pray: ℟.
- For sound judgment and steady leadership from those who hold political office, we pray: ℟.
- For all who have died and all who are grieving the loss of a loved one, we pray: ℟.

As we wait for the Blessed Hope, the Christ, to return, let us pray in the words he gave us.

Our Father . . .

O God,
you our strength.
Be with us today as we face the realities
of a life filled with both immense
beauty and terrible injustice.
Be our source of wisdom and fill us
with your grace.
Through Christ our Lord.
Amen.

✚ I will praise you, Lord,
among the nations.

Wednesday, December 4, 2024

✤ The Lord . . . will illumine what is hidden in darkness.

Psalm 71

page 376

Reading

Isaiah 25:6–8

On this mountain the LORD of hosts / will provide for all peoples / A feast of rich food and choice wines, / juicy, rich food and pure, choice wines. / On this mountain he will destroy / the veil that veils all peoples, / The web that is woven over all nations; / he will destroy death forever. / The Lord GOD will wipe away / the tears from all faces; / The reproach of his people he will remove / from the whole earth; for the LORD has spoken.

Reflection

"On this mountain" God will provide a feast, destroy that which veils all peoples, and even conquer death itself. What is our mountain? Where do we most closely encounter God's compassion and grace in our lives? Perhaps more importantly than where, how do we prepare ourselves to come to this place? What do we need to do to ready our hearts to encounter God in this most joyous and loving way?

Prayers

others may be added

In times of difficulty, it is you, O God, to whom we turn. You nurture and guide us. Hear us now as we offer you our prayers:

℟. **Redeeming God, hear our prayer.**

- That our hearts may be open to receive the grace that is so freely offered to us, we pray: ℟.
- That children around the world may know the security of a family who loves and cares for them, we pray: ℟.
- That all peoples may be advocates for justice and help to prepare this world for the coming of Jesus, we pray: ℟.

As we wait for the Blessed Hope,
the Christ, to return, let us pray
in the words he gave us.

Our Father . . .

O God,
you offer us your love and the fullness of redemption.
Help us to follow the path that you lay out for us.
Lead us to that holy place within ourselves
where we may enjoy the celebrations of your feast
and know the joy of your salvation.
Through Christ our Lord.
Amen.

✤ The Lord . . . will illumine what is hidden in darkness.

✚ You, O Lord, are close,
and all your ways are truth.

Psalm 46

page 372

Reading

Matthew 7:21, 24–27

Jesus said to his disciples: "Not everyone who says to me, 'Lord, Lord,' will enter the Kingdom of heaven, but only the one who does the will of my Father in heaven.

"Everyone who listens to these words of mine and acts on them will be like a wise man who built his house on rock. The rain fell, the floods came, and the winds blew and buffeted the house. But it did not collapse; it had been set solidly on rock. And everyone who listens to these words of mine but does not act on them will be like a fool who built his house on sand. The rains fell, the floods came, and the winds blew and buffeted the house. And it collapsed and was completely ruined."

Reflection

Christ invites us to consider the foundation of our life and faith this day. A life (or house) built on rock is solid; one built on sand remains vulnerable and is prone to movement. Christ is our firm foundation, unchanging and solid. We are invited to hear the words of the Gospel, embrace the example of Christ, and act in love of neighbor. While this foundation does not guarantee us a life free from challenges and struggles, it offers us the tools to withstand the storms of life and remain surefooted and strong in the midst of them.

Prayers

others may be added

O God, you are the foundation that holds us firm through the storms of life. Listen now to our prayers:

℟. God our strength, hear our prayer.

- For all who are living in isolation or loneliness, we pray: ℟.
- For those who suffer from dementia and for their caregivers, we pray: ℟.
- For the wisdom always to seek God in times of difficulty, we pray: ℟.
- For those who have passed on from this world; that they may have eternal peace, we pray: ℟.

As we wait for the Blessed Hope,
the Christ, to return, let us pray
in the words he gave us.

Our Father . . .

Sustaining God,
as we continue prepare our hearts
for the coming of your Son,
be present to us.
Help us to draw strength
from the firm foundation
of our spiritual lives.
Through Christ our Lord.
Amen.

✚ You, O Lord, are close,
and all your ways are truth.

Advent Weekday

Friday, December 6, 2024

✚ Behold, the Lord will come.

Psalm 126 *page 387*

Reading *Matthew 9:27–31*

As Jesus passed by, two blind men followed him, crying out, "Son of David, have pity on us!" When he entered the house, the blind men approached him and Jesus said to them, "Do you believe that I can do this?" "Yes, Lord," they said to him. Then he touched their eyes and said, "Let it be done for you according to your faith." And their eyes were opened. Jesus warned them sternly, "See that no one knows about this." But they went out and spread word of him through all that land.

Reflection

The two blind men recognized Christ passing by and cried out to him in their moment of need. He heard their cry, healed them, and warned them not to talk about the incident. Despite that warning, they spread the message throughout the land. Like these blind men, we cry out to God in our time of need, and he responds by showering us with his grace, mercy, and love. We, too, should not keep silent about how he has transformed our lives. Take time this day to sing God's praises and proclaim his name to your family and friends for the blessings he has showered upon you.

Prayers *others may be added*

O God, you love us beyond all understanding and we trust that you know our inmost needs. Hear the prayers we offer to you:

℟. O God, hear us.

- For the Church and all who make decisions, we pray: ℟.
- For the healing of broken relationships between and within countries, we pray: ℟.
- For all who struggle with feelings of low self-worth, poor body image, or lack of self-esteem, we pray: ℟.
- For open-mindedness and understanding between groups of different race, gender, or sexual identity, we pray: ℟.

As we wait for the Blessed Hope,
the Christ, to return, let us pray
in the words he gave us.

Our Father . . .

Compassionate God,
you know us and love us.
You heal our wounds, inspire acts
of charity, and guide us on our paths.
During this season of inner reflection,
help us to know and learn from
ourselves more deeply.
Help us to understand our own dignity
and worth
as well as the dignity and worth
of those around us.
Through Christ our Lord.
Amen.

✚ Behold, the Lord will come.

✤ The Lord [fills us] with the spirit of wisdom and understanding.

Psalm 80

page 377

Reading

Isaiah 30:23–26

He will give rain for the seed / that you sow in the ground, / And the wheat that the soil produces / will be rich and abundant. / On that day your flock will be given pasture / and the lamb will graze in spacious meadows; / The oxen and the asses that till the ground / will eat silage tossed to them / with shovel and pitchfork. / Upon every high mountain and lofty hill / there will be streams of running water. / On the day of the great slaughter, / when the towers fall, / The light of the moon will be like that of the sun / and the light of the sun will be seven times greater / like the light of seven days. / On the day the LORD binds up the wounds of his people, / he will heal the bruises left by his blows.

Reflection

In the midst of their trials, God offered a promise to his people. They would have a fruitful harvest, be refreshed in streams of running water, be people of the light, and have their wounds and bruises healed. We are invited to take comfort in this promise as well. When we turn our eyes to the Lord and acknowledge his presence in our midst, he provides all that we need. Throughout this season of Advent, we wait in joyful hope and expectation for the day of the Lord's coming, when all his promises will be fulfilled, and we will walk united with him.

Prayers

others may be added

Trusting in a God who listens to our cries, we pray: ℟.

℟. Lord, hear our prayer.

- For leaders of the Church, that their hearts may be open to the needs of those they serve, we pray: ℟.
- For all who are grieving the loss of a loved one, we pray: ℟.
- For those who have lost jobs or are struggling to find employment, we pray: ℟.
- For all who are without a home, especially those in cold winter climates, we pray: ℟.

As we wait for the Blessed Hope, the Christ, to return, let us pray in the words he gave us.

Our Father . . .

O God,
your people cry out to you in times of sorrow.
Hear our prayers and answer us.
Help us to be open to the ways
that you are tending to our hearts.
Through Christ our Lord.
Amen.

✤ The Lord [fills us] with the spirit of wisdom and understanding.

✣ The Lord will make the glory of his voice heard / in the joy of your heart.

Psalm 72 *page 376*

Reading *Luke 3:3–6*

John went throughout the whole region of the Jordan, proclaiming a baptism of repentance for the forgiveness of sins, as it is written in the book of the words of the prophet Isaiah: *A voice of one crying out in the desert: / "Prepare the way of the Lord, / make straight his paths. / Every valley shall be filled / and every mountain and hill shall be made low. / The winding roads shall be made straight, / and the rough ways made smooth, / and all flesh shall see the salvation of God."*

Reflection

God's Word always comes to specific human beings in concrete situations. It's not airy, floating in the clouds. All around the world, as Advent begins, Christians undertake intensified prayer and preparation. This is how they prepare the way and make the paths straight. There is a collective power in millions turning from the culture's hype, seeking instead a way of peace, emptiness, and mystery.

Prayers *others may be added*

Let us place our trust in our God
who loves us as we pray:

℟. O God, hear our prayer.

- That our Advent journey may be filled with hope and a deeper understanding of the challenges of this world, we pray: ℟.
- That all people who live in a perpetual state of fear may feel the comfort of God's love in their hearts, we pray: ℟.
- That our political leaders may be of sound moral judgement, we pray: ℟.
- That all who have died may know eternal peace in the presence of the One who created us, we pray: ℟.

As we wait for the Blessed Hope,
the Christ, to return, let us pray
in the words he gave us.

Our Father . . .

Redeeming God,
as we await the coming of your Son
into this world,
we acknowledge the many fears
and pains that exist around us.
Guide us to help make a more
peaceable world
in which every human person is treated
with dignity and respect.
Through Christ our Lord.
Amen.

✣ The Lord will make the glory of his voice heard / in the joy of your heart.

✠ My God is the joy of my soul.

Psalm 96

page 380

Reading

Luke 1:26–29, 38

The angel Gabriel was sent from God to a town of Galilee called Nazareth, to a virgin betrothed to a man named Joseph, of the house of David, and the virgin's name was Mary. And coming to her, he said, "Hail, full of grace! The Lord is with you." But she was greatly troubled at what was said and pondered what sort of greeting this might be. Mary said, "Behold, I am the handmaid of the Lord. May it be done to me according to your word."

Reflection

Gabriel's greeting and Mary's response to his message are familiar words for us. We hear a version of this greeting, "The Lord be with you" throughout the Mass and respond faithfully "And with your Spirit." The Lord is always present in our midst—in our lives, our relationships, and our encounters with one another. He calls us to recognize him and to respond to him in faith. Mary's fiat, her "may it be done," serves as an example for how we are to respond when God reveals himself to us. As you listen for and recognize God's greeting for you this day, what words will you use to respond to him?

Prayers

others may be added

Joining our hearts with Mary and all the saints in heaven, we offer our prayers to God.

℟. O God, in your love, hear us.

- That all Christians may live by Mary's example of discipleship, we pray: ℟.
- That all expectant mothers and their infants may be given love, nourishment, and care, we pray: ℟.
- That all parents who have lost a child will experience God's comfort and strength, we pray: ℟.
- That all who have died may rest in the peace of God's heavenly embrace, we pray: ℟.

As we wait for the Blessed Hope, the Christ, to return, let us pray in the words he gave us.

Our Father . . .

O God,
you gave us Mary as an example
of how to be bearers of Christ's
divine light.
Give us the courage to carry
Christ's light
that it may shine forth in our world.
Through Christ our Lord.
Amen.

✠ My God is the joy of my soul.

Tuesday, December 10, 2024

✠ Behold, the Lord will come, . . . / and on that day there will be a great light.

Psalm 33 *page 369*

Reading *Isaiah 40:1–2*

Comfort, give comfort to my people, / says your God. / Speak tenderly to Jerusalem, and proclaim to her / that her service is at an end, / her guilt is expiated; / Indeed, she has received from the hand of the LORD / double for all her sins.

Reflection

Today's reading invites us to consider how God comforts his people and ministers to his people in their time of need. The prophet reminds us that the people receive not only what they need, but an overabundance of compassion and mercy. As recipients of God's grace, we are called to offer that same comfort to others. Consider those in your family, circle of friends, parish, and wider community who are hurting or in need of healing this day. What are ways that you might be able to share God's compassion and comfort with them?

Prayers *others may be added*

Trusting in the Lord, we offer to him our prayers:

℟. **Comfort, give comfort, O God, to your people.**

- For those who minister to the grieving, we pray: ℟.
- For those throughout the world who are displaced from their homes due to war, violence, or oppression, we pray: ℟.
- For those who are experiencing the pain of loss, especially during this holiday season, we pray: ℟.

As we wait for the Blessed Hope,
the Christ, to return, let us pray
in the words he gave us.

Our Father . . .

Sustaining God,
you console your people
and give comfort to those in need.
Help us to be compassionate to others
and to live by Christian example.
Through Christ our Lord.
Amen.

✠ Behold, the Lord will come, . . . / and on that day there will be a great light.

✣ The Lord will come
and he will not delay.

Psalm 71 *page 376*

Reading *Isaiah 40:25–31*

To whom can you liken me as an equal? / says the Holy One. / Lift up your eyes on high / and see who has created these things: / He leads out their army and numbers them, / calling them all by name. / By his great might and the strength of his power / not one of them is missing! / Why, O Jacob, do you say, / and declare, O Israel, / "My way is hidden from the LORD, / and my right is disregarded by my God"? / Do you not know / or have you not heard? / The LORD is the eternal God, / creator of the ends of the earth. / He does not faint nor grow weary, / and his knowledge is beyond scrutiny. / He gives strength to the fainting; / for the weak he makes vigor abound. / Though young men faint and grow weary, / and youths stagger and fall, / They that hope in the LORD will renew their strength, / they will soar as with eagles' wings; / They will run and not grow weary, / walk and not grow faint.

Reflection

We are filled with joyful hope this day through the words of the prophet. God knows our name and calls us by it. Although there is none equal to God, he does not place himself above us or hide himself from us. Rather, he is right here with us, integrally present in our daily activities. As the eternal God, creator and sustainer of all creation, he never grows tired or weary, even when we cry out to him for strength and courage. When we are tired and weary, he strengthens us so that we may be renewed to proclaim his praise and glorify his name.

Prayers *others may be added*

Placing our hope in God, who gives strength to those in need, we pray:

℟. **Renew us with your love, O God.**

- That the Church may always be a place of hope and renewal for those in need, we pray: ℟.
- That world leaders will have the wisdom and strength to guide their people with peace, we pray: ℟.
- That those who need shelter from the cold or inclement weather will find the warmth and hospitality they need, we pray: ℟.
- That those who are nearing the end of life may find comfort and hope in what is to come, we pray: ℟.

As we wait for the Blessed Hope,
the Christ, to return, let us pray
in the words he gave us.

Our Father . . .

God of hope,
you renew us with hope.
Help us to place our trust in you
and draw from your endless strength
in times of need.
Through Christ our Lord.
Amen.

✣ The Lord will come
and he will not delay.

Feast of Our Lady of Guadalupe
Thursday, December 12, 2024

✣ A great sign appeared in the sky,
a woman clothed with the sun.

Psalm 96

page 380

Reading

Luke 1:39–45

Mary set out and traveled to the hill country in haste to a town of Judah, where she entered the house of Zechariah and greeted Elizabeth. When Elizabeth heard Mary's greeting, the infant leaped in her womb, and Elizabeth, filled with the Holy Spirit, cried out in a loud voice and said, "Most blessed are you among women, and blessed is the fruit of your womb. And how does this happen to me, that the mother of my Lord should come to me? For at the moment the sound of your greeting reached my ears, the infant in my womb leaped for joy. Blessed are you who believed that what was spoken to you by the Lord would be fulfilled."

Reflection

Mary, having learned of Elizabeth's condition, not only traveled to visit her, but did so in haste. While Luke is silent about Mary's reasons for visiting Elizabeth, we can glean from this account the importance of visiting and caring for our relatives and those who are in need. When we learn about the joys or sorrows of another, how do we respond? Like Mary, we are invited to go in haste to be with them. "Going" might look different today than it did for Mary, with technology spanning great distances. Consider how you might "go in haste" this day to someone in your life who needs a visit.

Prayers

others may be added

With humility, we offer to God
our prayers:

℟. **Open our hearts, O God.**

- May the Church open her doors to those who have been marginalized or forgotten, we pray: ℟.
- May all peoples work to build a more peaceful and inclusive world, we pray: ℟.
- May nations reconcile acts of hatred and oppression shown toward native peoples, we pray: ℟.
- May we have the courage to bring Christ's message of love to the people we encounter every day, we pray: ℟.

As we wait for the Blessed Hope,
the Christ, to return, let us pray
in the words he gave us.

Our Father . . .

O God,
open the hearts of your Church
and teach us to be a more loving people,
that we may go in haste
to those in our communities who need our presence.
Through Christ our Lord.
Amen.

✣ A great sign appeared in the sky,
a woman clothed with the sun.

✤ Give us a new heart, O Lord.

Psalm 126

page 387

Reading

Isaiah 48:17–19

Thus says the LORD, your redeemer, / the Holy One of Israel: / I, the LORD, your God, / teach you what is for your good, / and lead you on the way you should go. / If you would hearken to my commandments, / your prosperity would be like a river, / and your vindication like the waves of the sea; / Your descendants would be like the sand, / and those born of your stock like its grains, / Their name never cut off / or blotted out from my presence.

Reflection

Isaiah proclaims the invitation to follow the Lord and the blessings that will be ours if we do so. While these promises were first given to the Israelites, they hold true for us today. The Lord teaches, guides, and leads us in the right path; all that he offers is for our good. When we follow his commands, we are granted prosperity and vindication. What powerful words these are for us as we come to understand that our God loves us and wants us to succeed. Take a moment to reflect on how you are recognizing and following God in the events of your day.

Prayers

others may be added

Trusting that God will hear us,
we pray:

℟. Loving God, hear our prayer.

- For an increase in vocations to lay ecclesial ministries, the deaconate, priesthood, and religious orders, we pray: ℟.
- For refugees around the world, especially children who have been separated from their parents, we pray: ℟.
- For those who experience times of spiritual darkness and struggle to know God's love, we pray: ℟.
- For all who have died and all who are grieving the loss of a loved one, we pray: ℟.

As we wait for the Blessed Hope,
the Christ, to return, let us pray
in the words he gave us.

Our Father . . .

Redeeming God,
you promise our prosperity
to be like a river
if only we listen to your commands
and follow in the path that you lay out
for us.
Give us wisdom to know your will
and strength to stay true to you.
Through Christ our Lord.
Amen.

✤ Give us a new heart, O Lord.

Memorial of St. John of the Cross,
Priest and Doctor of the Church
Saturday, December 14, 2024

✣ May I never boast, / except in the cross of our Lord Jesus Christ.

Psalm 80

page 377

Reading

Sirach 48:1–4, 9–11

In those days, / like a fire there appeared the prophet Elijah / whose words were as a flaming furnace. / Their staff of bread he shattered, / in his zeal he reduced them to straits; / By the Lord's word he shut up the heavens / and three times brought down fire. / How awesome are you, Elijah, in your wondrous deeds! / Whose glory is equal to yours? / You were taken aloft in a whirlwind of fire, / in a chariot with fiery horses. / You were destined, it is written, in time to come / to put an end to wrath before the day of the LORD, / To turn back the hearts of fathers toward their sons, / and to re-establish the tribes of Jacob. / Blessed is he who shall have seen you / and who falls asleep in your friendship.

Reflection

This recounting of Elijah's life invites us to reflect on how following God when he calls and doing his will offers great rewards. Through his actions and words, Elijah helped the Israelites recognize the presence of God in their midst and overcome challenges to their faith. He spoke the Word of God and called down fire from heaven. While our words may not be powerful enough to light a blaze, when we speak God's truth, people will listen and turn their hearts toward him. What words has God given you to share this day?

Prayers

others may be added

Summoning the strength to call out to God, we offer our prayers:

℟. **Hear us, O God.**

- That all voices of the Church may be heard and respected, we pray: ℟.
- That people in all areas of the world have access to the healthcare services they need, we pray: ℟.
- That as Christian people we might find the strength to speak out against all forms of oppression, we pray: ℟.
- That all who have died may find peace in the eternal embrace of our heavenly Father, we pray: ℟.

As we wait for the Blessed Hope, the Christ, to return, let us pray in the words he gave us.

Our Father . . .

O God,
you sent the prophets to reveal
your word
so that we may be filled with the fire
of your love.
Guide us so that we too may speak
your truth
in a way that inspires others to justice.
Through Christ our Lord.
Amen.

✣ May I never boast, / except in the cross of our Lord Jesus Christ.

✤ Rejoice in the Lord always.

Psalm 72
page 376

Reading
Luke 3:15–18

[T]he people were filled with expectation, and all were asking in their hearts whether John might be the Christ. John answered them all, saying, "I am baptizing you with water, but one mightier than I is coming. I am not worthy to loosen the thongs of his sandals. He will baptize you with the Holy Spirit and fire. His winnowing fan is in his hand to clear his threshing floor and to gather the wheat into his barn, but the chaff he will burn with unquenchable fire." Exhorting them in many other ways, he preached good news to the people.

Reflection

As we continue to wait in anticipation for Christ's coming, we are like the people who asked whether John was the Messiah. We are drawn to the people who reveal Christ to us, for in them we recognize his presence. In his words and actions, John preached Good News and pointed the way to the one who was yet to come. John understood his role in helping people prepare their hearts for the Messiah. Like John, we are called to be prophets pointing the way to Christ. As you reflect this day, consider how you might be John-like, allowing your words and actions to lead others to Christ's love.

Prayers
others may be added

Putting the needs of others into the forefront of our hearts, we turn to God with our prayers:

℟. O God, hear our prayer.

- That our Church may be a place of warmth and hospitality for those in need, we pray: ℟.
- That war-torn countries may find wisdom in their negotiations toward peace, we pray: ℟.
- That we may give of our excess to those who are in need, we pray: ℟.
- That our local governments will prioritize the needs of the most vulnerable, impoverished, and needy, we pray: ℟.

As we wait for the Blessed Hope, the Christ, to return, let us pray in the words he gave us.

Our Father . . .

Compassionate God,
you call us to be good stewards
  of our resources
and to show love and compassion
  to our neighbors.
Help us to open our eyes to the needs
  of others
and give us strength to sacrifice for
  the greater good of our communities.
Through Christ our Lord.
Amen.

✤ Rejoice in the Lord always.

Advent Weekday

Monday, December 16, 2024

✣ Behold, our Savior will come;
you need no longer fear.

Psalm 24 *page 367*

Reading *Matthew 21:23–27*

When Jesus had come into the temple area, the chief priests and the elders of the people approached him as he was teaching and said, "By what authority are you doing these things? And who gave you this authority?" Jesus said to them in reply, "I shall ask you one question, and if you answer it for me, then I shall tell you by what authority I do these things. Where was John's baptism from? Was it of heavenly or of human origin?" They discussed this among themselves and said, "If we say 'Of heavenly origin,' he will say to us, 'Then why did you not believe him?' But if we say, 'Of human origin,' we fear the crowd, for they all regard John as a prophet." So they said to Jesus in reply, "We do not know." He himself said to them, "Neither shall I tell you by what authority I do these things."

Reflection

Jesus rarely directly answered any question that was put before him. Rather, he turned the tables and invited the questioner to become the respondent. As we pause to ponder our own heart this day, we are invited to consider why it is that we follow Christ. There are no easy answers and sometimes the best answer is the one the chief priests and elders gave, "we do not know." This answer allows for the movement and working of the Holy Spirit and acknowledges that there are some aspects of faith that can and should remain a mystery.

Prayers *others may be added*

In humility, we bring our prayers
before a God who loves us:

℟. Teach us your ways, O God.

- For the Church, may we learn more than we teach, we pray: ℟.
- For the world, may we give more than we take, we pray: ℟.
- For the oppressed, may we heal more than we harm, we pray: ℟.
- For those we encounter through daily life, may we humble ourselves more than we judge, we pray: ℟.

As we wait for the Blessed Hope,
the Christ, to return, let us pray
in the words he gave us.

Our Father . . .

God our wisdom and strength,
we thank you for the many ways
that you reveal yourself to us each day.
May we never lose sight of the great
mystery that is our faith
and remain open to how we might be
transformed anew.
Through Christ our Lord.
Amen.

✣ Behold, our Savior will come;
you need no longer fear.

✤ Our Lord will come to show mercy to the poor.

Psalm 33 *page 369*

Reading *Genesis 49:2, 8–10*

Jacob called his sons and said to them: / "Assemble and listen, sons of Jacob, / listen to Israel, your father.

"You, Judah, shall your brothers praise /—your hand on the neck of your enemies; / the sons of your father shall bow down to you. / Judah, like a lion's whelp, / you have grown up on prey, my son. / He crouches like a lion recumbent, / the king of beasts—who would dare rouse him? / The scepter shall never depart from Judah, / or the mace from between his legs, / While tribute is brought to him, / and he receives the people's homage."

Reflection

At the heart of today's reading is the invitation for us to stop and pause, to assemble and listen. Jacob instructed Judah that he was to receive the gifts that were given to him. When our days are filled with activities, responsibilities, and choices it may seem that there is no time to pause and listen for the voice of the Lord. When we do so, though, we are filled with grace, as well as the strength to accomplish all that is before us. Take a few moments to ponder the God who invites you into his presence and allow him to speak to your heart.

Prayers *others may be added*

In hope and anticipation for what is to come, we offer to God our prayers:

℟. **God, in your wisdom,
hear our prayer.**

- Direct our religious leaders to lead with humility and curiosity, we pray: ℟.
- Prosper efforts to make food, clean water, and necessary resources available to all people, we pray: ℟.
- Give peace of mind and security to those who have suffered from the trauma of an abusive relationship, we pray: ℟.
- Lead those who are dying and their loved ones into a place of hope and acceptance, we pray: ℟.

As we wait for the Blessed Hope,
the Christ, to return, let us pray
in the words he gave us.

Our Father . . .

O God,
our hearts are filled with longing
for your coming.
Be with us as we journey through
these days of waiting.
Give us patience and strength.
Help us to keep our minds and hearts
oriented toward the day of your coming.
Through Christ our Lord.
Amen.

✤ Our Lord will come to show mercy to the poor.

Wednesday, December 18, 2024

✤ Christ our King is coming.

Psalm 71

page 376

Reading

Matthew 1:18–21

Now this is how the birth of Jesus Christ came about. When his mother Mary was betrothed to Joseph, but before they lived together, she was found with child through the Holy Spirit. Joseph her husband, since he was a righteous man, yet unwilling to expose her to shame, decided to divorce her quietly. Such was his intention when, behold, the angel of the Lord appeared to him in a dream and said, "Joseph, son of David, do not be afraid to take Mary your wife into your home. For it is through the Holy Spirit that this child has been conceived in her. She will bear a son and you are to name him Jesus, because he will save his people from their sins."

Reflection

Joseph was a faithful and righteous man who wanted to do what was right and proper. He made a decision without knowing all the facts. When the angel of the Lord appeared to him and revealed how God was at work, Joseph heeded the message. When we are in a situation where we are asked to make a decision, we are challenged to acknowledge that God may be at work in ways we cannot fathom. We should open our minds to all aspects, as well as pause and place our need and decision before God, asking for his guidance and wisdom, so that we might act in accordance with his will for us and for others.

Prayers

others may be added

Placing our trust in God,
we offer our prayers:

℟. God of all ages, hear our prayer.

- For an increase in vocations
  to lay ministry, religious life,
  and priesthood, we pray: ℟.
- For the advancement of medical
  research in the development of
  vaccines and the curing of diseases,
  we pray: ℟.
- For those who are homeless and
  for an improvement in social services,
  we pray: ℟.
- For those who live in nursing facilities
  and senior housing and for their
  caretakers, we pray: ℟.

As we wait for the Blessed Hope,
the Christ, to return, let us pray
in the words he gave us.

Our Father . . .

God of Israel,
you have shown your presence
throughout the ages
and assured us of your love
and saving power.
In these days of preparation,
may our hearts grow continuously
more ready
to receive your ultimate gift.
Through Christ our Lord.
Amen.

✤ Christ our King is coming.

✤ He who is to come will come
and will not delay.

Psalm 46 *page 372*

Reading *Luke 1:13–17*

But the angel said to him, “Do not be afraid, Zechariah, because your prayer has been heard. Your wife Elizabeth will bear you a son, and you shall name him John. And you will have joy and gladness, and many will rejoice at his birth, for he will be great in the sight of the Lord. He will drink neither wine nor strong drink. He will be filled with the Holy Spirit even from his mother’s womb, and he will turn many of the children of Israel to the Lord their God. He will go before him in the spirit and power of Elijah to turn the hearts of fathers toward children and the disobedient to the understanding of the righteous, to prepare a people fit for the Lord.”

Reflection

The foundation is being laid in today’s reading for an understanding of the significance of John the Baptist and God’s plan for salvation. The Gospel writer, Luke, has provided connections to the prophesies of the Old Testament. In doing so, Luke reminds us of the importance of the one who comes before the Messiah; the one who readies the way by preparing the hearts of the people. As we sit with today’s message, may John’s prophetic spirit transform our own hearts as we prepare to receive our Lord.

Prayers *others may be added*

In trust and anticipation, we pray: ℟.

℟. Redeeming God, hear our prayer.

- That the Church might embody John’s evangelizing spirit, preparing hearts to receive Christ, we pray: ℟.
- That refugees, migrants, and all who have had to flee their homes may find safety and shelter, we pray: ℟.
- That those who are transitioning toward less independence may find acceptance and the help they need, we pray: ℟.
- That all who have died may know the eternal peace and comfort of God, we pray: ℟.

As we wait for the Blessed Hope,
the Christ, to return, let us pray
in the words he gave us.

Our Father . . .

Saving God,
as we continue to prepare our hearts
for the coming of your Son,
guide us, inspire us,
and give us strength.
May all of our actions reflect the love
we have for you
so that we might inspire others toward
a more faith-filled life.
Through Christ our Lord.
Amen.

✤ He who is to come will come
and will not delay.

Friday, December 20, 2024

✚ The glory of the Lord will fill
the whole earth / and all flesh
will see the salvation of God.

Psalm 126 *page 387*

Reading *Isaiah 7:10–14*

The LORD spoke to Ahaz: Ask for a sign from the LORD, your God; let it be deep as the nether world, or high as the sky! But Ahaz answered, "I will not ask! I will not tempt the LORD!" Then Isaiah said: Listen, O house of David! Is it not enough for you to weary men, must you also weary my God? Therefore the Lord himself will give you this sign: the virgin shall conceive and bear a son, and shall name him Emmanuel.

Reflection

Even though the Lord encouraged Ahaz to ask for a sign, Ahaz hesitated and refused to ask, calling it an occasion to tempt the Lord. This sign, though, was to be freely given to the people so that they might come to believe more deeply. In our own lives, we may also hesitate to question God or ask him to show us his power and might. Yet, our God is a God of love who desires his people to know, love, and serve him. We must ask for what we need in quiet and gentle faith, recognizing that our God will reveal himself to us, as he answers our prayers and guides us to life with him.

Prayers *others may be added*

Let us turn to the God who loves us and offer our prayers:

℟. **Come to us and hear us, O God.**

- That those in positions of decision-making within the Church might remain open to the needs of her people, we pray: ℟.
- That advancements in science and environmentalism might lead to policies and practices that better care for our earth, we pray: ℟.
- That our systems will better support families who struggle to put food on their tables, we pray: ℟.
- That our minds might be opened to more fully to understand the significance of Christ's birth, we pray: ℟.

As we wait for the Blessed Hope,
the Christ, to return, let us pray
in the words he gave us.

Our Father . . .

O God,
you hold the keys to
the eternal kingdom.
We wait joyfully for your coming.
Be present to us in this time of waiting.
Give us wisdom, strength, and courage
to face each new day.
May we rejoice in the gift of your love
and presence.
Through Christ our Lord.
Amen.

✚ The glory of the Lord will fill
the whole earth / and all flesh
will see the salvation of God.

✣ The Lord and Ruler will be
coming soon.

Psalm 80

page 377

Reading

Luke 1:39–45

Mary set out in those days and traveled to the hill country in haste to a town of Judah, where she entered the house of Zechariah and greeted Elizabeth. When Elizabeth heard Mary's greeting, the infant leaped in her womb, and Elizabeth, filled with the Holy Spirit, cried out in a loud voice and said, "Most blessed are you among women, and blessed is the fruit of your womb. And how does this happen to me, that the mother of my Lord should come to me? For at the moment the sound of your greeting reached my ears, the infant in my womb leaped for joy. Blessed are you who believed that what was spoken to you by the Lord would be fulfilled."

Reflection

Today we hear of the first encounter between Jesus and John the Baptist. Elizabeth, carrying John in her womb, is filled with joy as she expresses her excitement that, "the mother of [the] Lord" has come to her. Immediately she acknowledges the significance of Mary's decision to listen to what the angel had said to her and to carry out this prophetic birth. How might we find ways to express such a deep level of excitement and gratitude for what Mary's yes brought forth in God's plan of salvation?

Prayers

others may be added

In joyful anticipation and gratitude,
we offer to God our prayers:

℟. Hear us, O God.

- For a broader vision of what it means to be Church as many places smaller congregations, we pray: ℟.
- For justice to be served in crimes of war and against humanity, we pray: ℟.
- For those living in abusive or harmful relationships, that they might find resources and safety, we pray: ℟.
- For expecting mothers, that they have the care and support they need, we pray: ℟.

As we wait for the Blessed Hope,
the Christ, to return, let us pray
in the words he gave us.

Our Father . . .

O Radiant Dawn,
we await your coming in
joyful anticipation.
Fill our hearts with the Spirit
of your love,
that as we continue to prepare
for your coming
we might remain focused on building
your kingdom in the here and now.
Who live and reign for ever and ever.
Amen.

✣ The Lord and Ruler will be
coming soon.

Sunday, December 22, 2024

✚ Let the earth be opened
and bring forth a Savior.

Psalm 72 *page 376*

Reading *Luke 1:39–45*

Mary set out and traveled to the hill country in haste to a town of Judah, where she entered the house of Zechariah and greeted Elizabeth. When Elizabeth heard Mary's greeting, the infant leaped in her womb, and Elizabeth, filled with the Holy Spirit, cried out in a loud voice and said, "Blessed are you among women, and blessed is the fruit of your womb. And how does this happen to me, that the mother of my Lord should come to me? For at the moment the sound of your greeting reached my ears, the infant in my womb leaped for joy. Blessed are you who believed that what was spoken to you by the Lord would be fulfilled."

Reflection

What does it mean to do the will of God? This is the question that is posed for us in our reading today. To do God's will, we must first know it and know him. We accomplish this by looking to Christ as our example and model. He offered his own life as a sacrifice, in obedience to the will of the Father. We are called, therefore, to follow Christ, to serve in faithfulness and mercy, and to know the Father. As we do so, we recognize that sacrifices are not what God desires, but hearts, minds, and voices raised in service to our neighbors.

Prayers *others may be added*

In hope we offer to God our prayers:

℟. O King of all nations, hear us.

- For an increase in vocations
  in the Church, we pray: ℟.
- For a renewed dedication to protecting the earth and all our natural resources, we pray: ℟.
- For those who lack secure and comfortable housing, we pray: ℟.
- For local governments and leaders, that human dignity may be at the forefront of their decision making, we pray: ℟.

As we wait for the Blessed Hope,
the Christ, to return, let us pray
in the words he gave us.

Our Father . . .

O King of Nations,
you formed us and gave us life.
Hear us as we offer our prayers to you
and guide us as we strive to live a life
of Christian discipleship.
We continue to joyfully wait
for your coming
and trust in your eternal love.
Through Christ our Lord.
Amen.

✚ Let the earth be opened
and bring forth a Savior.

✚ A child shall be born for us, / and
he will be called God, the Almighty.

Psalm 24

page 367

Reading

Luke 1:57–66

When the time arrived for Elizabeth to have her child she gave birth to a son. Her neighbors and relatives heard that the Lord had shown his great mercy toward her, and they rejoiced with her. When they came on the eighth day to circumcise the child, they were going to call him Zechariah after his father, but his mother said in reply, "No. He will be called John." But they answered her, "There is no one among your relatives who has this name." So they made signs, asking his father what he wished him to be called. He asked for a tablet and wrote, "John is his name," and all were amazed.

Reflection

Elizabeth and Zechariah's neighbors and relatives could not understand why they were naming their son John as it did not follow the established cultural and traditional patterns. Yet Elizabeth and John were following what God had asked them to do. Following God is often countercultural and requires us to be steadfast in faith. Rather than embracing the busyness of society, we are encouraged this day to take a few moments to be present to God, listening for and heeding his voice. What must be accomplished so that we can pause to wait in joyful hope for Christ's coming?

Prayers

others may be added

In hope and gladness we offer
our prayers to our loving God:

℟. **Emmanuel, hear our prayer.**

- For parish ministers and volunteers as they prepare for the coming Christmas celebrations, we pray: ℟.
- For peace around the world, especially in these coming days, we pray: ℟.
- For those without a home or place to be during this holiday season, we pray: ℟.
- For all women who are laboring and for those who provide them care, we pray: ℟.

As we wait for the Blessed Hope,
the Christ, to return, let us pray
in the words he gave us.

Our Father . . .

O Emmanuel,
we know that you are here:
in our past, our present,
and in all that is to come.
Pour out your Spirit of love
on your faithful people
and lead us into truth and light.
Through Christ our Lord.
Amen.

✚ A child shall be born for us, / and
he will be called God, the Almighty.

Tuesday, December 24, 2024

✠ Behold, when the fullness of time had come, God sent his Son into the world.

Psalm 33 *page 369*

Reading *Luke 1:67, 73–79*

Zechariah his father, filled with the Holy Spirit, prophesied, saying: . . . / "This was the oath he swore to our father Abraham: / to set us free from the hand of our enemies, / free to worship him without fear, / holy and righteous in his sight all the days of our life. / You, my child, shall be called the prophet of the Most High, / for you will go before the Lord to prepare his way, / to give his people knowledge of salvation / by the forgiveness of their sins. / In the tender compassion of our God / the dawn from on high shall break upon us, / to shine on those who dwell in darkness and the shadow of death, / and to guide our feet into the way of peace."

Reflection

It's hard to be alone at Christmas. If you are, remember: you are so infinitely precious to God that Jesus became human—and would have done it for you alone. Gather in grateful prayer all who have ever loved you, including the deceased. They make up a fine company; savor the memories. Then do something kind for yourself today. Old Zechariah, in today's Gospel, had failed to appreciate the grace of the angel's announcement: his wife, also elderly, would indeed bear a son. Today, however, he is redeemed, and sings a beautiful canticle to our merciful God.

Prayers *others may be added*

We turn our hearts toward the dawn of eternal light as we lift up our prayers to God:

℟. **Eternal God, hear our prayer.**

- That those who serve the Church may be beacons of Christ's light to all who live in darkness, we pray: ℟.
- That people around the world will open their hearts to the needs of those around them, we pray: ℟.
- That we may seek ways to end gun violence, we pray: ℟.
- That all who have died may experience eternal peace in Christ, we pray: ℟.

As we wait for the Blessed Hope,
the Christ, to return, let us pray
in the words he gave us.

Our Father . . .

O God,
who has been our help in ages past,
we know that you have been with us
through all of history
and continue to be present to us today
and for all days to come.
Fill our hearts
and help us to rise tomorrow with
the dawn of your eternal light.
Through Christ our Lord.
Amen.

✠ Behold, when the fullness of time had come, God sent his Son into the world.

✚ Today true peace has come down to us from heaven.

Psalm 96 *page 380*

Reading *John 1:1–5, 9–10*

In the beginning was the Word, / and the Word was with God, / and the Word was God. / He was in the beginning with God. / All things came to be through him, / and without him nothing came to be. / What came to be / through him was life, / and this life was the light of the human race; / the light shines in the darkness, / and the darkness has not overcome it. / The true light, which enlightens everyone, was coming into the world. / He was in the world, / and the world came to be through him, / but the world did not know him. / He came to what was his own, / but his own people did not accept him.

Reflection

The true light has come into the world! This is the light that we have been anticipating, and yet the Gospel makes it clear that the light has been present since the very beginning of time. Today we celebrate the ultimate revelation of that which has been gradually shown to us through Advent. Let our hearts rejoice while we open ourselves to the truth of this divine reality, which has always been there and will continue through all of eternity.

Prayers *others may be added*

With joyful hearts, we offer these prayers:

℟. Christ our light, hear our prayer.

That the Church will open her doors this Christmas to all people, especially those who have become estranged, we pray: ℟.

That the light of Christ will find its way into the darkest corners of our world, we pray: ℟.

That we may all open our hearts to the needs of others, we pray: ℟.

That all who are mourning the loss of a loved one will be graced by God's comforting presence, we pray: ℟.

Let us offer together the prayer that Emmanuel, our God-with-us, gave us.

Our Father . . .

Eternal God,
you demonstrated the strength
of your love
through the gift of your Son
becoming human.
Fill our world with light and truth.
We praise you and we thank you!
Lead us onward in this
Christian journey,
as we commit ourselves to being
Christ's light for all to see.
Who lives and reigns for ever and ever.
Amen.

✚ Today true peace has come down to us from heaven.

Feast of St. Stephen, The First Martyr

Thursday, December 26, 2024

✚ Stephen . . . was found to be first among the number of the martyrs.

Psalm 111

page 384

Reading

Matthew 10:17–22

Jesus said to his disciples: "Beware of men, for they will hand you over to courts and scourge you in their synagogues, and you will be led before governors and kings for my sake as a witness before them and the pagans. When they hand you over, do not worry about how you are to speak or what you are to say. You will be given at that moment what you are to say. For it will not be you who speak but the Spirit of your Father speaking through you. Brother will hand over brother to death, and the father his child; children will rise up against parents and have them put to death. You will be hated by all because of my name, but whoever endures to the end will be saved."

Reflection

Here we are the day after Christmas still in celebration mode, and the readings and feast shift to martyrdom and handing loved ones over to death. Yet in the shadow of death, Jesus encourages us not to be afraid to speak—to be the voice for the voiceless. As we hold onto the news of the messianic birth, may we not shy away from proclaiming that joy to the ends of the earth. May we be a sign of hope for all peoples.

Prayers

others may be added

Placing our faith in God,
we offer these prayers:

℟. **Redeeming God, hear our prayer.**

- For the Church, that she may use her voice to spread the Good News, we pray: ℟.
- For an end to human trafficking and the treatment of people as commodities, we pray: ℟.
- For people who do not have the presence of families to support them through both difficult and celebratory times, we pray: ℟.
- For couples who are yearning to conceive a child, we pray: ℟.

Let us offer together the prayer that Emmanuel, our God-with-us, gave us.

Our Father . . .

God our wisdom and strength,
your Spirit guides us,
if only we open our hearts
to know your will.
Give us the words to speak your truth
and the courage to use our voices
to spread the joyous news
of your Son's birth.
Who lives and reigns for ever and ever.
Amen.

✚ Stephen . . . was found to be first among the number of the martyrs.

✤ The Lord filled [John] with the spirit of wisdom and understanding.

Psalm 100

page 382

Reading

1 John 1:1–4

Beloved: What was from the beginning, what we have heard, what we have seen with our eyes, what we looked upon and touched with our hands concerns the Word of life—for the life was made visible; we have seen it and testify to it and proclaim to you the eternal life that was with the Father and was made visible to us—what we have seen and heard we proclaim now to you, so that you too may have fellowship with us; for our fellowship is with the Father and with his Son, Jesus Christ. We are writing this so that our joy may be complete.

Reflection

John's perspective on salvation history brings us back to the beginning of time. His poetic and visual descriptions tell us how God created the universe and came as the true light into the world, overcoming all darkness. At Christmas we honor that light and yet, in the Northern Hemisphere, we are only just past the shortest day and our world still appears dark. It is our task then, as we celebrate this season, to be the world's Christ-light presence.

Prayers

others may be added

Christ, our light and salvation,
hear us as we offer you these prayers:

℟. Fill us with your light, O God.

- For deepening ecumenical relations and dialogue, we pray: ℟.
- For a greater love and appreciation for all of our world's natural resources, we pray: ℟.
- For an increase in respect for the culture and history of our indigenous populations, we pray: ℟.
- For those who live in our own home communities and do not feel safe or welcome, we pray: ℟.

Let us offer together the prayer that Emmanuel, our God-with-us, gave us.

Our Father . . .

God of all ages,
you came into this world so that there might be light.
Help us to discover within ourselves the place where that light resides
and may we have the strength and courage to carry that light
into the darkest corners of this world.
Through Christ our Lord.
Amen.

✤ The Lord filled [John] with the spirit of wisdom and understanding.

Saturday, December 28, 2024

✠ The innocents were slaughtered
as infants for Christ.

Psalm 91

page 379

Reading

Matthew 2:13–15a, 16–18

[T]he angel of the Lord appeared to Joseph . . . and said, "Rise, take the child and his mother, flee to Egypt, and stay there until I tell you." . . . Joseph rose and took the child and his mother by night and departed for Egypt. He stayed there until the death of Herod . . .

When Herod realized that he had been deceived by the magi, he became furious. He ordered the massacre of all the boys in Bethlehem and its vicinity two years old and under, in accordance with the time he had ascertained from the magi. Then was fulfilled what had been said through Jeremiah the prophet: / *"A voice was heard in Ramah, / sobbing and loud lamentation; / Rachel weeping for her children, / and she would not be consoled, / since they were no more."*

Reflection

The Feast of the Holy Innocents follows so quickly after Christmas that it stands in stark contrast to the celebrations that we might expect. In today's Gospel, we hear the tragic story of the innocent children who were executed at King Herod's command in his anger about being deceived. There is much discomfort in a reading like this, yet the dichotomy of suffering and death alongside light and birth mirrors our journey through the Triduum. These stories of martyrdom that we hear during the Octave of the Nativity of the Lord remind us to not lose sight of the paschal mystery—the wood of the cradle leads to the wood of the cross.

Prayers

others may be added

We bring our prayers before
a God who loves us.

℟. **In your compassion,**
hear our prayer.

- Inspire those in parish leadership to find creative ways to reach out to those on the margins, we pray: ℟.
- Make known the needs of the most vulnerable to world leaders and government officials, we pray: ℟.
- Fill the hearts of all people with hospitality and love for those in greater need than themselves, we pray: ℟.
- Give peace to and ease the suffering of those grieving the loss of a loved one, we pray: ℟.

Let us offer together the prayer that Emmanuel, our God-with-us, gave us.

Our Father . . .

Loving God,
we thank you for the gift of your Son.
Help us to hold the tension in this world
where abundant beauty and deep
suffering coexist.
May we always remember that life and
resurrection will ultimately reign.
Through Christ our Lord.
Amen.

✠ The innocents were slaughtered
as infants for Christ.

✠ The Lord is my light
and my salvation.

Psalm 96

page 380

Reading

Luke 2:43–51

After three days [Jesus' parents] found him in the temple, sitting in the midst of the teachers, listening to them and asking them questions, and all who heard him were astounded at his understanding and his answers. When his parents saw him, they were astonished, and his mother said to him, "Son, why have you done this to us? Your father and I have been looking for you with great anxiety." And he said to them, "Why were you looking for me? Did you not know that I must be in my Father's house?" But they did not understand what he said to them. He went down with them and came to Nazareth, and was obedient to them; and his mother kept all these things in her heart.

Reflection

When my son was a year and a half, I learned the hard way that he had taught himself how to open exterior doors, and one day he let himself out. He couldn't have been gone long, but he was fast. We searched for him and found him near a pond. The three minutes that he was missing is nothing compared to the three days that Mary and Joseph searched for Jesus. However, desperate searching is a reminder that God seeks far more than we seek God. As we celebrate the Holy Family today, may we allow ourselves to be sought out and discovered by a God who loves us beyond understanding.

Prayers

others may be added

We offer our prayers to a God
who knows our inmost hearts.

℟. God our Father, hear our prayer.

- For a Church that hears and responds to the needs of all families, we pray: ℟.
- For families who have been separated by war or deportation, we pray: ℟.
- For parents who are waiting in the adoption process, we pray: ℟.
- For children who do not have proper nutrition or go to bed hungry, we pray: ℟.

Let us offer together the prayer that Emmanuel, our God-with-us, gave us.

Our Father . . .

Loving God,
you search us and know us.
Your love has surrounded us
since we were in our mother's womb.
Help us to respond with respect
and care to our own families,
living by the model given to us
by the Holy Family.
Through Christ our Lord.
Amen.

✠ The Lord is my light
and my salvation.

Sixth Day within the Octave of the Nativity of the Lord

Monday, December 30, 2024

✤ Your all-powerful Word, O Lord,
bounded from heaven's royal throne.

Psalm 111

page 384

Reading

Luke 2:36–40

There was a prophetess, Anna, the daughter of Phanuel, of the tribe of Asher. She was advanced in years, having lived seven years with her husband after her marriage, and then as a widow until she was eighty-four. She never left the temple, but worshiped night and day with fasting and prayer. And coming forward at that very time, she gave thanks to God and spoke about the child to all who were awaiting the redemption of Jerusalem.

When they had fulfilled all the prescriptions of the law of the Lord, they returned to Galilee, to their own town of Nazareth. The child grew and became strong, filled with wisdom; and the favor of God was upon him.

Reflection

You can sense the eagerness of both Anna and those who "await the redemption of Jerusalem." They wait, trusting that God will hear their prayers. Imagine being so attuned to God's Spirit that you can recognize the presence of God in this tiny child. Imagine being so convinced that you proclaim it to those who wait for such good news. Do I really expect to meet God in the flesh—in unexpected people and places?

Prayers

others may be added

We turn to God as we offer
these prayers:

**℟. In your loving mercy,
hear our prayer.**

- That, inspired by practices of prayer and fasting, all may be moved to proclaim God's truth, we pray: ℟.
- That all children, regardless of gender or economic status, may receive a good education, we pray: ℟.
- That all who have experienced adverse childhood events or trauma will have the support they need in their healing, we pray: ℟.
- That all who have died will know the eternal peace of God, we pray: ℟.

Let us offer together the prayer that Emmanuel, our God-with-us, gave us.

Our Father . . .

God of Wisdom and Spirit of Truth,
you have inspired prophets throughout
the ages.
Open our hearts to a fuller
understanding of your presence
in this world.
Open our minds and our lips
to proclaim our faith.
Through Christ our Lord.
Amen.

✤ Your all-powerful Word, O Lord,
bounded from heaven's royal throne.

✤ A child is born for us,
and a son is given to us.

Psalm 148

page 390

Reading

John 1:1–5, 14

In the beginning was the Word, / and the Word was with God, / and the Word was God. / He was in the beginning with God. / All things came to be through him, / and without him nothing came to be. / What came to be through him was life, / and this life was the light of the human race; / the light shines in the darkness, / and the darkness has not overcome it. . . .

And the Word became flesh / and made his dwelling among us, / and we saw his glory, / the glory as of the Father's only-begotten Son, / full of grace and truth.

Reflection

We receive light, truth, and grace from Christ. As we prepare ourselves for the beginning of a new year, what better way to ready our hearts than to remind ourselves of these gifts and to reflect on how we might open ourselves to embodying them. We are called to be filled with God's grace, walk in Christ's light, and proclaim the truth that he gives us. On this threshold of the calendar year, how might we continue to live this Christmas message? How might be allow ourselves to become transformed so that we might not live in darkness but live in the light and lead others to this same light?

Prayers

others may be added

Turning our hearts towards Christ's light, we offer our prayers:

℟. Lead us to your truth, O God.

✦ Invigorate the Church's advocacy of justice for the poor, the vulnerable, and the voiceless, we pray: ℟.

✦ Prosper efforts for peaceful dialogue among leaders of nations, we pray: ℟.

✦ Strengthen the resolve of those recovering from addiction, we pray: ℟.

✦ Comfort those who are mourning the loss of a loved one, we pray: ℟.

Let us offer together the prayer that Emmanuel, our God-with-us, gave us.

Our Father . . .

Eternal God,
you sent your Son into the world
that we might receive his light, truth,
and grace.
Open our hearts
so that we might walk this earth as
beacons of that light for all to see.
Through Christ our Lord.
Amen.

✤ A child is born for us,
and a son is given to us.

✠ Hail, Holy Mother, who gave birth to the King.

Psalm 98 *page 381*

Reading *Luke 2:16–21*

The shepherds went in haste to Bethlehem and found Mary and Joseph, and the infant lying in the manger. When they saw this, they made known the message that had been told them about this child. All who heard it were amazed by what had been told them by the shepherds. And Mary kept all these things, reflecting on them in her heart. Then the shepherds returned, glorifying and praising God for all they had heard and seen, just as it had been told to them.

When eight days were completed for his circumcision, he was named Jesus, the name given him by the angel before he was conceived in the womb.

Reflection

For any new parent, those first days of an infant's life are precious, and it's no different for Mary. Having a baby is a blessing unto itself, and that blessing is multiplied by the love that is poured out by those who come to welcome him or her into the world. Like Mary, may we hold in our hearts the joy and enthusiasm people had for Jesus. May we allow this encounter to inspire and guide us.

Prayers *others may be added*

Trusting in God's love we offer these prayers:

℟. God of all ages, hear our prayer.

- For a Church that proclaims the Good News with the same energy and joy as the shepherds, we pray: ℟.
- For all women and girls to have accessible education, we pray: ℟.
- For new mothers who are struggling with postpartum depression or lack the feelings of joy they expected, we pray: ℟.
- For women and men who long to celebrate the birth of their own child but struggle to conceive, we pray: ℟.

Let us offer together the prayer that Emmanuel, our God-with-us, gave us.

Our Father . . .

Loving God,
at the birth of your Son,
you filled the world with awe and joy.
Gift us with that same joy,
so that in celebrating his birth
we may inspire others in faith and love.
Through Christ our Lord.
Amen.

✠ Hail, Holy Mother, who gave birth to the King.

✠ Let the peoples recount the wisdom of the saints.

Psalm 104

page 383

Reading

John 1:19–23

This is the testimony of John. When the Jews from Jerusalem sent priests and Levites to him to ask him, "Who are you?" he admitted and did not deny it, but admitted, "I am not the Christ." So they asked him, "What are you, then? Are you Elijah?" And he said, "I am not." "Are you the Prophet?" He answered, "No." So they said to him, "Who are you, so we can give an answer to those who sent us? What do you have to say for yourself?" He said: / "I am the *voice of one crying out in the desert,* / *'Make straight the way of the Lord,'* / as Isaiah the prophet said."

Reflection

The two saints honored today were born in the same area, Cappadocia, in the same year, 330, and both studied in Athens. Later, both became bishops. Gregory wrote of his friend: "We became everything to each other . . . We seemed to be two bodies with a single spirit . . . Our great pursuit, the great name we wanted, was to be Christians." How do you live out your Christian discipleship? How do you extend the light of Christ to others?

Prayers

others may be added

Faithful God, your love endures forever. And so, in confidence we pray:

℟. God, in your wisdom, hear us.

- That the work of your Church may bear the fruit of love and justice in the world, we pray: ℟.
- That leaders of nations may take action to bring peace to our world, we pray: ℟.
- That all who are ill or dying may have the medical support they need and deserve, we pray: ℟.
- That children, teachers, and staff in schools may be safe from gun violence, we pray: ℟.

Let us offer together the prayer that Emmanuel, our God-with-us, gave us.

Our Father . . .

God of salvation,
awaken our hearts to your
divine presence.
Help us to recognize and honor
your presence
in ourselves and in one another
that all we say and do might be
for the greater glory of your name.
Through Christ our Lord.
Amen.

✠ Let the peoples recount the wisdom of the saints.

Friday, January 3, 2025

✤ Come, you nations,
and adore the Lord.

Psalm 100 *page 382*

Reading *1 John 3:1–3*

See what love the Father has bestowed on us that we may be called the children of God. Yet so we are. The reason the world does not know us is that it did not know him. Beloved, we are God's children now; what we shall be has not yet been revealed. We do know that when it is revealed we shall be like him, for we shall see him as he is. Everyone who has this hope based on him makes himself pure, as he is pure.

Reflection

It is a lifelong journey uncovering our true selves. Parents can easily recall vivid details about the birth of their children—especially the first few moments looking into their newborn's eyes. Their eyes reflect back to us so much information—their unique soul and identity as well as resemblances to the mother or father. The child is a beautiful reflection of the love the parents share. This newborn child is beloved and cherished by the new parents. But above all, the child is a reflection of God's image and the love he has for us. All of God's children are first and foremost his beloved children.

Prayers *others may be added*

We humbly come before our God, offering these prayers:

℟. Hear us, O God

- That the Church may exemplify what it means to live as witnesses to God's love, we pray: ℟.
- That all people may work toward cleaner and more sustainable practices, we pray: ℟.
- That victims of abuse may receive the care and protection they need, we pray: ℟.
- That those facing death, and their loved ones, may be comforted, we pray: ℟.

Let us offer together the prayer that Emmanuel, our God-with-us, gave us.

Our Father . . .

God of love,
you created us in your image
and likeness.
Help us to recognize your presence
within us,
a presence that continues to be revealed
to us in new and surprising ways.
Through Christ our Lord.
Amen.

✤ Come, you nations,
and adore the Lord.

✤ Behold a wise woman who has built her house.

Psalm 91

page 379

Reading

John 1:35–42

John was standing with two of his disciples, and as he watched Jesus walk by, he said, "Behold, the Lamb of God." The two disciples heard what he said and followed Jesus. Jesus turned and saw them following him and said to them, "What are you looking for?" They said to him, "Rabbi" (which translated means Teacher), "where are you staying?" He said to them, "Come, and you will see." So they went and saw where he was staying, and they stayed with him that day. It was about four in the afternoon. Andrew, the brother of Simon Peter, was one of the two who heard John and followed Jesus. He first found his own brother Simon and told him, "We have found the Messiah," which is translated Christ. Then he brought him to Jesus. Jesus looked at him and said, "You are Simon the son of John, you will be called Cephas," which is translated Peter.

Reflection

St. Elizabeth Ann Seton was the first native born North American saint. She suffered tremendous loss throughout her life yet she persevered with faith. Several of her immediate family members died when she was a child, she was widowed at a young age, and she lost children of her own. Yet in the midst of her grief Elizabeth not only remained faithful but accomplished tremendous work in the name of Christ's Church. Anyone who has the courage to love will undoubtedly experience loss and grief. How can we allow the pain of losing a loved one transform us into a deeper commitment to Christian discipleship?

Prayers

others may be added

With humble hearts, we turn to God and pray:

℟. Loving God, hear our prayer.

- For an increase in vocations
  to monastic and religious life,
  we pray: ℟.
- For strong education for girls and boys around the world, we pray: ℟.
- For victims of gun violence and those living with the trauma of violent events, we pray: ℟.
- For all who are grieving the loss of a loved one, we pray: ℟.

Let us offer together the prayer that Emmanuel, our God-with-us, gave us.

Our Father . . .

Lord Jesus,
you wept at the death of a friend,
and you understand the grief we carry
from the loss of someone we love.
Comfort us in our grief.
Give us peace
and help us to transform our pain
into action toward the building up
of your kingdom.
Through Christ our Lord.
Amen

✤ Behold a wise woman who has built her house.

✠ Behold, the Lord, the Mighty One, has come.

Psalm 96

page 380

Reading

Isaiah 60:1–4

Rise up in splendor, Jerusalem! Your light has come, / the glory of the LORD shines upon you. / See, darkness covers the earth, / and thick clouds cover the peoples; / but upon you the LORD shines, / and over you appears his glory. / Nations shall walk by your light, / and kings by your shining radiance. / Raise your eyes and look about; / they all gather and come to you: / your sons come from afar, / and your daughters in the arms of their nurses.

Reflection

During a season when sunshine is limited for North Americans, today's readings brim with light. They counter the dark paranoia of Herod, shared by his people: "He was frightened, and all Jerusalem with him." What do they dread? This baby born to poverty in an obscure village? They must sense a power they do not understand. To all appearances, Herod's wealth and power, a murderous army at his beck and call, sharply contrasts with the vulnerability of the infant Christ. Yet we know that while Herod's influence is confined to a small patch of turf, Jesus' authority is universal. By showing the Gentiles worshiping him first, Matthew stresses that Jesus comes to all people. While the foreign visitors are overjoyed, Jesus' own people, the insiders, seem hostile or unaware. What assumptions could we insiders rethink? What stars are shining in our skies?

Prayers

others may be added

In confidence we offer our prayers
to a God who loves us.

℟. **Light of the world, hear our prayer.**

- Guide our Church to trust in the light of Christ, we pray: ℟.
- Give wisdom and courage to world leaders so that their actions may work toward peace, we pray: ℟.
- Embolden people to speak up for justice for all people who live on the margins, we pray: ℟.
- Strengthen the relationships and build trust among neighbors and community members, we pray: ℟.

Let us offer together the prayer that
Emmanuel, our God-with-us, gave us.

Our Father . . .

Word-Made-Flesh,
you are the light that has conquered
the darkness.
Inspire us to give to others
in a spirit of love
and help us to trust that wherever we go
your light will guide us.
Who live and reign for ever and ever.
Amen.

✠ Behold, the Lord, the Mighty One, has come.

✚ A holy day has dawned upon us.

Psalm 111

page 384

Reading

Matthew 4:23–25

Jesus began to preach and say, "Repent, for the Kingdom of heaven is at hand." He went around all of Galilee, teaching in their synagogues, proclaiming the Gospel of the Kingdom, and curing every disease and illness among the people. His fame spread to all of Syria, and they brought to him all who were sick with various diseases and racked with pain, those who were possessed, lunatics, and paralytics, and he cured them. And great crowds from Galilee, the Decapolis, Jerusalem, and Judea, and from beyond the Jordan followed him.

Reflection

The Church celebrates the fact that the secret is out: the longed-for Messiah of the chosen people has come, not just for the Jews, but for the whole world. He is "a great light" that reaches even into the darkest places, a land "overshadowed by death," a "people who sit in darkness." In our world, there are still many lands overshadowed by death—by famine, by disease, by war, by oppression and injustice. And all around us there are people who still sit in the darkness of poverty, of depression, of chronic mental or physical illness. What can we do that the light of Christ may arise for them?

Prayers

others may be added

Trusting in the God who conquers
the darkness, we pray:

℟. **Light in our darkness,**
hear our prayer.

- For all ministers who are engaged in the work of teaching, preaching, and healing, we pray: ℟.
- For more diversity among leaders and decision makers, we pray: ℟.
- For those who are suffering from the personal darkness of depression, we pray: ℟.
- For all who have died and all who are grieving the recent loss of a loved one, we pray: ℟.

Let us offer together the prayer
that Jesus taught us.

Our Father . . .

God of all goodness,
your teachings and good works
attracted your followers
as you called them to participate
in building the Kingdom.
Help all of us to transform
our own hearts
as we learn to live out our call
as disciples of your love.
Through Christ our Lord.
Amen.

✚ A holy day has dawned upon us.

Tuesday, January 7, 2025

✤ The Lord is God and has given us light.

Psalm 148 *page 390*

Reading *Mark 6:34–44*

When Jesus saw the vast crowd, his heart was moved with pity for them, for they were like sheep without a shepherd; and he began to teach them many things. By now it was already late and his disciples approached him and said, "This is a deserted place and it is already very late. Dismiss them so that they can go to the surrounding farms and villages and buy themselves something to eat." He said to them in reply, "Give them some food yourselves." But they said to him, "Are we to buy two hundred days' wages worth of food and give it to them to eat?" He asked them, "How many loaves do you have? Go and see." And when they had found out they said, "Five loaves and two fish." So he gave orders to have them sit down in groups on the green grass. The people took their places in rows by hundreds and by fifties. Then, taking the five loaves and the two fish and looking up to heaven, he said the blessing, broke the loaves, and gave them to his disciples to set before the people; he also divided the two fish among them all. They all ate and were satisfied. And they picked up twelve wicker baskets full of fragments and what was left of the fish. Those who ate of the loaves were five thousand men.

Reflection

Quick—with which phrase in today's Gospel do you instinctively identify: "his heart was moved with pity for them," or "dismiss them"? We all want to think we're filled with compassion. But often we're annoyed by unexpected intrusions. Remember the context: Jesus invites his disciples to a quiet place to recover. They leave by boat, but, in the charming King James translation, the crowd "outwent them"—as if you escaped for a quiet retreat and discovered the world's most irritating neighbor in your room.

Prayers *others may be added*

We humble ourselves before God,
as we offer these prayers:

℟. God of Love, hear us.

- That the Church may always remain open to new ways that the Spirit is at work in our world, we pray: ℟.
- That we work together as a global community to support areas that have experienced natural disaster, we pray: ℟.
- That hearts and homes may be opened with love to those who need shelter and support, we pray: ℟.
- That those who are experiencing the loss of a loved one may know God's presence and peace, we pray: ℟.

Let us offer together the prayer that Emmanuel, our God-with-us, gave us.

Our Father . . .

Comforting God,
you teach us to love.
Open our hearts to serve you
in this world.
Through Christ our Lord.
Amen.

✤ The Lord is God and has given us light.

✤ A people who walked in darkness
has seen a great light.

Psalm 98 *page 381*

Reading *Mark 6:45–52*

After the five thousand had eaten and were satisfied, Jesus made his disciples get into the boat and precede him to the other side toward Bethsaida, while he dismissed the crowd. And when he had taken leave of them, he went off to the mountain to pray. When it was evening, the boat was far out on the sea and he was alone on shore. Then he saw that they were tossed about while rowing, for the wind was against them. About the fourth watch of the night, he came toward them walking on the sea. He meant to pass by them. But when they saw him walking on the sea, they thought it was a ghost and cried out. They had all seen him and were terrified. But at once he spoke with them, "Take courage, it is I, do not be afraid!" He got into the boat with them and the wind died down. They were completely astounded.They had not understood the incident of the loaves. On the contrary, their hearts were hardened.

Reflection

In today's Gospel, we see Jesus attending to peoples' physical needs, feeding them first. Then he knows he must dismiss the crowd and withdraw for prayer. That pattern throughout his life, alternating action and reflection, fed his ministry. But when he senses his friends' distress on the water, he comes to them. Apparently he has forgiven their exasperated "send them away." If we identified with that dismissal yesterday, Jesus must see behind it our heartbreak, illness, or fatigue. Whatever storms we face, he weathers them with us.

Prayers *others may be added*

Rejoicing in the miracle of God's presence in our lives, we pray:

℟. O God, hear us.

- Strengthen your people to be Christ's hands, feet, and compassionate presence in the world, we pray: ℟.
- Open our eyes to the beauty of this world that we may grow stronger in our conviction to protect natural resources, we pray: ℟.
- Lead us to recognize the needs of all people and give us the courage to respond, we pray: ℟.
- Broaden our views of inclusion so that all people we meet may be welcomed with hospitality and love, we pray: ℟.

Let us offer together the prayer that Emmanuel, our God-with-us, gave us.

Our Father . . .

O God,
you showed us your love
through the miracles of your Son
who fed the hungry
and calmed those in fear.
Help us to turn to you
in our own times of turmoil
and trust in your loving, and calming,
presence.
Through Christ our Lord.
Amen.

✤ A people who walked in darkness
has seen a great light.

Christmas Weekday

Thursday, January 9, 2025

✣ In the beginning and before all ages, the Word was God.

Psalm 104

page 383

Reading

Luke 4:17–22

[Jesus] unrolled the scroll and found the passage where it was written:

The Spirit of the Lord is upon me, / because he has anointed me / to bring glad tidings to the poor. / He has sent me to proclaim liberty to captives / and recovery of sight to the blind, / to let the oppressed go free, / and to proclaim a year acceptable to the Lord.

Rolling up the scroll, he handed it back to the attendant and sat down, and the eyes of all in the synagogue looked intently at him. He said to them, "Today this Scripture passage is fulfilled in your hearing." And all spoke highly of him and were amazed at the gracious words that came from his mouth.

Reflection

Jesus comes right out and tells people that he is the fulfillment of Isaiah's prophecy. The people are amazed. And yet, we know they will soon turn against him. Consider your vantage point today. We always hear and interpret the Scriptures through a post-Resurrection lens. We *know* that Jesus is the Messiah. We *believe* he is the fulfillment of Isaiah's prophecy. How does knowing the end of the story and believing in its truth affect how this Scripture is fulfilled today in *your* hearing?

Prayers

others may be added

With trust, we turn to God and pray:

℟. God of all ages, hear our prayer.

- That the Church may always be filled with awe at the revelation of God's Word, we pray: ℟.
- That communities around the world most affected by climate change will receive the necessary support, we pray: ℟.
- That those who hunger will find nourishment through the generosity of others, we pray: ℟.
- That those who live in group homes and nursing facilities will be cared for with dignity and respect, we pray: ℟.

Let us offer together the prayer that Emmanuel, our God-with-us, gave us.

Our Father . . .

O God,
we are grateful for the ways that
you have revealed—and continue
to reveal—yourself to us.
Inspire us to live devotedly your Word,
that in doing so we may be examples
of Christian love
to all whom we encounter.
Through Christ our Lord.
Amen.

✣ In the beginning and before all ages, the Word was God.

✤ A light has risen in the darkness
for the upright of heart.

Psalm 100 *page 382*

Reading *Luke 5:12–16*

It happened that there was a man full of leprosy in one of the towns where Jesus was; and when he saw Jesus, he fell prostrate, pleaded with him, and said, "Lord, if you wish, you can make me clean." Jesus stretched out his hand, touched him, and said, "I do will it. Be made clean." And the leprosy left him immediately. Then he ordered him not to tell anyone, but "Go, show yourself to the priest and offer for your cleansing what Moses prescribed; that will be proof for them." The report about him spread all the more, and great crowds assembled to listen to him and to be cured of their ailments, but he would withdraw to deserted places to pray.

Reflection

Consider today's reading through the experience of the COVID-19 pandemic. Jesus was brave when he touched the man with leprosy. Think about those who worked in health care during the pandemic! Much like the man who had been cast out by society because of disease, the patients in hospitals who suffered from COVID before the vaccine was available were isolated and cut off from their loved ones. They could not be with loved ones when intubated. They could not be with loved ones when they took their last breath. The doctors, nurses, and other healthcare staff who cared for them showed faith, not because they weren't afraid, but because they understood the sacredness of each life they treated. We may not all be called to that kind of healing work, yet all of us can show love to those who need healing.

Prayers *others may be added*

Safe in God's love we pray:

℟. O God, come to our aid.

- For the courage Church leaders need to open their doors and be a safe place for all who seek God's love, we pray: ℟.
- For refugees, immigrants, and all who have been displaced from their homes or families, we pray: ℟.
- For those who have been victim to police brutality and for greater efforts toward public safety, we pray: ℟.
- For those who serve the sick in hospitals, clinics, nursing facilities, and homes, we pray: ℟.

Let us offer together the prayer that Emmanuel, our God-with-us, gave us.

Our Father . . .

God of courage,
you inspire and guide us in all we do.
Help us to set aside our anxieties
and fear.
May we always place our trust in you
and in the belief that you will never
abandon us.
Through Christ our Lord.
Amen.

✤ A light has risen in the darkness
for the upright of heart.

Saturday, January 11, 2025

✚ God sent his Son, born of a woman,
so that we might receive adoption
as children.

Psalm 91 *page 379*

Reading *John 3:22–30*

Jesus and his disciples went into the region of Judea, where he spent some time with them baptizing. John was also baptizing in Aenon near Salim, because there was an abundance of water there, and people came to be baptized, for John had not yet been imprisoned. Now a dispute arose between the disciples of John and a Jew about ceremonial washings. So they came to John and said to him, "Rabbi, the one who was with you across the Jordan, to whom you testified, here he is baptizing and everyone is coming to him." John answered and said, "No one can receive anything except what has been given from heaven. You yourselves can testify that I said that I am not the Christ, but that I was sent before him. The one who has the bride is the bridegroom; the best man, who stands and listens for him, rejoices greatly at the bridegroom's voice. So this joy of mine has been made complete. He must increase; I must decrease."

Reflection

There was a time in my life when it was all about me. Childhood, of course, carries a sense of the world revolving around us. But I think especially of college and young adulthood as I discerned my vocation and networked. I was increasing—more education, more success, more friends. Then I joined my husband in marriage and life beautifully became *less* mine. And in becoming a mother nothing in the world mattered more than the little lives of our children. Increasing and decreasing happen naturally and are not mutually exclusive. As we *decrease* a sense of self-centered individuality, we *increase* in love by a life that has been given to us by God.

Prayers *others may be added*

Placing our trust in God, we pray:

℟. **God of love, hear our prayer.**

- That Church leaders may be resilient in service, we pray: ℟.
- That the world may grow in awareness of our interdependence on one another and treat each other and our earth with respect, we pray: ℟.
- That women, children, and all who have been the victims of human trafficking may find safety and help, we pray: ℟.
- That all who have died may know eternal peace as they rest in God's heavenly embrace, we pray: ℟.

Let us offer together the prayer that Emmanuel, our God-with-us, gave us.

Our Father . . .

Eternal God,
you are here with us in all that we do.
Help us to decrease that which distracts
us from you
so that we might increase in our love
and charity.
Through Christ our Lord.
Amen.

✚ God sent his Son, born of a woman,
so that we might receive adoption
as children

✣ After the Lord was baptized,
the heavens were opened.

Psalm 96

page 380

Reading

Luke 3:15–16, 21–22

The people were filled with expectation, and all were asking in their hearts whether John might be the Christ. John answered them all, saying, "I am baptizing you with water, but one mightier than I is coming. I am not worthy to loosen the thongs of his sandals. He will baptize you with the Holy Spirit and fire."

After all the people had been baptized and Jesus also had been baptized and was praying, heaven was opened and the Holy Spirit descended upon him in bodily form like a dove. And a voice came from heaven, "You are my beloved Son; with you I am well pleased."

Reflection

The first line of today's Gospel sets the tone: "As the people were filled with expectation . . ." Anticipation seems the necessary prelude to all that follows. John can't do it alone: his listeners must take ownership of their conversions. How many people would pay for expensive theatre or concert tickets, then ignore the performance, play computer games, check social media? When they've made a large investment in time or money, it's as though the audience stands on tiptoe as the curtain opens. Are we equally excited about God's revelations in our lives? This is not a performance designed for thousands; this is God writing our unique stories. Have we grown so used to the surprising reversals and unexpected graces that we yawn, blasé? What would make us pay attention? Be aware that Jesus is present in the ordinary. Wherever his people are, Jesus is too. Even with us. Even here. Even now.

Prayers

others may be added

In hope, we bring our payers to a God who loves us:

℟. **God of all, hear our prayer.**

- Open the hearts of your Church's members to the fullness of your existence in the world, we pray: ℟.
- Guide the hearts and minds of world leaders so that their decisions might lead to a more peaceful place to live, we pray: ℟.
- Strengthen the efforts of nonprofit organizations that work for justice and promote the dignity of all people, we pray: ℟.
- Welcome the faithful departed into your loving embrace and give comfort and peace to those who grieve, we pray: ℟.

Let us offer together the prayer that Emmanuel, our God-with-us, gave us.

Our Father . . .

O God,
may your presence give us the strength
and the wisdom that we need to face
the challenges of each new day.
Through Christ our Lord.
Amen.

✣ After the Lord was baptized,
the heavens were opened.

Monday, January 13, 2025

✚ You are the God who works wonders.

Psalm 24

page 367

Reading

Mark 1:14–20

After John had been arrested, Jesus came to Galilee proclaiming the Gospel of God: "This is the time of fulfillment. The Kingdom of God is at hand. Repent, and believe in the Gospel."

As he passed by the Sea of Galilee, he saw Simon and his brother Andrew casting their nets into the sea; they were fishermen. Jesus said to them, "Come after me, and I will make you fishers of men." Then they left their nets and followed him. He walked along a little farther and saw James, the son of Zebedee, and his brother John. They too were in a boat mending their nets. Then he called them. So they left their father Zebedee in the boat along with the hired men and followed him.

Reflection

Call and response. Consider what the future apostles were doing when they heard Jesus' call. For them it was an ordinary work day. And yet Jesus found them. Every day we continue to do our work and pursue our passion. If we remain attentive, we might hear God's call within the ordinary. These men left their nets. What is our response? Perhaps we might respond to God's call by continuing to do what we do and doing it well. How do I announce God's kingdom is at hand in the context of my daily work?

Prayers

others may be added

With a sincere heart we ask the grace to respond to your call as we pray:

℟. **Strengthen us, O God.**

- For the Church, that she may always respond to God's call and be faithful followers, we pray: ℟.
- For leaders of the world, that they may respond with justice to the needs of the people they serve, we pray: ℟.
- For those who suffer or are marginalized, that they may be the beneficiaries of God's kingdom coming into being, we pray: ℟.
- For those with whom we live and work, may they see us as God's presence and love in their midst, we pray: ℟.

Let us offer together the prayer that Jesus taught us.

Our Father . . .

Loving God,
you call us to follow you.
With Jesus as our example,
may we follow in his footsteps
to make your kingdom a reality
for all those who wait in hope.
Through Christ our Lord.
Amen

✚ You are the God who works wonders.

✤ God is my rock; I take refuge in him.

Psalm 27

page 368

Reading

Mark 1:21–28

Jesus came to Capernaum with his followers, and on the sabbath he entered the synagogue and taught. The people were astonished at his teaching, for he taught them as one having authority and not as the scribes. In their synagogue was a man with an unclean spirit; he cried out, "What have you to do with us, Jesus of Nazareth? Have you come to destroy us? I know who you are—the Holy One of God!" Jesus rebuked him and said, "Quiet! Come out of him!" The unclean spirit convulsed him and with a loud cry came out of him. All were amazed and asked one another, "What is this? A new teaching with authority. He commands even the unclean spirits and they obey him." His fame spread everywhere throughout the whole region of Galilee.

Reflection

Jesus spoke with authority. One understanding of authority is to empower someone or give approval. Jesus' words were not to exercise power over but to share with those who dared to follow him the power to join in and continue the work he was doing. To be in his presence and to hear his words was to recognize a power within oneself to do the will of God. When I look into myself, how do I best use the power given to me at baptism to continue the work of Jesus?

Prayers

others may be added

Empowered by God's words,
we pray with confidence:

℟. **Hear us, O Lord.**

- For the Church, that she may continue the teaching of Christ with authority and wisdom, we pray: ℟.
- For leaders of all countries, that they may use their authority to create a just and peaceful world, we pray: ℟.
- For those who are the victims of abuse of power by those in positions of governmental leadership; may they receive relief and a return to active citizenship, we pray: ℟.
- For places of education, health care, and opportunity; may they flourish under good leadership, we pray: ℟.

Let us offer together the prayer
that Jesus taught us.

Our Father . . .

Almighty God,
you gave your Son authority to teach,
preach and heal.
May we who seek to share in his work
be blessed with your grace, which
brings all good things to fulfillment.
Through Christ our Lord.
Amen.

✤ God is my rock; I take refuge in him.

✥ He created me, and through all eternity I shall not cease to be.

Psalm 30

page 369

Reading

Mark 1:29–31

On leaving the synagogue Jesus entered the house of Simon and Andrew with James and John. Simon's mother-in-law lay sick with a fever. They immediately told him about her. He approached, grasped her hand, and helped her up. Then the fever left her and she waited on them.

Reflection

Peter's mother-in-law, an unnamed woman, serves as a model disciple. Jesus restores her to health and immediately she rises up to serve. Despite our brokenness we too are called to serve. Then Jesus teaches us that in doing God's will and serving others we are strengthened by rest and prayer. Healing and restoration, service to others, refreshing the soul with prayer and solitude. How can I incorporate all these aspects of responding to the call of Jesus into my life?

Prayers

others may be added

O God, we rely on your healing power as we bring our broken selves before you and pray:

℟. Heal us, O God.

- For those in the Church who have not lived as models of service to others, we pray: ℟.
- For people around the world who continue to be victims of endless wars and famine, we pray: ℟.
- For those who are excluded from the services that enable them to live a healthy and fruitful life, we pray: ℟.
- For first responders who rush to the aid of those in peril and save them from injury and death, we pray: ℟

Let us offer together the prayer that Jesus taught us.

Our Father . . .

Loving God,
you heal our bodies and bring peace
  to our restless spirits.
We bring to you our brokenness
so that you may create us anew.
Refresh us with your love and strength
so that we might rise up and do
  your will.
Through Christ our Lord.
Amen.

✥ He created me, and through all eternity I shall not cease to be.

✤ You are worthy, O Lord our God.

Psalm 51
page 373

Reading
Hebrews 3:7–14

The Holy Spirit says: / *Oh, that today you would hear his voice, / "Harden not your hearts as at the rebellion / in the day of testing in the desert, / where your ancestors tested and tried me / and saw my works for forty years. / Because of this I was provoked with generations / and I said, 'They have always been of erring heart, / and they do not know my ways.' / As I swore in my wrath, / 'They shall not enter into my rest.'"* / Take care, brothers and sisters, that none of you may have an evil and unfaithful heart, so as to forsake the living God. Encourage yourselves daily while it is still "today," so that none of you may grow hardened by the deceit of sin. We have become partners of Christ if only we hold the beginning of the reality firm until the end.

Reflection
Our days begin with an idea of what we need to accomplish. Often that ideal is intruded upon by someone in need, an invitation to spend time with a friend, an unexpected suggestion that leads us to discover a more creative thought or direction. Can it be that God's voice is heard in what we might consider interruptions? In these moments we can become "partners of Christ." Christ who, to the dismay of his apostles, responded to the person in front of him, teaching them and us to address others' needs instead of ours.

Prayers
others may be added

Eager to hear God's voice, we open our ears and our hearts as we pray:

℟. **Speak to us, O God.**

- That the Church, may always be the true voice of God in the world, we pray: ℟.
- That world leaders, hearing God's voice, might respond to the needs of their people, we pray: ℟.
- May those who hear and respond to God's voice become true advocates for those who have no voice of their own, we pray: ℟.
- For the children in our community; may they feel cared for and supported when they hear the voice of someone who loves them, we pray: ℟.

Let us offer together the prayer
that Jesus taught us.

Our Father . . .

Lord Jesus,
your voice is gentle and merciful.
Help us to listen to your words
and let them lead us to do what is right
and just
for our sisters and brothers in need.
You who live and reign for ever and ever.
Amen.

✤ You are worthy, O Lord our God.

✚ The just will flourish like
the palm tree.

Psalm 34

page 370

Reading

Hebrews 4:1–5, 11

Let us be on our guard while the promise of entering into his rest remains, that none of you seem to have failed. For in fact we have received the Good News just as our ancestors did. But the word that they heard did not profit them, for they were not united in faith with those who listened. For we who believed enter into that rest, just as he has said: / *As I swore in my wrath,* / *"They shall not enter into my rest,"* / and yet his works were accomplished at the foundation of the world. For he has spoken somewhere about the seventh day in this manner, / *And God rested on the seventh day from all his works;* / and again, in the previously mentioned place, / *They shall not enter into my rest.* /

Therefore, let us strive to enter into that rest, so that no one may fall after the same example of disobedience.

Reflection

"And God rested." We often hear that we are "co-creators" with God—caring for creation, nurturing it, building upon it, using it in service to the good of others. If we are called to aid in creation then we are also called to follow the example of God's resting. The Sabbath is not just a requirement, it is essential to the continuation of God's work. Without a restored, renewed, and refreshed spirit we might not have the strength to complete our work. How can I "enter into" God's rest?

Prayers

others may be added

As a shepherd cares for his sheep,
the Lord leads us to restful waters,
as we pray:

℟. **Renew us, O Lord.**

✦ For those in the Church who work tirelessly to spread God's Word, may they be granted peaceful rest, we pray: ℟.

✦ For organizations that travel the globe to feed, clothe, and shelter those who have no country, may their numbers increase, we pray: ℟.

✦ For those who are homeless and struggle each day to find a place to rest their heads, we pray: ℟.

✦ For those who work tirelessly in order to feed their families, may they experience gratitude from them and a chance to relax with them, we pray: ℟.

Let us offer together the prayer
that Jesus taught us.

Our Father . . .

Creator God,
you have given us this beautiful world
and invite us to join you in continuing
to build it and make it holy.
Help us to know that resting in your care
and taking time to be with you in
prayer is also part of your will for us.
Through Christ our Lord.
Amen.

✚ The just will flourish like
the palm tree.

✤ Proclaim the marvels he has done.

Psalm 23

page 367

Reading

Mark 2:13–17

Jesus went out along the sea. All the crowd came to him and he taught them. As he passed by, he saw Levi, son of Alphaeus, sitting at the customs post. Jesus said to him, "Follow me." And he got up and followed Jesus. While he was at table in his house, many tax collectors and sinners sat with Jesus and his disciples; for there were many who followed him. Some scribes who were Pharisees saw that Jesus was eating with sinners and tax collectors and said to his disciples, "Why does he eat with tax collectors and sinners?" Jesus heard this and said to them, "Those who are well do not need a physician, but the sick do. I did not come to call the righteous but sinners."

Reflection

"I did not come to call the righteous but sinners." How lucky for us! It is comforting for us to consider with gratitude God's mercy toward us. But we often find ourselves standing with the Pharisees judging others to be the sinners. It is when we become self-righteous that we risk losing our own place among those who are forgiven. Today, let us see others with the eyes of Jesus and a heart that is patient and forgiving. That is when we truly respond to God's call to "Follow me."

Prayers

others may be added

Lord, in your mercy forgive us our sins. Give us your forgiving heart and understanding spirit as we pray:

℟. Forgive us, O God.

- When we have forsaken our call to holiness and turned away from you, we pray: ℟.
- When we have put our own greed and sense of self-importance in front of the needs of others, we pray: ℟.
- When we have looked the other way instead of into the face of the poor, we pray: ℟.
- When we have wasted an opportunity to participate in community activities that strengthen the ties among us, we pray: ℟.

Let us offer together the prayer
that Jesus taught us.

Our Father . . .

Forgiving God,
you do not judge us
but call us to your loving heart.
Help us to treat our neighbors
with the same openness and forgiveness
that you offer so freely to us.
Through Christ our Lord.
Amen.

✤ Proclaim the marvels he has done.

Sunday, January 19, 2025

✤ Behold the Lamb of God.

Psalm 46 *page 372*

Reading *John 2:1–8, 10*

There was a wedding at Cana in Galilee, and the mother of Jesus was there. Jesus and his disciples were also invited to the wedding. When the wine ran short, the mother of Jesus said to him, "They have no wine." And Jesus said to her, "Woman, how does your concern affect me? My hour has not yet come." His mother said to the servers, "Do whatever he tells you." Now there were six stone water jars there for Jewish ceremonial washings, each holding twenty to thirty gallons. Jesus told them, "Fill the jars with water." So they filled them to the brim. Then he told them, "Draw some out now and take it to the headwaiter." So they took it. . . . [T]he headwaiter called the bridegroom and said to him, "Everyone serves good wine first, and then when people have drunk freely, an inferior one; but you have kept the good wine until now."

Reflection

Three signs, three revelations: the Epiphany to the Magi, Jesus' baptism in the Jordan, and the Wedding at Cana. Each one invites us to experience a new insight into this person who is called "the Christ." We learn that this Messiah comes for all, that he is to be known as the Son of God and that his power will be demonstrated through many signs and wonders. But these are not the last nor the only revelations. We experience God's revelations to us even now. What has God revealed to you today?

Prayers *others may be added*

O God, you reveal yourself to us in many ways. We continue to seek you as we pray:

℟. Open our eyes, O Lord.

- That the Church may continue to help people recognize the ways in which Christ continues to reveal himself to the whole world, we pray: ℟.
- That the beauty created by artists of all kinds reveal to us the creative power of God, we pray: ℟.
- That we may begin to see and serve the needs of others as a way to reveal God's love and care through our words and actions, we pray: ℟.
- That we may see our efforts to save the earth revealed as God's promise to future generations, we pray: ℟.

Let us offer together the prayer that Jesus taught us.

Our Father . . .

Gentle Jesus,
you revealed yourself in signs
and wonders
when you walked this earth.
Continue to share yourself with us today
and help us to recognize your presence
among us.
Who live and reign for ever and ever.
Amen.

✤ Behold the Lamb of God.

✚ Whatever you do, do all for the glory of God.

Psalm 47 *page 372*

Reading *Mark 2:18–22*

The disciples of John and of the Pharisees were accustomed to fast. People came to him and objected, "Why do the disciples of John and the disciples of the Pharisees fast, but your disciples do not fast?" Jesus answered them, "Can the wedding guests fast while the bridegroom is with them? As long as they have the bridegroom with them they cannot fast. But the days will come when the bridegroom is taken away from them, and then they will fast on that day. No one sews a piece of unshrunken cloth on an old cloak. If he does, its fullness pulls away, the new from the old, and the tear gets worse. Likewise, no one pours new wine into old wineskins. Otherwise, the wine will burst the skins, and both the wine and the skins are ruined. Rather, new wine is poured into fresh wineskins."

Reflection

Can I be open to change and a new vision? Do I let my old ways limit me? Often, we become stuck in the patterns and restrictions that we have fixed for ourselves. What might we be able to accomplish if we are willing to let go of the usual, the old, and explore what is possible? Jesus challenges us and calls us to look at the world with new eyes. How can I serve others in different ways? How can I renew my prayer life? What do I see today that I might not have thought possible yesterday?

Prayers *others may be added*

O, God, ever new, ever changing,
lead us to discipleship as we pray:

℟. Renew us, O God.

- That those who lead us in the Church may always challenge us with a vision of what is possible in the future, we pray: ℟.
- That artists and musicians lead us to recognize the multiple ways that beauty can lift our spirits and change our perspectives, we pray: ℟.
- That we may come to realize that poverty and homelessness are not a given if only we have the vision to see things differently, we pray: ℟.
- That we may learn to accept and love all those whom we may see as strangers and enemies until we can call them neighbors and friends, we pray: ℟.

Let us offer together the prayer
that Jesus taught us.

Our Father . . .

O God, our loving Father,
lead us, your children, out of
our slumber
and into the light of a new day.
Help us to realize that you are a God
who always calls us forward and who
leads us in your ways.
Through Christ our Lord.
Amen.

✚ Whatever you do, do all for the glory of God.

Memorial of St. Agnes, Virgin and Martyr

Tuesday, January 21, 2025

✚ Those who live in love, live in God.

Psalm 71

page 376

Reading

Mark 2:28–38

As Jesus was passing through a field of grain on the sabbath, his disciples began to make a path while picking the heads of grain. At this the Pharisees said to him, "Look, why are they doing what is unlawful on the sabbath?" He said to them, "Have you never read what David did when he was in need and he and his companions were hungry? How he went into the house of God when Abiathar was high priest and ate the bread of offering that only the priests could lawfully eat, and shared it with his companions?" Then he said to them, "The sabbath was made for man, not man for the sabbath. That is why the Son of Man is lord even of the sabbath."

Reflection

Jesus is not afraid to challenge. And his ability to challenge stems from his deep knowledge and understanding of the Scriptures and tradition. It is important for us to become familiar with the Scriptures through reading and reflection. We must strengthen our participation in and understanding of our beautiful traditions. It is only then that we can build on that foundation and create even more meaningful ways of living out our faith. How will I advance my own faith?

Prayers

others may be added

Hearing your voice in your Word and witnessing you alive today in our traditions, we pray:

℟. **Teach us, O Lord.**

- That the Church, in sharing Scripture and teaching traditions, might lead us to live out our faith more deeply, we pray: ℟.
- That leaders of the world might learn from their history to build a more generous future for all their citizens, we pray: ℟.
- That the laws and customs we have used to treat immigrants will be replaced with more humane and compassionate ways to welcome them among us, we pray: ℟.
- That the importance of education for our young is given priority among the pressing issues of our local communities, we pray: ℟.

Let us offer together the prayer that Jesus taught us.

Our Father . . .

God of life,
help us to recognize that when
    we refuse to change,
our lives risk becoming empty.
Give us the grace and courage
to create a deeper understanding of
    our faith grounded in your Word.
Through Christ our Lord.
Amen.

✚ Those who live in love, live in God.

✤ The Lord . . . has redeemed us in his love.

Psalm 62

page 374

Reading

Mark 3:1–6

Jesus entered the synagogue. There was a man there who had a withered hand. They watched Jesus closely to see if he would cure him on the sabbath so that they might accuse him. He said to the man with the withered hand, "Come up here before us." Then he said to the Pharisees, "Is it lawful to do good on the sabbath rather than to do evil, to save life rather than to destroy it?" But they remained silent. Looking around at them with anger and grieved at their hardness of heart, Jesus said to the man, "Stretch out your hand." He stretched it out and his hand was restored. The Pharisees went out and immediately took counsel with the Herodians against him to put him to death.

Reflection

To do good rather than evil. To save life rather than destroy it. Jesus offers us the choice. It is up to us to consider Jesus' words in each of our actions. This choice is neither simple nor easy in most cases. Those who opposed Jesus' logic went out and plotted his death. We must be willing to stand firm in the face of opposition. Let us always consider how to advance life through all our actions rather than diminish it out of fear of opposition.

Prayers

others may be added

Recognizing the sanctity and beauty of every life, we pledge our commitment and pray:

℟. **Protect us, O Lord.**

- That the Church may always stand as the defender of life in all its stages, we pray: ℟.
- That people in all countries will secure the value of life from birth to death by protecting their citizens from all that would harm them, we pray: ℟.
- That the unborn, those who are disabled, those in their older years, and those challenged by mental and emotional issues may find defenders in us, we pray: ℟.
- That we may search for ways to defend our communities from violence and from those who would choose to harm life rather than enhance it, we pray: ℟.

Let us offer together the prayer that Jesus taught us.

Our Father . . .

God of life,
you breathe your spirit into each person.
May we respect the life you have
given us,
protect the lives of those around us and
work to create a more fulfilling life
for all.
Through Christ our Lord.
Amen.

✤ The Lord . . . has redeemed us in his love.

Thursday, January 23, 2025

✤ We shall find compassion and grace to help us in time of need.

Psalm 63

page 375

Reading

Mark 3:7–12

Jesus withdrew toward the sea with his disciples. A large number of people followed from Galilee and from Judea. Hearing what he was doing, a large number of people came to him also from Jerusalem, from Idumea, from beyond the Jordan, and from the neighborhood of Tyre and Sidon. He told his disciples to have a boat ready for him because of the crowd, so that they would not crush him. He had cured many and, as a result, those who had diseases were pressing upon him to touch him. And whenever unclean spirits saw him they would fall down before him and shout "You are the Son of God." He warned them sternly not to make him known.

Reflection

It seems that even Jesus gets tired. How often we feel the same. We wish we could get in a boat and float away. We do our best and it leads others to continue asking us for help. It seems the answer might be to rely on others. To ask for help ourselves enables us to create some distance and reduce stress. We must disarm ourselves of the notion that we can do it all. Jesus is recognized by his work as being the Son of God. We are not. We do best when we recognize our limitations.

Prayers

others may be added

Realizing our own limitations and admitting our need for rest, we pray:

℟. Refresh us, O God.

- In gratitude for the Church that offers us the opportunity to rest and keep holy the Lord's day, we pray: ℟.
- For countries that invite their citizens to celebrate special days that renew their spirits and strengthen their allegiances, we pray: ℟.
- For volunteers, who continue the tireless efforts of organizations that tend to the needs of others, we pray: ℟.
- For parks and beaches, for museums and displays of art that soar with beauty and help us to renew our spirits, we pray: ℟.

Let us offer together the prayer
that Jesus taught us.

Our Father . . .

Lord Jesus,
you knew what it was like to be weary.
Give us the wisdom to know that our
work is important.
Give us the energy to work,
but also the ability to say, "enough,
it is time for rest."
Help us to follow your example.
Who live and reign for ever and ever.
Amen.

✤ We shall find compassion and grace to help us in time of need.

✣ Let us love God, for he first loved us.

Psalm 67

page 375

Reading

Mark 3:13–19

Jesus went up the mountain and summoned those whom he wanted and they came to him. He appointed Twelve, whom he also named Apostles, that they might be with him and he might send them forth to preach and to have authority to drive out demons: He appointed the Twelve: Simon, whom he named Peter; James, son of Zebedee, and John the brother of James, whom he named Boanerges, that is, sons of thunder; Andrew, Philip, Bartholomew, Matthew, Thomas, James the son of Alphaeus; Thaddeus, Simon the Cananean, and Judas Iscariot who betrayed him.

Reflection

These are the workers. Yesterday we heard that Jesus was weary. This is the answer. He summoned those he trusted to work with him, to accomplish more because they were empowered by him. We should follow this example. Rather than deplete our own energy we must learn to rely on others. Who are the people you trust and rely on? Jesus' number was twelve. We might not have that many, but let us name those whom we recognize as our helpers and pray for them with gratitude.

Prayers

others may be added

Realizing that we have been given a mission and purpose, and grateful for those who have been our faithful helpers and friends, we pray:

℟. **Bless them, O God.**

- For clergy and laity who do the work that Christ called us to do, we pray: ℟.
- For leaders who tirelessly work for their citizens and invite participation from those who are able, we pray: ℟.
- For those who work in hospitals, homeless shelters, food pantries, and childcare centers and share the burdens carried by many families, we pray: ℟.
- For those who serve on school boards, townships, and city administrations and who assist in providing services to their communities, we pray: ℟.

Let us offer together the prayer
that Jesus taught us.

Our Father . . .

Lord Jesus,
you summoned those who would be
your helpers and friends.
Give us the wisdom to recognize when
we need to reach out to others
and the courage to ask for their
assistance in doing your work.
You live and reign for ever and ever.
Amen.

✣ Let us love God, for he first loved us.

✤ Christ loved us, and gave himself up to death for us.

Psalm 84

page 378

Reading

Acts 22:6–11

[Paul said:] ". . . [A]s I drew near to Damascus, about noon a great light from the sky suddenly shone around me. I fell to the ground and heard a voice saying to me, 'Saul, Saul, why are you persecuting me?' I replied, 'Who are you, sir?' And he said to me, 'I am Jesus the Nazorean whom you are persecuting.' My companions saw the light but did not hear the voice of the one who spoke to me. I asked, 'What shall I do, sir?' The Lord answered me, 'Get up and go into Damascus, and there you will be told about everything appointed for you to do.' Since I could see nothing because of the brightness of that light, I was led by hand by my companions and entered Damascus.

Reflection

Paul's story is important for us because it is so like our own story. The call comes to each person in its own unique way. Some are called in their workplace. Some have an amazing life-changing experience. The call came to Peter, to the three thousand baptized at Pentecost, and to Paul. It comes to each one of us too. But we are not the last. Through our lives and our prayer, we become part of this long line of followers that invite others to become one with us. How do you do this in your life?

Prayers

others may be added

God who calls each of us in our own unique way, help us to answer you as we pray:

℟. Here I am, Lord.

- For our local parishes, that they may be places where people are welcomed and community is formed by those who seek to belong, we pray: ℟.
- That communities will always be places where citizens are challenged to create fellowship, support, and acceptance of each individual, we pray: ℟.
- That our response to God's call will be lived out in lives of dedication to the least among us, we pray: ℟.
- That participation in our neighborhoods and local communities will be a source of life and growth for the youngest among us, we pray: ℟.

Let us offer together the prayer that Jesus taught us.

Our Father . . .

Loving God,
you call us out of love
and invite each of us to be a connector
between those who have gone before
and those who will come after.
Help us to pass on your desire
that we all may become one in you.
Through Christ our Lord.
Amen.

✤ Christ loved us, and gave himself up to death for us.

✣ Christ prays for us: he is our priest.

Psalm 85 *page 379*

Reading *Luke 4:14–21*

Jesus returned to Galilee in the power of the Spirit, and news of him spread throughout the whole region. He taught in their synagogues and was praised by all.

He came to Nazareth, where he had grown up, and went according to his custom into the synagogue on the sabbath day. He stood up to read and was handed a scroll of the prophet Isaiah. He unrolled the scroll and found the passage where it was written:

The Spirit of the Lord / is upon me, / because he has anointed me to bring glad tidings to the poor. / He has sent me to proclaim liberty to captives / and recovery of sight to the blind, / to let the oppressed go free, / and to proclaim a year acceptable to the Lord. / Rolling up the scroll, he handed it back to the attendant and sat down, and the eyes of all in the synagogue looked intently at him. He said to them, "Today this Scripture passage is fulfilled in your hearing."

Reflection

Jesus does not hesitate to proclaim who he is and the mission he has been sent to accomplish. And we all know the hometown's response to Jesus' proclamation. They drove him from their midst. This reading calls us to examine our call and our mission. More importantly, it urges us to stand firm in our place, building the kingdom. Not everyone will respond positively. We may not finish our work. But we are not allowed to quit. We are called to be faithful to the end.

Prayers *others may be added*

Knowing who you are, Jesus, and forming our own identity in your image we ask for your aid and pray:

℟. Strengthen us, O Lord.

- May leaders of the Church never shirk from proclaiming their role as the presence of Christ in the world, we pray: ℟.
- That truth and service will become the foundations of those who seek leadership in the world, we pray: ℟.
- That we may humbly accept our role in feeding the hungry, sheltering the homeless, and comforting those in need, we pray: ℟.
- For our local parish, that it may become a place of comfort and peace, and a source of nourishment for body and soul of all who live and work in it, we pray: ℟.

Let us offer together the prayer
that Jesus taught us.

Our Father . . .

Lord Jesus,
you proclaimed who you were
and did not shrink from your call.
Help us to discover our true selves
and live out our mission without fear
of rejection and with love for all.
Who live and reign for ever and ever.
Amen.

✣ Christ prays for us: he is our priest.

Monday, January 27, 2025

✚ Christ loved the Church,
and gave himself up for her.

Psalm 91 *page 379*

Reading *Mark 3:22–30*

The scribes who had come from Jerusalem said of Jesus, "He is possessed by Beelzebul," and "By the prince of demons he drives out demons."

Summoning them, he began to speak to them in parables, "How can Satan drive out Satan? If a kingdom is divided against itself, that kingdom cannot stand. And if a house is divided against itself, that house will not be able to stand. And if Satan has risen up against himself and is divided, he cannot stand; that is the end of him. But no one can enter a strong man's house to plunder his property unless he first ties up the strong man. Then he can plunder his house. Amen, I say to you, all sins and all blasphemies that people utter will be forgiven them. But whoever blasphemes against the Holy Spirit will never have forgiveness, but is guilty of an everlasting sin." For they had said, "He has an unclean spirit."

Reflection

Jesus is facing the ultimate evil, someone possessed by Satan. Jesus' power is victorious. Even then, those who would challenge his authority seek to accuse him of working with demons. But Jesus does not flinch. He speaks the truth that his power comes from the Spirit and nothing else. To deny the power of the Spirit is a serious sin. We who are confirmed in our faith have been anointed with the Holy Spirit and called to act with the abundant gifts bestowed on us by that Spirit. Let us stand firm in the Spirit who brings us life.

Prayers *others may be added*

Anointed with the Holy Spirit and
showered with its abundant gifts
we dare to pray:

℟. Come, Holy Spirit.

- That the Church will model the gifts of wisdom and right judgment so that the world may benefit from her teachings, we pray: ℟.
- That good people around the world will offer understanding for those who are in danger and be given the courage to address their situation and bring them protection, we pray: ℟.
- That all teachers might share their gift of knowledge with those who seek the truth, we pray: ℟.
- That all people may embody the gifts of reverence, wonder, and awe as they begin to appreciate the world that God has created for them, we pray: ℟.

Let us offer together the prayer
that Jesus taught us.

Our Father . . .

Loving God,
you pour out your Spirit upon us that
we might renew the face of the earth.
Help us to always be faithful
to your Spirit
who brings us life and invites us
to live it abundantly.
Through Christ our Lord.
Amen.

✚ Christ loved the Church,
and gave himself up for her.

✠ The Lord loved me and gave himself up to death for me.

Psalm 95

page 380

Reading

Wisdom 7:7–10, 15–16

Today's reading is from the Proper of Saints.

I prayed, and prudence was given me; / I pleaded, and the spirit of Wisdom came to me. / I preferred her to scepter and throne, / And deemed riches nothing in comparison with her, / nor did I liken any priceless gem to her; / Because all gold, in view of her, is a little sand, / and before her, silver is to be accounted mire. / Beyond health and comeliness I loved her, / And I chose to have her rather than the light, / because the splendor of her never yields to sleep.

Now God grant I speak suitably / and value these endowments at their worth: / For he is the guide ofWisdom / and the director of the wise. / For both we and our words are in his hand, / as well as all prudence and knowledge of crafts.

Reflection

What do we hold in highest esteem? If we reflect on this question honestly, what would we list as our top three? Today's reading rejects what others may see as worthy—gold, beauty, even health—in favor of wisdom. How do we acquire wisdom? Openness, prayer, dialogue. Once we are granted wisdom then we are commissioned to speak wisely and act accordingly. How can I advance my knowledge and understanding today? Who is a wise friend I can learn from? How can I use my words wisely?

Prayers

others may be added

In the shadow of your great saint, Thomas Aquinas, we ask your guidance, O Lord, as we pray:

℟. Teach us, O Lord.

- That the Church may continue to raise up models of study, prayer, and practice, we pray: ℟.
- That professors, teachers, guidance counselors, and parents may always lead those in their care to a deeper understanding of the world and of you, we pray: ℟.
- That researchers and thinkers will use their skills to solve the many troubling issues of life in our cities and towns, we pray: ℟.
- That each citizen will discover their gifts and talents and offer to use them in service to the people in their neighborhood schools and places of learning, we pray: ℟.

Let us offer together the prayer that Jesus taught us.

Our Father . . .

Almighty God,
in every age you raise up thinkers
and writers,
people of great wisdom to share
their learning with all.
Help us to see the value in learning,
and work to improve the lives of others
with our knowledge.
Through Christ our Lord.
Amen.

✠ The Lord loved me and gave himself up to death for me.

Weekday

Wednesday, January 29, 2025

✤ By [Christ's] wounds we are healed.

Psalm 98 *page 381*

Reading *Mark 4:1, 3–9*

On another occasion Jesus began to teach by the sea. . . . "Hear this! A sower went out to sow. And as he sowed, some seed fell on the path, and the birds came and ate it up. Other seed fell on rocky ground where it had little soil. It sprang up at once because the soil was not deep. And when the sun rose, it was scorched and it withered for lack of roots. Some seed fell among thorns, and the thorns grew up and choked it and it produced no grain. And some seed fell on rich soil and produced fruit. It came up and grew and yielded thirty, sixty, and a hundredfold." He added, "Whoever has ears to hear ought to hear."

Reflection

Parables teach important lessons. They use ordinary, everyday things to express profound insights into the kingdom of God. They hold more truth than any one explanation can give. The sower and seed are so familiar we might feel we have wrung out all their meaning. But let us consider this. The parable ends with the admonition, "Whoever has ears to hear ought to hear." Read it again with new eyes. Hear it with new ears. What keeps a seed from growing? What enhances it? What part of the growth am I responsible for?

Prayers *others may be added*

With a desire to learn the secrets of
your kingdom, O Lord, we beg you
to open our eyes and ears as we pray:

℟. **Enlighten us, O Lord.**

- That the Church will share with all her people the secrets of God's kingdom through study and exploration of the Scriptures, we pray: ℟.
- That all people in the world might look upon the simple things they encounter and discover a deeper meaning that brings them closer to God, we pray: ℟.
- That we might recognize those who are poor as a beautiful unfolding of the truth of God's kingdom among us and learn from their lives and example, we pray: ℟.
- That parents might introduce their children to the secrets of God hidden in the beauty of nature, we pray: ℟.

Let us offer together the prayer
that Jesus taught us.

Our Father . . .

Lord Jesus,
you taught us in parables
so that we might slowly discover
the richness of your kingdom.
Help us to reflect on the many facets
of your teaching
and always seek to know more
about you.
Who live and reign for ever and ever.
Amen.

✤ By [Christ's] wounds we are healed.

✠ Seek, and you will find, / knock on the door, and it will be opened to you.

Psalm 103
page 382

Reading
Mark 4:21–25

Jesus said to his disciples, "Is a lamp brought in to be placed under a bushel basket or under a bed, and not to be placed on a lampstand? For there is nothing hidden except to be made visible; nothing is secret except to come to light. Anyone who has ears to hear ought to hear." He also told them, "Take care what you hear. The measure with which you measure will be measured out to you, and still more will be given to you. To the one who has, more will be given; from the one who has not, even what he has will be taken away."

Reflection

Light and darkness. Do we live as people of the light? Do we examine what comes to light in our world and ask, is it true, is it trustworthy, is it life-giving? What do we do if it is not? The warning in today's reading admonishes us to "take care what you hear." For as we hear and act, so our lives will be judged. Let us examine our lives in the light of Christ. What we take in and what we give out must always contribute to bringing the kingdom of God to light.

Prayers
others may be added

Lord of all, you declare each of us to be light for the world. Enable us to share our light with others, as we pray:

℟. **Lord, may your light shine through us.**

- For those who seek a relationship with God, may the Church always be welcoming and living example, we pray: ℟.
- For the courageous people who bring light to the darkest places in the world, places covered by war and famine, hatred and violence, we pray: ℟.
- For those who huddle in the darkness of addiction and struggle with mental illness; may they encounter the light of hope, we pray: ℟.
- For families who suffer discord, may the light of reconciliation and peace dispel the darkness, we pray: ℟.

Let us offer together the prayer that Jesus taught us.

Our Father . . .

God of Light,
you show us the way to you.
Fill us with the desire to always do good
and follow in your footsteps.
Help us to fill the world with the light
of your love
and scatter the darkness that still
surrounds us.
Through Christ our Lord.
Amen.

✠ Seek, and you will find, / knock on the door, and it will be opened to you.

Memorial of St. John Bosco, Priest

Friday, January 31, 2025

✚ Be strong and steadfast, / for the Lord your God is going with you.

Psalm 115

page 385

Reading

Mark 4:30–34

[Jesus] said, "To what shall we compare the Kingdom of God, or what parable can we use for it? It is like a mustard seed that, when it is sown in the ground, is the smallest of all the seeds on the earth. But once it is sown, it springs up and becomes the largest of plants and puts forth large branches, so that the birds of the sky can dwell in its shade." With many such parables he spoke the word to them as they were able to understand it. Without parables he did not speak to them, but to his own disciples he explained everything in private.

Reflection

Today's reading is puzzling. A seed grows on its own, seemingly without any help from the sower. It appears to discount our responsibility beyond just scattering the seed. Or, perhaps, it is more a lesson in trust. We do what we can but success is not totally dependent on us. We do the work; God brings about the fullness. It is also a lesson in humility. We do our work realizing the work is not ours alone. It is God who brings all good seed to "harvest." The seed that grows without our help teaches us to acknowledge our dependence on God.

Prayers

others may be added

God of the harvest, look upon our labors and bless us with abundance as we pray:

℟. **Gather us in, O Lord.**

- May the seeds of faith sown among us produce a rich harvest for God's kingdom, we pray: ℟.
- May the abundant harvests in the rich countries of the earth be shared with those who experience hunger, famine, and drought we pray: ℟.
- May our richly filled cupboards be shared with those who seek food and shelter in our neighborhoods, we pray: ℟.
- May families work to reduce their wants so that others may fill their needs, we pray: ℟.

Let us offer together the prayer that Jesus taught us.

Our Father . . .

God of growth,
we sow the seeds of faith that feed
our spirits
and the seeds of crops that feed
our bodies.
Help us to realize that it is you who
brings us abundant goodness.
Teach us to be grateful for our bounty
and be determined to share it.
Through Christ our Lord.
Amen.

✚ Be strong and steadfast, / for the Lord your God is going with you.

✚ The Lord is the refuge of my life.

Psalm 121 *page 386*

Reading *Hebrews 11:1–2, 8, 12–14*

Brothers and sisters: Faith is the realization of what is hoped for and evidence of things not seen. Because of it the ancients were well attested.

By faith Abraham obeyed when he was called to go out to a place that he was to receive as an inheritance; he went out, not knowing where he was to go.

So it was that there came forth from one man, himself as good as dead, descendants as numerous as the stars in the sky and as countless as the sands on the seashore.

All these died in faith. They did not receive what had been promised but saw it and greeted it from afar and acknowledged themselves to be strangers and aliens on earth, for those who speak thus show that they are seeking a homeland.

Reflection

Faith. What a profound word. It defies definition and is beyond understanding. If we have faith, we can leave a comfortable place for an uncertain future. We can believe that life is possible where only barrenness exists. We can believe that we are destined for greater things that are promised not only to us but our descendants. The experiences of our ancestors in faith strengthen our own belief. What is it that I hope for? What am I able to see that others might not? Faith, what a gift from our God!

Prayers *others may be added*

God of all those who believe,
strengthen our faith as we pray:

℟. Lord, hear our prayer.

- For the Church who calls all to faith in Jesus, we pray: ℟.
- For the success of those who believe in and work to build a better future for their citizens, we pray: ℟.
- For those who suffer violence, may their faith in a future built on peace become a reality, we pray: ℟.
- That the children among us can look forward to a future of security, abundance, and peace, we pray: ℟.

Let us offer together the prayer
that Jesus taught us.

Our Father . . .

O God,
you call us into the unknown without
 fear because of our trust in you.
Help us to become partners with you
in building a better future for
 our children
and our children's children.
Through Christ our Lord.
Amen.

✚ The Lord is the refuge of my life.

✤ I live now by faith in the Son of God.

Psalm 122

page 387

Reading

Luke 2:22, 39–40

When the days were completed for their purification according to the law of Moses, Mary and Joseph took Jesus up to Jerusalem to present him to the Lord.

When they had fulfilled all the prescriptions of the law of the Lord, they returned to Galilee, to their own town of Nazareth. The child grew and became strong, filled with wisdom; and the favor of God was upon him.

Reflection

Mary and Joseph, faithful to the law, bring Jesus to the temple. Their child, recognized as God's chosen one, was formed in the faith by his parents. Imagine the home that prayed, obeyed the law, and practiced charity to all as the place where Jesus learned his "faith." At this early age his is recognized as a light for revelation. Let us pray that all parents model for their children how to live their faith. In the light of this day let us examine how we have led our children and those whom we influence to be a light to the world.

Prayers

others may be added

Jesus, Light of the world, we look
to you and pray:

℟. **Send your light upon us, O Lord.**

- For members of the Church, may we spread the light of Christ to all the world, we pray: ℟.
- For the success of people committed to justice who are called to shine the light of compassion in the darkest places in the world, we pray: ℟.
- For those who are deprived of education and learning and are kept in darkness, may they be enlightened through the teaching of others, we pray: ℟.
- For those who work to protect our environment from destruction, may they give us the light of hope in a flourishing and verdant future, we pray: ℟.

Let us offer together the prayer
that Jesus taught us.

Our Father . . .

Creator God,
you began your work of creation
  by speaking "Let there be light."
Continue to share your light with us.
Show us the way to partner in
  your creation
by working to remove darkness
  wherever it lingers.
Through Christ our Lord.
Amen.

✤ I live now by faith in the Son of God.

✤ May the Lord be generous.

Psalm 24 *page 367*

Reading *Mark 5:1–10*

Jesus and his disciples came to the other side of the sea, to the territory of the Gerasenes. When he got out of the boat, at once a man from the tombs who had an unclean spirit met him. The man had been dwelling among the tombs, and no one could restrain him any longer, even with a chain. In fact, he had frequently been bound with shackles and chains, but the chains had been pulled apart by him and the shackles smashed, and no one was strong enough to subdue him. Night and day among the tombs and on the hillsides he was always crying out and bruising himself with stones. Catching sight of Jesus from a distance, he ran up and prostrated himself before him, crying out in a loud voice, "What have you to do with me, Jesus, Son of the Most High God? I adjure you by God, do not torment me!" (He had been saying to him, "Unclean spirit, come out of the man!") He asked him, "What is your name?" He replied, "Legion is my name. There are many of us." And he pleaded earnestly with him not to drive them away from that territory.

Reflection

Legions of evil spirits, possession, and swineherds. The tragedy of this one man ends on a positive note. Through the mercy of God, he is relieved of his evil spirits. Filled with gratitude he asks to stay with Jesus. But that is not his mission. We often receive great relief from our own troubles. In response, we want to stay with this generous God. But, like the man, it is our greater task to announce to others what has been done for us. Our own life example becomes a foundation for others to believe in this healing Christ

Prayers *others may be added*

We give you thanks, O God, for freeing us from whatever keeps us from doing your work, as we pray:

℟. Restore our spirits, O God.

✦ For the Church that is commissioned to spread the Word of God's great works, we pray: ℟.

✦ For leaders who address the needs of their citizens without asking for "gratitude," we pray: ℟.

✦ For counselors, social workers, and doctors who journey with and treat those who suffer with depression, anxiety, and any mental illness, we pray: ℟.

✦ For school personnel who address the needs of students who struggle to succeed, we pray: ℟.

Let us offer together the prayer that Jesus taught us.

Our Father . . .

Merciful God,
you are the source of all goodness.
Grant us your healing touch
and free us from all torment.
Through Christ our Lord.
Amen.

✤ May the Lord be generous.

Weekday

Tuesday, February 4, 2025

✠ Christ has been raised to life.

Psalm 27

page 368

Reading

Mark 5:25–34

There was a woman afflicted with hemorrhages for twelve years. She had suffered greatly at the hands of many doctors and had spent all that she had. Yet she was not helped but only grew worse. She had heard about Jesus and came up behind him in the crowd and touched his cloak. She said, "If I but touch his clothes, I shall be cured." Immediately her flow of blood dried up. She felt in her body that she was healed of her affliction. Jesus, aware at once that power had gone out from him, turned around in the crowd and asked, "Who has touched my clothes?" But his disciples said to him, "You see how the crowd is pressing upon you, and yet you ask, Who touched me?" And he looked around to see who had done it. The woman, realizing what had happened to her, approached in fear and trembling. She fell down before Jesus and told him the whole truth. He said to her, "Daughter, your faith has saved you. Go in peace and be cured of your affliction."

Reflection

What a remarkable woman! Is it possible for any of us to follow her courageous example? Never discouraged by her years of suffering and knowing that to touch Jesus might incur his wrath, she nonetheless took the risk. And that risk was rewarded. What troubles you, discourages you, disables you? Can you summon your courage to reach out to Jesus and ask for healing? Perhaps the only thing prolonging your "struggle" is your fear of action. Let us witness this woman's faith and make it our own.

Prayers

others may be added

Healing Lord, we dare to bring our broken bodies and spirits to you as we pray:

℟. **Heal us, O God.**

- That we might look to the sacraments of the Church as sources of healing for body and spirit, we pray: ℟.
- That medical professionals around the world will continue to discover treatments for diseases that ravage communities, we pray: ℟.
- That the poor who are deprived of adequate medical care may receive the attention and treatment they deserve, we pray: ℟.
- That caregivers may be supported in their efforts to ease the pain and suffering of those they serve, we pray: ℟.

Let us offer together the prayer that Jesus taught us.

Our Father . . .

Lord Jesus,
you healed those who were lame
and blind
and all who came to you for relief
of pain and sickness.
Be merciful and free us from all illness
that we may serve you with strength
and compassion.
Who live and reign for ever and ever.
Amen.

✠ Christ has been raised to life.

✚ Bless the Lord God at all times.

Psalm 30

page 369

Reading

Mark 6:1–6

Jesus departed from there and came to his native place, accompanied by his disciples. When the sabbath came he began to teach in the synagogue, and many who heard him were astonished. They said, "Where did this man get all this? What kind of wisdom has been given him? What mighty deeds are wrought by his hands! Is he not the carpenter, the son of Mary, and the brother of James and Joseph and Judas and Simon? And are not his sisters here with us?" And they took offense at him. Jesus said to them, "A prophet is not without honor except in his native place and among his own kin and in his own house." So he was not able to perform any mighty deed there, apart from curing a few sick people by laying his hands on them. He was amazed at their lack of faith.

Reflection

It is astounding to think how truly important our own faith is to the success of Jesus' mission. God works through us but how can this happen if we do not believe it? We might be discouraged or doubtful about our ability to create change, to heal ills, to transform the world, but Jesus shows us that we do have the power. To truly believe in Jesus is also to acknowledge the power that is ours given in baptism and nourished through Eucharist.

Prayers

others may be added

Lord Jesus, we believe in you. Affirm our faith as we pray:

℟. We put our trust in you, O Lord.

- In gratitude for the gifts of baptism and Eucharist, we pray: ℟.
- In gratitude for the many ways that citizens of all countries work to create a better world, and have faith in their ability to succeed, we pray: ℟.
- In gratitude for those who seem to work miracles for those in need because of their belief in you and in their abilities, we pray: ℟.
- In gratitude for families who believe in and trust one another and enable their members to grow, we pray: ℟.

Let us offer together the prayer that Jesus taught us.

Our Father . . .

Faithful God,
fill us with your grace and your power
to do good.
Help us to realize that if we have faith
in you and in ourselves,
we can indeed change the world.
Through Christ our Lord.
Amen.

✚ Bless the Lord God at all times.

✚ The Lord will come to be glorified in his holy ones.

Psalm 51

page 373

Reading

Mark 6:7–13

Jesus summoned the Twelve and began to send them out two by two and gave them authority over unclean spirits. He instructed them to take nothing for the journey but a walking stick—no food, no sack, no money in their belts. They were, however, to wear sandals but not a second tunic. He said to them, "Wherever you enter a house, stay there until you leave. Whatever place does not welcome you or listen to you, leave there and shake the dust off your feet in testimony against them." So they went off and preached repentance. The Twelve drove out many demons, and they anointed with oil many who were sick and cured them.

Reflection

This passage challenges us. If we take this instruction seriously, we are to begin our mission armed mainly with trust in God and a willingness to spread the word. We need not feel overly responsible for the people who hear or reject our message. If we reflect for a moment, we might recognize that is the way Jesus worked. He relied on God, spoke God's Word with power, and touched those who needed healing. Then he moved on. We are the instruments of God's work. We are not to worry about what we might need. We have all we need when we rely on God.

Prayers

others may be added

Loving God, you give us all we need, and so we pray:

℟. Make us worthy, O Lord.

- You sent the Spirit to be with your Church to help her members spread your Word. Help us respond to your call, we pray: ℟.
- Your Spirit calls us to renew the face of the earth. Help us humbly begin the mission given to us, we pray: ℟.
- Your Spirit calls us to give sight to the blind, liberty to captives, and to let the oppressed go free. Fill us also with the confidence to complete this work, we pray: ℟.
- Your Spirit enables us to create community and honor neighbors of all races and creeds so that we all may be one. Let us never tire of this work until it is accomplished, we pray: ℟.

Let us offer together the prayer that Jesus taught us.

Our Father . . .

Faithful God,
you give us a command to be your
presence in the world.
Strengthen our trust in you
so that we might fulfill your command
to humbly do your work.
Help us to be faithful to the work
you have entrusted to us.
Through Christ our Lord.
Amen.

✚ The Lord will come to be glorified in his holy ones.

✚ The Lord is faithful in all his words /
and loving in all his deeds.

Psalm 34

page 370

Reading

Hebrews 13:1–8

Let brotherly love continue. Do not neglect hospitality, for through it some have unknowingly entertained angels. Be mindful of prisoners as if sharing their imprisonment, and of the ill-treated as of yourselves, for you also are in the body. Let marriage be honored among all and the marriage bed be kept undefiled, for God will judge the immoral and adulterers. Let your life be free from love of money but be content with what you have, for he has said, / *I will never forsake you or abandon you.* / Thus we may say with confidence: / *The Lord is my helper,* / *and I will not be afraid.* / *What can anyone do to me?* Remember your leaders who spoke the word of God to you. Consider the outcome of their way of life and imitate their faith. Jesus Christ is the same yesterday, today, and forever.

Reflection

"Christ, yesterday, today and forever." Although the authorship of this letter is uncertain the message of this passage is beautiful. It is a blueprint for how we should approach life in Christ. Love allows us to live a beautiful life that includes gracious hospitality, empathy for those in prison, faithfulness in our commitments, lack of greed. Who wouldn't want to live with or near someone who behaved in this manner? Let us determine that we will become such persons because of our love for God and others.

Prayers

others may be added

God of love, teach us that your love enables us to achieve all that is good, as we pray:

℟. Fill us with your love, O Lord.

- For the Church, that she may always be a place of welcome for all who seek Christ's presence, we pray: ℟.
- For leaders and citizens, may they welcome and provide for those who seek asylum and shelter within their borders, we pray: ℟.
- For places that shelter those without homes and those who have been abused; may their doors always remain open to care for those who enter seeking their help, we pray: ℟.
- For those who are imprisoned by mental illness, addiction, and loneliness; may they find a welcoming place that offers acceptance, recovery, and peace, we pray: ℟.

Let us offer together the prayer
that Jesus taught us.

Our Father . . .

Loving God,
you teach us how to live a life
of generosity and compassion.
Help us never shirk from
our responsibilities toward
our neighbors.
Give us the strength to build up
our communities.
Through Christ our Lord.
Amen.

✚ The Lord is faithful in all his words /
and loving in all his deeds.

Saturday, February 8, 2025

✤ The Lord has blessed [us] in all that [we] have done.

Psalm 23

page 367

Reading

Mark 6:30–34

The Apostles gathered together with Jesus and reported all they had done and taught. He said to them, "Come away by yourselves to a deserted place and rest a while." People were coming and going in great numbers, and they had no opportunity even to eat. So they went off in the boat by themselves to a deserted place. People saw them leaving and many came to know about it. They hastened there on foot from all the towns and arrived at the place before them.

When Jesus disembarked and saw the vast crowd, his heart was moved with pity for them, for they were like sheep without a shepherd; and he began to teach them many things.

Reflection

Sometimes it is important to take a step back and rest. It is even good to reflect with others on the good work you have done. Not with pride or boasting but a humble review of your accomplishments. If we continue to work without rest, we run the risk of pushing ourselves beyond the limits of productivity. Acknowledging our achievements enables us to build upon them. And, as we read today, people who need us will always be there to call us again to action. Then we will be rested and ready.

Prayers

others may be added

Creator God, who rested on the seventh day, be our model as we pray:

℟. Grant us your peace, O Lord.

- As the Church gathers to pray at the end of each week, may she be a reminder that we are called to rest at the end of our labors, we pray: ℟.
- That employers and organization heads will pay just wages so their workers can have resources that enable them to rest and renew their bodies and spirits, we pray: ℟.
- For those who struggle to earn enough money to support their families, may they find adequate employment and support in their work, we pray: ℟.
- May all families enjoy free time together to rejoice in one another's presence and benefit from each person's gifts, we pray: ℟.

Let us offer together the prayer that Jesus taught us.

Our Father . . .

Lord Jesus,
you sent out your apostles
to do your work
and welcomed them back
to a place of rest.
Continue to reward our labors with
times of renewal and appreciation
for what we have accomplished
in your name.
Who live and reign for ever and ever.
Amen.

✤ The Lord has blessed [us] in all that [we] have done.

✤ You are the light of the world.

Psalm 46 *page 372*

Reading *Luke 5:4–11*

After [Jesus] had finished speaking, he said to Simon, "Put out into deep water and lower your nets for a catch." Simon said in reply, "Master, we have worked hard all night and have caught nothing, but at your command I will lower the nets." When they had done this, they caught a great number of fish and their nets were tearing. They signaled to their partners in the other boat to come to help them. They came and filled both boats so that the boats were in danger of sinking. When Simon Peter saw this, he fell at the knees of Jesus and said, "Depart from me, Lord, for I am a sinful man." For astonishment at the catch of fish they had made seized him and all those with him, and likewise James and John, the sons of Zebedee, who were partners of Simon. Jesus said to Simon, "Do not be afraid; from now on you will be catching men." When they brought their boats to the shore, they left everything and followed him.

Reflection

Every day, like the fishermen in this story, we are astonished by the great works of God. Measuring ourselves against God's goodness we feel unworthy to continue his work. It is then that Jesus looks upon us with confidence and calls us to do even greater things than we are doing. For Peter and the others, it was to become fishers of men instead of fish. What am I doing now in the name of God? What greater things does God call me to do? With trust and courage, we must walk confidently into the future to which God calls us.

Prayers *others may be added*

O God, you call us to do great things in your name. Help us to respond with courage and not with fear, as we pray

℟. Empower us O, Lord.

- For all members of the Church who are willing to respond to God's call to work in his name, we pray: ℟.
- For all people in positions of power, that they will instill in their citizens the willingness to participate in the work of building community, we pray: ℟.
- For the powerless, that they may be supported by those who have the authority to make their lives better, safer, and more productive, we pray: ℟.
- For all children, that we may see their talents and goodness and encourage them to take their rightful place among us, we pray: ℟.

Let us offer together the prayer that Jesus taught us.

Our Father . . .

All-knowing God,
give us the insight to appreciate
the gifts within us
and call us to bravely put them
at the service of others.
Through Christ our Lord.
Amen.

✤ You are the light of the world.

Monday, February 10, 2025

✠ By the grace of God, I am what I am.

Psalm 47 *page 372*

Reading *Luke 10:38–42*

Today's reading is from the Proper of Saints.

Jesus entered a village where a woman whose name was Martha welcomed him. She had a sister named Mary who sat beside the Lord at his feet listening to him speak. Martha, burdened with much serving, came to him and said, "Lord, do you not care that my sister has left me by myself to do the serving? Tell her to help me." The Lord said to her in reply, "Martha, Martha, you are anxious and worried about many things. There is need of only one thing. Mary has chosen the better part and it will not be taken from her."

Reflection

This reading is appropriate for the Memorial of St. Scholastica. She and her brother, St. Benedict, each founded a group of followers who were entrusted with the practice of hospitality. Strangers were greeted and welcomed as if they were Christ knocking at the begging entrance. Can I follow the example of these holy siblings and welcome the stranger, provide nourishment for the hungry, reach out to the one who is lonely? This is the message heard at the feet of Jesus and the work of each of us that is required make it a reality

Prayers *others may be added*

Lord Jesus, you love the worker and the attentive disciple. Bring balance into our lives, as we pray:

℟. Teach us to serve you, O Lord.

- For those in the Church who spread your Word and those who do your work, we pray: ℟.
- For leaders who reflect on the needs of their people and the many citizens who daily work to meet them, we pray: ℟.
- For those who offer themselves to protect us from violence and those who march and work for a peaceful world, we pray: ℟.
- For those who plan a future for our communities and those who work to build it, we pray: ℟.

Let us offer together the prayer that Jesus taught us.

Our Father . . .

Gracious God,
you give each of us different talents
and you bless them all.
Help us to see the value in what we do
and to work tirelessly to put ourselves
at the service of others.
Help us to find a purpose for our work
in your word.
Through Christ our Lord.
Amen.

✠ By the grace of God, I am what I am.

✣ We have believed in Christ Jesus /
so that we might be made holy.

Psalm 71

page 376

Reading

Genesis 1:24–27

Then God said, "Let the earth bring forth all kinds of living creatures: cattle, creeping things, and wild animals of all kinds." And so it happened: God made all kinds of wild animals, all kinds of cattle, and all kinds of creeping things of the earth. God saw how good it was. Then God said: "Let us make man in our image, after our likeness. Let them have dominion over the fish of the sea, the birds of the air, and the cattle, and over all the wild animals and all the creatures that crawl on the ground." God created man in his image; / in the divine image he created him; / male and female he created them.

Reflection

"And God saw how good it was." Why can we not see the earth as God sees it? God created it to be good and beautiful, for every plant and living thing to be fertile and multiply. Then God created us in God's image to have "dominion" over creation. If we are made in God's image, do we not have to treat the earth as God does and recognize its beauty and our charge to keep t that way? Our God is a good God who has given us all that we need for our lives. Let us be grateful and responsible with this gift.

Prayers

others may be added

Creator God, we thank you for all
the plants and creatures of the earth,
as we pray:

℟. **Help us to care for your gifts,
O Lord.**

- That the Church may strive to protect God's creation, we pray: ℟.
- That countries may preserve their natural resources so that their citizens may live safe and abundant lives, we pray: ℟.
- That those who have plenty will share with those who have nothing, we pray: ℟.
- For gardeners and farmers, for grocers and florists, may they help us all to see how good and plentiful the harvest of the earth can be, we pray: ℟.

Let us offer together the prayer
that Jesus taught us.

Our Father . . .

Lord Jesus,
you gave us the example of the birds
of the air and the lilies of the field
to show us how much you care for us.
Help us not to worry and hoard
our resources
but share them with all our brothers
and sisters.
You who live and reign for ever
and ever.
Amen.

✣ We have believed in Christ Jesus /
so that we might be made holy.

Wednesday, February 12, 2025

✚ There is neither Jew nor Greek;
[we] are all made one in Christ Jesus.

Psalm 62

page 374

Reading

Genesis 2:4b–9, 15–17

At the time when the LORD God made the earth and the heavens—while as yet there was no field shrub on earth and no grass of the field had sprouted, for the LORD God had sent no rain upon the earth and there was no man to till the soil, but a stream was welling up out of the earth and was watering all the surface of the ground—the LORD God formed man out of the clay of the ground and blew into his nostrils the breath of life, and so man became a living being.

Then the LORD God planted a garden in Eden, in the east, and he placed there the man whom he had formed. Out of the ground the LORD God made various trees grow that were delightful to look at and good for food, with the tree of life in the middle of the garden and the tree of the knowledge of good and evil.

Reflection

God breathes into us the breath of life and we become living beings. But to be truly alive we must be more than one who just breathes and eats, works and rests. What makes me truly alive? Am I able to look at all that God has given me and use it well? How do I care for the earth? How do I respond to God's creatures who are our helpers and companions? How do I treat every living being who is created with God's breath? We are called to live fully. Let us ask God to help us appreciate the life we have been given.

Prayers

others may be added

O God, you share your own life with us. Help us to use this gift to continue your creation, as we pray:

℟. Inspire us, O God.

- Through the gift of baptism may we become more like you in word and deed, we pray: ℟.
- With the gift of citizenship, may we work for the good of all who live in our country and offer welcome to all those who seek entry, we pray: ℟.
- With the gift of compassion, may we reach out to those whose lives are burdened or limited and free them to live more fully, we pray: ℟.
- With the gift of friendship, may we always enrich the lives of those we love and those who love us, we pray: ℟.

Let us offer together the prayer that Jesus taught us.

Our Father . . .

Living God,
you breathe into us your own life
that we might be like you.
Help us to fulfill your desire for us to be fully alive in you and filled with abundant joy.
Through Christ our Lord.
Amen.

✚ There is neither Jew nor Greek;
[we] are all made one in Christ Jesus.

✤ The Lord is the Spirit, / and where the Spirit of the Lord is, there is freedom.

Psalm 63 *page 375*

Reading *Genesis 2:18–23*

The LORD God said: "It is not good for the man to be alone. I will make a suitable partner for him." So the LORD God formed out of the ground various wild animals and various birds of the air, and he brought them to the man to see what he would call them; whatever the man called each of them would be its name. The man gave names to all the cattle, all the birds of the air, and all the wild animals; but none proved to be the suitable partner for the man.

So the LORD God cast a deep sleep on the man, and while he was asleep, he took out one of his ribs and closed up its place with flesh. The LORD God then built up into a woman the rib that he had taken from the man. When he brought her to the man, the man said: "This one, at last, is bone of my bones / and flesh of my flesh; / this one shall be called 'woman,' / for out of 'her man' this one has been taken."

Reflection

Having someone with whom to share our lives is a great gift! Not all people find this companionship in marriage. Those who are single, make religious vows, or are ordained still have someone who shares their spirit and their friendship and love. God created us so that we would not be alone. Who in your life fills the role? What is it that draws you two together? How can I show my gratitude for this person who leads me to God?

Prayers *others may be added*

Knowing that it is not good for us to be alone in life we ask you to fulfill us with love and friendship, as we pray:

℟. Make us whole, O God.

- In celebration of the sacrament of marriage that blesses the union of two people with God's grace, we pray: ℟.
- In gratitude for organizations that offer assistance to households so that they too can contribute to their community, we pray: ℟.
- With compassion for those who are alone and struggle with physical obstacles, may they find someone who will be their partner and friend, we pray: ℟.
- In celebration of single people, may they discover and honor their own richness and share their gifts with all who fill their lives, we pray: ℟.

Let us offer together the prayer that Jesus taught us.

Our Father . . .

God of all people,
help us to grow into who we are meant
to be in your creation.
Bless all those become our friends
and companions.
Through Christ our Lord.
Amen.

✤ The Lord is the Spirit, / and where the Spirit of the Lord is, there is freedom.

✚ The signs of the Spirit's presence are love, joy, and peace.

Psalm 67
page 375

Reading
Mark 7:31–37

Again Jesus left the district of Tyre and went by way of Sidon to the Sea of Galilee, into the district of the Decapolis. And people brought to him a deaf man who had a speech impediment and begged him to lay his hand on him. He took him off by himself away from the crowd. He put his finger into the man's ears and, spitting, touched his tongue; then he looked up to heaven and groaned, and said to him, "*Ephphatha*!" (that is, "Be opened!") And immediately the man's ears were opened, his speech impediment was removed, and he spoke plainly. . . . They were exceedingly astonished and they said, "He has done all things well. He makes the deaf hear and the mute speak."

Reflection

"Be opened!" The story of the man who was deaf and had a speech impediment is our story too. Physical deafness is not the only kind of impediment to our lives. We can be deaf to many things: the cries of the poor and the immigrant, the call of those who suffer violence and fear, the words of those we look at as enemies because they have a different perspective on the world. Could we "be open"? The man's friends brought him to Jesus to be healed. We too might rely on friends to bring us to awareness of our deafness. Then when we can truly hear we might also be freed to speak God's word of love and acceptance to others.

Prayers
others may be added

As you healed the deaf man, we pray:

℟. **Help us to hear, O Lord.**

- That the Church may continue to teach the Gospel of Christ, we pray: ℟.
- That leaders around the world might create venues for their citizens to speak their concerns and be willing to address them with openness, we pray: ℟.
- That the cries of the oppressed will reach the ears of those who can become their helpers, we pray: ℟.
- That communities will provide sufficient resources for their youngest so that the cries of joy and growth will be heard from their children, we pray: ℟.

Let us offer together the prayer that Jesus taught us.

Our Father . . .

Lord Jesus,
you opened the ears of the man
who could not hear.
Open our ears and our hearts
that we might hear from those who cry
for help.
Let us speak words of comfort and hope
to all.
Who live and reign for ever and ever.
Amen.

✚ The signs of the Spirit's presence are love, joy, and peace.

✤ It is the Spirit that gives life.

Psalm 84 *page 378*

Reading *Mark 8:2–9*

[Jesus said], "My heart is moved with pity for the crowd, because they have been with me now for three days and have nothing to eat. If I send them away hungry to their homes, they will collapse on the way, and some of them have come a great distance." His disciples answered him, "Where can anyone get enough bread to satisfy them here in this deserted place?" Still he asked them, "How many loaves do you have?" They replied, "Seven." He ordered the crowd to sit down on the ground. Then, taking the seven loaves he gave thanks, broke them, and gave them to his disciples to distribute, and they distributed them to the crowd. They also had a few fish. He said the blessing over them and ordered them distributed also. They ate and were satisfied. They picked up the fragments left over—seven baskets. There were about four thousand people.

Reflection

This story appears in some form in each of the four Gospel accounts. From that, we learn the story is very important and carries a serious lesson for our life of faith. Mark is the only one that writes that there were seven left over. The other three Gospel accounts speak about twelve. The number varies but the lesson is clear. Jesus nourishes us—nourishes all—and his bounty is never depleted. With Jesus there is always enough and more. Let us be grateful for God's bounty as we approach the Eucharistic table. Let us fill ourselves and share our bounty with others.

Prayers *others may be added*

Lord Jesus, you teach us that if we believe in you, we will always live with abundance, and so we pray:

℟. Nourish us, O Lord.

- For the young people among us preparing for first Communion, may they come to know God's abundant love, we pray: ℟.
- For lands where bread is abundant, may they share with those whose fields are empty, we pray: ℟.
- For those who seek food and shelter, may we share the little we have so that everyone may have some, we pray: ℟.
- In gratitude for bakeries and bread makers, for those who plant grain and for those who harvest it, we pray: ℟.

Let us offer together the prayer
that Jesus taught us.

Our Father . . .

O God,
you give us your own self in the Bread
and Wine that we share.
Help us realize that when the bread
and wine are changed,
we too must become changed.
Help us to become bread broken
for others
and wine poured out for those in need.
Through Christ our Lord.
Amen.

✤ It is the Spirit that gives life.

✤ The word of the Lord endures
for ever.

Psalm 85

page 379

Reading

Luke 6:20–26

[R]aising his eyes toward his disciples [Jesus] said: / "Blessed are you who are poor, / for the kingdom of God is yours. / Blessed are you who are now hungry, / for you will be satisfied. / Blessed are you who are now weeping, / for you will laugh. / Blessed are you when people hate you, / and when they exclude and insult you, / and denounce your name as evil on account of the Son of Man. / Rejoice and leap for joy on that day! Behold, your reward will be great in heaven. For their ancestors treated the prophets in the same way. / But woe to you who are rich, / for you have received your consolation. / Woe to you who are filled now, / for you will be hungry. / Woe to you who laugh now, / for you will grieve and weep. / Woe to you when all speak well of you, / for their ancestors treated the false prophets in this way."

Reflection

Luke has a different take on the Beatitudes than Matthew. There are only four and he has Jesus deliver them on a plain to his disciples rather than on a mount to the crowds. And there are Woes! And woe to us if we do not listen to his words. Luke has Jesus address the real physical needs of the people. Blessed are the poor as opposed to poor in spirit. The hungry instead of those who hunger for righteousness. Jesus asks us as his followers to take stock of our current condition and ask ourselves which is more important, our good or the good of the kingdom.

Prayers

others may be added

God of the poor, you call your disciples to care for others before themselves. Help us to respond to your command, as we pray:

℟. Fill us with compassion, O Lord.

- That the Church may preach and live the Beatitudes of Jesus, we pray: ℟.
- That the poor of the world will become a priority for leaders of all countries, we pray: ℟.
- That those who are excluded from the good things of the earth may receive the justice they deserve from those who have much, we pray: ℟.
- That those who weep from loneliness or sorrow will be comforted and given joy through the compassion and kindness of others, we pray: ℟.

Let us offer together the prayer
that Jesus taught us.

Our Father . . .

Lord Jesus,
you stand on the plain
and call us to rise to your level
of compassion for others.
Teach us to look with love upon those
who are in need
and share with them our abundance.
That is your will, that all may be filled.
You who live and reign for ever and ever.
Amen.

✤ The word of the Lord endures
for ever.

✤ Lord, if you will, you can make me clean.

Psalm 91

page 379

Reading

Genesis 4:8–12

Cain said to his brother Abel, "Let us go out in the field." When they were in the field, Cain attacked his brother Abel and killed him. Then the LORD asked Cain, "Where is your brother Abel?" He answered, "I do not know. Am I my brother's keeper?" The LORD then said: "What have you done! Listen: your brother's blood cries out to me from the soil! Therefore you shall be banned from the soil that opened its mouth to receive your brother's blood from your hand. If you till the soil, it shall no longer give you its produce. You shall become a restless wanderer on the earth."

Reflection

Jealousy, rivalry, the desire to be the favored one in the eyes of God. This story from Genesis is still relevant today. Each day we are faced with how we can overcome these desires. We sometimes wish we would be better than others instead of working to become the best of ourselves. Our thoughts and actions against others only lead to guilt in ourselves. We are our brother's and sister's keepers. We must acknowledge the best in them and use it as an incentive to bring out our best. What will I improve in myself today?

Prayers

others may be added

God who loves us all, give us the grace to appreciate and love our brothers and sisters, and so we pray

℟. **Help us to love, O God.**

- For the Church, that she will continue to teach that we are all children of God and equal in his eyes, we pray: ℟.
- For those who grow things and those who care for flocks, may they honor each other's skills and rights so that all may benefit, we pray: ℟.
- For those who work in the field but do not benefit from its bounty, may they receive justice and their fill, we pray: ℟.
- For gardeners to rejoice in the harvest and for pet guardians to benefit from the companionship of their animals, we pray: ℟.

Let us offer together the prayer
that Jesus taught us.

Our Father . . .

Loving God,
in your creation you filled the earth
with vegetation
and every type of living creature.
You created us in your image
to care for the earth and all things on it.
Give us the grace to work tirelessly
to protect all your creation
and with the work of our own hands
help it to flourish.
Through Christ our Lord.
Amen.

✤ Lord, if you will, you can make me clean.

Tuesday, February 18, 2025

✚ In the beginning was the Word.

Psalm 95 *page 380*

Reading *Genesis 6:5–8*

When the LORD saw how great was man's wickedness on earth, and how no desire that his heart conceived was ever anything but evil, he regretted that he had made man on the earth, and his heart was grieved.

So the LORD said: "I will wipe out from the earth the men whom I have created, and not only the men, but also the beasts and the creeping things and the birds of the air, for I am sorry that I made them." But Noah found favor with the LORD.

Reflection

Children love to hear about the animals boarding the ark two by two. But the story of the flood is not a child's tale. It is a story of destruction but also of a new creation. The people have turned against God except for one just man. God looks upon what has become of his creation and decides to do it all over again. But the just man is rewarded with salvation for himself and his family, and he is given care of all the creatures. The actions of a single person are important. Let us strive to always do God's work and by doing it help to renew the earth.

Prayers *others may be added*

God of second chances, help us to always do your will. We ask your protection as we pray:

℟. **Preserve us from harm, O Lord.**

- For members of the Church, may they always follow God's commandments and be judged as just and worthy of salvation, we pray: ℟.
- For leaders around the world, may they turn from ways of hatred and violence and focus their citizens on the task of creating a new and better world, we pray: ℟.
- For those who protect the environment and the animals created by God who are in danger of extinction; may their work be considered worthy of our support, we pray: ℟.

Let us offer together the prayer that Jesus taught us.

Our Father . . .

O God,
you are just and yet merciful.
Help us to take advantage of your
generous love
and repent of our sins.
May we live again in the shelter
of your love.
Through Christ our Lord.
Amen.

✚ In the beginning was the Word.

✤ Wisdom has built herself a house.

Psalm 98

page 381

Reading

Mark 8:22–26

When Jesus and his disciples arrived at Bethsaida, people brought to him a blind man and begged him to touch him. He took the blind man by the hand and led him outside the village. Putting spittle on his eyes he laid his hands on the man and asked, "Do you see anything?" Looking up he replied, "I see people looking like trees and walking." Then he laid hands on the man's eyes a second time and he saw clearly; his sight was restored and he could see everything distinctly. Then he sent him home and said, "Do not even go into the village."

Reflection

There are many forms of blindness. What in my life am I blind to? Opening our eyes is difficult. Even Jesus needs to touch the blind man twice before he can truly see. We are often resistant to changing our ideas and our beliefs. We need to rely on others to help us get a clear perspective. The friends of the blind man advocated for him. Who in my life helps me to see clearly? How would you answer the question, "Do you see anything?" Let us pray for the ability to see things aright.

Prayers

others may be added

Lord Jesus, you restored sight to the blind man. Look upon our blindness and touch us with your compassion, as we pray:

℟. Open our eyes, O Lord.

- For the times we fail to see the way forward when we try to do your will, we pray: ℟.
- For the times leaders turn a blind eye to the needs of their people, we pray: ℟.
- For those whom we fail to see because they are poor or homeless or struggle with addiction, we pray: ℟.
- For the times we neglect to see the beauty in our world and as a result fail to protect it, we pray: ℟.

Let us offer together the prayer that Jesus taught us.

Our Father . . .

O God, you created us in your image.
Help us to see the world
and our brothers and sisters as you
see them.
Give us a new vision,
so that we might move forward
toward the future with clarity and love.
Through Christ our Lord.
Amen.

✤ Wisdom has built herself a house.

Thursday, February 20, 2025

✚ The law of God is in [our] heart.

Psalm 103

page 382

Reading

Mark 8:27–33

Jesus and his disciples set out for the villages of Caesarea Philippi. Along the way he asked his disciples, "Who do people say that I am?" They said in reply, "John the Baptist, others Elijah, still others one of the prophets." And he asked them, "But who do you say that I am?" Peter said to him in reply, "You are the Christ." Then he warned them not to tell anyone about him.

He began to teach them that the Son of Man must suffer greatly and be rejected by the elders, the chief priests, and the scribes, and be killed, and rise after three days. He spoke this openly. Then Peter took him aside and began to rebuke him. At this he turned around and, looking at his disciples, rebuked Peter and said, "Get behind me, Satan. You are thinking not as God does, but as human beings do."

Reflection

This passage poses a question to all of us, "But who do you say that I am?" Children often answer this question so differently. They have so many ideas since they have so many different life experiences. As we come to understand Jesus more, we recognize that even our answers change throughout our lives. How did you answer as a child? What is your answer today? What will it be years from now?

Prayers

others may be added

Lord Jesus, you reveal yourself to us in many ways. Help us to acknowledge your presence in our lives, as we pray:

℟. **Lord, help us to know you better.**

- In gratitude for the Church, who through her liturgy and sacraments unites us with Christ the Messiah, we pray: ℟.
- In gratitude for citizens in countries around the world who are the face of Jesus to those in need, we pray: ℟.
- In gratitude for those who serve the least among us by demonstrating God's love and compassion, we pray: ℟.
- In gratitude for parents and catechists who introduce children to Jesus and also learn from them, we pray: ℟.

Let us offer together the prayer that Jesus taught us.

Our Father . . .

Lord Jesus,
you are the Messiah.
Help us to recognize you
and your saving actions in our
own lives.
Let us always be willing to profess our
belief in you with conviction.
Through Christ our Lord.
Amen.

✚ The law of God is in [our] heart.

✤ Take delight in the Lord.

Psalm 115 *page 385*

Reading *Genesis 11:5–8*

The LORD came down to see the city and the tower that they had built. Then the LORD said: "If now, while they are one people, all speaking the same language, they have started to do this, nothing will later stop them from doing whatever they presume to do. Let us then go down and there confuse their language, so that one will not understand what another says." Thus the LORD scattered them from there all over the earth, and they stopped building the city.

Reflection

What if the whole world spoke the same language? What if everyone used the same words and agreed on the same, truthful meaning? In one sense that would be ideal. But what about diversity? Is it possible that even though we live in different places, follow different customs, and speak different languages we can still strive for unity? The celebration of Pentecost gives us hope. There, amid all the differences there was understanding and truth. The Spirit of God is still present among us. Let us pray that it helps us to find communion with all our sisters and brothers.

Prayers *others may be added*

O God, we come to you speaking many languages, living different lives. Bring us together in your love, as we pray:

℟. Lord, help us to love.

✦ For the Church, that she will find common ground with all peoples, we pray: ℟.

✦ For countries around the world, that they might always work toward unity and peace while honoring differences, we pray: ℟.

✦ For those without a voice to speak for themselves, may their advocates find the words and the will to address their needs, we pray: ℟.

✦ For writers and filmmakers, for poets and songwriters, may their creative talents unite those who are entertained by their creative works, we pray: ℟.

Let us offer together the prayer
that Jesus taught us.

Our Father . . .

Loving God,
you created us in your image.
No matter where we live,
how we speak or how we are governed,
help us to understand that we are
all neighbors
because we are all your children.
Through Christ our Lord.
Amen.

✤ Take delight in the Lord.

✤ [Our] lamp will never go out.

Psalm 121

page 386

Reading

1 Peter 5:1–4

Beloved: I exhort the presbyters among you, as a fellow presbyter and witness to the sufferings of Christ and one who has a share in the glory to be revealed. Tend the flock of God in your midst, overseeing not by constraint but willingly, as God would have it, not for shameful profit but eagerly. Do not lord it over those assigned to you, but be examples to the flock. And when the chief Shepherd is revealed, you will receive the unfading crown of glory.

Reflection

Today we celebrate the Feast of the Chair of Peter. Through the symbol of the Chair, we come to understand that all who succeed Peter as head of the Church on earth are charged with an important mission. The pope is called by God to preserve the unity of the Church and by being faithful to the Gospel exemplify compassionate care for the people of God. Let us pray for our pope as he works tirelessly to fulfill this mission.

Prayers

others may be added

Peter was chosen by you to lead your people, the Church. We ask your blessing on his successor as we pray for him and for us:

℟. **Lord, make us one in you.**

- For the pope, that he might be the light of unity to all those who seek God, we pray: ℟.
- For all leaders, that they might work for unity among nations and peace among all people, we pray: ℟.
- For refugees who are without home or country, may they be welcomed and cared for with compassion, we pray: ℟.
- For communities, filled with people of many faiths, may they seek unity by working together as they learn to love one another, we pray: ℟.

Let us offer together the prayer that Jesus taught us.

Our Father . . .

O God,
you bless your Church with
strong leaders.
Help us be attentive to your Word
that all may be one in you.
Give us the grace to live the Gospel
with fidelity
and respond to the example
of our leaders.
Through Christ our Lord.
Amen.

✤ [Our] lamp will never go out.

✣ Love one another as I have loved you.

Psalm 122 *page 387*

Reading *Luke 6:27–31, 35*

Jesus said to his disciples: "To you who hear I say, love your enemies, do good to those who hate you, bless those who curse you, pray for those who mistreat you. To the person who strikes you on one cheek, offer the other one as well, and from the person who takes your cloak, do not withhold even your tunic. Give to everyone who asks of you, and from the one who takes what is yours do not demand it back. Do to others as you would have them do to you . . . love your enemies and do good to them, and lend expecting nothing back; then your reward will be great and you will be children of the Most High, for he himself is kind to the ungrateful and the wicked."

Reflection

Once, when presenting this passage to some fifth-graders, one of the students responded, "But God doesn't mean terrorists!" Suggesting that there might have been a qualifier we missed reading, we reread the passage. Not finding any difference the student's response was the same. The question then became, "Does my response change God's word?" He agreed not. How wise and honest. We decided then it was up to us to live into this challenge by becoming more like our God. Dare we become like this struggling but determined ten-year-old.

Prayers *others may be added*

God, you call us to be like you even in the most difficult of actions. Be with us, as we pray:

℟. **Give us courage, O Lord.**

- That members of the Church will view all people as friends and not enemies, we pray: ℟.
- That nations may change their weapons of war into ploughshares to sustain and feed their people, we pray: ℟.
- That all those who are held captive in prisons of steel or prisons of hatred will someday be embraced by love, we pray: ℟.
- That children from the earliest age will learn to cooperate and build friendships by watching the example of the adults in their lives, we pray: ℟.

Let us offer together the prayer
that Jesus taught us.

Our Father . . .

Crucified Lord,
you forgave your enemies—
even on the cross.
You ask us to do only what you have
already done.
Fill us with your Spirit and your love
so that we might walk in your footsteps
and share your love and forgiveness
with all people.
Who live and reign for ever and ever.
Amen.

✣ Love one another as I have loved you.

Weekday

Monday, February 24, 2025

✤ I am the light of the world.

Psalm 24

page 367

Reading

Sirach 1:1–8

All wisdom comes from the LORD / and with him it remains forever, and is before all time / The sand of the seashore, the drops of rain, / the days of eternity: who can number these? / Heaven's height, earth's breadth, / the depths of the abyss: who can explore these? / Before all things else wisdom was created; / and prudent understanding, from eternity. / The word of God on high is the fountain of wisdom / and her ways are everlasting. / To whom has wisdom's root been revealed? / Who knows her subtleties? / To whom has the discipline of wisdom been revealed? / And who has understood the multiplicity of her ways? / There is but one, wise and truly awe-inspiring, / seated upon his throne: / There is but one, Most High / all-powerful creator-king and truly awe-inspiring one, / seated upon his throne and he is the God of dominion.

Reflection

Pope Francis

The wisdom the Holy Spirit grants is the grace of being able to see things through God's eyes. It is seeing the world, situations, problems, everything, with the eyes of God. And obviously this derives from intimacy with God, from the relationship of a son with his Father. When we are in communion with the Lord, it is through the Holy Spirit that our heart transforms and we are able to perceive all its warmth and predilection.

Prayers

others may be added

God of wisdom, you fill the earth with your works of wonder and give them to us as a gift. Fill us with wonder and awe, as we pray:

℟. Help us appreciate your gifts, O Lord.

- For an awareness of the daily miracles of our world bestowed upon us, we pray: ℟.
- For the beauty of different lands and the wonders of different peoples around the world, we pray: ℟.
- For those who live diminished lives due to depression or illness, may those who care for them bring joy back into their lives, we pray: ℟.
- For each of us, that every day we might find a reason for joy in our lives that inspires us to share God's gifts with others, we pray: ℟.

Let us offer together the prayer that Jesus taught us.

Our Father . . .

God of wonder and awe,
you created us to share in your wisdom
and your creativity.
Inspire us to use our gifts wisely
and share in your creative acts
for the benefit of all.
Through Christ our Lord.
Amen.

✤ I am the light of the world.

✠ There is a season for everything.

Psalm 27 *page 368*

Reading *Sirach 2:1–5*

My son, when you come to serve the LORD, / stand in justice and fear, / prepare yourself for trials. / Be sincere of heart and steadfast, / incline your ear and receive the word of understanding, / undisturbed in time of adversity. / Wait on God, with patience, cling to him, forsake him not; / thus will you be wise in all your ways. / Accept whatever befalls you, / when sorrowful, be steadfast, / and in crushing misfortune be patient; / For in fire gold and silver are tested, / and worthy people in the crucible of humiliation.

Reflection

Who among us has not known trouble? Even as we relate or share our own troubles with a friend we come to realize that they too have their own suffering. It enables us to comfort one another. It gives us hope that as we see another survive life's tragedies, we might also find strength. We should not expect our lives to be easy. But we can trust in God because we have seen that those who do are not disappointed. The one who became like us will not abandon us to sorrow.

Prayers *others may be added*

Compassionate God, you promise that if we trust in you, we will not be disappointed, and so we pray:

℟. **Be with us, O God.**

- For the Church, that she might be a beacon of hope for all those who are in trouble, we pray: ℟.
- For leaders of countries that they might serve their citizens by enacting laws that protect their rights and support their livelihoods, we pray: ℟.
- For those affected by storms and drought, fires and floods, may they be assisted in their troubles by those who commit their lives to helping those in danger, we pray: ℟.
- For those who staff homeless shelters and women's shelters may they share God's compassion and care as they reach out to those in trouble and sorrow, we pray: ℟.

Let us offer together the prayer that Jesus taught us.

Our Father . . .

O God,
you promise that all who call upon you
will be heard and answered.
You promise that if we hope for good
things we will be fulfilled.
We believe and trust in you.
Help us to always put our faith in you
and show us that our hope is not
in vain.
Through Christ our Lord.
Amen.

✠ There is a season for everything.

Weekday

Wednesday, February 26, 2025

✤ I have put my trust in you, O Lord.

Psalm 30 *page 369*

page 369

Reading *Mark 9:38–40*

John said to Jesus, "Teacher, we saw someone driving out demons in your name, and we tried to prevent him because he does not follow us." Jesus replied, "Do not prevent him. There is no one who performs a mighty deed in my name who can at the same time speak ill of me. For whoever is not against us is for us."

Reflection

Who is for us? Who are the ones I rely on? Who are the ones who rely on me? How are we called to work together for the good of all? The line after this short passage ends gives us a simple measure of judgment. It tells us that even anyone who gives another a cup of water in Christ's name will be rewarded. Let us put away our grand ideas of service that often paralyze us into inaction. Rather, let us think of simple ways to make life better for others and put those ideas into action. What three things can I do today?

Prayers *others may be added*

God of small things, you ask us to do great things in simple ways. Help us to image ways in which to serve you, as we pray:

℟. Inspire us, O God.

- That the Church around the world may always find ways to serve people every day as Christ did, we pray: ℟.
- That leaders of countries will look to the daily needs of people with the hope that their work will strengthen and support their citizens to do greater things, we pray: ℟.
- That those who need drink and food, clothing and shelter, visits when they are sick and imprisoned will receive comfort from those who are willing to do simple things well, we pray: ℟.
- That parents and caregivers may always recognize and respond to the simple needs of those who depend on them, we pray: ℟.

Let us offer together the prayer
that Jesus taught us.

Our Father . . .

O God,
you ask us to be neighbor to all those
  who need us.
Help us to not look at our differences
but recognize that we must do the things
that help us be there for one another
  in your name.
Through Christ our Lord.
Amen.

✤ I have put my trust in you, O Lord.

✤ God . . . is faithful and just.

Psalm 51 *page 373*

Reading *Mark 9: 42–45*

[Jesus said:] "Whoever causes one of these little ones who believe in me to sin, it would be better for him if a great millstone were put around his neck and he were thrown into the sea. If your hand causes you to sin, cut it off. It is better for you to enter into life maimed than with two hands to go into Gehenna, into the unquenchable fire. And if your foot causes you to sin, cut if off. It is better for you to enter into life crippled than with two feet to be thrown into Gehenna.

Reflection

Mark's Gospel tells us that whatever keeps us from doing God's will should be abandoned; if not, we will be punished. More than worrying about ourselves we must keep our focus on not letting our behavior scandalize and lead others to sin. Our good lives are not only necessary for our own salvation but for the purpose of saving our community.

Prayers *others may be added*

Merciful God, we rely on your mercy;
yet we know that we are responsible
for our actions. Help us to lead lives
of goodness, as we pray:

℟. Forgiving God, hear our prayer.

- For the Church, that she may always provide the opportunity to celebrate reconciliation with our God and our neighbor, we pray: ℟.
- For the world, that its leaders may come together to discover ways to create peace among those who would continue to wage war, we pray: ℟.
- For those of us who look away from those in need, may we ask God's mercy to help us turn our face toward them and respond with love, we pray: ℟.
- When there are disputes between families and neighbors, may we work toward harmony and forgiveness rather than hold grudges and continue feuds, we pray: ℟.

Let us offer together the prayer
that Jesus taught us.

Our Father . . .

Loving Father,
you care for us as your children.
Help us to consider not only our
own salvation
but to look toward being a good example
to others
instead of a source of their sin.
Through Christ our Lord.
Amen.

✤ God . . . is faithful and just.

Friday, February 28, 2025

✢ The Lord is at my right hand.

Psalm 34 *page 370*

Reading *Sirach 6:15–17*

A faithful friend is a sturdy shelter; / he who finds one finds a treasure. / A faithful friend is beyond price, / no sum can balance his worth. / A faithful friend is a life-saving remedy, / such as he who fears God finds; / For he who fears God behaves accordingly, / and his friend will be like himself.

Reflection

Who is your friend? Sirach teaches us that a good and faithful friend is beyond price. It is easy for us to believe that is true if we have known good friendships. But let us consider, "To whom am I a friend?" What I consider as important in friendship requires the same of me. Take some time today to thank God for the good friends in your life. Let us pray that we can develop and share the qualities of friendship with others and, perhaps, extend our friendship to a wider circle of people not yet among those counted as our friends.

Prayers *others may be added*

God of love, you bless us with people we call friends. Help each us to be a friend as well, as we ask your guidance and pray:

℟. Create in me a kind heart, O God.

- May the example of Christ and his disciples, Mary and Martha, teach us the joys and challenges of friendship, we pray: ℟.
- May justice abound in the world so that even those we consider enemies might be served with fairness and understanding, and lead toward reducing hatred and fear, we pray: ℟.
- May we choose to become friends with those who have none, we pray: ℟.
- May we be an example of friendship to the young people in our lives so that they might develop a variety of friendships, we pray: ℟.
- May each of us pass on the qualities of a good friend by always acting like one, we pray: ℟.

Let us offer together the prayer that Jesus taught us.

Our Father . . .

Lord Jesus,
you taught us the lesson of friendship
when you gave us the example
of the Good Samaritan.
Teach us to go the extra mile
not only for those we like but also those in need.
May we never count the cost of the good we can do.
You who live and reign for ever and ever.
Amen.

✢ The Lord is at my right hand.

✚ Your presence fills me with joy.

Psalm 23

page 367

Reading

Mark 10:13–16

People were bringing children to Jesus that he might touch them, but the disciples rebuked them. When Jesus saw this he became indignant and said to them, "Let the children come to me; do not prevent them, for the Kingdom of God belongs to such as these. Amen, I say to you, whoever does not accept the Kingdom of God like a child will not enter it." Then he embraced the children and blessed them, placing his hands on them.

Reflection

"People were bringing their children to Jesus." Isn't that what we still do? Whether they are our children or children who are entrusted to our care, we bring them to Jesus with our word and our example. But we look to them also, for they teach us to accept the kingdom with open arms. They trust in God and so should we. They depend on God and so should we. They love God with innocent hearts and so should we. The kingdom belongs to them and to us. Let us cherish the children in our lives and all the children of the world.

Prayers

others may be added

Loving Father, we are all your children.
Receive us and bless us as we pray:

℟. **Welcoming God, hear us.**

- For all those preparing for baptism at Easter, may they be received by the Church with loving arms, we pray: ℟.
- For all children around the world, may they be cared for and nourished so they may become strong future leaders, we pray: ℟.
- For all children who are abandoned or abused, homeless or victims of war, may we protect them, provide them with safe shelter, and be someone to love and care for them, we pray: ℟.
- For all the children in our community, may we be a source of their good education, exposure to the arts, and examples of service to others, we pray: ℟.

Let us offer together the prayer
that Jesus taught us.

Our Father . . .

God our Father,
as you love Jesus your Son,
look upon us, your children,
and make us one with you.
Help us to keep your commandments
and remain in your love until
we are with you forever.
Through Christ our Lord.
Amen.

✚ Your presence fills me with joy.

Sunday, March 2, 2025

✤ Seek first the kingdom of God.

Psalm 46 *page 372*

Reading *Luke 6:43–45*

Jesus told his disciples a parable, "A good tree does not bear rotten fruit, nor does a rotten tree bear good fruit. For every tree is known by its own fruit. For people do not pick figs from thornbushes, nor do they gather grapes from brambles. A good person out of the store of goodness in his heart produces good, but an evil person out of a store of evil produces evil; for from the fullness of the heart the mouth speaks."

Reflection

A lilac bush in our yard lost some of its branches during a hard winter. Many of them lay strewn across the yard. Spring cleanup time came and the dead branches were still there. Passing the bush one day I noticed one of the broken branches on the ground had begun to bloom. How was that possible? Examining it more closely, a single strip of bark was still attached to the bush. That was all it needed to flourish! Connection is an important part of any relationship. If we stay connected to Jesus we can produce good fruit.

Prayers *others may be added*

God of the harvest, you look forward to gathering all good things we produce. Help us to stay connected to you, our source of life, as we pray

℟. Gather us to you, O Lord.

- For all members of the Church; may our unity with Jesus help us to produce good fruit, we pray: ℟.
- For farmers and growers around the world; may their labor yield a harvest that will feed all people, we pray: ℟.
- For migrant workers, that their hard work will be rewarded with just wages and times of rest, we pray: ℟.
- For grocers and gardeners; may their supplies and harvests be abundant; we pray: ℟.
- For workers, that they may rejoice as they witness the results of their labors enjoyed by those who benefit from their work, we pray: ℟.

Let us offer together the prayer that Jesus taught us.

Our Father . . .

Creator God,
you gave us every kind of plant
and seed, tree and vegetation.
Bless those who till the earth
for our benefit
and grant them an abundant harvest.
May we share the fruits of the earth
with those who hunger.
Through Christ our Lord.
Amen.

✤ Seek first the kingdom of God.

✠ Blessed be the name of the Lord.

Psalm 47 *page 372*

page 372

Reading *Mark 10:17–22*

As Jesus was setting out on a journey, a man ran up, knelt down before him, and asked him, "Good teacher, what must I do to inherit eternal life?" Jesus answered him, "Why do you call me good? No one is good but God alone. You know the commandments: *You shall not kill; you shall not commit adultery; you shall not steal; you shall not bear false witness; you shall not defraud; honor your father and your mother.*" He replied and said to him, "Teacher, all of these I have observed from my youth." Jesus, looking at him, loved him and said to him, "You are lacking in one thing. Go, sell what you have, and give to the poor and you will have treasure in heaven; then come, follow me." At that statement his face fell, and he went away sad, for he had many possessions.

Reflection

We may not consider ourselves among the rich but we can certainly identify with the man in this story. As we count our possessions, which would we be willing to do without? Perhaps we are just meant to keep our things but not make them the most important in our lives. What exactly do we owe to the poor? These are questions we must each answer for ourselves, remembering Jesus' words.

Prayers *others may be added*

God of the rich and the poor, teach us to value your love and your word above all else, as we pray:

℟. **Grant us eternal life, O Lord.**

- That all Christians may follow the teachings of Jesus that lead us to a place in his kingdom, we pray: ℟.
- That the rich of the world will assess their possessions and be inspired to share the goods of the earth more justly, we pray: ℟.
- That those who search for jobs may be rewarded with employment and just wages, we pray: ℟.
- That homeless shelters, shelters for battered women and children, and other organizations that help the poor may receive donations of clothing and household items so they can be reused by those in need, we pray: ℟.

Let us offer together the prayer
that Jesus taught us.

Our Father . . .

O God,
you always challenge us to do more,
  to be more.
You ask much of us but it is for our good
  and our growth.
Help us to develop a generous spirit
  and a loving heart
that allows us to give what we have
  and not count the cost.
Through Christ our Lord.
Amen.

✠ Blessed be the name of the Lord.

Tuesday, March 4, 2025

✤ Lord, you have probed me
and you know me.

Psalm 71 *page 376*

Reading *Mark 10:28–31*

Peter began to say to Jesus, "We have given up everything and followed you." Jesus said, "Amen, I say to you, there is no one who has given up house or brothers or sisters or mother or father or children or lands for my sake and for the sake of the Gospel who will not receive a hundred times more now in this present age: houses and brothers and sisters and mothers and children and lands, with persecutions, and eternal life in the age to come. But many that are first will be last, and the last will be first."

Reflection

Peter asks the question we all consider at some time. What do we get for all that we do? Jesus assures us that we will be rewarded. Perhaps we might step back and consider if that is the right question to ask. In the liturgy one of the prayers asks, "What will I give back to the Lord for all that has been given to me?" This question is the reverse of Peter's question. Let us first count the multiple blessings we have received. We might determine that all we have done is not yet enough. Then we might learn to give without asking for a reward.

Prayers *others may be added*

Generous God, help us to be like you and give generously—even when not asked, as we pray:

℟. **Give us a generous heart, O Lord.**

- For the Holy Father as he receives our donations throughout the year and distributes them to needy groups around the world, we pray: ℟.
- For the success of all non-governmental organizations who rely on our support and who work tirelessly under dangerous and difficult situations, we pray: ℟.
- For those who feel unappreciated, unnoticed, and unloved, may we reach out to them with kindness and fill them with a feeling of self-worth, we pray: ℟.
- For the courage of first responders, who put their lives on the line to keep us safe and bring us to safety when needed, may we give them our support, we pray: ℟.

Let us offer together the prayer
that Jesus taught us.

Our Father . . .

Patient God,
you wait for us to understand what it
means to follow you.
Help us not to always list the things
we have done
but to look for the things we have
yet to do in your name.
Through Christ our Lord.
Amen.

✤ Lord, you have probed me
and you know me.

✤ You are merciful to all, O Lord.

Psalm 42

page 371

Reading

Matthew 6:1–2, 5–6, 16–18

Jesus said to his disciples: "Take care not to perform righteous deeds in order that people may see them; otherwise, you will have no recompense from your heavenly Father. When you give alms, do not blow a trumpet before you, as the hypocrites do in the synagogues and in the streets to win the praise of others. . . .

"When you pray, do not be like the hypocrites, who love to stand and pray in the synagogues and on street corners so that others may see them. Amen, I say to you, they have received their reward. But when you pray, go to your inner room, close the door, and pray to your Father in secret. And your Father who sees in secret will repay you.

"When you fast, do not look gloomy like the hypocrites. They neglect their appearance, so that they may appear to others to be fasting. Amen, I say to you, they have received their reward. But when you fast, anoint your head and wash your face, so that you may not appear to be fasting, except to your Father who is hidden. And your Father who sees what is hidden will repay you."

Reflection

The righteous deeds of praying, giving alms, and fasting are an offering to God, not to man. Jesus' directions remind us of this fact. We offer these practices to God because we love him and we want to make recompense for our sinfulness and the sinfulness of the world. These righteous deeds should arise from an interior desire to please God. May we foster the interior movements of our hearts so that we will become closer to God. May this ever-growing love of God move us to pray, to fast, and to give alms for his glory.

Prayers

others may be added

Lord, we place ourselves in your presence and offer to you our prayers.

℟. **In your mercy, hear our prayer.**

- For the Church throughout the world, that she may guide all souls to God, we pray: ℟.
- For leaders of nations, that they may seek the common good of all, we pray: ℟.
- For the poor and the oppressed, that our righteous deeds will alleviate their suffering, we pray: ℟
- For our neighbors, both locally and globally, that they may be transformed by our prayers, fasting, and almsgiving, we pray: ℟.

As one body, we pray in the words our merciful Lord gave us.

Our Father . . .

God our Father,
as we begin this holy season of Lent,
strengthen us to reject the world,
discipline our bodies and minds,
and direct our thoughts to our final end
in heaven with you.
Through Christ our Lord.
Amen.

✤ You are merciful to all, O Lord.

Thursday, March 6, 2025

✤ The Lord . . . rescued me from those who attack me.

Psalm 141

page 389

Reading

Luke 9:22–25

Jesus said to his disciples: "The Son of Man must suffer greatly and be rejected by the elders, the chief priests, and the scribes, and be killed and on the third day be raised."

Then he said to all, "If anyone wishes to come after me, he must deny himself and take up his cross daily and follow me. For whoever wishes to save his life will lose it, but whoever loses his life for my sake will save it. What profit is there for one to gain the whole world yet lose or forfeit himself?"

Reflection

Throughout the Lenten season, the cross of Christ is always before us. The cross was not an interruption in the life of Jesus or an obstacle to be overcome. The cross was the whole point. It is the same for all who are baptized into the death of Jesus Christ. Jesus tells us that if we follow him, we will surely carry the cross. Truly living our baptism means realizing that the suffering we encounter in our daily lives is not a mistake. Rather, it is the means by which we grow in holiness; it is the only way to follow Christ.

Prayers

others may be added

Lord, we humbly come before you and beg that you hear our prayers:

℟. In your mercy, hear our prayer.

- That the Church may light our path to God in times of darkness and confusion, we pray: ℟.
- That leaders of nations will light the path of peace and refuge to those seeking a better life, we pray: ℟.
- That all peoples may recognize their solidarity with the poor and the oppressed we pray: ℟.
- That our community may be renewed by our acts of true charity, we pray: ℟.

As one body, we pray in the words our merciful Lord gave us.

Our Father . . .

God of wisdom,
you offer clear direction for how we are to live our lives,
yet we still lose our way.
Forgive us our selfish habits and lead us in the path of humility.
Through Christ our Lord..
Amen.

✤ The Lord . . . rescued me from those who attack me.

✚ The Lord heard and had mercy on me.

Psalm 139
page 389

Reading
Isaiah 58:3c–9a

Lo, on your fast day you carry out your own pursuits, / and drive all your laborers. / Yes, your fast ends in quarreling and fighting, / striking with wicked claw. / Would that today you might fast / so as to make your voice heard on high! / Is this the manner of fasting I wish, / of keeping a day of penance: / That a man bow his head like a reed / and lie in sackcloth and ashes? / Do you call this a fast, / a day acceptable to the LORD? / This, rather, is the fasting that I wish: / releasing those bound unjustly, / untying the thongs of the yoke; / Setting free the oppressed, / breaking every yoke; / Sharing your bread with the hungry, / sheltering the oppressed and the homeless; / Clothing the naked when you see them, / and not turning your back on your own. / Then your light shall break forth like the dawn, / and your wound shall quickly be healed; / Your vindication shall go before you, / and the glory of the LORD shall be your rear guard. / Then you shall call, and the LORD will answer, / you shall cry for help, and he will say: Here I am!

Reflection
The Lord tells the people that their fasting is false. The people are attached to worldly pursuits and this corruption is revealed with their mutual interaction. God tells them to live in true solidarity with their neighbors. Solidarity helps us to see that all people are equal in the eyes of God; therefore, the exploitation and oppression of others should not happen. Through our Lenten practices, may our relationship with our neighbors be transformed into one of solidarity.

Prayers
others may be added

Lord, we place ourselves in your presence, as we turn to you in prayer.

℟. **In your mercy, hear our prayer.**

- That the Church may help us live in solidarity with one another, we pray: ℟.
- That leaders of nations become aware of the needs of the voiceless, we pray: ℟.
- That our eyes will be opened to see in our neighbor God's own image, we pray: ℟.
- That our community may be transformed by our Lenten witness, we pray: ℟.

As one body, we pray in the words our merciful Lord gave us.

Our Father . . .

God our Father,
during this holy season of Lent,
strengthen us to love our neighbor
as we love ourselves.
Through Christ our Lord.
Amen.

✚ The Lord heard and had mercy on me.

Saturday, March 8, 2025

✠ In the abundance of your mercies,
look upon [me].

Psalm 126

page 387

Reading

Isaiah 58:9b–12

Thus says the LORD: / If you remove from your midst oppression, / false accusation and malicious speech; / If you bestow your bread on the hungry / and satisfy the afflicted; / Then light shall rise for you in the darkness, / and the gloom shall become for you like midday; / Then the LORD will guide you always / and give you plenty even on the parched land. / He will renew your strength, / and you shall be like a watered garden, / like a spring whose water never fails. / The ancient ruins shall be rebuilt for your sake, / and the foundations from ages past you shall raise up; / "Repairer of the breach," they shall call you, / "Restorer of ruined homesteads."

Reflection

The Lord continually invites us to love him by loving our neighbor. "If you remove from your midst oppression, / false accusation and malicious speech; / If you bestow your bread on the hungry / and satisfy the afflicted; / Then light shall rise for you in the darkness." The goods of this world are meant for everybody. We are called to share these goods with those who have little. Our interior dispositions need to be purged of all improperly ordered attachments so we may give freely and generously of that which God meant for all.

Prayers

others may be added

Lord, you desire that we love one another and so we humbly bring these petitions to you:

℟. **In your mercy, hear our prayer.**

- That the Church throughout the world may guide us to serve those on the peripheries, we pray: ℟.
- That leaders of nations may build a civilization of love, we pray: ℟.
- That those who are poor and oppressed may be a constant reminder of our need to love and serve one another, we pray: ℟.
- That we may become aware of our flaws and biases and resolve to correct them, we pray: ℟.

As one body, we pray in the words our merciful Lord gave us.

Our Father . . .

God our Father,
as we begin this holy season of Lent,
order our desires so we may love
and serve our neighbors
according to your holy will.
Through Christ our Lord.
Amen.

✠ In the abundance of your mercies,
look upon [me].

✚ When [the Lord] calls on me,
I will answer him.

Psalm 51 *page 373*

Reading *Deuteronomy 26:4–10*

Moses spoke to the people, saying: “The priest shall receive the basket from you and shall set it in front of the altar of the LORD, your God. Then you shall declare before the LORD, your God, ‘My father was a wandering Aramean who went down to Egypt with a small household and lived there as an alien. But there he became a nation great, strong, and numerous. When the Egyptians maltreated and oppressed us, imposing hard labor upon us, we cried to the LORD, the God of our fathers, and he heard our cry and saw our affliction, our toil and our oppression. He brought us out of Egypt with his strong hand and outstretched arm, with terrifying power, with signs and wonders; and bringing us into this country, he gave us this land flowing with milk and honey. Therefore, I have now brought you the firstfruits of the products of the soil which you, O LORD, have given me.’ And having set them before the Lord, your God, you shall bow down in his presence.”

Reflection

Sometimes we can become so overburdened by the worries of our day that we forget that God is with us. He is present to us in every trial; even the most trivial. In today’s reading, we hear the Israelites recall with great detail their sufferings that transformed into joy. Out of thankfulness and praise, the Israelites return to God the first bounty from their land. Can you recall a time when you were worried and realized God helped you through this time of struggle? Praise him right now for it. Try to make it a regular practice to be aware of the generous gifts that God has blesssed you with. Doing so may further amplify your great love for him. May this great love inspire you to avoid sin and be moved to perform acts of charity toward your neighbor.

Prayers *others may be added*

Lord, we remember your great deeds
and humbly present to you the needs
of the world:

℟. **Lord, have mercy.**

✦ For the People of God, that they may find sustenance in the Word of God, we pray: ℟.

✦ For people of all nations, that love will overpower fear and despair, we pray: ℟.

✦ For all who are struggling to trust in God, we pray: ℟.

✦ For the recognition that all people are imbued with dignity, we pray: ℟.

As one body, we pray in the words
our merciful Lord gave us.

Our Father . . .

God our Father,
may we freely give of ourselves
and of our excess
for the good of all people and the glory
of your name.
Through Christ our Lord.
Amen.

✚ When [the Lord] calls on me,
I will answer him.

Monday, March 10, 2025

✤ Have mercy on us, Lord, have mercy.

Psalm 115

page 385

Reading

Matthew 25:42–46

Jesus said to his disciples: "'. . . For I was hungry and you gave me no food, I was thirsty and you gave me no drink, a stranger and you gave me no welcome, naked and you gave me no clothing, ill and in prison, and you did not care for me.' Then they will answer and say, 'Lord, when did we see you hungry or thirsty or a stranger or naked or ill or in prison, and not minister to your needs?' He will answer them, 'Amen, I say to you, what you did not do for one of these least ones, you did not do for me.' And these will go off to eternal punishment, but the righteous to eternal life."

Reflection

This is the plain truth. When we pass from this world we will face God's judgment. We now have the choice to order our lives according to God's will and avail ourselves of his unfathomable mercy. This entire season of Lent is an opportunity to purge ourselves of sin. The Church reminds us to take courage and travel the lifelong path to conversion. Conversion not only involves faith in God, but expressing that faith in our good works.

Prayers

others may be added

Lord, aware of our weakness we approach you in humility and ask for your help:

℟. Lord, have mercy.

- That the Church may offer support and assistance to those in need, we pray: ℟.
- That the plight of the forgotten ones—those who are poor, or elderly, or children, or imprisoned—may be made known and their needs be met, we pray: ℟.
- That we may we work to repair the bonds of humanity that sin has broken, we pray: ℟.
- That we may see the presence of God in those who are poor and those who suffer oppression, we pray: ℟.

As one body, we pray in the words our merciful Lord gave us.

Our Father . . .

God of love,
let us seek all those who are lost,
feed all who are hungry,
and cloth all those who are naked
in the garment of your love.
May we serve you in all we do.
Through Christ our Lord.
Amen.

✤ Have mercy on us, Lord, have mercy.

✣ O Lord, you have been our refuge.

Psalm 130

page 388

Reading

Matthew 6:7–15

Jesus said to his disciples: "In praying, do not babble like the pagans, who think that they will be heard because of their many words. Do not be like them. Your Father knows what you need before you ask him.

"This is how you are to pray: / Our Father who art in heaven, / hallowed be thy name, / thy Kingdom come, / thy will be done, / on earth as it is in heaven. / Give us this day our daily bread; / and forgive us our trespasses, / as we forgive those who trespass against us; / and lead us not into temptation, / but deliver us from evil.

"If you forgive men their transgressions, your heavenly Father will forgive you. But if you do not forgive men, neither will your Father forgive your transgressions."

Reflection

St. Teresa of Ávila once said that the soul is like a castle made entirely out of a single diamond or very clear crystal. In this crystal castle there are many rooms. In the center is a dwelling place in which secret connections take place between God and the soul. One enters this dwelling place through prayer. St. Teresa said that prayer opens the door to encounter the mystery of God. Prayer is absolutely essential for this enounter, whether the prayer is said quietly in our minds or verbalized out loud. Let us take up the practice of prayer and persevere, for through it we are united with God.

Prayers

others may be added

Lord, aware of our weakness we approach you in humility and ask for your help as we pray:

℟. Lord of mercy, hear our prayer.

- For the Church throughout the world, that may she offer to God constant prayers, we pray: ℟.
- For all inhabitants of the world, may they continually offer God praise, we pray: ℟.
- For the poor and the oppressed, that they will cry out to the Lord with their needs, we pray: ℟.
- For us, that we may pray through Christ, with Christ, and in Christ, at all times, we pray: ℟.

As one body, we pray in the words our merciful Lord gave us.

Our Father . . .

God our Father,
you are present in us.
May we pray with rapt attention
so that the castle of our soul becomes
a dwelling place for God.
Through Christ our Lord.
Amen.

✣ O Lord, you have been our refuge.

Wednesday, March 12, 2025

✚ Remember your compassion, O Lord.

Psalm 42

page 371

Reading

Jonah 3:7–10

[The king of Nineveh said:]: "Neither man nor beast, neither cattle nor sheep, shall taste anything; they shall not eat, nor shall they drink water. Man and beast shall be covered with sackcloth and call loudly to God; every man shall turn from his evil way and from the violence he has in hand. Who knows, God may relent and forgive, and withhold his blazing wrath, so that we shall not perish." When God saw by their actions how they turned from their evil way, he repented of the evil that he had threatened to do to them; he did not carry it out.

Reflection

Pope Francis

We know that the state of sin distances us from God. But in fact, sin is the way that we distance ourselves from him. Yet that does not mean that God distances himself from us. The state of weakness and confusion that results from sin is one more reason for God to remain close to us. . . . The certainty of this should accompany us throughout our lives. His grace is constantly at work in us, to strengthen our hope that his love will never be lacking, in spite of any sin we may have committed by rejecting his presence in our lives. . . . Let us now ask the Lord for the grace to know the greatness of his love, which wipes away our every sin. Let us allow ourselves to be purified by love, in order to recognize true love!

Prayers

others may be added

Lord, aware of our weakness we approach you in humility and ask for your help.

℟. Be merciful to us, O Lord.

- That the Church be open to the Word of God, we pray: ℟.
- That leaders of nations listen to the voices of the poor, we pray: ℟.
- That those who are poor and oppressed may find comfort and healing, we pray: ℟.
- That we may we work together to build a culture of life, we pray: ℟.

As one body, we pray in the words our merciful Lord gave us.

Our Father . . .

O merciful God,
open wide your mercy to us and
  to all generations,
for we so desperately need your
  loving forgivness.
Help us cast out violence, greed,
  and selfishness,
that we may live peacefully, generously,
  and in unity.
Through Christ our Lord.
Amen.

✚ Remember your compassion, O Lord.

✤ You are Peter, and upon this rock
I will build my Church.

Psalm 141
page 389

Reading
Matthew 7:7–12

Jesus said to his disciples: "Ask and it will be given to you; seek and you will find; knock and the door will be opened to you. For everyone who asks, receives; and the one who seeks, finds; and to the one who knocks, the door will be opened. Which one of you would hand his son a stone when he asked for a loaf of bread, or a snake when he asked for a fish? If you then, who are wicked, know how to give good gifts to your children, how much more will your heavenly Father give good things to those who ask him.

"Do to others whatever you would have them do to you. This is the law and the prophets."

Reflection

"How much more will your heavenly Father give good things to those who ask him." Certainly it is fine to ask the Lord for help when we worry or struggle financially. But what good things should we ask of him? What will aid us in the spiritual life? St. Francis de Sales once said that we should ask God to help us understand the effects that sin has on our soul. Knowledge of our sins along with God's grace will help to enliven our contrition. True contrition begets humility. With true humily we will follow God's path.

Prayers
others may be added

The Lord has commanded us to pray, and so we come before him with our needs.

℟. Lord, hear us.

- That the Church throughout the world may offer unceasing prayers to God, we pray: ℟.
- That all may work together for peace and unity, we pray: ℟.
- That catechumens preparing for baptism may feel the strength of the community's prayer, we pray: ℟.
- That our own prayer to God may grow more constant and profound, we pray: ℟.

As one body, we pray in the words our merciful Lord gave us.

Our Father . . .

Gracious God,
your love and truth surround us.
If we would know you,
we must call your name;
if we would be loved,
we must love on another,
even as you love us.
Let us but knock,
and as your sons and daughters,
we will be welcomed into your kingdom.
Through Christ our Lord.
Amen.

✤ You are Peter, and upon this rock
I will build my Church.

✤ Set me free from my distress, O Lord.

Psalm 139

page 389

Reading

Ezekiel 18:21–23

Thus says the Lord GOD: If the wicked man turns away from all the sins he committed, if he keeps all my statutes and does what is right and just, he shall surely live, he shall not die. None of the crimes he committed shall be remembered against him; he shall live because of the virtue he has practiced. Do I indeed derive any pleasure from the death of the wicked? says the Lord GOD. Do I not rather rejoice when he turns from his evil way that he may live?

Reflection

Some might find this reading from Ezekiel rather consoling. God desires our conversion and does not relish punishing us with death. He is just and his ways are true but because of our fallen nature we may see his justice as unfair instead of seeing his mercy as wholly undeserved. The Lord confirms that we will have everlasting life if we turn away from sinful ways. God gives us so much help and helps us to encounter him in so many ways, especially through participation in the sacraments. We need only be open to the gifts he blesses us with and serve him in the world. Let us persevere in the faith and understand that true conversion is our life's work.

Prayers

others may be added

Called to be saints, we offer our prayers for the good of all:

℟. **Hear our prayer, O Lord.**

- That the Church may be an instrument of reconciliation and peace in a world torn by violence, we pray:℟.
- That all who have suffered at the hands of others may find the courage to forgive, we pray: ℟.
- That during this Lenten season we will seek reconciliation with those whom we have hurt, we pray: ℟.
- That members of our community may be doers of the Word rather than just hearers of the Word, we pray: ℟.

As one body, we pray in the words our merciful Lord gave us.

Our Father . . .

God of all consolation,
fill us with your love
so that envy and hatred will find
no place, no dwelling within us.
Teach us to forgive one another
so that we may approach you
with clean hearts.
Through Christ our Lord.
Amen.

✤ Set me free from my distress, O Lord.

✠ The law of the Lord is perfect;
it revives the soul.

Psalm 126 *page 387*

Reading *Matthew 5:43–48*

Jesus said to his disciples: "You have heard that it was said, / *You shall love your neighbor and hate your enemy.* / But I say to you, love your enemies, and pray for those who persecute you, that you may be children of your heavenly Father, for he makes his sun rise on the bad and the good, and causes rain to fall on the just and the unjust. For if you love those who love you, what recompense will you have? Do not the tax collectors do the same? And if you greet your brothers and sisters only, what is unusual about that? Do not the pagans do the same? So be perfect, just as your heavenly Father is perfect."

Reflection *Pope John Paul II*

One's neighbor is . . . not only a human being with his or her own rights and a fundamental equality with everyone else, but becomes the living image of God the Father, redeemed by the blood of Jesus Christ and placed under the permanent action of the Holy Spirit. One's neighbor must therefore be loved, even if an enemy, with the same love with which the Lord loves him or her; and for that person's sake one must be ready for sacrifice, even the ultimate one: to lay down one's life for the brethren.

Prayers *others may be added*

Called to love all people, we offer to the Lord our prayers:

℟. **Lord, hear our prayer.**

- May Christians love all people, even their enemies, we pray: ℟.
- May God's grace pour out upon our world and overflow in abundance, we pray: ℟.
- May the poor and the oppressed find comfort in their strugglges, we pray: ℟.
- May peace flourish within our communities, we pray: ℟.

As one body, we pray in the words our merciful Lord gave us.

Our Father . . .

God of love,
help us to see that our enemies are also
created in your image and likeness.
May we find them worthy and
deserving of our love.
Through Christ our Lord.
Amen.

✠ The law of the Lord is perfect;
it revives the soul.

Sunday, March 16, 2025

✤ Remember your compassion, O Lord.

Psalm 51

page 373

Reading

Luke 9:28B–36

Jesus took Peter, John, and James and went up the mountain to pray. While he was praying his face changed in appearance and his clothing became dazzling white. And behold, two men were conversing with him, Moses and Elijah, who appeared in glory and spoke of his exodus that he was going to accomplish in Jerusalem. Peter and his companions had been overcome by sleep, but becoming fully awake, they saw his glory and the two men standing with him. As they were about to part from him, Peter said to Jesus, "Master, it is good that we are here; let us make three tents, one for you, one for Moses, and one for Elijah." But he did not know what he was saying. While he was still speaking, a cloud came and cast a shadow over them, and they became frightened when they entered the cloud. Then from the cloud came a voice that said, "This is my chosen Son; listen to him." After the voice had spoken, Jesus was found alone. They fell silent and did not at that time tell anyone what they had seen.

Reflection

For Catholic Christians, Jesus is the ultimate sign and sacrament. Last Sunday, Jesus showed us how to handle temptation. This Sunday he points to our final goal: transformation into the glory of our Father and Creator. If we've wandered lost or confused, he restores our direction: "Look, you were made for this brilliant light!" He reminds us that no matter how much we struggle or suffer, we are still God's beloved children. To our Father, we are as dazzling as Jesus on the mountaintop was to Peter, James, and John.

Prayers

others may be added

Let us approach the Lord and ask for the grace to hear his Word and respond to his will:

℟. Lord, hear us.

- Fill the Church with your light,
  we pray: ℟.
- Shine on those who live in the shadow
  of war, violence, and oppression,
  we pray: ℟.
- Enlighten the hearts and minds
  of those preparing for baptism,
  we pray: ℟.
- Help us to give witness to the glory
  of your resurrection, we pray: ℟.

As one body, we pray in the words
our merciful Lord gave us.

Our Father . . .

God our Father,
help us to hear your voice
and do your will.
Through Christ our Lord.
Amen.

✤ Remember your compassion, O Lord.

✠ Redeem me, O Lord, and have mercy on me.

Psalm 115 *page 385*

Reading *Daniel 9:4b–10*

"Lord, great and awesome God, you who keep your merciful covenant toward those who love you and observe your commandments! We have sinned, been wicked and done evil; we have rebelled and departed from your commandments and your laws. We have not obeyed your servants the prophets, who spoke in your name to our kings, our princes, our fathers, and all the people of the land. Justice, O Lord, is on your side; we are shamefaced even to this day: we, the men of Judah, the residents of Jerusalem, and all Israel, near and far, in all the countries to which you have scattered them because of their treachery toward you. O Lord, we are shamefaced, like our kings, our princes, and our fathers, for having sinned against you. But yours, O Lord, our God, are compassion and forgiveness! Yet we rebelled against you and paid no heed to your command, O Lord, our God, to live by the law you gave us through your servants the prophets."

Reflection

Today's reading from Daniel illustrates how we should confess our sins. Admit them. Don't give excuses or soft-pedal your sins. Admit that you have freely chosen to rebel against God. Don't blame other people. Then, the priest, like a physician, can prescribe the right medicine, the right penance, to heal your relationship with God. If you want to be healed, show God where you are ill and hurting. When we confess our sins, we realize how much we are in need of God's grace and rejoice when we receive forgiveness.

Prayers *others may be added*

Called to be merciful and forgiving,
we offer to the Lord our prayers:

℟. **Lord, deliver us from evil.**

- That the Church may share God's gift of mercy with all peoples, we pray: ℟.
- That through forgiveness and mutual understanding, nations may find true and lasting peace, we pray: ℟.
- That those who have been hurt may know the peace that comes from forgiveness, we pray: ℟.
- That we may share the good things we have received with those in need, we pray: ℟.

As one body, we pray in the words
our merciful Lord gave us.

Our Father . . .

O God,
you are great and awesome,
and you bestow mercy upon us.
Stir up in us great sorrow for our sins
that we may approach you in
the sacrament of reconciliation
and be fully healed.
Through Christ our Lord.
Amen.

✠ Redeem me, O Lord, and have mercy on me.

Tuesday, March 18, 2025

✠ Give light to my eyes lest I fall asleep in death.

Psalm 130

page 388

Reading

Matthew 23:1–12

Jesus spoke to the crowds and to his disciples, saying, "The scribes and the Pharisees have taken their seat on the chair of Moses. Therefore, do and observe all things whatsoever they tell you, but do not follow their example. For they preach but they do not practice. They tie up heavy burdens hard to carry and lay them on people's shoulders, but they will not lift a finger to move them. All their works are performed to be seen. They widen their phylacteries and lengthen their tassels. They love places of honor at banquets, seats of honor in synagogues, greetings in marketplaces, and the salutation 'Rabbi.' As for you, do not be called 'Rabbi.' You have but one teacher, and you are all brothers. Call no one on earth your father; you have but one Father in heaven. Do not be called 'Master'; you have but one master, the Christ. The greatest among you must be your servant. Whoever exalts himself will be humbled; but whoever humbles himself will be exalted."

Reflection

Again and again, Jesus tells his disciples that our right relationship with God is bound up in our right relationship with those around us. He condemns the scribes and the Pharisees who are more concerned with laying down the law for others than in observing it for themselves. They do good works not for the glory of God but in order to be praised by their fellow human beings. He also tells us that no other human being can be our teacher, our father, our master. That does not mean that we cannot teach each other and learn from each other. It means that we must do so with humility of heart, aware that God is the Father and Teacher of all.

Prayers

others may be added

The Lord call us to be humble servants, and so we pray:

℟. **Lord, may we return to you.**

- May all the Church's wayward children repent and return to the flock, we pray: ℟.
- May the hearts and actions of world leaders be transformed for the good of their people, we pray: ℟.
- May our witness of love be a sign of hope for all peoples, we pray: ℟.
- May we work together for the common good, we pray: ℟.

As one body, we pray in the words our merciful Lord gave us.

Our Father . . .

All-knowing God,
your love is truth and light.
Make us transparent servants,
so that your glory may shine through us
and be magnified for ever.
Through Christ our Lord.
Amen.

✠ Give light to my eyes lest I fall asleep in death.

✤ Behold, a faithful servant
and prudent steward.

Psalm 96

page 380

Reading

Matthew 1:16, 18–21, 24a

Jacob was the father of Joseph, the husband of Mary. Of her was born Jesus who is called the Christ.

Now this is how the birth of Jesus Christ came about. When his mother Mary was betrothed to Joseph, but before they lived together, she was found with child through the Holy Spirit. Joseph her husband, since he was a righteous man, yet unwilling to expose her to shame, decided to divorce her quietly. Such was his intention when, behold, the angel of the Lord appeared to him in a dream and said, "Joseph, son of David, do not be afraid to take Mary your wife into your home. For it is through the Holy Spirit that this child has been conceived in her. She will bear a son and you are to name him Jesus, because he will save his people from their sins." When Joseph awoke, he did as the angel of the Lord had commanded him and took his wife into his home.

Reflection

Surely Joseph was surprised at his role in the plan of salvation. Are we, too, surprised at our role? Do we try to respectfully decline? Does God offer us uncomfortably bold opportunities to serve? Joseph can be our model and inspiration at accepting our responsibilities in the plan of salvation. We can enter situations fraught with danger and turmoil confident that Jesus' earthly father has walked before us.

Prayers

others may be added

Joining our prayers to St. Joseph,
the universal patron of the Church,
we come before our Lord:

℟. Hear us, O God.

- That the Church may continue to grow in holiness and trust in God's promises, we pray: ℟.
- That all fathers and grandfathers may be filled with the wisdom and gentleness of St. Joseph, we pray: ℟.
- That couples preparing for marriage may turn to God together in all their joys and sorrows, we pray: ℟.
- That the prayers of St. Joseph may lead us ever closer to the one who was called the carpenter's son, we pray: ℟.

As one body, we pray in the words
our merciful Lord gave us.

Our Father . . .

Loving God,
you chose Joseph to be the foster father
and teacher of our Lord.
Let our labors bear witness
to the Gospel,
so that the peace of Christ is present
in all we do.
Who lives and reigns for ever and ever.
Amen.

✤ Behold, a faithful servant
and prudent steward.

Thursday, March 20, 2025

✤ Lead me in the way everlasting.

Psalm 141 *page 389*

Reading *Luke 16:19–26*

Jesus said to the Pharisees: "There was a rich man who dressed in purple garments and fine linen and dined sumptuously each day. And lying at his door was a poor man named Lazarus, covered with sores, who would gladly have eaten his fill of the scraps that fell from the rich man's table. Dogs even used to come and lick his sores. When the poor man died, he was carried away by angels to the bosom of Abraham. The rich man also died and was buried, and from the netherworld, where he was in torment, he raised his eyes and saw Abraham far off and Lazarus at his side. And he cried out, 'Father Abraham, have pity on me. Send Lazarus to dip the tip of his finger in water and cool my tongue, for I am suffering torment in these flames.' Abraham replied, 'My child, remember that you received what was good during your lifetime while Lazarus likewise received what was bad; but now he is comforted here, whereas you are tormented. Moreover, between us and you a great chasm is established to prevent anyone from crossing who might wish to go from our side to yours or from your side to ours.'"

Reflection *St. Gregory of Nazianzen*

The Lord of all asks for mercy, not sacrifice. . . . Let us then show him mercy in the persons of the poor and those who today are lying on the ground, so that when we come to leave this world they may receive us into everlasting dwelling places.

Prayers *others may be added*

The Lord hears the cry of the poor,
and so we pray:

℟. Lord, hear our prayer.

- That the Church will accompany the People of God through every trial, we pray: ℟.
- That leaders and lawmakers may be mindful of those who are poor, we pray: ℟.
- That the rich will share their abundance with those in need, we pray: ℟.
- That we may not be deceived by the glamours of the world, we pray: ℟.
- That the poor and oppressed may hold fast to God amid their trials, we pray: ℟.
- That we may endeavor to rebuild the bonds of the human family that have been broken by sin, we pray: ℟.

As one body, we pray in the words
our merciful Lord gave us.

Our Father . . .

God our Father,
do not permit us to be deceived by
the fleeting glamour of our world.
Give us true sight so we see its emptiness
and folly.
Transform our hearts,
that we may know the joy of giving
with chairty, generosity, and love.
Through Christ our Lord.
Amen.

✤ Lead me in the way everlasting.

✤ In you, O Lord, I put my trust.

Psalm 139 *page 389*

Reading *Matthew 21:33–41*

[Jesus said:] "There was a landowner who planted a vineyard, put a hedge around it, dug a wine press in it, and built a tower. Then he leased it to tenants and went on a journey. When vintage time drew near, he sent his servants to the tenants to obtain his produce. But the tenants seized the servants and one they beat, another they killed, and a third they stoned. Again he sent other servants, more numerous than the first ones, but they treated them in the same way. Finally, he sent his son to them, thinking, 'They will respect my son.' But when the tenants saw the son, they said to one another, 'This is the heir. Come, let us kill him and acquire his inheritance.' They seized him, threw him out of the vineyard, and killed him. What will the owner of the vineyard do to those tenants when he comes?" They answered him, "He will put those wretched men to a wretched death and lease his vineyard to other tenants who will give him the produce at the proper times."

Reflection

How many times does Jesus warn of the harm that will come from not following the way of God? The Pharisees and scribes hear Jesus preach and yet they plot to kill him instead of repenting for their ill ways. What does the Lord say to us that we would rather not hear and heed? During this season of Lent, let us try to conform our minds, hearts, and wills to the ways of the Lord. Let us listen more attentively to God and ask for his help so we may repent and transform our lives.

Prayers *others may be added*

As servants of the Lord, we pray:

℟. **Lord, hear our prayer.**

- That the Church may be a light
  to all those who walk in darkness,
  we pray: ℟.
- That God's voice may be heard
  throughout all lands, we pray: ℟.
- That the poor and the oppressed
  will be loved as God's own children,
  we pray: ℟.
- That we may heed God's voice
  and share it with our neighbors,
  we pray: ℟.

As one body, we pray in the words
our merciful Lord gave us.

Our Father . . .

God our Father,
may our hearts and ears be attentive
to your voice
so that we may do what is pleasing
to you.
Through Christ our Lord.
Amen.

✤ In you, O Lord, I put my trust.

✚ The Lord is kind and full of compassion.

Psalm 126

page 387

Reading

Micah 7:14–15, 18–20

Shepherd your people with your staff, / the flock of your inheritance, / That dwells apart in a woodland, / in the midst of Carmel. / Let them feed in Bashan and Gilead, / as in the days of old; / As in the days when you came from the land of Egypt, / show us wonderful signs.

Who is there like you, the God who removes guilt / and pardons sin for the remnant of his inheritance; / Who does not persist in anger forever, / but delights rather in clemency, / And will again have compassion on us, / treading underfoot our guilt? / You will cast into the depths of the sea all our sins; / You will show faithfulness to Jacob, / and grace to Abraham, / As you have sworn to our fathers / from days of old.

Reflection

Pope Francis

God gives every Christian the grace to write a story of good in the life of his or her brothers and sisters, especially of those who have done something regrettable or wrong. With a word, an embrace, a smile, we can pass on to others the most precious thing we have received. What is the most precious thing we have received? Forgiveness, which we too must be able to give to others.

Prayers

others may be added

O Lord, there is none like you. You pardon our sin and lead us to life, and so we pray.

℟. **Lord, be merciful.**

- We pray for the Church, that she may be strengthened in her ministry to reconcile sinners, we pray: ℟.
- We pray for the world, may all the people come to embrace the mercy of God, we pray: ℟.
- We pray for the poor and oppressed, may we serve them constantly, we pray ℟.
- We pray for our local community, that we be examples of God's mercy by forgiving those who trespass against us, we pray: ℟.

As one body, we pray in the words our merciful Lord gave us.

Our Father . . .

God our Father,
you reconcile sinners and pardon them with grace.
May we never forget your great mercy and love for us
and extend these gifts to others.
Through Christ our Lord.
Amen.

✚ The Lord is kind and full of compassion.

✤ Turn to me [O Lord,] and have mercy on me.

Psalm 51

page 373

Reading

Luke 13:1–9

Some people told Jesus about the Galileans whose blood Pilate had mingled with the blood of their sacrifices. Jesus said to them in reply, "Do you think that because these Galileans suffered in this way they were greater sinners than all other Galileans? By no means! But I tell you, if you do not repent, you will all perish as they did! Or those eighteen people who were killed when the tower at Siloam fell on them—do you think they were more guilty than everyone else who lived in Jerusalem? By no means! But I tell you, if you do not repent, you will all perish as they did!"

And he told them this parable: "There once was a person who had a fig tree planted in his orchard, and when he came in search of fruit on it but found none, he said to the gardener, 'For three years now I have come in search of fruit on this fig tree but have found none. So cut it down. Why should it exhaust the soil?' He said to him in reply, 'Sir, leave it for this year also, and I shall cultivate the ground around it and fertilize it; it may bear fruit in the future. If not you can cut it down.'"

Reflection

Pope Francis

The rediscovery of nature can never be at the cost of the freedom and responsibility of human beings who, as part of the world, have the duty to cultivate their abilities in order to protect it and develop its potential. If we acknowledge the value and the fragility of nature and, at the same time, our God-given abilities, we can finally leave behind the modern myth of unlimited material progress. A fragile world, entrusted by God to human care, challenges us to devise intelligent ways of directing, developing and limiting our power.

Prayers

others may be added

Bearing the fruit of our faith, we offer to the Lord our prayers:

℟. **Lord of love, hear our prayer.**

- That the Church help her children produce good fruit for God, we pray: ℟.
- That we may see the world as the garden of God and plant the seeds of faith everywhere, we pray: ℟.
- That we may protect creation and allow it to produce great fruit according to God's design, we pray: ℟.
- That the poor and oppressed may be liberated from their sufferings, we pray: ℟.
- That God will bless and protect the peoples of this world, we pray: ℟.

As one body, we pray in the words our merciful Lord gave us.

Our Father . . .

God our Father,
help us to cultivate the gifts you have
given us
and to share their fruit with
the entire world.
Through Christ our Lord.
Amen.

✤ Turn to me [O Lord,] and have mercy on me.

Monday, March 24, 2025

✚ My heart and my flesh cry out
to the living God.

Psalm 115 *page 385*

Reading *Luke 4:24–30*

Jesus said to the people in the synagogue at Nazareth: "Amen, I say to you, no prophet is accepted in his own native place. Indeed, I tell you, there were many widows in Israel in the days of Elijah when the sky was closed for three and a half years and a severe famine spread over the entire land. It was to none of these that Elijah was sent, but only to a widow in Zarephath in the land of Sidon. Again, there were many lepers in Israel during the time of Elisha the prophet; yet not one of them was cleansed, but only Naaman the Syrian." When the people in the synagogue heard this, they were all filled with fury. They rose up, drove him out of the town, and led him to the brow of the hill on which their town had been built, to hurl him down headlong. But he passed through the midst of them and went away.

Reflection

Have you ever heard someone complain that their penances were too easy? Perhaps they stopped going to confession. How foolish! Why forgo God's healing because of your own ego? Naaman almost missed out on being healed because the prescription was not to his liking. He wanted something more spectacular. Let us be sensible and thankful for God's mercy and if we need something hard to do then try avoiding the near occasion of sin and resist temptation so we do not fall back into the same sins.

Prayers *others may be added*

We are called to live what we believe, and so we turn to the Lord now with our prayers:

℟. **Lord, hear our prayer.**

- That the Church may listen to the prophetic voices of our times, we pray: ℟.
- That our world may be renewed by the mercy of God, we pray: ℟.
- That the nations of the world may find peace through mutual understanding and respect, we pray: ℟.
- That those who have drifted away from the practice of their faith may find their way home to God, we pray: ℟.
- That we will be agents of God's mercy to all who are suffering, we pray: ℟.

As one body, we pray in the words our merciful Lord gave us.

Our Father . . .

God of healing,
may we be ever grateful for your mercy
and loving kindness toward us.
Strengthen and steady us
that we may walk with you,
even against the tide of doubt.
Through Christ our Lord.
Amen.

✚ My heart and my flesh cry out
to the living God.

✤ Behold, I come to do your will, O God.

Psalm 96

page 380

Reading

Luke 1:38

Mary said, "Behold, I am the handmaid of the Lord. May it be done to me according to your word."

Reflection

In today's Gospel, humanity's future hangs on Mary's answer to the angel's question. Her yes transformed her life, starting with uncomfortable journeys, birth in a stable, her son's growth and leading to his eventual death. He would follow her lead. "Jesus Christ . . . was not 'yes' and 'no,' but 'yes' has been in him" (2 Corinthians 1:19). When do I say yes? It may seem small and insignificant, but it can represent one's best efforts and affect many other lives. When do I need to say no to projects that drain energy, so that my yesses can be fuller, more life- affirming?

Prayers

others may be added

The Almighty has done great things for us, and so we pray:

℟. **Lord, keep us faithful.**

- ✦ May the Lord fill the Church with faith and humility, we pray: ℟.
- ✦ May the Lord cast down the mighty from their thrones and lift up the lowly, we pray: ℟.
- ✦ May the Lord fill the hungry of the earth with good things, we pray: ℟.
- ✦ May the Lord remember his mercy and bestow his goodness on all peoples, we pray: ℟.

As one body, we pray in the words our merciful Lord gave us.

Our Father . . .

God of love and mercy,
let us praise you;
for in your Son you came as a servant,
born of a humble virgin.
Let us glorify you;
for you have lifted up the lowly
and cast down the proud and
the arrogant.
Let us magnify your holy Name;
for you have defeated death
and kept your promise of salvation
and eternal life.
Through Christ our Lord.
Amen.

✤ Behold, I come to do your will, O God.

Wednesday, March 26, 2025

✚ Let my steps be guided
by your promise.

Psalm 42 *page 371*

Reading *Deuteronomy 4:9*

Moses spoke to the people and said: . . . "[T]ake care and be earnestly on your guard not to forget the things which your own eyes have seen, nor let them slip from your memory as long as you live, but teach them to your children and to your children's children."

Prayers *Go and Make Disciples*

We must evangelize because the Lord Jesus commanded us to do so. He gave the Church the unending task of evangelizing as a restless power, to stir and to stimulate all its actions until all nations have heard his Good News and until every person has become his disciple (paragraph 28; see Matthew 23:37).

Prayers *others may be added*

Remembering the promises of God and responding in faith, we pray:

℟. **Lord, may we remember your greatness.**

- That the Church may remind her flock of God's generosity and greatness, we pray: ℟.
- That we may remember who created the world and make efforts to sustain it, we pray: ℟.
- That the poor and the oppressed may find strength in the promises of God, we pray: ℟.
- That we may we share the Gospel with our neighbors by the witness of our life, we pray: ℟.

As one body, we pray in the words
our merciful Lord gave us.

Our Father . . .

Lord our God,
may we always remember what
you have done for us
and spread the Good News in every part
of our life.
Through Christ our Lord.
Amen.

✚ Let my steps be guided
by your promise.

✤ Cleanse your people, Lord.

Psalm 95

page 380

Reading

Luke 11:14–23

Jesus was driving out a demon that was mute, and when the demon had gone out, the mute man spoke and the crowds were amazed. Some of them said, "By the power of Beelzebul, the prince of demons, he drives out demons." Others, to test him, asked him for a sign from heaven. But he knew their thoughts and said to them, "Every kingdom divided against itself will be laid waste and house will fall against house. And if Satan is divided against himself, how will his kingdom stand? For you say that it is by Beelzebul that I drive out demons. If I, then, drive out demons by Beelzebul, by whom do your own people drive them out? Therefore they will be your judges. But if it is by the finger of God that I drive out demons, then the Kingdom of God has come upon you. When a strong man fully armed guards his palace, his possessions are safe. But when one stronger than he attacks and overcomes him, he takes away the armor on which he relied and distributes the spoils. Whoever is not with me is against me, and whoever does not gather with me scatters."

Reflection

Psalm 95 reminds us of our relationship with God and that we are called to have open hearts and praise God joyfully. We can soften our hearts by being attentive to God when we pray and ask for the grace to do his will. Let us be open and strive to be ready for God when he calls us.

Prayers

others may be added

Let us turn to God and ask for an awareness of his presence in our lives, as we pray:

℟. Lord, soften our hearts.

- That the Church may condition us to hear the voice of the Lord and, through softened hearts, respond lovingly to his call, we pray: ℟.
- That the nations of this world may never blot out the voice of the Lord, we pray: ℟.
- That we may serve the poor with love, we pray: ℟.
- That we may listen to what God is telling us, we pray: ℟.

As one body, we pray in the words our merciful Lord gave us.

Our Father . . .

God of goodness,
may we soften our hearts when
you call us.
Let us turn to you and always do
your will, a will that is love itself.
Through Christ our Lord.
Amen.

✤ Cleanse your people, Lord.

Friday, March 28, 2025

✚ Among the gods there is none like you, O Lord.

Psalm 139

page 389

Reading

Mark 12:28–34

One of the scribes came to Jesus and asked him, "Which is the first of all the commandments?" Jesus replied, "The first is this: / *Hear, O Israel! / The Lord our God is Lord alone! / You shall love the Lord your God with all your heart, / with all your soul, / with all your mind, / and with all your strength.* / The second is this: / *You shall love your neighbor as yourself.* / There is no other commandment greater than these." The scribe said to him, "Well said, teacher. You are right in saying, / *He is One and there is no other than he. / And to love him with all your heart, / with all your understanding, / with all your strength, / and to love your neighbor as yourself* / is worth more than all burnt offerings and sacrifices." And when Jesus saw that he answered with understanding, he said to him, "You are not far from the Kingdom of God." And no one dared to ask him any more questions.

Reflection

How are your Lenten practices going? Don't despair if you have not been keeping up with the prayers, fasting, and almsgiving. Begin again today. Fittingly, the Church reminds us today of the commandment to love God over all the gods and to love our neighbor as ourselves. In short, we are reminded why we do the Lenten practices—to get closer to God. How we can do that is by loving our neighbor. What might that look like? Providing food and clothing for a homeless shelter or diapers for a pregnancy center or maybe providing meals for an elderly neighbor would be a good start.

Prayers

others may be added

The Lord calls us to love,
and so we pray:

℟. **Lord, hear us.**

✦ That the Church may go to the peripheries to serve the Lord, we pray: ℟.

✦ That world leaders may be renewed in their efforts to preserve justice, we pray: ℟.

✦ That we may live in solidarity with those who are poor and oppressed, we pray: ℟.

✦ That we may always be attentive to the needs of our neighbors, we pray: ℟.

As one body, we pray in the words our merciful Lord gave us.

Our Father . . .

God of love,
you call us to love all peoples and all creatures of this world.
Soften our hearts so that we may seve you with love
Through Christ our Lord.
Amen.

✚ Among the gods there is none like you, O Lord.

✣ Bless the Lord, O my soul.

Psalm 126

page 387

Reading

Hosea 6:1–6

"Come, let us return to the LORD, / it is he who has rent, but he will heal us; / he has struck us, but he will bind our wounds. / He will revive us after two days; / on the third day he will raise us up, / to live in his presence. / Let us know, let us strive to know the LORD; / as certain as the dawn is his coming, / and his judgment shines forth like the light of day! / He will come to us like the rain, / like spring rain that waters the earth."

What can I do with you, Ephraim? / What can I do with you, Judah? / Your piety is like a morning cloud, / like the dew that early passes away. / For this reason I smote them through the prophets, / I slew them by the words of my mouth; / For it is love that I desire, not sacrifice, / and knowledge of God rather than burnt offerings.

Reflection

St. Francis de Sales says that in order to live a devout life, one must love God. God does not want rote sacrifices—love means truly living the faith. God can see our hearts. He knows when are just going through the motions. Exterior practices mean nothing if we are not motivated by love for God. Spend time reflecting on God's beauty, truth, and goodness to arouse in yourself love and awe of God.

Prayers

others may be added

Returning to the Lord in prayer,
we offer the needs of our world:

℟. **Lord, have mercy on us.**

- That the Church may reach out with love to the sinful and the doubting, we pray: ℟.
- That those who are burdened by sin may lift up thir hearts to the God of forgiveness, we pray: ℟.
- That all who bear the name of Christian may be like Christ, meek and humble of heart, we pray: ℟.
- That we may have the grace to see God's presence shining in those around us, we pray: ℟.

As one body, we pray in the words
our merciful Lord gave us.

Our Father . . .

Loving God,
you are generous in mercy.
Forgive us and grant us peace;
drive away our shame and weakness
as you enfold us in the strength
of your love.
Through Christ our Lord.
Amen.

✣ Bless the Lord, O my soul.

Sunday, March 30, 2025

✤ Rejoice, Jerusalem, and all who love her.

Psalm 51

page 373

Reading

2 Corinthians 5:17–21

Brothers and sisters: Whoever is in Christ is a new creation: the old things have passed away; behold, new things have come. And all this is from God, who has reconciled us to himself through Christ and given us the ministry of reconciliation, namely, God was reconciling the world to himself in Christ, not counting their trespasses against them and entrusting to us the message of reconciliation. So we are ambassadors for Christ, as if God were appealing through us. We implore you on behalf of Christ, be reconciled to God. For our sake he made him to be sin who did not know sin, so that we might become the righteousness of God in him.

Prayers

Virgil Michel, OSB

A Chrisian Lent can never be entirely sad. With the fourth Sunday the pent up spiritual joy in the true members of Christ burst forth in anticipation of the Easter joy to come. "Rejoice, O Jerusalem, and come together all that love her; rejoice with joy, you that have been in sorrow" (introit).

Prayers

others may be added

Ambassadors for Christ, we offer to the Lord our prayers:

℟. Lord, have mercy on us.

- Guide your Church and make her a place of mercy and forgiveness, we pray: ℟.
- Lead our world leaders in the ways of justice, charity, and peace, we pray: ℟.
- Bless those preparing for baptism, that they may behold what new things await them, we pray: ℟.
- Open our hearts to the ways of mercy, we pray: ℟.

As one body, we pray in the words our merciful Lord gave us.

Our Father . . .

God of love,
may the truth of your mercy
radiate throughout the world
and be a beacon for those without
knowledge of you.
Help us to be your advocates and
witnesses in our broken world.
Through Christ our Lord.
Amen.

✤ Rejoice, Jerusalem, and all who love her.

✤ Let me be glad and rejoice
in your mercy.

Psalm 115

page 385

Reading

John 4:46–54

Now there was a royal official whose son was ill in Capernaum. When he heard that Jesus had arrived in Galilee from Judea, he went to him and asked him to come down and heal his son, who was near death. Jesus said to him, "Unless you people see signs and wonders, you will not believe." The royal official said to him, "Sir, come down before my child dies." Jesus said to him, "You may go; your son will live." The man believed what Jesus said to him and left. While the man was on his way back, his slaves met him and told him that his boy would live. He asked them when he began to recover. They told him, "The fever left him yesterday, about one in the afternoon." The father realized that just at that time Jesus had said to him, "Your son will live," and he and his whole household came to believe. Now this was the second sign Jesus did when he came to Galilee from Judea.

Reflection

In today's Gospel, notice how directly the royal official states his longing: "Sir, come down before my little boy dies." He must have had enormous trust in Jesus' word because without any proof of healing, he "started on his way." What can we learn from him about directness and confidence in prayer?

Prayers

others may be added

The Lord heals us from every ill,
and so we pray:

℟. **Lord, in your mercy,
hear our prayer.**

- ✦ That the Church will always spread the message of the Gospel , we pray: ℟.
- ✦ That those of our world may embrance the message of the Gospel and embrace the Lord , we pray: ℟.
- ✦ That the Lord will lift up the poor and the suffering, and heal them of their pain, we pray: ℟.
- ✦ That we who have received the message of the Gospel will go and glorify the Lord by our life, we pray: ℟.

As one body, we pray in the words
our merciful Lord gave us.

Our Father . . .

Healing God,
you wish for all to come to you
and be healed.
Inspire us to share the truth
of your mercy
with all peoples of this world.
Through Christ our Lord.
Amen.

✤ Let me be glad and rejoice
in your mercy.

Tuesday, April 1, 2025

✤ All you who are thirsty,
come to the waters.

Psalm 130

page 388

Reading

John 5:1–9

There was a feast of the Jews, and Jesus went up to Jerusalem. Now there is in Jerusalem at the Sheep Gate a pool called in Hebrew Bethesda, with five porticoes. In these lay a large number of ill, blind, lame, and crippled. One man was there who had been ill for thirty-eight years. When Jesus saw him lying there and knew that he had been ill for a long time, he said to him, "Do you want to be well?" The sick man answered him, "Sir, I have no one to put me into the pool when the water is stirred up; while I am on my way, someone else gets down there before me." Jesus said to him, "Rise, take up your mat, and walk." Immediately the man became well, took up his mat, and walked.

Reflection

The invalid never answers Jesus's question, "Do you want to be made well?" How would we answer? While "yes" may seem obvious, sometimes people trapped in unhealthy situations fail to recognize the payoffs that hold them there. Some enjoy the "victim" stance, others like attention, and still others are shackled by inertia. What challenges might the cured person in today's Gospel encounter after thirty-eight years? What challenges might you meet if you were cured?

Prayers

others may be added

We come before our God of healing grace asking him to hear the prayers of our hearts:

℟. **Lord, in your mercy,
hear our prayer.**

- That the Church may lead all peoples to conversion of heart, we pray: ℟.
- That those of our world may always feel the healing power of God, we pray: ℟.
- That the Lord will heal the sick and lift them from their suffering, we pray: ℟.
- That we may we spread the news of God's healing power, we pray: ℟.

As one body, we pray in the words our merciful Lord gave us.

Our Father . . .

Healing Lord,
we may grow weary on our lonely path,
for sin has weakened us
and thrown obstacles in our way.
Hold out your loving hand,
that we may rise and walk again.
Heal us in your life-giving waters
and by your mercy make us whole.
Through Christ our Lord.
Amen.

✤ All you who are thirsty,
come to the waters.

✠ In your great mercy, answer me,
O God.

Psalm 42 *page 371*

Reading *Isaiah 49:8–15*

Thus says the LORD: / In a time of favor I answer you, / on the day of salvation I help you; / and I have kept you and given you as a covenant to the people, / To restore the land / and allot the desolate heritages, / Saying to the prisoners: Come out! / To those in darkness: Show yourselves! / Along the ways they shall find pasture, / on every bare height shall their pastures be. / They shall not hunger or thirst, / nor shall the scorching wind or the sun strike them; / For he who pities them leads them / and guides them beside springs of water. / I will cut a road through all my mountains, / and make my highways level. / See, some shall come from afar, / others from the north and the west, / and some from the land of Syene. Sing out, O heavens, and rejoice, O earth, / break forth into song, you mountains. For the Lord comforts his people / and shows mercy to his afflicted.

But Zion said, "The LORD has forsaken me; / my Lord has forgotten me." / Can a mother forget her infant, / be without tenderness for the child of her womb? / Even should she forget, / I will never forget you.

Reflection

Think about the tenderness and joy a new mother shares with her infant. Her attention to the needs and well-being of the child are constant. Love motivates her. It is reassuring to meditate on the fact that God is present to us and attentive to us like a mother is to her infant. He loves us deeply. We are not alone. In moments of struggle, remember that God is like an attentive mother. He is always with you! Cry out to him like a child and ask God to cradle and nurse you like a newborn's mother.

Prayers *others may be added*

The Lord does not forget his people. Let us turn to him now in prayer:

℟. **Lord, in your mercy,
hear our prayer.**

- That the Church may be filled with the love of God, we pray: ℟.
- That the world may be filled with the peace of God, we pray: ℟.
- That those who are afflicted may be filled with the compassion of God, we pray: ℟.
- That we may be filled with the goodness of God, we pray: ℟.

As one body, we pray in the words our merciful Lord gave us.

Our Father . . .

God our Father,
you comfort your people
and show mercy to all those
who are afflicted and suffering.
Make your presence known to us
so that we may feel your abiding love.
Through Christ our Lord.
Amen.

✠ In your great mercy, answer me,
O God.

Thursday, April 3, 2025

✚ Let the hearts that seek
the Lord rejoice.

Psalm 141 *page 389*

Reading *John 5:39–47*

[Jesus said:] "You search the Scriptures, because you think you have eternal life through them; even they testify on my behalf. But you do not want to come to me to have life.

"I do not accept human praise; moreover, I know that you do not have the love of God in you. I came in the name of my Father, but you do not accept me; yet if another comes in his own name, you will accept him. How can you believe, when you accept praise from one another and do not seek the praise that comes from the only God? Do not think that I will accuse you before the Father: the one who will accuse you is Moses, in whom you have placed your hope. For if you had believed Moses, you would have believed me, because he wrote about me. But if you do not believe his writings, how will you believe my words?"

Reflection

Jesus needs no elaborate words; he simply points to the testimony of his life. Could we say the same? Or do we need words to disguise little action? Jesus then asks, "How can you believe, when you accept praise from one another and do not seek the praise that comes from the only God?" Are we so quick to seek human applause that we do not spend time in quiet, listening for God's affirmation, the only one that counts?

Prayers *others may be added*

Remember your servants, O Lord,
as we come before you in prayer.

℟. **Lord, hear us.**

- That the Church may give to the poor with the reckless generosity of God, we pray: ℟.
- That those who suffer persecution and violence may know freedom and peace, we pray: ℟.
- That the elect may be filled with joy and awe as they prepare for baptism, we pray: ℟.
- That, as we continue our Lenten journey, we may be renewed wtih faith and love, we pray: ℟.

As one body, we pray in the words
our merciful Lord gave us.

Our Father . . .

Loving God,
teach us to listen with open hearts,
for you teach us how to live in the light.
Through Christ our Lord.
Amen.

✚ Let the hearts that seek
the Lord rejoice.

✣ O God, hear my prayer; give ear to the words of my mouth.

Psalm 139 *page 389*

Reading *John 7:1–2, 10, 25–30*

Jesus moved about within Galilee; he did not wish to travel in Judea, because the Jews were trying to kill him.

But the Jewish feast of Tabernacles was near. But when his brothers had gone up to the feast, he himself also went up, not openly but as it were in secret.

Some of the inhabitants of Jerusalem said, "Is he not the one they are trying to kill? And look, he is speaking openly and they say nothing to him. Could the authorities have realized that he is the Christ? But we know where he is from. When the Christ comes, no one will know where he is from." So Jesus cried out in the temple area as he was teaching and said, "You know me and also know where I am from. Yet I did not come on my own, but the one who sent me, whom you do not know, is true. I know him, because I am from him, and he sent me." So they tried to arrest him, but no one laid a hand upon him, because his hour had not yet come.

Reflection

Confronting a divine mystery, the people of today's Gospel argue, question authority, categorize, check origins and credentials, and demonize. The resulting frustration can almost be heard in Jesus' voice. He wants to give a gift; they want to fit him into a neat mental construct. Have any recent experiences moved beyond your own established frameworks? How did you receive them? Today, ask for grace to welcome surprises.

Prayers *others may be added*

Turning toward truth, we offer to the Lord our prayers:

℟. Lord, hear us.

- For radical honesty among Christians, we pray: ℟.
- For courage among elected officials to serve with humility and to promote justice, we pray: ℟.
- For integrity among those tempted to ignore or deny sin and wrong doing, we pray: ℟.
- For careful examination of our own guilt, we pray: ℟.

As one body, we pray in the words our merciful Lord gave us.

Our Father . . .

Lord Jesus, Prince of Truth,
you proclaimed the reign of God
in the light of day and in the dark
of night.
May truth be our shield in the fight
against sin and evil,
and may we have the courage to see our
own sin
and our complicity in the sin of others.
Show us the way of repentance, leading
us back to the Father.
You who live and reign for ever
and ever.
Amen.

✣ O God, hear my prayer; give ear to the words of my mouth.

Saturday, April 5, 2025

✤ May the working of your mercy,
O Lord, . . . direct our hearts.

Psalm 126

page 387

Reading

Jeremiah 11:18–20

I knew their plot because the LORD informed me; / at that time you, O LORD, showed me their doings.

Yet I, like a trusting lamb led to slaughter, / had not realized that they were hatching plots against me: / "Let us destroy the tree in its vigor; / let us cut him off from the land of the living, / so that his name will be spoken no more."

But, you, O Lord of hosts, O just Judge, / searcher of mind and heart, / Let me witness the vengeance you take on them, / for to you I have entrusted my cause!

Reflection

I keep thinking about God as the searcher of mind and heart. He sees all things. Perhaps we are afraid because he can see all our sinfulness and imperfections. Let us not be afraid but see this as an opportunity to ask for help. Let us ask him to heal our minds and hearts. Purge all things that are displeasing to him. Let us ask for God's grace in doing this and be assured that he sees us completely and knows our hearts and minds more intimately than we do. So with all confidence let us turn to God and implore him to heal us!

Prayers

others may be added

O God, you search me and you know me. You know the prayers of our hearts, so we turn to you now and voice our needs:

℟. Lord, hear us.

- May the Church guard the faith, we pray: ℟.
- May the world be purged of all that is displeasing to God , we pray: ℟.
- May we constantly seek to ameliorate the sufferings of the poor, we pray: ℟.
- May we find Christ in our neighbors, we pray: ℟.

As one body, we pray in the words our merciful Lord gave us.

Our Father . . .

Lord of hosts,
you see us for who we really are
and love us just the same.
Heal us and help us.
May we love you with complete
devotion.
Through Christ our Lord.
Amen.

✤ May the working of your mercy,
O Lord, . . . direct our hearts.

✠ Give me justice, O God, . . .
for you . . . are my strength.

Psalm 51 *page 373*

Reading *John 8:1–11*

Jesus went to the Mount of Olives. But early in the morning he arrived again in the temple area, and all the people started coming to him, and he sat down and taught them. Then the scribes and the Pharisees brought a woman who had been caught in adultery and made her stand in the middle. They said to him, "Teacher, this woman was caught in the very act of committing adultery. Now in the law, Moses commanded us to stone such women. So what do you say?" They said this to test him, so that they could have some charge to bring against him. Jesus bent down and began to write on the ground with his finger. But when they continued asking him, he straightened up and said to them, "Let the one among you who is without sin be the first to throw a stone at her." Again he bent down and wrote on the ground. And in response, they went away one by one, beginning with the elders. So he was left alone with the woman before him. Then Jesus straightened up and said to her, "Woman, where are they? Has no one condemned you?" She replied, "No one, sir." Then Jesus said, "Neither do I condemn you. Go, and from now on do not sin any more."

Reflection

Today's reading raises so many questions. Why isn't the man who sinned present? Why is it only the woman? What was Jesus writing on the ground? Perhaps he wrote a list of the sins of all present. The people were certainly aware of their own sins without Jesus exposing them. They knew to walk away when he suggested that the one who without sin should cast the first stone. Jesus is patient and merciful with them and and he is with us. Instead of judging and focusing on the sins of others, may we go forth and sin no more.

Prayers *others may be added*

In faith, we turn to our merciful and loving God with our prayers:

℟. **Lord, have mercy on us.**

- That the Church may reach out to those who have strayed with love and forgiveness, we pray: ℟.
- That those who have sinned may seek God's forgiveness in the sacrament of reconciliation, we pray: ℟.
- That we may not judge lest we be judged, we pray: ℟.
- That all peoples may be shown mercy and love, we pray: ℟.

As one body, we pray in the words our merciful Lord gave us.

Our Father . . .

God of love,
you are merciful to us.
May we always extend the same mercy
to our neighbors.
Through Christ our Lord.
Amen.

✠ Give me justice, O God, . . .
for you . . . are my strength.

Monday, April 7, 2025

✚ Have mercy on me, O God.

Psalm 115

page 385

Reading

John 11:17–18, 20–27

When Jesus arrived, he found that Lazarus had already been in the tomb for four days. Now Bethany was near Jerusalem, only about two miles away . . . When Martha heard that Jesus was coming, she went to meet him; but Mary sat at home. Martha said to Jesus, "Lord, if you had been here, my brother would not have died. But even now I know that whatever you ask of God, God will give you." Jesus said to her, "Your brother will rise." Martha said, "I know he will rise, in the resurrection on the last day." Jesus told her, "I am the resurrection and the life; whoever believes in me, even if he dies, will live, and everyone who lives and believes in me will never die. Do you believe this?" She said to him, "Yes, Lord. I have come to believe that you are the Christ, the Son of God, the one who is coming into the world."

Reflection

Jesus reveals himself as "the resurrection and the life," who has come to give us life that lasts forever. In Lazarus, buried for four days, past all hope, we see that it is never too late for us to seek the new life that comes from Christ. In Martha, we see the hope that trusts in Christ, no matter what. The Church asks the elect, and all of us, to find ourselves in this story as we approach Easter—the feast of Resurrection.

Prayers

others may be added

As instruments of God's compassion, we turn to him in prayer for the needs of our world:

℟. Lord of mercy, hear us.

- That the Church may be a place of refuge for those who are abused or assaulted, we pray: ℟.
- That laws and policies will be put in place to protect people from assault and harassment, we pray: ℟.
- That those who have been raped, attacked, victimized, or harassed may find healing and comfort in the mercy of God, we pray: ℟.
- That that peace and reconciliation prevail, even in the face of persecution, we pray: ℟.

As one body, we pray in the words our merciful Lord gave us.

Our Father . . .

Loving God,
you give us hope in our darkness;
healing in our suffering.
May we have the courage to find
strength in you
during times of great pain.
Through Christ our Lord.
Amen.

✚ Have mercy on me, O God.

✣ Wait for the Lord; be strong.

Psalm 130 *page 388*

Reading *Numbers 21:4–9*

From Mount Hor the children of Israel set out on the Red Sea road, to bypass the land of Edom. But with their patience worn out by the journey, the people complained against God and Moses, "Why have you brought us up from Egypt to die in this desert, where there is no food or water? We are disgusted with this wretched food!"

In punishment the LORD sent among the people saraph serpents,which bit the people so that many of them died. Then the people came to Moses and said, "We have sinned in complaining against the LORD and you. Pray the LORD to take the serpents away from us." So Moses prayed for the people, and the LORD said to Moses, "Make a saraph and mount it on a pole, and whoever looks at it after being bitten will live." Moses accordingly made a bronze serpent and mounted it on a pole, and whenever anyone who had been bitten by a serpent looked at the bronze serpent, he lived.

Reflection

How often do we, like the grumbling Israelites, forget our blessings? Why do we need to experience something worse to remember our blessings? The people came to their senses, admitted they were wrong, and asked for relief from the serpents. Yet again, God is so merciful with them. He is also merciful to us. If we admit our sins and ask for his mercy, God will heal us. Moses lifted up an image of the serpent for the people to see and be healed. Christ was lifted up on the cross and healed our sin. We just need to look, repent, and be reconciled with God.

Prayers *others may be added*

Awed by God, we have the courage to pray:

℟. Lord, have mercy.

- That the Church's teachers convey a sense of the wideness of God's mercy and depth of his love, we pray: ℟.
- That the majesty of God and his works provide a humbling perspective to world leaders, we pray: ℟.
- That the mysteries of the faith are not a deterrent but an inspiration to skeptics, we pray: ℟.
- That our faith may be humble, grateful, and intrigued by the greatness of God, we pray: ℟.

As one body, we pray in the words our merciful Lord gave us.

Our Father . . .

God our Father,
you bless us abundantly.
Open our eyes to see your
many blessings
and fill our hearts with gratitude
and love for you.
Through Christ our Lord.
Amen.

✣ Wait for the Lord; be strong.

Wednesday, April 9, 2025

✠ Enlighten, O God of compassion,
the hearts of your children.

Psalm 42

page 371

Reading

Daniel 3:14–18

King Nebuchadnezzar said: "Is it true, Shadrach, Meshach, and Abednego, that you will not serve my god, or worship the golden statue that I set up? Be ready now to fall down and worship the statue I had made, whenever you hear the sound of the trumpet, flute, lyre, harp, psaltery, bagpipe, and all the other musical instruments; otherwise, you shall be instantly cast into the white-hot furnace; and who is the God who can deliver you out of my hands?" Shadrach, Meshach, and Abednego answered King Nebuchadnezzar, "There is no need for us to defend ourselves before you in this matter. If our God, whom we serve, can save us from the white-hot furnace and from your hands, O king, may he save us! But even if he will not, know, O king, that we will not serve your god or worship the golden statue that you set up."

Reflection

The words of Shadrach, Meshach, and Abednego are excellent reminders of how we should respond when we are pressured to reject our faith. Refuse! We may face social or financial consequences when we follow God. May we become detached from the things of this world and be bound more tightly to God.

Prayers

others may be added

Trusting in the Lord, we offer to him our prayers:

℟. Lord, come to our aid.

- That the Church may help her children stand firm in the face of persecution, we pray: ℟.
- That the false promises of the world will not overtake God's children, we pray: ℟.
- That the poor will have faith in the promises of God, we pray ℟.
- That we may always be reconciled to Christ, we pray: ℟.

As one body, we pray in the words our merciful Lord gave us.

Our Father . . .

God our Father.
we face many demands to conform
to the fashions and whims of the world.
May we always live in accordance
to your will.
Strengthen us in our resolve to have
faith in you.
Through Christ our Lord.
Amen.

✠ Enlighten, O God of compassion,
the hearts of your children.

✥ Be near, O Lord, to those who plead before you.

Psalm 141 *page 389*

Reading *Genesis 17:3–9*

When Abram prostrated himself, God spoke to him: "My covenant with you is this: you are to become the father of a host of nations. No longer shall you be called Abram; your name shall be Abraham, for I am making you the father of a host of nations. I will render you exceedingly fertile; I will make nations of you; kings shall stem from you. I will maintain my covenant with you and your descendants after you throughout the ages as an everlasting pact, to be your God and the God of your descendants after you. I will give to you and to your descendants after you the land in which you are now staying, the whole land of Canaan, as a permanent possession; and I will be their God."

God also said to Abraham: "On your part, you and your descendants after you must keep my covenant throughout the ages."

Reflection *Pope Francis*

At the heart of the new covenant is our realization that, in Christ, we are embraced by God's mercy and compassion, and that our lives must bear witness to his love for all our brothers and sisters. . . . Prepared for in the Old Testament and established by Christ in the fullness of time, the Church is a new people, founded on a new covenant . . . sealed with the blood of Jesus.

Prayers *others may be added*

Our God is generous with his promises, and so we pray:

℟. Lord, make us faithful to you.

- For a continuation of God's promise that Abraham's descendants will be as numerous as the stars, we pray: ℟.
- For inhabitants of the world, that laws and policies may safeguard the human dignity of all, we pray: ℟.
- For a fulfillment of God's promise to lead all his people out of suffering, we pray: ℟.
- For confidence in God's promise to be with us until the end of time, we pray: ℟.

As one body, we pray in the words our merciful Lord gave us.

Our Father . . .

Lord of hosts,
you give us the promise of eternal life.
May your covenant be ever present
in our hearts,
freeing us from sin and bringing us
into the land of promise.
Through Christ our Lord.
Amen.

✥ Be near, O Lord, to those who plead before you.

Friday, April 11, 2025

✤ Have mercy on me, O Lord.

Psalm 139 *page 389*

Reading *Jeremiah 20:10–13*

I hear the whisperings of many: "Terror on every side! Denounce! let us denounce him!" All those who were my friends are on the watch for any misstep of mine. "Perhaps he will be trapped; then we can prevail, and take our vengeance on him." But the LORD is with me, like a mighty champion: my persecutors will stumble, they will not triumph. In their failure they will be put to utter shame, to lasting, unforgettable confusion. O LORD of hosts, you who test the just, who probe mind and heart, Let me witness the vengeance you take on them, for to you I have entrusted my cause. Sing to the LORD, praise the LORD, For he has rescued the life of the poor from the power of the wicked!

Reflection

When we walk with God, we have nothing to fear. St. Teresa of Ávila prayed: "Let nothing disturb you, let nothing frighten you. All things are passing away. God never changes. Patience obtains all things. Whoever has God lacks nothing; God alone suffices." We may have many anxieties in life—perhaps you had a falling out with a friend or spouse, there is bad weather, you or a loved one have fallen ill. But, do not fear! God is with you, "like a mighty champion." May you allow God to fill your heart and bring you peace.

Prayers *others may be added*

Confident in faith and free from fear,
we offer to the Lord our prayers.

℟. Lord, hear our prayer.

- That Christians may always sing the praise of the Lord in action and word, we pray: ℟.
- That God will help us in our duty to care for his gift of creation, we pray: ℟.
- That we will always serve those who are poor and oppressed with generosity and love, we pray: ℟.
- That we may live together in justice and peace, we pray: ℟.

As one body, we pray in the words
our merciful Lord gave us.

Our Father . . .

God our Father,
you comfort us in our worry.
Be present to us always
so that nothing will disturb us,
nothing will frighten us,
and that we will have patience
in all things.
Through Christ our Lord.
Amen.

✤ Have mercy on me, O Lord.

✚ O Lord, do not stay afar off.

Psalm 126 *page 387*

Reading *John 11:49–53*

Caiaphas, who was high priest that year, said to [the Jews], "You know nothing, nor do you consider that it is better for you that one man should die instead of the people, so that the whole nation may not perish." He did not say this on his own, but since he was high priest for that year, he prophesied that Jesus was going to die for the nation, and not only for the nation, but also to gather into one the dispersed children of God. So from that day on they planned to kill him.

Reflection

As we draw near to Palm Sunday, the Gospel begins to tell the story of Jesus' passion, taking us step by step to the Mount of Calvary. Today we learn that word has spread of the raising of Lazarus. While many come to believe in Jesus, others are afraid of his power. The chief priests and the Pharisees see Jesus as a political threat—if the people follow him, will the Roman occupiers oppress the Jewish people more than ever? And Caiaphas, the high priest, unwittingly becomes a prophet when he suggests that one man, Jesus, should die instead of the whole nation. Jesus will bear the punishment of all "the dispersed children of God." The decision is made to arrest Jesus and have him killed. The passion has begun.

Prayers *others may be added*

We turn now to the Lord who gives us life:.

℟. **Lord, hear our prayer.**

- That the Church may hear and heed the prophetic voices of our own time, we pray: ℟.
- That those who are persecuted for their faith may be strengthened by God, we pray: ℟.
- That those preparing for baptism may grown in the love of God, we pray: ℟.
- That our Lenten observance may open our hearts to those in need, we pray: ℟.

As one body, we pray in the words our merciful Lord gave us.

Our Father . . .

God our Father,
order our steps according to your Word.
Help us to live according to your
divine will.
Through Christ our Lord.
Amen.

✚ O Lord, do not stay afar off.

✣ Hosanna to the Son of David;
blessed is he who comes
in the name of the Lord.

Psalm 22
page 366

Reading
Luke 24:53–56

After [John] had taken the body down, he wrapped it in a linen cloth and laid him in a rock-hewn tomb in which no one had yet been buried. It was the day of preparation, and the sabbath was about to begin. The women who had come from Galilee with him followed behind, and when they had seen the tomb and the way in which his body was laid in it, they returned and prepared spices and perfumed oils. Then they rested on the sabbath according to the commandment.

Reflection

Today's celebration has been known by several names through its long history. It has been called "Palm Sunday," and it has been called "Passion Sunday." Today, it is called "Palm Sunday of the Passion of the Lord," a title that reflects the dual nature of this day, the great beginning of Holy Week. Our liturgy begins with the joyful waving of palm branches, proclaiming Jesus the Messiah as he rides humbly into Jerusalem. But it continues with the reading of the passion according to Luke, when the same crowds who welcomed Jesus with joy assent to his torture and crucifixion. Our joyful entrance into Jerusalem becomes the way of the cross.

Prayers
others may be added

We have set out with Jesus Christ, our King, on his journey to Jerusalem. In love, let us turn to the Lord in prayer:

℟. **Lord, hear us.**

- That the Church will guide her children with care during this Holy Week, we pray: ℟.
- That the saving power of God will wash over our world, we pray: ℟.
- That those preparing for baptism will be transformed by the love of God, we pray: ℟.
- That all Christians may be filled with renewed faith and hope during this Holy Week, we pray: ℟.

As one body, we pray in the words
our merciful Lord gave us.

Our Father . . .

Lord Jesus,
let your soothing oil flow over us.
As you ransomed us with your life,
let us return our love to you freely
and generously;
let us shower one another with mercy
and kindness.
Who live and reign for ever and ever.
Amen.

✣ Hosanna to the Son of David;
blessed is he who comes
in the name of the Lord.

✣ Arise in my defense, O Lord.

Psalm 13 *page 365*

Reading *John 12:1–8*

Six days before Passover Jesus came to Bethany, where Lazarus was, whom Jesus had raised from the dead. They gave a dinner for him there, and Martha served, while Lazarus was one of those reclining at table with him. Mary took a liter of costly perfumed oil made from genuine aromatic nard and anointed the feet of Jesus and dried them with her hair; the house was filled with the fragrance of the oil. Then Judas the Iscariot, one of his disciples, and the one who would betray him, said, "Why was this oil not sold for three hundred days' wages and given to the poor?" He said this not because he cared about the poor but because he was a thief and held the money bag and used to steal the contributions. So Jesus said, "Leave her alone. Let her keep this for the day of my burial. You always have the poor with you, but you do not always have me."

Reflection

Love without limits. That is the message of this passage from the Gospel according to John. Mary, perhaps in gratitude to Jesus for the raising of her brother Lazarus, takes a liter of perfumed oil, perhaps the most valuable thing she owned, and pours it over Jesus' feet. Judas is shocked at the gesture, which he sees as wasteful, but Jesus rebukes him. We cannot love God too much. When it comes to God, we can give with abandon and love without limits. During the Sacred Triduum, we will see the unconditional love of Jesus, who gives himself to us and for us with radical generosity.

Prayers *others may be added*

Trusting in the love of Christ, we offer our prayers to God.

℟. **Lord, have mercy on us.**

✦ That Christ may bring the Church
to the passover feast of heaven,
we pray: ℟.

✦ That Christ, lifted high on the cross,
may heal our wounds, we pray: ℟.

✦ That Christ may grant to those to be reborn in baptism the fruit of his holy cross, we pray: ℟.

✦ That Christ, who forgave the repentant thief, may forgive our sins, we pray: ℟.

As one body, we pray in the words
our merciful Lord gave us.

Our Father . . .

Lord Jesus, our Savior,
you show us how to trust God,
even in the darkest and most
desperate situations.
Be our light in the darkness
especially when the obstacles we face
seem insurmountable.
Help us continue to believe and love
as you did.
Who live and reign for ever and ever.
Amen.

✣ Arise in my defense, O Lord.

Tuesday, April 15, 2025

✤ Do not leave me to the will of my foes, O Lord.

Psalm 13 *page 365*

Reading *John 13:31-33*

When [Judas] had left, Jesus said, "Now is the Son of Man glorified, and God is glorified in him. If God is glorified in him, God will also glorify him in himself, and he will glorify him at once. My children, I will be with you only a little while longer. You will look for me, and as I told the Jews, 'Where I go you cannot come,' so now I say it to you."

Reflection

In today's Gospel, when Jesus speaks of being glorified, he refers to a specific Hebrew understanding of the word "glorified": it means perceiving God's presence through our senses. For example, the cloud that stayed with the people after they fled Egypt (see Exodus 16:10) represented God's remaining with them. His crucifixion will be a unique sign that God is still with us.

Prayers *others may be added*

With faith in God, we turn to him now in prayer.

℟. Lord, help us persevere in faith.

- That all the baptized people of God may remain faithful to the very end, we pray: ℟.
- That those who live in the shadow of violence, death, and war may keep the light of Christ alive in their hearts, we pray: ℟.
- That those who suffer may see in their affliction a share in the glorious cross of Christ, we pray: ℟.
- That we may trust always in the God who brings good out of evil, we pray: ℟.

As one body, we pray in the words our merciful Lord gave us.

Our Father . . .

Lord Jesus,
you came into our midst,
bearing the priceless gift of salvation
and eternal life,
but we did not know you.
Awaken us to your presence among us
and drive all sin from our hearts.
Who live and reign for ever and ever.
Amen.

✤ Do not leave me to the will of my foes, O Lord.

✠ At the name of Jesus,
every knee should bend.

Psalm 13

page 365

Reading

Matthew 26:20–25

When it was evening, [Jesus] reclined at table with the Twelve. And while they were eating, he said, "Amen, I say to you, one of you will betray me." Deeply distressed at this, they began to say to him one after another, "Surely it is not I, Lord?" He said in reply, "He who has dipped his hand into the dish with me is the one who will betray me. The Son of Man indeed goes, as it is written of him, but woe to that man by whom the Son of Man is betrayed. It would be better for that man if he had never been born." Then Judas, his betrayer, said in reply, "Surely it is not I, Rabbi?" He answered, "You have said so."

Reflection

Judas is a warning to us. We can perform all the exterior acts of devotion and appear to be close to God but inside be rotten and deceitful. Judas was constantly in the presence of Jesus and yet he betrayed him for money. How can we avoid being like Judas? We must have humility and cling tightly to God, the sacraments, and the teachings of the Church. Let us remember that the supreme principle on which all human beings should make their choices is the will of God. The will of God can at times call us to painful sacrifices. But they are made sweet if our will is conformed to God's.

Prayers

others may be added

Let us pray to the Lord who redeemed us by his blood.

℟. **Lord, have mercy on us.**

- For the Church, that temptation may be conquered by faithfulness to Christ, we pray: ℟.
- For betrayers of countries, of promises, of families, and of friendships, that they may repent and return to lives of integrity, we pray: ℟.
- For strength in moments of temptation, we pray: ℟.
- For those who have died in the state of sin, we pray: ℟.

As one body, we pray in the words our merciful Lord gave us.

Our Father . . .

God our Father,
your Son ransomed us with his life.
Let us be imbued with that love
and offer it to others freely
and generously.
Let us shower one another with mercy
and kindness.
Through Christ our Lord.
Amen.

✠ At the name of Jesus,
every knee should bend.

✚ To [Jesus Christ] be glory and power for ever.

Psalm 34

page 370

Reading

John 13:2–4

During supper, fully aware that the Father had put everything into his power and that he had come from God and was returning to God, [Jesus] rose from supper and took off his outer garments. He took a towel and tied it around his waist. Then he poured water into a basin and began to wash the disciples' feet and dry them with the towel around his waist.

Reflection

Every time we say "yes" by saying "Amen" when receiving the Body and Blood of Christ in the Eucharist, we agree to share in his life. In the Gospel according to John, Jesus shows us tangibly how we are to follow in his steps: by washing the feet of others. Find a way during the Paschal Triduum to say yes to God through humble and loving service toward others.

Prayers

others may be added

Rejoicing in all who follow the Lord,
we offer to him our prayers.

℟. **Lord, nourish your people.**

✦ For leaders of the Church, that they may serve in Jesus' name and follow in his footsteps, we pray: ℟.

✦ For the leaders of nations, that they may bow down to the poorest among them, hearing their pleas, and working for the common good, we pray: ℟.

✦ For teachers and parents, that they may model leadership with humility and love, we pray: ℟.

✦ For each of us, that we may bow down before Lord with acts of service and charity, we pray: ℟.

Let us offer together the prayer
that Jesus taught us.

Our Father . . .

God our Father,
you offer yourself to us as spiritual food
and drink
in the sacrament of the Eucharist.
Fill our hearts with love and awe,
that we may approach your
grace worthily.
Through Christ our Lord.
Amen.

✚ To [Jesus Christ] be glory and power for ever.

✠ Behold the wood of the Cross,
on which hung the salvation
of the world.

Psalm 22

page 366

Reading

Isaiah 53:7–10

Though he was harshly treated, he submitted / and opened not his mouth; / like a lamb led to the slaughter / or a sheep before the shearers, / he was silent and opened not his mouth. / Oppressed and condemned, he was taken away, / and who would have thought any more of his destiny? / When he was cut off from the land of the living, / and smitten for the sin of his people, / a grave was assigned him among the wicked / and a burial place with evildoers, / though he had done no wrong / nor spoken any falsehood. / But the LORD was pleased / to crush him in infirmity.

If he gives his life as an offering for sin, / he shall see his descendants in a long life, / and the will of the LORD shall be accomplished through him.

Reflection

Any time we feel alone, when our pain and suffering is unbearable, or we lose faith in God's presence, this is the passage we should read. We see the incredible strength, love, and mercy of our Savior expressed in these words describing God's Suffering Servant. He knows our pain; he knows our loneliness; he knows our despair. No matter how alone or despairing we may feel, he is there. He took on our suffering in order to conquer it forever.

Prayers

others may be added

We bring our prayers before the crucified Lord:

℟. **Lord, have mercy on us.**

- For the holy Church of God, for our Holy Father, for the bishops, priests, deacons, religious, and lay faithful, we pray: ℟.
- For those preparing for baptism, that the cross that they accepted as catechumens may lead them to new life, we pray: ℟.
- For those who do not believe in God, we pray: ℟.
- For the sick, the dying, those unjustly deprived of liberty, and those suffering the ravages of war, we pray: ℟.

Let us offer together the prayer
that Jesus taught us.

Our Father . . .

God our Father,
your Son and our Lord Jesus Christ
suffered and died for us
that we might have eternal life.
Help us to cherish this gift
and help us conform our wills to yours.
Through Christ our Lord.
Amen.

✠ Behold the wood of the Cross,
on which hung the salvation
of the world.

✠ By his holy / and glorious wounds, / may Christ the Lord / guard us / and protect us.

Psalm 13

page 365

Reading

Isaiah 54:7; 9-10

For a brief moment I abandoned you, / but with great tenderness I will take you back. / In an outburst of wrath, for a moment / I hid my face from you; / but with an enduring love I take pity on you, / says the LORD, your redeemer. / This is for me like the days of Noah, when I swore that the waters of Noah / should never again deluge the earth; / so I have sworn not to be angry with you, / or to rebuke you. / Though the mountains leave their place / and the hills be shaken, / my love shall never leave you / nor my covenant of peace be shaken, / says the LORD, who has mercy on you.

Reflection

We are part of a long line of God's people. He has been with us through dangers, battles, darkness, and confusion. God has taken us back time after time when we have wandered, sinned, and lost our way. This Easter night we trace our story as children of God. In the incarnation, we know we are deeply loved. In the crucifixion, we know we will never be alone. In the resurrection of our Lord, we know that we will never die, but instead we will live with God forever. Rejoice!

Prayers

others may be added

The Lord will raise us to new life,
and so we pray.

℟. **Lord, restore the world.**

- For the faithful who, despite many trials, continue to follow God, we pray: ℟.
- For humanity, that the wisdom and compassion of God may wash over all people, we pray: ℟.
- For those who enter the Church this night, that the light of Christ may burn brightly in their lives, we pray: ℟.
- For all the baptized, that we may rejoice in our destiny as children of God, we pray: ℟.
- For all who have died, that they may be reunited with the love of God in heaven, we pray: ℟.

Let us offer together the prayer
that Jesus taught us.

Our Father . . .

Magnificent God,
roll the stone away from the graves
of our sin,
that we may rise to see your Son in glory;
and let us rejoice in eternal life.
We ask this through Christ our Lord.
Amen.

✠ By his holy / and glorious wounds, / may Christ the Lord / guard us / and protect us.

✚ The Lord is truly risen, alleluia.

Psalm 148 *page 390*

Reading *John 20:1–9*

On the first day of the week, Mary of Magdala came to the tomb early in the morning, while it was still dark, and saw the stone removed from the tomb. So she ran and went to Simon Peter and to the other disciple whom Jesus loved, and told them, "They have taken the Lord from the tomb, and we don't know where they put him." So Peter and the other disciple went out and came to the tomb. They both ran, but the other disciple ran faster than Peter and arrived at the tomb first; he bent down and saw the burial cloths there, but did not go in. When Simon Peter arrived after him, he went into the tomb and saw the burial cloths there, and the cloth that had covered his head, not with the burial cloths but rolled up in a separate place. Then the other disciple also went in, the one who had arrived at the tomb first, and he saw and believed. For they did not yet understand the Scripture that he had to rise from the dead.

Reflection

Who is the other disciple in this remarkable Easter story? How was he able to run a bit faster than Peter, yet could not go into the empty tomb? Was there still some fear inside him, some confusion? We can relate so much to his abiding fear and confusion. Did Jesus really rise from the dead, like he said he would? How could this happen? In living our Easter faith, we might share his confusion at this awesome mystery. In the end, he believed. Let us let go of fear this Easter and believe in our risen Lord.

Prayers *others may be added*

Our Lord Jesus is risen from the dead! With joy, let us offer our prayers to God.

℟. **Risen Lord, hear our prayer.**

- For an increase in Easter faith in our Church, we pray: ℟.
- For an increase of Easter hope in our world, we pray: ℟.
- For an increase in Easter love for those on the margins in our lives, we pray: ℟.
- For the lonely and forgotten on this Easter Sunday, we pray: ℟.
- For those who are dying, and those who will die today, we pray: ℟.

Let us offer together the prayer that Jesus taught us.

Our Father . . .

Lord Jesus,
you conquered sin and death through
your resurrection,
help us run to you with Easter joy
as did the disciple you loved.
Give us the grace and courage to share
our Easter joy with others this day
and throughout the Easter season.
You who live and reign for ever.
Amen.

✚ The Lord is truly risen, alleluia.

Monday within the Octave of Easter

Monday, April 21, 2025

✣ The Lord has risen from the dead.

Psalm 98

page 381

Reading

Matthew 28:8–14

Mary Magdalene and the other Mary went away quickly from the tomb, fearful yet overjoyed, and ran to announce the news to his disciples. And behold, Jesus met them on their way and greeted them. They approached, embraced his feet, and did him homage. Then Jesus said to them, "Do not be afraid. Go tell my brothers to go to Galilee, and there they will see me."

While they were going, some of the guard went into the city and told the chief priests all that had happened. The chief priests assembled with the elders and took counsel; then they gave a large sum of money to the soldiers, telling them, "You are to say, 'His disciples came by night and stole him while we were asleep. And if this gets to the ears of the governor, we will satisfy him and keep you out of trouble.'"

Reflection

Mary Magdalene was "fearful, yet overjoyed" at the truth of Jesus' resurrection. Two things helped her overcome fear. First, she wasn't alone—she had at least one other faithful woman with her. And two, meeting Jesus gave her even more courage so that she could share the Good News with the disciples. How often does fear overcome us? How might you embrace Jesus' message to not be afraid?

Prayers

others may be added

Without fear, we approach the Lord in prayer:

℟. **Risen Lord, hear our prayer.**

- For all who minister in the Church, we pray: ℟.
- For leaders of nations, that they may not govern out of fear, we pray: ℟.
- For those who go without the necessities of life, we pray: ℟.
- For an increase in the virtue of hope, we pray: ℟.
- For those who are dying, and those who will die today, we pray: ℟.

The Lord is risen and present among us and so we pray as he taught us.

Our Father . . .

Risen Lord,
you sent Mary Magdalene and other faithful women
to be the first to proclaim your resurrection.
Overcome our fear with joy
in proclaiming you to a world in need of your love.
Give us courage to love you and all peoples.
Who live and reign for ever and ever.
Amen.

✣ The Lord has risen from the dead.

✤ O God, . . . endow your people
with heavenly gifts.

Psalm 96 *page 380*

page 380

Reading *Acts 2:36–41*

On the day of Pentecost, Peter said to the Jewish people, "Let the whole house of Israel know for certain that God has made him both Lord and Christ, this Jesus whom you crucified."

Now when they heard this, they were cut to the heart, and they asked Peter and the other Apostles, "What are we to do, my brothers?" Peter said to them, "Repent and be baptized, every one of you, in the name of Jesus Christ, for the forgiveness of your sins; and you will receive the gift of the Holy Spirit. For the promise is made to you and to your children and to all those far off, whomever the Lord our God will call." He testified with many other arguments, and was exhorting them, "Save yourselves from this corrupt generation." Those who accepted his message were baptized, and about three thousand persons were added that day.

Reflection

Did you witness and participate in the baptism of adults or children during your parish's celebration of the Triduum? Imagine if three thousand people had been baptized! Peter's message must have been powerful and influential for so many people to have come to Jesus and be baptized. Imagine how dramatic Jesus' appearances must have been in order for Peter and the other disicples to have shared their faith with such conviction! Do you share your faith with conviction so that others are led to Jesus by your words and witness? How might your life be a living witness to the truth of Christ's resurrection?

Prayers *others may be added*

With faith in Jesus' resurrection,
we turn to him now in prayer:

℟. **Risen Lord, hear our prayer.**

- For the Church throughout the world, we pray: ℟.
- For peace among nations, we pray: ℟.
- For immigrants, refugees, and those seeking a better life for themselves, we pray: ℟.
- For those in our families who are struggling, we pray: ℟.
- For those who are dying, and those who will die today, we pray: ℟.

The Lord is risen and present among us and so we pray as he taught us.

Our Father . . .

Risen Lord,
you inspired your disciples to share
their faith
and grow the early Church.
Give us the courage to share with others
the joy of your resurrection.
Who live and reign for ever and ever.
Amen.

✤ O God, . . . endow your people
with heavenly gifts.

Wednesday, April 23, 2025

✠ Come, you blessed . . . / receive
the kingdom prepared for you.

Psalm 138

page 388

Reading

Acts 3:2–10

A man crippled from birth was carried and placed at the gate of the temple called "the Beautiful Gate" every day to beg for alms from the people who entered the temple. When he saw Peter and John about to go into the temple, he asked for alms. But Peter looked intently at him, as did John, and said, "Look at us." He paid attention to them, expecting to receive something from them. Peter said, "I have neither silver nor gold, but what I do have I give you: in the name of Jesus Christ the Nazorean, rise and walk." Then Peter took him by the right hand and raised him up, and immediately his feet and ankles grew strong. He leaped up, stood, and walked around, and went into the temple with them, walking and jumping and praising God. When all the people saw him walking and praising God, they recognized him as the one who used to sit begging at the Beautiful Gate of the temple, and they were filled with amazement and astonishment at what had happened to him.

Reflection

You might pass people begging for alms on a regular basis. How we respond to these situations can be complicated. Do we give them money? Do we bring them food, blankets, or clothing? Do engage in conversation? Or do we simply walk on by and pretend the people do not exist? In the reading today, Peter and John encounter a crippled man but they have no alms to give him. Instead, they give the crippled man something better—the healing power of Jesus! Simply revealing Jesus' holy name brought forth miraculous healing. We all need healing. We are all crippled in some way. What do you bring to Jesus today for healing? How might you bring Jesus' healing to others?

Prayers

others may be added

Not with silver or gold, O Lord, do
we pray, but with all that we are and
with all that you have created us to
be do we pray:

℟. **Risen Lord, hear our prayer.**

- For Church leaders to have courage, we pray: ℟.
- For world leaders to act with integrity, we pray: ℟.
- For those who are poor, homeless, and unemployed or underemployed, we pray: ℟.
- For those who are dying, and those who will die today, we pray: ℟.

The Lord is risen and present among
us and so we pray as he taught us.

Our Father . . .

Risen Jesus,
your holy name is the source of healing.
Give us honesty to acknowledge where
we need your healing in our lives
and the faith to believe that you can
bring us to wholeness.
Who live and reign for ever and ever.
Amen.

✠ Come, you blessed . . . / receive
the kingdom prepared for you.

✣ May [we] be one in the faith
of [our] hearts.

Psalm 47

page 372

Reading

Acts 3:11–16

As the crippled man who had been cured clung to Peter and John, all the people hurried in amazement toward them in the portico called "Solomon's Portico." When Peter saw this, he addressed the people, "You children of Israel, why are you amazed at this, and why do you look so intently at us as if we had made him walk by our own power or piety? The God of Abraham, the God of Isaac, and the God of Jacob, the God of our fathers, has glorified his servant Jesus whom you handed over and denied in Pilate's presence, when he had decided to release him. You denied the Holy and Righteous One and asked that a murderer be released to you. The author of life you put to death, but God raised him from the dead; of this we are witnesses. And by faith in his name, this man, whom you see and know, his name has made strong, and the faith that comes through it has given him this perfect health, in the presence of all of you.

Reflection

The people are so astonished that the crippled man was healed. How did this happen, they ask? How could he be healed so quickly? The people simply needed a reminder that the God of Abraham, Isaac, and Jacob was still present among them in Christ Jesus, the risen Lord. What spiritual reminders do we need today to remember that God is present to us and acting in our lives?

Prayers

others may be added

With faith in the name of the Lord,
we offer our prayers:

℟. Risen Lord, hear our prayer.

- For the Church, that we may always be ministers of Christ's healing love, we pray: ℟.
- For world leaders, that they provide health care for their citizens, we pray:
- For those who deny the healing powers of God,
- For reminders of how God is working in our lives, we pray: ℟.
- For those who are dying, and those who will die today, we pray: ℟.

The Lord is risen and present among us and so we pray as he taught us.

Our Father . . .

Loving God,
you formed a covenant with
the Israelites
and fulfilled this promise in Jesus.
Help us to be aware of your presence
in our lives
and give us the grace to follow
where you lead us.
Through Christ our Lord.
Amen.

✣ May [we] be one in the faith
of [our] hearts.

Friday, April 25, 2025

✤ The Lord led his people in hope.

Psalm 63

page 375

Reading

Acts 4:1–4

After the crippled man had been cured, while Peter and John were still speaking to the people, the priests, the captain of the temple guard, and the Sadducees confronted them, disturbed that they were teaching the people and proclaiming in Jesus the resurrection of the dead. They laid hands on Peter and John and put them in custody until the next day, since it was already evening. But many of those who heard the word came to believe and the number of men grew to about five thousand.

Reflection

Peter must have known his healing of the crippled man would cause a stir. Didn't he know that it might get him into trouble? Sure enough, he was arrested for going against the leaders. Yet even in the face of persecution he stood strong and spoke with faith and conviction. Living our faith comes with a cost. Sure, it's easier to just go along with others in order to get along. But living our faith means to be countercultural. Where are the situations in your life in which being true to your faith is difficult, when your faith comes with a cost? How do you find God's strength in these situations?

Prayers

others may be added

Lord, we have heard your Word and believe, and so we pray:

℟. **Risen Lord, hear our prayer.**

- For all bishops, priests, deacons, and lay ministers in our Church, we pray: ℟.
- For peace in our world, we pray: ℟.
- For an end to gun violence in our communities, we pray: ℟.
- For those experiencing a diminishment of their minds or bodies, and those who care for them, we pray: ℟.
- For those who are dying, and those who will die today, we pray: ℟.

The Lord is risen and present among us and so we pray as he taught us.

Our Father . . .

God our Father,
you reveal the path to love.
Help us to share that love with others
especially when doing so is difficult
or comes with a cost.
Through Christ our Lord.
Amen.

✤ The Lord led his people in hope.

✚ The Lord brought out his people with joy.

Psalm 30 *page 369*

Reading *Mark 16:9–15*

When Jesus had risen, early on the first day of the week, he appeared first to Mary Magdalene, out of whom he had driven seven demons. She went and told his companions who were mourning and weeping. When they heard that he was alive and had been seen by her, they did not believe.

After this he appeared in another form to two of them walking along on their way to the country. They returned and told the others; but they did not believe them either.

But later, as the Eleven were at table, he appeared to them and rebuked them for their unbelief and hardness of heart because they had not believed those who saw him after he had been raised. He said to them, "Go into the whole world and proclaim the Gospel to every creature."

Reflection

Some of the most frustrating moments for parents are repeating instructions over and over again. It must have been so frustrating for Mary Magdalene. No one would believe her! She must have felt like parents do when their children do not listen. Yet aren't we, at times, like the disciples in todays reading? Do we sometimes forget what it means to be a Christian? Do we recognize Christ's presence in others? In ourselves? Jesus rebukes the disciples for their unbelief. We must be open to the presence of Christ in our lives and have the courage to "go out into the whole world and proclaim the Gospel to every creature." How? By the very witness of our lives.

Prayers *others may be added*

Glorifying the Lord by our lives,
we offer to him our prayers:

℟. **Risen Lord, hear our prayer.**

- That we will walk with Christ at all times, we pray: ℟.
- That citizens call upon their leaders to rid the world of injustice and abuse, we pray:
- That we believe that Christ has the words of life, we pray: ℟.
- That, when we are tempted to walk away from Christ, others' example may invite us back, we pray: ℟.

The Lord is risen and present among us and so we pray as he taught us.

Our Father . . .

Lord Jesus,
you send us out to proclaim the Gospel
to all people.
Give us faith to believe all that we have
been taught,
and courage to share it with others.
Help us to recognize your presence
among us.
Who live and reign for ever and ever.
Amen.

✚ The Lord brought out his people with joy.

Second Sunday of Easter /
Sunday of Divine Mercy
Sunday, April 27, 2025

✚ Receive the joy of your glory,
giving thanks to God.

Psalm 118

page 386

Reading

John 20:24–29

Thomas, called Didymus, one of the Twelve, was not with them when Jesus came. So the other disciples said to him, "We have seen the Lord." But he said to them, "Unless I see the mark of the nails in his hands and put my finger into the nailmarks and put my hand into his side, I will not believe."

Now a week later his disciples were again inside and Thomas was with them. Jesus came, although the doors were locked, and stood in their midst and said, "Peace be with you." Then he said to Thomas, "Put your finger here and see my hands, and bring your hand and put it into my side, and do not be unbelieving, but believe." Thomas answered and said to him, "My Lord and my God!" Jesus said to him, "Have you come to believe because you have seen me? Blessed are those who have not seen and have believed."

Reflection

Many have experienced a "dark night of the soul"—an experience in which one desires greatly to know and feel God's presence, yet feels very much alone. Certainly Thomas felt that way. The disciples tell Thomas that the Lord has risen! They have seen him! But Thomas didn't believe. Jesus himself appeared to Thomas, and yet he still didn't believe. Thomas needed a tangible, physical sign that Jesus was with him. We all struggle at times. But Jesus gives us peace. His peace delivers us from our anxieties and doubt. We need only be open to the grace and let him calm our troubles. Jesus is present! Let us believe.

Prayers

others may be added

O Lord, we may not see you, but we do believe, and so we pray:

℟. Healer of all, hear our prayer.

- For all leaders in the Church who struggle with doubt, we pray: ℟.
- For harmony among all nations, we pray: ℟.
- For the grace to offer mercy and healing to those who have wronged us, we pray: ℟.
- For respect to be given to all human life, we pray: ℟.
- For those who are dying, and those who will die today, we pray: ℟.

The Lord is risen and present among us and so we pray as he taught us.

Our Father . . .

Lord Jesus,
you love us despite our doubts.
Help our unbelief.
Increase our faith in you today
so that we may share it with others
and lead all to your eternal glory.
Who live and reign for ever and ever.
Amen.

✚ Receive the joy of your glory,
giving thanks to God.

✠ Christ, having risen from the dead, dies now no more.

Psalm 111 *page 384*

Reading *John 3:1–8*

There was a Pharisee named Nicodemus, a ruler of the Jews. He came to Jesus at night and said to him, "Rabbi, we know that you are a teacher who has come from God, for no one can do these signs that you are doing unless God is with him." Jesus answered and said to him, "Amen, amen, I say to you, unless one is born from above, he cannot see the Kingdom of God." Nicodemus said to him, "How can a man once grown old be born again? Surely he cannot reenter his mother's womb and be born again, can he?" Jesus answered, "Amen, amen, I say to you, unless one is born of water and Spirit he cannot enter the Kingdom of God. What is born of flesh is flesh and what is born of spirit is spirit. Do not be amazed that I told you, 'You must be born from above.' The wind blows where it wills, and you can hear the sound it makes, but you do not know where it comes from or where it goes; so it is with everyone who is born of the Spirit."

Reflection *Pope Francis*

Baptism permits Christ to live in us, and to live united with him in order to collaborate in the Church, each according to his or her own condition, to the transformation of the world. . . . No one merits baptism, which is always a free gift to all, adults and newborns. But as happens with a small seed full of life, this gift takes root and bears fruit in land nourished by faith.

Prayers *others may be added*

Rejoice in the Lord for he has risen! Let us come before him with our prayers.

℟. In your mercy, hear us, O Lord.

- That all the baptized may give witness to Christ by the integrity and compassion of their lives, we pray: ℟.
- That the Spirit of God may bless the world with peace, we pray: ℟.
- That those seeking baptism may be strengthened in their resolve to follow Christ, we pray: ℟.
- That all who are opppressed because of their beliefs may worship God in freedom, we pray: ℟.

The Lord is risen and present among us and so we pray as he taught us.

Our Father . . .

Loving God,
by your power we are created,
and through baptism we inherit
your kingdom.
Let us stand in awe of you;
let us praise you and thank you
for the gift of salvation.
Through Christ our Lord.
Amen.

✠ Christ, having risen from the dead, dies now no more.

✤ Here is a wise virgin . . . who
went forth with lighted lamp
to meet Christ.

Psalm 95
page 380

Reading
Acts 4:32–37

The community of believers was of one heart and mind, and no one claimed that any of his possessions was his own, but they had everything in common. With great power the Apostles bore witness to the resurrection of the Lord Jesus, and great favor was accorded them all. There was no needy person among them, for those who owned property or houses would sell them, bring the proceeds of the sale, and put them at the feet of the Apostles, and they were distributed to each according to need.

Thus Joseph, also named by the Apostles Barnabas (which is translated "son of encouragement"), a Levite, a Cypriot by birth, sold a piece of property that he owned, then brought the money and put it at the feet of the Apostles.

Reflection

Catherine of Siena and Teresa of Avila were the first women to be declared "Doctors of the Church." Today's Gospel is fitting for Catherine, insofar as strong winds buffeted the Church in the fourteenth century. Catherine's profound dedication to the Eucharist inspired her to be an ambassador of peace and unity. A remarkable woman for any generation, she worked tirelessly to restore peace among the papal states and was instrumental in the return of the seat of the papacy from France to Italy. In iconography, Catherine is sometimes depicted as carrying the "Bark of Peter," the Church, on her shoulders.

Prayers
others may be added

Bearing witness to the Lord, we turn to him in prayer:

℟. **God of love, hear our prayer.**

- For all leaders in the Church who are persecuted for their faith, we pray: ℟.
- For world leaders to protect the religious freedom of all peoples, we pray: ℟.
- For an end to climate change, and for those who suffer from its effects, we pray: ℟.
- For patience within our families and with those who challenge us, we pray: ℟.
- For those who are dying, and those who will die today, we pray: ℟.

The Lord is risen and present among us and so we pray as he taught us.

Our Father . . .

God of Providence,
in every generation
you provide refuge and strength
to your people.
As you once called St. Catherine of Siena,
so today open our hearts and minds
to work
for peace and unity in your Church
and in the world,
Through Christ our Lord.
Amen.

✤ Here is a wise virgin . . . who
went forth with lighted lamp
to meet Christ.

✚ I will praise you, Lord,
among the nations.

Psalm 96 *page 380*

Reading *John 3:16–21*

God so loved the world that he gave his only-begotten Son, so that everyone who believes in him might not perish but might have eternal life. For God did not send his Son into the world to condemn the world, but that the world might be saved through him. Whoever believes in him will not be condemned, but whoever does not believe has already been condemned, because he has not believed in the name of the only-begotten Son of God. And this is the verdict, that the light came into the world, but people preferred darkness to light, because their works were evil. For everyone who does wicked things hates the light and does not come toward the light, so that his works might not be exposed. But whoever lives the truth comes to the light, so that his works may be clearly seen as done in God.

Reflection

You cannot watch a professional sporting event without seeing a John 3:16 sign. Even though we see this reference often, do we fully embrace its meaning? God did not send Jesus to condemn the world but to love the world. Yet how often do we condemn others for the color of their skin, immigration status, political party affiliation, economic status, sexuality, or other issues? Or how often might we feel condemned by others? God loves us. So much so that he sent his only Son to redeem us. Our call in this world is simple—let us love.

Prayers *others may be added*

God loves the world and we, by also loving the world, show our love for God, so we pray:

℟. **Savior of all, hear our prayer.**

- For Church leaders, that their ministry be imbued with the love of God, we pray: ℟.
- For world leaders to strive for peace rather than discord, we pray: ℟.
- For those who only feel condemned by others, we pray: ℟.
- For holy bonds of friendship to be shared among all peoples, we pray: ℟.
- For those who are dying, and those who will die today, we pray: ℟.

The Lord is risen and present among us and so we pray as he taught us.

Our Father . . .

God our Father,
out of great love for all people
you sent Jesus, your Son,
to be the bearer of salvation—
even to the point of death.
As your image and likness,
may we embody the call to love
with everyone we encounter.
Through Christ our Lord.
Amen.

✚ I will praise you, Lord,
among the nations.

Easter Weekday

Thursday, May 1, 2025

✠ O God, who for the salvation of the world / brought about the paschal sacrifice.

Psalm 121

page 386

Reading

Acts 5:27–33

When the court officers had brought the Apostles in and made them stand before the Sanhedrin, the high priest questioned them, "We gave you strict orders did we not, to stop teaching in that name. Yet you have filled Jerusalem with your teaching and want to bring this man's blood upon us." But Peter and the Apostles said in reply, "We must obey God rather than men. The God of our ancestors raised Jesus, though you had him killed by hanging him on a tree. God exalted him at his right hand as leader and savior to grant Israel repentance and forgiveness of sins. We are witnesses of these things, as is the Holy Spirit whom God has given to those who obey him."

When they heard this, they became infuriated and wanted to put them to death.

Reflection

The apostles are given "strict" instructions to stop preaching in the name of Jesus. The apostles' response is simple—they must obey God. In any number of ways, we can be told subtly (and not so subtly) to reject our faith or to live it quietly. Jesus gives us strict instructions—proclaim the Gospel to the ends of the earth. Will we follow them like the apostles did?

Prayers

others may be added

In the name of Jesus, we offer our prayers:

℟. **Risen Christ, hear our prayer.**

- For Church leaders to boldly proclaim the Gospel, we pray: ℟.
- For an end to violent conflicts in the world, we pray: ℟.
- For those who are without adequate shelter, we pray: ℟.
- For those who are silenced because of their religious beliefs, we pray: ℟.
- For those who are dying, and those who will die today, we pray: ℟.

The Lord is risen and present among us and so we pray as he taught us.

Our Father . . .

God our Father,
you call us to be faithful to you.
Give us courage when it is difficult
to follow you.
Bless us with strong communities
of faith
who will proclaim your Gospel.
Through Christ our Lord.
Amen.

✠ O God, who for the salvation of the world / brought about the paschal sacrifice.

✣ The Lord filled him with the spirit
of wisdom and understanding.

Psalm 148 *page 390*

Reading *John 6:5–13*

When Jesus raised his eyes and saw that a large crowd was coming to him, he said to Philip, "Where can we buy enough food for them to eat?" He said this to test him, because he himself knew what he was going to do. Philip answered him, "Two hundred days' wages worth of food would not be enough for each of them to have a little." One of his disciples, Andrew, the brother of Simon Peter, said to him, "There is a boy here who has five barley loaves and two fish; but what good are these for so many?" Jesus said, "Have the people recline." Now there was a great deal of grass in that place. So the men reclined, about five thousand in number. Then Jesus took the loaves, gave thanks, and distributed them to those who were reclining, and also as much of the fish as they wanted. When they had had their fill, he said to his disciples, "Gather the fragments left over, so that nothing will be wasted." So they collected them, and filled twelve wicker baskets with fragments from the five barley loaves that had been more than they could eat.

Reflection

The 2003 movie, *Seabiscuit*, is based on the true story of an underdog racehorse. In one scene, the horse's owner says: "The little guy [the horse], when he doesn't know he's the little guy, can do great big things." That is what happens in today's Gospel story. The boy gives what food he has to Jesus. Jesus takes the offering of a few loaves of bread and a little fish and does great things with them. Just like the boy, we are called to serve God in simple ways. God will make something big out of what little we have to offer. What can you offer to God today that can be transformed into something more?

Prayers *others may be added*

Rejoicing in the Lord because he fills our every need, we offer to him our prayers:

℟. **Risen Lord, hear our prayer.**

- For the Church, that all will share their gifts in generosity, we pray: ℟.
- For a greater willingness to share resources among nations, we pray: ℟.
- For those who lack access to clean water, we pray: ℟.
- For greater respect for God's gift of creation, we pray: ℟.
- For those who are dying, and those who will die today, we pray: ℟.

The Lord is risen and present among us and so we pray as he taught us.

Our Father . . .

Lord Jesus,
you took five loaves and two fish
and fed a multitude.
Help us to share our gifts in gratitude
and generosity.
Help us to trust that our blessings from
you are always enough.
Who live and reign for ever and ever.
Amen.

✣ The Lord filled him with the spirit
of wisdom and understanding.

✤ These are the holy men / whom the Lord chose in his own perfect love.

Psalm 46

page 372

Reading

John 14:8–14

Philip said to [Jesus], "Master, show us the Father, and that will be enough for us." Jesus said to him, "Have I been with you for so long a time and you still do not know me, Philip? Whoever has seen me has seen the Father. How can you say, 'Show us the Father'? Do you not believe that I am in the Father and the Father is in me? The words that I speak to you I do not speak on my own. The Father who dwells in me is doing his works. Believe me that I am in the Father and the Father is in me, or else, believe because of the works themselves. Amen, amen, I say to you, whoever believes in me will do the works that I do, and will do greater ones than these, because I am going to the Father. And whatever you ask in my name, I will do, so that the Father may be glorified in the Son. If you ask anything of me in my name, I will do it."

Reflection

Philip, born in Bethsaida, was initially a disciple of John the Baptist. Later he became a follower of Christ. Prompted by the Spirit, Philip accosted the Godfearing Ethiopian official on the Gaza road, baptizing him after instruction as the first member of the Church from outside the tradition of Israel. On the other hand, James, a cousin of the Lord and the son of Alphaeus, ruled over the Church in Jerusalem after Peter left Jerusalem to go on mission to Rome. James penned an epistle and converted many of the Jewish people to the faith. He led an austere life and suffered martyrdom in the year 62. Together James and Philip represent the churches of the Jewish and Gentile followers of Christ. Much like Peter and Paul, they are complementary figures.

Prayers

others may be added

Holding fast to God's Word we have the courage to pray:

℟. **Risen Lord, hear our prayer.**

- That ministers of the Church will stay true to the faith given us from the apostles, we pray: ℟.
- That nations will pass legislation to protect the rights of workers, we pray: ℟.
- That workers will recognize that their work is a cooperation with the work of God, we pray:
- That those who are dying will be embraced by the peace of Christ, we pray: ℟.

The Lord is risen and present among us and so we pray as he taught us.

Our Father . . .

Jesus the Christ,
you reveal to us the great love
of the Father.
Increase our belief in you
that we may glorify you in all
our earthly works.
Who live and reign for ever.
Amen.

✤ These are the holy men / whom the Lord chose in his own perfect love.

✤ Cry out with joy to God, all the earth.

Psalm 33 *page 369*

Reading *John 21:12–14*

Jesus said to [his disciples], "Come, have breakfast." And none of the disciples dared to ask him, "Who are you?" because they realized it was the Lord. Jesus came over and took the bread and gave it to them, and in like manner the fish. This was now the third time Jesus was revealed to his disciples after being raised from the dead.

Reflection *Pope Francis*

Jesus is able to feed everyone. . . . The Lord can do a lot with the little that we put at his disposal. Jesus can do a lot with our prayers, gestures of kindness and offering up our suffering, working miracles with them. This is how God loves to act: he does great things, starting from those small things, those freely-given ones.

Prayers *others may be added*

The Lord is present among us. As his disciples, we offer to him our prayers:

℟. **Good Shepherd, hear our prayer.**

- For all leaders in the Church, that they joyfully lead in service to others, we pray: ℟.
- For peace among all people of good will, we pray: ℟.
- For grace in following Jesus even where we do not want to go, we pray: ℟.
- For the lonely and forgotten members of our parish communities, we pray: ℟.
- For those who are dying, and those who will die today, we pray: ℟.

The Lord is risen and present among us and so we pray as he taught us.

Our Father . . .

Lord Jesus, our Bread of LIfe,
you know our hunger and thirst.
Fill and nourish us
that we might find strength in you.
Who live and reign for ever and ever.
Amen.

✤ Cry out with joy to God, all the earth.

Monday, May 5, 2025

✠ The Good Shepherd has risen, . . . /
and willingly died for his flock.

Psalm 98

page 381

Reading

Acts 6:8–15

Stephen, filled with grace and power, was working great wonders and signs among the people. Certain members of the so-called Synagogue of Freedmen, Cyreneans, and Alexandrians, and people from Cilicia and Asia, came forward and debated with Stephen, but they could not withstand the wisdom and the Spirit with which he spoke. Then they instigated some men to say, "We have heard him speaking blasphemous words against Moses and God." They stirred up the people, the elders, and the scribes, accosted him, seized him, and brought him before the Sanhedrin. They presented false witnesses who testified, "This man never stops saying things against this holy place and the law. For we have heard him claim that this Jesus the Nazorean will destroy this place and change the customs that Moses handed down to us." All those who sat in the Sanhedrin looked intently at him and saw that his face was like the face of an angel.

Reflection

Stephen is the first martyr recognized by the Church. Although we do not want to suffer the same fate as Stephen, we know that authentically living our faith will come at a cost. Early in his pontificate, Pope Francis implored us to live a "daily martyrdom." Pope Francis explained that being a martyr is not equal to being a hero, one who acts on his or her own. Rather, a martyr for Christ is a witness, and that witness is like a flower "blooming in a desert" and fruit that is ripe. How will our lives bloom with the love of Christ? How will our lives yield delicious fruit?

Prayers

others may be added

With wonder and awe at the great things God does for us, we offer to him our prayers:

℟. Risen Lord, hear our prayer.

- For all ministers of the Church, we pray: ℟.
- For world leaders, that they will lead their people with mercy, we pray: ℟.
- For the courage to always give witness to our faith, we pray: ℟.
- For those who are dying, and those who will die today, we pray: ℟.

The Lord is risen and present among us and so we pray as he taught us.

Our Father . . .

Lord Jesus,
you call us to follow you no matter
the cost.
Give us the courage to follow you
with joy.
May our lives reveal your fragrant love
and extend the gift of your presence
to all peoples.
Who live and reign for ever and ever.
Amen.

✠ The Good Shepherd has risen, . . . /
and willingly died for his flock.

✤ Sing praise to our God.

Psalm 96 *page 380*

Reading *John 6:30–35*

The crowd said to Jesus: "What sign can you do, that we may see and believe in you? What can you do? Our ancestors ate manna in the desert, as it is written: / *He gave them bread from heaven to eat.*"

So Jesus said to them, "Amen, amen, I say to you, it was not Moses who gave the bread from heaven; my Father gives you the true bread from heaven. For the bread of God is that which comes down from heaven and gives life to the world."

So they said to Jesus, "Sir, give us this bread always." Jesus said to them, "I am the bread of life; whoever comes to me will never hunger, and whoever believes in me will never thirst."

Reflection

Jesus is the ultimate sign and symbol for which we have been waiting. We have been given this sign once and for all. It is offered to us again and again through the sacraments and through our relationship with Jesus. We know him by the calming of our minds and the fulfillment of our hearts. We hear of him through the Word. We know him in baptism and in Eucharist. When our hunger is satisfied and our thirst is quenched, it will be because we have fully embraced God in the gift of Jesus Christ.

Prayers *others may be added*

Conscious of our needs, we come to the Lord in prayer:

℟. **Bread of Life, hear our prayer.**

- For the Church, that she will foster a greater understanding of the gift of the Eucharist, we pray: ℟.
- For world leaders, that they will ensure that no citizen is hungry and that justice and peace will reign, we pray: ℟.
- For those who struggle with doubt, we pray: ℟.
- For those in our communities who are poor, we pray: ℟.
- For those who are dying, and those who will die today, we pray: ℟.

The Lord is risen and present among us and so we pray as he taught us.

Our Father . . .

Lord Jesus,
you give yourself to us in the gift
of the Eucharist.
Help us to receive your love with faith
and devotion,
and to share it with others,
bringing them to your holy table.
Who live and reign for ever and ever.
Amen.

✤ Sing praise to our God.

Easter Weekday

Wednesday, May 7, 2025

✚ Let my mouth be filled
with your praise.

Psalm 138

page 388

Reading

Acts 8:1b–8

There broke out a severe persecution of the Church in Jerusalem, and all were scattered throughout the countryside of Judea and Samaria, except the Apostles. Devout men buried Stephen and made a loud lament over him. Saul, meanwhile, was trying to destroy the Church; entering house after house and dragging out men and women, he handed them over for imprisonment.

Now those who had been scattered went about preaching the word. Thus Philip went down to the city of Samaria and proclaimed the Christ to them. With one accord, the crowds paid attention to what was said by Philip when they heard it and saw the signs he was doing. For unclean spirits, crying out in a loud voice, came out of many possessed people, and many paralyzed and crippled people were cured. There was great joy in that city.

Reflection

Saul and Philip offer a stark contrast to one another. Saul was trying to destroy the early Church. Philip was doing what he could to help the Church spread through his acts of preaching and healing. Our lives of faith are not quite as dramatic as those of the disicples. Yet we can choose to live in a way that will attract others to consider a life of faith in the Church. Or we could do just the opposite and push them away from a life in Christ. Do we live authentic and faith-filled lives? Do we live in such a way that makes the idea of Christianity atttractive to others?

Prayers

others may be added

In truth and great joy, we offer
to the Lord our prayers:

℟. Lord of all, hear our prayer.

- For the Church, striving to live the Gospel daily, we pray: ℟.
- For respectful dialogue among leaders of all nations, we pray: ℟.
- For those with mental health struggles, we pray: ℟.
- For those who give witness to Christ, we pray: ℟.
- For those who are dying, and those who will die today, we pray: ℟.

The Lord is risen and present among us and so we pray as he taught us.

Our Father . . .

Lord Jesus,
give us the grace to live like Philip
and help the Church grow through
our acts of love.
May the very witness of our lives
inspire others to love you and believe
in you.
Who live and reign for ever and ever.
Amen.

✚ Let my mouth be filled
with your praise.

✚ The Lord is my strength
and my might.

Psalm 47

page 372

Reading

Acts 8:27b, 28–31, 35–36, 38

Now there was an Ethiopian eunuch, a court official of the Candace, that is, the queen of the Ethiopians, in charge of her entire treasury, who had come to Jerusalem to worship, and was returning home. Seated in his chariot, he was reading the prophet Isaiah. The Spirit said to Philip, "Go and join up with that chariot." Philip ran up and heard him reading Isaiah the prophet and said, "Do you understand what you are reading?" He replied, "How can I, unless someone instructs me?" So he invited Philip to get in and sit with him. Then Philip opened his mouth and, beginning with this Scripture passage, he proclaimed Jesus to him. As they traveled along the road they came to some water, and the eunuch said, "Look, there is water. What is to prevent my being baptized?" Then he ordered the chariot to stop, and Philip and the eunuch both went down into the water, and he baptized him.

Reflection

The Ethiopian eunuch would have faced lifelong exclusion for his deformity. No wonder he asks to be baptized once he understands what Jesus offers him—life, inclusion, and joy. We all crave these things, and we can accept them from Jesus as well as offer them to others.

Prayers

others may be added

In faith, we come before the Lord
with our needs:

℟. Risen Lord, hear our prayer.

✦ For all Christians to be open to sharing the faith, we pray: ℟.

✦ For peace in our world, we pray: ℟.

✦ For missionaries who spread the faith with respect and love, we pray: ℟.

✦ For parents who strive to share their faith with their children, we pray: ℟.

✦ For those who are dying, and those who will die today, we pray: ℟.

The Lord is risen and present among us and so we pray as he taught us.

Our Father . . .

God of compassion,
you know the human heart's longing
to be in relationship,
and sent your Son to unite all people
in your love.
May we continue to proclaim this joyful
news to all,
especially those at the margins
of our society.
Through Christ our Lord.
Amen.

✚ The Lord is my strength
and my might.

Friday, May 9, 2025

✣ Worthy is the Lamb who was slain.

Psalm 63

page 375

Reading

Acts 9:10–20

There was a disciple in Damascus named Ananias, and the Lord said to him in a vision, "Ananias." He answered, "Here I am, Lord." The Lord said to him, "Get up and go to the street called Straight and ask at the house of Judas for a man from Tarsus named Saul. He is there praying, and in a vision he has seen a man named Ananias come in and lay his hands on him,that he may regain his sight." But Ananias replied,"Lord, I have heard from many sources about this man, what evil things he has done to your holy ones in Jerusalem. And here he has authority from the chief priests to imprison all who call upon your name." But the Lord said to him, "Go, for this man is a chosen instrument of mine to carry my name before Gentiles, kings, and children of Israel, and I will show him what he will have to suffer for my name." So Ananias went and entered the house; laying his hands on him, he said, "Saul, my brother, the Lord has sent me, Jesus who appeared to you on the way by which you came, that you may regain your sight and be filled with the Holy Spirit." Immediately things like scales fell from his eyes and he regained his sight. He got up and was baptized, and when he had eaten, he recovered his strength.

Reflection

Paul literally needed to be knocked down from his high horse in order to hear God's voice and realize he was wrong for persecuting Christians. He also needed others, like Ananias, to help him see clearly that God wanted him to spread the Good News to the Gentiles. In your own life, who has helped you to hear God's voice? Who are the faithful people who helped remove the scales from your own eyes so that you could grow in faith and serve the Lord? How are you called to help others come to Christ just like Ananias helped Paul?

Prayers

others may be added

We are here before you, Lord. Hear the prayers we place in your hands:

℟. **Risen Savior, hear our prayer.**

- For the Church, that she will be open to conversion, we pray: ℟.
- For leaders of nations, that they may promote peace and justice for all, we pray: ℟.
- For those who help us when we are struggling to live our faith, we pray: ℟.
- For those who are dying, and those who will die today, we pray: ℟.

The Lord is risen and present among us and so we pray as he taught us.

Our Father . . .

God our Father,
you called Paul to a new life
of conversion in Christ.
May those of us who are baptized live
our faith with zeal and authenticity.
Through Christ our Lord.
Amen.

✣ Worthy is the Lamb who was slain.

✤ Keep safe those reborn in Christ.

Psalm 30

page 369

Reading

John 6:60–69

Many of the disciples of Jesus who were listening said, "This saying is hard; who can accept it?" Since Jesus knew that his disciples were murmuring about this, he said to them, "Does this shock you? What if you were to see the Son of Man ascending to where he was before? It is the Spirit that gives life, while the flesh is of no avail. The words I have spoken to you are Spirit and life. But there are some of you who do not believe." Jesus knew from the beginning the ones who would not believe and the one who would betray him. And he said, "For this reason I have told you that no one can come to me unless it is granted him by my Father."

As a result of this, many of his disciples returned to their former way of life and no longer walked with him. Jesus then said to the Twelve, "Do you also want to leave?" Simon Peter answered him, "Master, to whom shall we go? You have the words of eternal life. We have come to believe and are convinced that you are the Holy One of God."

Reflection

Those who stayed with Jesus were "convinced that he was the Holy One of God." How convinced are we about Jesus' identity? What signs do we need to be more convinced? In this season of resurrection, are we ready to share this truth with others—particularly those who struggle to believe? Do we live in a way that invites others to want to know Jesus? Or do we lead others away from him?

Prayers

others may be added

Convinced that our Lord Jesus is the Holy One of God, we offer our prayers:

℟. **Risen Savior, hear our prayer.**

- For the Church, that we will know with faith that Jesus is the Holy One of God, we pray: ℟.
- For harmony among all people of faith, and of no faith, we pray: ℟.
- For greater understanding of the gift of the Eucharist, we pray: ℟.
- For all those receiving Eucharist for the first time this year, and for those who guide them, we pray: ℟.
- For those who are dying, and those who will die today, we pray: ℟.

The Lord is risen and present among us and so we pray as he taught us.

Our Father . . .

Lord Jesus,
you reveal yourself as the Bread of Life.
Help us to receive this gift with faith
and understanding,
and help those who struggle with
this truth.
Who live and reign for ever and ever.
Amen.

✤ Keep safe those reborn in Christ.

Sunday, May 11, 2025

✤ The merciful love of the Lord fills the earth.

Psalm 118 *page 386*

Reading *John 10:27–30*

Jesus said: "My sheep hear my voice; I know them, and they follow me. I give them eternal life, and they shall never perish. No one can take them out of my hand. My Father, who has given them to me, is greater than all, and no one can take them out of the Father's hand. The Father and I are one."

Reflection

Being called a sheep is not a complement for it is often defined as a mindless follower. And yet Jesus holds up sheep as an example for how his disicples should be. In a Christian context, a sheep knows and follows the shepherd. Jesus is our Good Shepherd, he is the way, the truth, and the life. By following him we receive the greatest gift of all—the promise of eternal life. The Good Shepherd is so intimately connected to the Father that nothing can harm his flock. They shall never perish. What holds us back from accepting this gift?

Prayers *others may be added*

The Good Shepherd hears our voice. He knows our needs, even before we speak them, and so we pray:

℟. **Risen Lord, hear our prayer.**

- For all shepherds in the Church, that they always lead their flock to Christ, we pray: ℟.
- For all nations, that they will follow the way of peace and justice, we pray: ℟.
- For travelers, that they may be guided in the path of safety, we pray: ℟.
- For our communities, that they will be guided in the ways of faith, hope, and love, we pray: ℟.
- For those who are dying, and those who will die today, we pray: ℟.

The Lord is risen and present among us and so we pray as he taught us.

Our Father . . .

Good Shepherd,
you call us to follow you.
Help us to know your true voice
in our lives
and give us courage to follow you
each day.
Who live and reign for ever and ever.
Amen.

✤ The merciful love of the Lord fills the earth.

✤ Christ, having risen from the dead, dies now no more.

Psalm 111

page 384

Reading

John 10:7–10

Jesus said again, "Amen, amen, I say to you, I am the gate for the sheep. All who came before me are thieves and robbers, but the sheep did not listen to them. I am the gate. Whoever enters through me will be saved, and will come in and go out and find pasture. A thief comes only to steal and slaughter and destroy; I came so that they might have life and have it more abundantly."

Reflection

Pope Francis

[Jesus] is truly the Good Shepherd. And the most beautiful image of the Good Shepherd? The Word that becomes flesh to share in our life. Jesus is the Good Shepherd who comes to seek us right where we are: in our problems, in our suffering. . . . He comes there.

Prayers

others may be added

The Lord calls us by name,
and so we pray:

℟. **Risen Lord, show us the way.**

- When the Church tries to be faithful to the Word and also interact with the realities of modern life, we pray: ℟.
- When members of different religions and faiths come together to understand one another and the meaning of life, we pray: ℟.
- When we are overwhelmed by the variety of values held up by science, history, cultures, and religion, we pray: ℟.
- When we read scripture and listen for your wisdom, we pray: ℟.

The Lord is risen and present among us and so we pray as he taught us.

Our Father . . .

Lord Jesus,
you call us to follow you.
Help us to hear your voice, especially
when it is most difficult,
and help others to listen for your voice.
Who live and reign for ever and ever.
Amen.

✤ Christ, having risen from the dead, dies now no more.

Easter Weekday

Tuesday, May 13, 2025

✚ Let us rejoice and be glad
and give glory to God.

Psalm 95

page 380

Reading

Acts 11:19–24

Those who had been scattered by the persecution that arose because of Stephen went as far as Phoenicia, Cyprus, and Antioch, preaching the word to no one but Jews. There were some Cypriots and Cyrenians among them, however, who came to Antioch and began to speak to the Greeks as well, proclaiming the Lord Jesus. The hand of the Lord was with them and a great number who believed turned to the Lord. The news about them reached the ears of the Church in Jerusalem, and they sent Barnabas to go to Antioch. When he arrived and saw the grace of God, he rejoiced and encouraged them all to remain faithful to the Lord in firmness of heart, for he was a good man, filled with the Holy Spirit and faith. And a large number of people was added to the Lord.

Reflection

When was the last time you practiced your faith outside your comfort zone? The first followers of Jesus who shared the Good News with the Greeks and the Jews were delighted at the responsiveness of the people. With which people, and in what places, do you assume your faith is not welcome or needed?

Prayers

others may be added

We cannot contain our joy for the Lord! It propels us to be concerned for those in need, and so we pray:

℟. Risen Lord, hear our prayer.

- For the Church, that we will live as authentic Christians, we pray: ℟.
- For fruitful and honest dialogue among leaders of nations, and among our own civic leaders, we pray: ℟.
- For the courage to share our faith and the love of Jesus throughout our life, we pray: ℟.
- For all students of faith, who read Scripture, engage in worship, and participate in the community of faith, we pray: ℟.
- For those who are dying, and those who will die today, we pray: ℟.

The Lord is risen and present among us and so we pray as he taught us.

Our Father . . .

God our Father,
you love us as a parent and friend.
Help us to know this love more fully.
May we share that love with others.
Through Christ our Lord.
Amen.

✚ Let us rejoice and be glad
and give glory to God.

✤ The Lord chose us "and appointed [us] to go and bear fruit."

Psalm 96

page 380

Reading

Acts 1:20–26

"Therefore, it is necessary that one of the men who accompanied us the whole time the Lord Jesus came and went among us, beginning from the baptism of John until the day on which he was taken up from us, become with us a witness to his resurrection." So they proposed two, Joseph called Barsabbas, who was also known as Justus, and Matthias. Then they prayed, "You, Lord, who know the hearts of all, show which one of these two you have chosen to take the place in this apostolic ministry from which Judas turned away to go to his own place." Then they gave lots to them, and the lot fell upon Matthias, and he was counted with the Eleven Apostles

Reflection

What would it be like to replace Judas? How would it feel to replace the one who betrayed Jesus? Did Matthias hope one of the others would be chosen instead? How often do we wish that God would call someone else to forgive; someone else to proclaim the Gospel; someone else to feed the hungry, advocate for the immigrant, and so on? "It was not you who chose me, but I who chose you," says Jesus. What you are being called to today? How is Jesus calling you to follow him more closely?

Prayers

others may be added

The Lord chooses us; he calls us to serve, and so we pray:

℟. **Savior of all, hear our prayer.**

- For all Church leaders, that they will be faithful to God's Word, we pray: ℟.
- For all nations, that they may follow the way of peace and justice, we pray: ℟.
- For all peoples, that they will be imbued with a sense of peace and contentment, we pray: ℟.
- For those who are dying, and those who will die today, we pray: ℟.

The Lord is risen and present among us and so we pray as he taught us.

Our Father . . .

Lord Jesus,
you call each of us by name.
Give us the wisdom to hear your voice
and share our gifts with those in need.
Who live and reign for ever and ever.
Amen.

✤ The Lord chose us "and appointed [us] to go and bear fruit."

Thursday, May 15, 2025

✤ May you preserve the gifts /
of your enduring grace and blessing.

Psalm 121

page 386

Reading

Acts 13:13–18

From Paphos, Paul and his companions set sail and arrived at Perga in Pamphylia. But John left them and returned to Jerusalem. They continued on from Perga and reached Antioch in Pisidia. On the sabbath they entered into the synagogue and took their seats. After the reading of the law and the prophets, the synagogue officials sent word to them, "My brothers, if one of you has a word of exhortation for the people, please speak."

So Paul got up, motioned with his hand, and said, "Fellow children of Israel and you others who are God-fearing, listen. The God of this people Israel chose our ancestors and exalted the people during their sojourn in the land of Egypt. With uplifted arm he led them out, and for about forty years he put up with them in the desert."

Reflection

Wow! "For about forty years *he put up with them* in the desert." Isn't it great that God "puts up with" us, despite our shortcomings, failings, and sins? God put up with the Israelites and their many failings to live up to the Covenant. But he does more than that! Through Jesus, he loves us to the end and will raise us up on the last day. So too are we called to "put up with" those in our lives. Who are we called to "put up with" today, just as God does with us?

Prayers

others may be added

Speaking on behalf of the world,
we offer to the Lord our prayers:

℟. Risen Lord, hear our prayer.

- For those who minister in the Church, that they may always be filled with love for their flock, we pray: ℟.
- For the leaders of nations, that they bow down to the poorest among them, hearing their pleas, and working for the common good, we pray: ℟.
- For parents and teachers, that they may have patience with children, we pray: ℟.
- For each of us, that we honor ourselves in love and honor those around us, we pray: ℟.
- For those who are dying, and those who will die today, we pray: ℟.

The Lord is risen and present among us and so we pray as he taught us.

Our Father . . .

God our Father,
you "put up with" us despite
our failings.
Help us to love even those who cause us
difficulty or annoyance.
Grant us patience and a kind heart.
Through Christ our Lord.
Amen.

✤ May you preserve the gifts /
of your enduring grace and blessing.

✠ You have redeemed us, Lord,
by your Blood.

Psalm 148
page 390

Reading
John 14:1–6

Jesus said to his disciples, "Do not let your hearts be troubled. You have faith in God; have faith also in me. In my Father's house there are many dwelling places. If there were not, would I have told you that I am going to prepare a place for you? And if I go and prepare a place for you, I will come back again and take you to myself, so that where I am you also may be. Where I am going you know the way." Thomas said to him, "Master, we do not know where you are going; how can we know the way?" Jesus said to him, "I am the way and the truth and the life. No one comes to the Father except through me."

Reflection

Does death frighten you? There is great comfort in the image of the Father's house with its many rooms prepared for each of us. Jesus promises us a dwelling place with him. We know that those we have loved who have died have also been offered this eternal path. When we miss those who have passed on, we can allow ourselves to imagine the reunions that will take place after death in the heavenly kingdom. Let us not be afraid; our compassionate God will provide for our aching hearts and our desire to be with our beloved.

Prayers
others may be added

We are loved by the Lord and so
we have the courage to pray:

℟. **Loving Lord, hear our prayer.**

- That the compassion of Jesus permeate the Church's ministry to the dying and to those who mourn, we pray: ℟.
- That countries who have experienced violence and war find peace, we pray: ℟.
- That all who fear death turn to God for comfort, we pray: ℟.
- That all who have died find eternal peace, we pray: ℟.

The Lord is risen and present among us and so we pray as he taught us.

Our Father . . .

O God, Alpha and Omega,
you created us in love
and desire for us to return to you.
May our uncertainty and fears
about death
lead us on a journey toward
knowing you
and finding solace in your
compassionate community on earth.
Through Christ our Lord.
Amen.

✠ You have redeemed us, Lord,
by your Blood.

Saturday, May 17, 2025

✣ O chosen people, proclaim the mighty works of him.

Psalm 46 *page 372*

Reading *John 14:7–14*

Jesus said to his disciples: "If you know me, then you will also know my Father. From now on you do know him and have seen him." Philip said to Jesus, "Master, show us the Father, and that will be enough for us." Jesus said to him, "Have I been with you for so long a time and you still do not know me, Philip? Whoever has seen me has seen the Father. How can you say, 'Show us the Father'? Do you not believe that I am in the Father and the Father is in me? The words that I speak to you I do not speak on my own. The Father who dwells in me is doing his works. Believe me that I am in the Father and the Father is in me, or else, believe because of the works themselves. Amen, amen, I say to you, whoever believes in me will do the works that I do, and will do greater ones than these, because I am going to the Father. And whatever you ask in my name, I will do, so that the Father may be glorified in the Son. If you ask anything of me in my name, I will do it."

Reflection

Today's reading is comforting. Even the apostle Philip failed to understand Jesus' identity. We may not feel we really know Jesus, or we may struggle with questions of faith. Our tradition has a rich history of developing theology in response to questions. And yet Jesus asks us to believe. We are asked to follow him daily, and to do his will by proclaiming the kingdom and serving those most in need.

Prayers *others may be added*

Knowing that the Lord hears our prayers, we lift up to him our needs:

℟. Merciful Lord, hear our prayer.

- For the people of God who walk by faith, despite sometimes feeling lost or unsure, we pray: ℟.
- For the people of the world who do not have faith, that they may see how God is present to them, we pray: ℟.
- For those who are searching for answers, that they find them in God's gentle voice, we pray: ℟.
- For humility among us, we pray: ℟.
- For those who are dying, and those who will die today, we pray: ℟.

The Lord is risen and present among us and so we pray as he taught us.

Our Father . . .

Loving Lord,
you know us well,
just as you knew your apostles.
You are not shocked by our failings,
and teach us again and again
to follow you.
May we always find refuge in you.
Who live and reign for ever and ever.
Amen.

✣ O chosen people, proclaim the mighty works of him.

✤ Sing a new song to the Lord, /
for he has worked wonders.

Psalm 118

page 386

Reading

John 13:31–33A, 34–35

When Judas had left them, Jesus said, "Now is the Son of Man glorified, and God is glorified in him. If God is glorified in him, God will also glorify him in himself, and God will glorify him at once. My children, I will be with you only a little while longer. I give you a new commandment: love one another. As I have loved you, so you also should love one another. This is how all will know that you are my disciples, if you have love for one another."

Reflection

John's account of the Gospel is typically more abstract than the other Gospel accounts. Sometimes, there can be a temptation to ignore the difficult parts of this Gospel for the "easier" stories of Jesus in Matthew, Mark, and Luke. And still, John can be very practical. You may summarize John's account with one word that is not always popular in today's culture: Obedience. "As I have loved you, so you also should love one another," says Jesus. What is the commandment? We get it in today's Gospel. "Love one another." We will be known as followers of Jesus by how we love each other. How are we loving others today?

Prayers

others may be added

Glorifying the Lord by our lives,
we turn to him now in prayer:

℟. **Model of love, hear our prayer.**

- For the Church, that all will know us by our love for one another, we pray: ℟.
- For nations to show love and concern for their poorest citizens, we pray: ℟.
- For the grace to love those who are most difficult to love, we pray: ℟.
- For health care workers and all who strive to bring healing, we pray: ℟.
- For those who are dying, and those who will die today, we pray: ℟.

The Lord is risen and present among us and so we pray as he taught us.

Our Father . . .

Lord Jesus,
your obedience to the Father
was the ultimate gift of
self-sacrificing love.
Help us to offer ourselves
by loving our brothers and sisters
in this world.
Who live and reign for ever and ever.
Amen.

✤ Sing a new song to the Lord, /
for he has worked wonders.

Monday, May 19, 2025

✤ The Good Shepherd has risen, /
and willingly died for his flock.

Psalm 98

page 381

Reading

Acts 14:14–18

The Apostles Barnabas and Paul tore their garments when they heard this and rushed out into the crowd, shouting, "Men, why are you doing this? We are of the same nature as you, human beings. We proclaim to you good news that you should turn from these idols to the living God, / *who made heaven and earth and sea and all that is in them.* / In past generations he allowed all Gentiles to go their own ways; yet, in bestowing his goodness, he did not leave himself without witness, for he gave you rains from heaven and fruitful seasons, and filled you with nourishment and gladness for your hearts." Even with these words, they scarcely restrained the crowds from offering sacrifice to them.

Reflection

It can be tempting to be enamored of social media; the chance to get people to "like" or "love" you through your posts, thoughts, and ideas. It is all-consuming and self-serving to seek that type of admiration. Paul and Barnabas would probably have gotten many likes today! They could hardly restrain "the crowds from offering sacrifice to them." Yet, how remarkable it is that even in the face of this admiration, they stood firm and humble by not allowing the crowds to treat them as a god. Consider ways you can be more humble, and allow God to shine through you in a transparent way.

Prayers

others may be added

The Lord lives and dwells among us, inspiring us to care for one another, and so we pray:

℟. God of all people, hear our prayer.

- For the Church, that we may know and worship the one true God, we pray: ℟.
- For world leaders, that they may strive to serve and not to be served, we pray: ℟.
- For humble and contrite hearts, we pray: ℟.
- For peace in our families, we pray: ℟.
- For those who are dying, and those who will die today, we pray: ℟.

The Lord is risen and present among us and so we pray as he taught us.

Our Father . . .

God our Father,
you give us signs every day that show us you are the one true God.
Give us eyes to see and ears to hear you in our lives.
May we always serve you in humble and selfless ways.
Through Christ our Lord.
Amen.

✤ The Good Shepherd has risen, /
and willingly died for his flock.

✤ Now salvation and strength
have come.

Psalm 96 *page 380*

Reading *Acts 14:21–22*

After [Barnabas and Paul] had proclaimed the good news to that city and made a considerable number of disciples, they returned to Lystra and to Iconium and to Antioch. They strengthened the spirits of the disciples and exhorted them to persevere in the faith, saying, "It is necessary for us to undergo many hardships to enter the Kingdom of God."

Reflection

There is a shortage of good news in our lives. No wonder, then, that we often enjoy so intensely the visit of a missionary to our parish, or the opportunity to bless a young person heading off on a service trip. In a big church, we can lose sight of the many amazing stories of healing and conversion happening among us. We must bring stories of evangelization, miracles, and God's faithfulness before the community. In them, we will be renewed in faith and the desire to serve our God.

Prayers *others may be added*

Our world is full of hardships but it is through the Lord that peace will prevail. Let us now turn to him with our needs.

℟. **Risen Lord, hear our prayer.**

- That the Church find new and creative ways to spread the Good News, we pray: ℟.
- That opportunities are created for all peoples to live full and complete lives, we pray: ℟.
- That we may look for hidden signs of God's good news in our day to day encounters, we pray: ℟.
- That those who believe will find the time and means to share their stories of faith with others, we pray:

The Lord is risen and present among us and so we pray as he taught us.

Our Father . . .

God of power and might,
you are at work in numerous ways.
Open our eyes and ears to your
presence in our midst.
Give us the comfort we need
to share and celebrate stories
of your hand
at work in our lives and in the lives
of others.
Through Christ our Lord.
Amen.

✤ Now salvation and strength
have come.

Wednesday, May 21, 2025

✤ Let my mouth be filled with your praise, that I may sing aloud.

Psalm 138

page 388

Reading

John 15:1–8

Jesus said to his disciples: "I am the true vine, and my Father is the vine grower. He takes away every branch in me that does not bear fruit, and everyone that does he prunes so that it bears more fruit. You are already pruned because of the word that I spoke to you. Remain in me, as I remain in you. Just as a branch cannot bear fruit on its own unless it remains on the vine, so neither can you unless you remain in me. I am the vine, you are the branches. Whoever remains in me and I in him will bear much fruit, because without me you can do nothing. Anyone who does not remain in me will be thrown out like a branch and wither; people will gather them and throw them into a fire and they will be burned. If you remain in me and my words remain in you, ask for whatever you want and it will be done for you. By this is my Father glorified, that you bear much fruit and become my disciples."

Reflection

Like a good vine grower, God will clear away whatever does not bear fruit. The disciples were already "pruned" because they knew and followed Jesus and had the Word proclaimed to them. What in our own lives needs to be pruned away? What are we attached to that isn't life-giving? Relationships? Wealth? Success? Who has helped us prune away what has not been helpful, and who can be helpful to us today? And how can we stay close to Jesus, the vine, so we can be fruitful in God's Kingdom?

Prayers

others may be added

Jesus is the true vine, and we are his branches, so we pray:

℟. **Risen Lord, hear our prayer.**

- For the Church, that we stay true to Jesus and bear fruit, we pray: ℟.
- For world leaders, that they find ways to advance the common good, we pray: ℟.
- For catechists and religion teachers who teach us to stay close to Jesus, we pray: ℟.
- For those suffering from addictions, and those who care for them, we pray: ℟.
- For those who are dying, and those who will die today, we pray: ℟.

The Lord is risen and present among us and so we pray as he taught us.

Our Father . . .

Jesus the True Vine,
you promised that we will grow
much fruit
if we stay connected to you.
Help us to let go of whatever we need
to prune away in our lives,
and help us stay close to you and your
Word.
Who live and reign for ever and ever.
Amen.

✤ Let my mouth be filled with your praise, that I may sing aloud.

✣ Let my mouth be filled with your praise, that I may sing aloud.

Psalm 47

page 372

Reading

John 15:9–11

Jesus said to his disciples: "As the Father loves me, so I also love you. Remain in my love. If you keep my commandments, you will remain in my love, just as I have kept my Father's commandments and remain in his love.

"I have told you this so that my joy might be in you and your joy might be complete."

Reflection

Ok. Let's be honest. Who really likes to follow orders? Especially an order as strong as a *commandment*? With a commandment, there doesn't seem to be much room for the option to disagree or offer an alternative. Today Jesus gives us the most important commandment—to love. That's how we are to live as Christians, by loving each other and by loving God. But Jesus doesn't just give us a mandate with nothing in return. If we truly love—if we truly live as Christians—then we will find complete joy in eternal salvation. How can we say no to that? Why would we even want to live in a different way?

Prayers

others may be added

Remaining in Christ's love, we offer to him our prayers:

℟. **Risen Lord, hear our prayer.**

- That Christians may love others in a unique way, inspiring others to love, we pray: ℟
- That love will guide leaders of nations to work for charity and justice, we pray: ℟
- That our friendships may be long-lasting and life-giving, we pray: ℟
- That we may be inspired by the loving acts of friends, family, and strangers, we pray: ℟

The Lord is risen and present among us and so we pray as he taught us.

Our Father . . .

Lord our Savior,
you call us to obey you
so that our joy may be complete.
Help us let go of our egos and
follow you.
Help us always know the joy that comes
from following you.
Who live and reigns for ever and ever.
Amen.

✣ Let my mouth be filled with your praise, that I may sing aloud.

Easter Weekday
Friday, May 23, 2025

✤ Worthy is the Lamb who was slain.

Psalm 63 *page 375*

Reading *John 15:12–17*

Jesus said to his disciples: "This is my commandment: love one another as I love you. No one has greater love than this, to lay down one's life for one's friends. You are my friends if you do what I command you. I no longer call you slaves, because a slave does not know what his master is doing. I have called you friends, because I have told you everything I have heard from my Father. It was not you who chose me, but I who chose you and appointed you to go and bear fruit that will remain, so that whatever you ask the Father in my name he may give you. This I command you: love one another."

Reflection

Think of a friend you love dearly. Think of the ways you share your life, resources, and time with this friend. Think of sacrifices you have gladly made to help your friend. Jesus asks us to love like this every day. We are to open ourselves in great love to all our brothers and sisters. Are you willing to love?

Prayers *others may be added*

Loving as God loves, we offer to him our prayers.

℟. **Loving and merciful Lord,
hear our prayer.**

- For the Church, that we will always strive to love one another, we pray: ℟.
- For world leaders, that they will treat their citizens with respect, we pray: ℟.
- For the grace to love our enemies, we pray: ℟.
- For those suffering from a lack of love in our world, we pray: ℟.
- For those who are dying, and those who will die today, we pray: ℟.

The Lord is risen and present among us and so we pray as he taught us.

Our Father . . .

Lord our Savior,
you call us to love one another so that
we will be close to you.
Help us love those in our lives who are
most difficult to love
and bring others to know your love
for them.
Who lives and reigns for ever and ever.
Amen.

✤ Worthy is the Lamb who was slain.

✤ [We] have been buried with Christ in Baptism, through which [we] also rose again.

Psalm 30

page 369

Reading

John 15:18–21

Jesus said to his disciples: "If the world hates you, realize that it hated me first. If you belonged to the world, the world would love its own; but because you do not belong to the world, and I have chosen you out of the world, the world hates you. Remember the word I spoke to you, 'No slave is greater than his master.' If they persecuted me, they will also persecute you. If they kept my word, they will also keep yours. And they will do all these things to you on account of my name, because they do not know the one who sent me."

Reflection

Imagine a parent saying this to a child: "You do not belong to the world, and I have chosen you out of the world." The underlying message is that the child is precious, beloved, and created by God for a purpose. Our God speaks to us with deep love in these very words. God is our protective, nurturing, and attentive parent who reminds us of our eternal destiny. Rest in the embrace of God.

Prayers

others may be added

We belong to God; but we care for our world, and so we turn to him in prayer:

℟. Loving Lord, hear our prayer.

✦ That Christian parents instill a sense of dignity and purpose in their children, we pray: ℟.

✦ That leaders of nations may be guided by their commitment to charity and justice, we pray: ℟.

✦ That children without parents come to know themselves as children of God, we pray: ℟.

✦ That all members of our community will know that they are uniquely and wonderfully made in the image of God, we pray: ℟.

The Lord is risen and present among us and so we pray as he taught us.

Our Father . . .

Creator God,
even before we were made,
you knew us and you loved us.
You fashioned us with
  unconditional love.
Help us see in ourselves and others
  your beautiful image, uniquely and
  wonderfully made.
Through Christ our Lord.
Amen.

✤ [We] have been buried with Christ in Baptism, through which [we] also rose again.

Sunday, May 25, 2025

✚ Proclaim a joyful sound and let it be heard.

Psalm 118

page 386

Reading

John 14:23–29

Jesus said to his disciples: "Whoever loves me will keep my word, and my Father will love him, and we will come to him and make our dwelling with him. Whoever does not love me does not keep my words; yet the word you hear is not mine but that of the Father who sent me.

"I have told you this while I am with you. The Advocate, the Holy Spirit, whom the Father will send in my name, will teach you everything and remind you of all that I told you. Peace I leave with you; my peace I give to you. Not as the world gives do I give it to you. Do not let your hearts be troubled or afraid. You heard me tell you, 'I am going away and I will come back to you.' If you loved me, you would rejoice that I am going to the Father; for the Father is greater than I. And now I have told you this before it happens, so that when it happens you may believe."

Reflection

How difficult it must have been for the disciples to think of Jesus leaving them again. First, the disicples had to deal wtih the pain and confusion of losing Jesus in death. Then they rejoiced at his resurrection. Now Jesus is leaving again? What were they to think? How were they supposed to feel? Their emotions are probably all over the place. But Jesus, in his great mercy, leaves the disciples with peace. The Holy Spirit, the great Advocate, will come upon them—and us—so that they can continue Jesus' mission on earth. All we have to do is trust and receive. Are we willing to do that?

Prayers

others may be added

Out of love for the Lord we keep his word and so we offer to him our prayers for the needs of others:

℟. **Lord of peace, hear our prayer.**

- For the Church, that we will know the peace of Jesus and share it with others, we pray: ℟.
- For world leaders to engage each other in peace, we pray: ℟.
- For peace in our families, especially where there is discord, we pray: ℟.
- For peacemakers around the world, we pray: ℟.
- For those who are dying, and those who will die today, we pray: ℟.

The Lord is risen and present among us and so we pray as he taught us.

Our Father . . .

Lord Jesus,
you give us your gift of peace
and promise us the gift of the Holy Spirit.
Help us to be attentive to the Spirit
where it is present in our lives.
Help us know your peace in the midst
of our life struggles.
You who live and reign for ever
and ever.
Amen.

✚ Proclaim a joyful sound and let it be heard.

✚ The love of God has been poured into our hearts.

Psalm 98

page 381

Reading

John 15:26—16:4a

Jesus said to his disciples: "When the Advocate comes whom I will send you from the Father, the Spirit of truth who proceeds from the Father, he will testify to me. And you also testify, because you have been with me from the beginning.

"I have told you this so that you may not fall away. They will expel you from the synagogues; in fact, the hour is coming when everyone who kills you will think he is offering worship to God. They will do this because they have not known either the Father or me. I have told you this so that when their hour comes you may remember that I told you."

Reflection

Jesus warns the disciples that it's going to get difficult. Would you have been "tough enough" to stick around, knowing violent persecution lay ahead? Can we expect rough times in our lives and in our faith, but commit to staying in the race? Think through the persecutions or obstacles you have faced. What has been the key to making it through them? Has the Holy Spirit been behind, within, and around you? Pray for that grace in the future.

Prayers

others may be added

As believers in the Lord,
we offer to God our prayers.

℟. Be with us, O Lord.

- When the Church is maligned for her teachings on peace, justice, and respect for all life, we pray: ℟.
- When nations face war and division, poverty and inequality, we pray: ℟.
- When others hurt us by their words or actions, we pray: ℟.
- When migrants and refugees seek asylum in peaceful nations, we pray: ℟.
- When we face death and the fears of the unknown, we pray: ℟.

The Lord is risen and present among us and so we pray as he taught us.

Our Father . . .

God our Father,
you promised to send the Spirit
to be our Advocate.
May we be open to the places where
the Spirit is active in our world,
and share the fruits of the Spirit
with others.
Through Christ our Lord.
Amen.

✚ The love of God has been poured into our hearts.

Weekday

Tuesday, May 27, 2025

✚ Let us rejoice and be glad
and give glory to God.

Psalm 96

page 380

Reading

John 16:5–11

Jesus said to his disciples: "Now I am going to the one who sent me, and not one of you asks me, 'Where are you going?' But because I told you this, grief has filled your hearts. But I tell you the truth, it is better for you that I go. For if I do not go, the Advocate will not come to you. But if I go, I will send him to you. And when he comes he will convict the world in regard to sin and righteousness and condemnation: sin, because they do not believe in me; righteousness, because I am going to the Father and you will no longer see me; condemnation, because the ruler of this world has been condemned."

Reflection

Pope Francis

[Jesus] is always with us, looking at us, and "he always lives to make intercession" for us. To make the Father see his wounds, for us. In a word, Jesus intercedes. He is in a better "place," before his Father and ours, to intercede on our behalf.

Prayers

others may be added

The Lord sends us to serve others.
And so we offer to him our prayers:

℟. **Risen Lord, hear our prayer.**

- For the Church, that we may be open the Spirit that is with us, we pray: ℟.
- For world leaders, that they strive to find ways live in peace, we pray: ℟.
- For those who surprise us with their faith, we pray: ℟.
- For migrants and all on the move in our world today, we pray: ℟.
- For those who are dying, and those who will die today, we pray: ℟.

The Lord is risen and present among us and so we pray as he taught us.

Our Father . . .

Lord our Savior,
you said it was better for you to go so
that the Spirit would come to us.
May we be open to the places where
the Spirit is active in our world,
and share the fruits of the Spirit
with others.
You who live and reign for ever
and ever.
Amen.

✚ Let us rejoice and be glad
and give glory to God.

✣ I will praise you, Lord,
among the nations.

Psalm 138

page 388

Reading

John 16:12–15

Jesus said to his disciples: "I have much more to tell you, but you cannot bear it now. But when he comes, the Spirit of truth, he will guide you to all truth. He will not speak on his own, but he will speak what he hears, and will declare to you the things that are coming. He will glorify me, because he will take from what is mine and declare it to you. Everything that the Father has is mine; for this reason I told you that he will take from what is mine and declare it to you."

Reflection

After Jesus ascended to the Father in heaven, the apostles waited and prayed for the promised gift of the Spirit. On the great day of Pentecost, the Holy Spirit came upon the apostles, appearing as tongues of fire, and they went out proclaiming the Gospel, speaking new languages and performing mighty deeds for the glory of God. When we serve, it might not be as dramatic, but it's certainly just as important. How do you serve God? How will you allow the Holy Spirit to work through you?

Prayers

others may be added

The Spirit guides us to radical and compassionate living, and so we pray:

℟. **Lord of justice, hear our prayer.**

- For the Church, that we may be open the Spirit that is with us, we pray: ℟.
- For world leaders, that they strive for harmony among all nations, we pray: ℟.
- For police officers, firefighters, and all who work in public safety, we pray: ℟.
- For those who are dying, and those who will die today, we pray: ℟.

The Lord is risen and present among us and so we pray as he taught us.

Our Father . . .

Risen Savior,
you promised the Spirit will guide us
in all truth.
May we be open to the places where
the Spirit is leading us,
and share the fruits of the Spirit
with others.
You who live and reign for ever
and ever.
Amen.

✣ I will praise you, Lord,
among the nations.

Thursday, May 29, 2025

✤ Praise the Lord, who ascends
above the highest heavens.

Psalm 47

page 372

Reading

Luke 24:46–53

Jesus said to his disciples: "Thus it is written that the Christ would suffer and rise from the dead on the third day and that repentance, for the forgiveness of sins, would be preached in his name to all the nations, beginning from Jerusalem. You are witnesses of these things. And behold I am sending the promise of my Father upon you; but stay in the city until you are clothed with power from on high."

Then he led them out as far as Bethany, raised his hands, and blessed them. As he blessed them he parted from them and was taken up to heaven. They did him homage and then returned to Jerusalem with great joy, and they were continually in the temple praising God.

Reflection

Pope Francis

Before departing from his friends, Jesus, referring to the event of his death and Resurrection, said to them: "You are witnesses of these things" (v. 48). In other words the disciples, the Apostles, were witnesses of the death and Resurrection of Christ, on that day, also of the Ascension of Christ. . . . This is the witness—born not only with words but with everyday life—the witness that every Sunday should flow from our churches so as to enter during the week into homes, offices, schools, meeting and recreational places, hospitals, prisons, homes for the elderly, in places crowded with immigrants, in the peripheries of the city. . . . We must bear this witness every week: Christ is with us: Jesus rose to heaven, he is with us: Christ lives!

Prayers

others may be added

Praying for others praises God, and so, let us now turn to God with our needs:

℟. Ascended Lord, hear our prayer.

- For the Church, for trust in the promise of the Spirit, we pray: ℟.
- For those who live in underprivelaged lands, may their leaders protect and safeguard their human rights, pray: ℟.
- For the grace of joy in living our faith, we pray: ℟.
- For those for whom we have promised to pray, we pray: ℟.
- For those who are dying, and those who will die today, we pray: ℟.

The Lord is risen and present among us and so we pray as he taught us.

Our Father . . .

Lord Jesus,
today you leave a blessing for us
as you ascend to your Faither.
Give us the grace to know the blessings
in our lives,
and to share the joy we have with others
so they may know your blessings.
Who live and reign for ever and ever.
Amen.

✤ Praise the Lord, who ascends
above the highest heavens.

✠ You have . . . made us into
a kingdom, priests for our God.

Psalm 63

page 375

Reading

John 16:20–23

Jesus said to his disciples: "Amen, amen, I say to you, you will weep and mourn, while the world rejoices; you will grieve, but your grief will become joy. When a woman is in labor, she is in anguish because her hour has arrived; but when she has given birth to a child, she no longer remembers the pain because of her joy that a child has been born into the world. So you also are now in anguish. But I will see you again, and your hearts will rejoice, and no one will take your joy away from you. On that day you will not question me about anything. Amen, amen, I say to you, whatever you ask the Father in my name he will give you."

Reflection

Pope Francis

Do not be afraid! Trust in the Father who wants to give you all you truly need. He has already given you his Son, his kingdom, and he always accompanies you with his providence, taking care of you every day. Fear not: this is the certainty that your hearts should be attached to! Fear not.

Prayers

others may be added

Whataver we ask the Father through Jesus, the Father will give us, and so we pray:

℟. **Christ our light, hear our prayer.**

- For the Church, that we trust the promises of God, we pray: ℟.
- For world leaders, that they work to care for God's creation, we pray: ℟.
- For all who work for the common good, we pray: ℟.
- For those struggling with mental illness and for their caregivers, we pray: ℟.
- For those who are dying, and those who will die today, we pray: ℟.

The Lord is risen and present among us and so we pray as he taught us.

Our Father . . .

Ascended Lord,
you promised that whatever we ask
the Father will be given to us.
Give us hope in this promise,
and patience to trust that God always
gives us what we need.
Who live and reign for ever and ever.
Amen.

✠ You have . . . made us into
a kingdom, priests for our God.

✣ All generations will call me blessed, / for he who is mighty has done great things for me.

Psalm 98

page 381

Reading

Luke 1:39–45

Mary set out and traveled to the hill country in haste to a town of Judah, where she entered the house of Zechariah and greeted Elizabeth. When Elizabeth heard Mary's greeting, the infant leaped in her womb, and Elizabeth, filled with the Holy Spirit, cried out in a loud voice and said, "Blessed are you among women, and blessed is the fruit of your womb. And how does this happen to me, that the mother of my Lord should come to me? For at the moment the sound of your greeting reached my ears, the infant in my womb leaped for joy. Blessed are you who believed that what was spoken to you by the Lord would be fulfilled."

Reflection

If you invited Mary into your home today, what would you serve her? How would you make time for her? Think of all the ways you treat a special guest. Notice your reaction to being selected for her visit. Do you feel humbled, honored, or do you rise to the occasion with greater faithfulness and commitment to God than you had the day before? What could you learn from her? Make an effort to develop a relationship with her and see her as family, as someone sent to help you become closer to God. Listen to all she has to teach you in prayer.

Prayers

others may be added

Glorifying the Lord with our prayers we now turn to him with the needs of our world:

℟. **Ascended Lord, hear our prayer.**

- For the Church, that Mary may be our model of faith and service, we pray: ℟.
- For refugees in camps and foreign lands, that they may feel the companionship of Mary, we pray: ℟.
- For travelers and visitors to our homes, that we may welcome them as Elizabeth welcomed Mary, we pray: ℟.
- For open hearts among us, that we may learn from Mary and Elizabeth, we pray: ℟.

The Lord is risen and present among us and so we pray as he taught us.

Our Father . . .

God of providence,
you filled Mary with faith
and blessed her among all women.
We are honored to have her example
and to know that she intercedes
 on our behalf.
May we walk in her footsteps of faith.
Through Christ our Lord.
Amen.

✣ All generations will call me blessed, / for he who is mighty has done great things for me.

✚ Praise the Lord, who ascends above the highest heavens.

Psalm 118 *page 386*

Reading *John 17:20–26*

Lifting up his eyes to heaven, Jesus prayed, saying: "Holy Father, I pray not only for them, but also for those who will believe in me through their word, so that they may all be one, as you, Father, are in me and I in you, that they also may be in us, that the world may believe that you sent me. And I have given them the glory you gave me, so that they may be one, as we are one, I in them and you in me, that they may be brought to perfection as one, that the world may know that you sent me, and that you loved them even as you loved me. Father, they are your gift to me. I wish that where I am they also may be with me, that they may see my glory that you gave me, because you loved me before the foundation of the world. Righteous Father, the world also does not know you, but I know you, and they know that you sent me. I made known to them your name and I will make it known, that the love with which you loved me may be in them and I in them."

Reflection *Pope Francis*

God is love. And we move toward the light to find the love of God. But is God's love within us, even in the dark moments? Is the love of God there, hidden away? Yes, always! The love of God never leaves us. It is always with us. Do we trust in this love?

Prayers *others may be added*

Lifting our eyes to heaven, we offer our prayers for the world:

℟. **Ascended Lord, hear our prayer.**

- For the Church, that we will strive for unity, we pray: ℟.
- For world leaders to be united in justice and peace, we pray: ℟.
- For conversion of heart for those who strive to sow discord, we pray: ℟.
- For those who have no one to pray for them, we pray: ℟.
- For those who are dying, and those who will die today, we pray: ℟.

The Lord is risen and present among us and so we pray as he taught us.

Our Father . . .

Lord Jesus,
you and the Father are one, and you call
us to unity with each other.
Help us strive for unity in our
broken world.
Give us wisdom to know how we can
work to heal
and restore your vision to all the places
in our world that need it.
Who live and reign for ever and ever.
Amen.

✚ Praise the Lord, who ascends above the highest heavens.

Monday, June 2, 2025

✠ [We] will receive the power of the Holy Spirit coming among [us].

Psalm 111 *page 384*

Reading *Acts 19:1–8*

While Apollos was in Corinth, Paul traveled through the interior of the country and down to Ephesus where he found some disciples. He said to them, "Did you receive the Holy Spirit when you became believers?" They answered him, "We have never even heard that there is a Holy Spirit." He said, "How were you baptized?" They replied, "With the baptism of John." Paul then said, "John baptized with a baptism of repentance, telling the people to believe in the one who was to come after him, that is, in Jesus." When they heard this, they were baptized in the name of the Lord Jesus. And when Paul laid his hands on them, the Holy Spirit came upon them, and they spoke in tongues and prophesied. Altogether there were about twelve men.

He entered the synagogue, and for three months debated boldly with persuasive arguments about the Kingdom of God.

Reflection

"We have never even heard that there is a Holy Spirit." How much of our lives do we live like this? How much could our lives, and world, be different if all Christians truly believed in the power of the Spirit, and lived out the Spirit's gifts and fruits? Paul knew the power of the Spirit in his life. The Spirit was with him throughout his journeys, struggles, imprisonment, preaching, healing, and death. Where can we find the Spirit active in our lives today, and what is the Spirit calling us to in these final days of the Easter season?

Prayers *others may be added*

Baptized into Christ, we now have the courage to pray:

℟. **Ascended Lord, hear our prayer:**

- For the Church, all bishops, priests, deacons, and lay leaders, we pray: ℟.
- For those facing intense pressures in the military, governemnt, and law enforcement, we pray: ℟.
- For those struggling with eating disorders and caring for themselves, we pray: ℟.
- For those who are dying, and those who will die today, we pray: ℟.

The Lord is risen and present among us and so we pray as he taught us.

Our Father . . .

Merciful God,
you are with us always.
Help us to find you within our hearts
as we approach the end of this
Easter season,
and live out your calling in our lives
and world today.
Through Christ our Lord.
Amen.

✠ [We] will receive the power of the Holy Spirit coming among [us].

✚ Behold, [God is] alive for ever and ever.

Psalm 95

page 380

Reading

Acts 20:21–22, 25–27

[Paul said:] "I earnestly bore witness for both Jews and Greeks to repentance before God and to faith in our Lord Jesus. But now, compelled by the Spirit, I am going to Jerusalem. . . .

"But now I know that none of you to whom I preached the kingdom during my travels will ever see my face again. And so I solemnly declare to you this day that I am not responsible for the blood of any of you, for I did not shrink from proclaiming to you the entire plan of God."

Reflection

Pope Francis

The witness of a Christian life involves a journey of holiness, based on Baptism, which makes us "sharers in the divine nature. In this way they are really made holy" (*Lumen gentium*, 40). A holiness that is not reserved to the few; that is a gift from God and demands to be listened to and made to bear fruit for ourselves and for others. Chosen and beloved by God, we must bring this love to others. . . . It springs from the heart that is filled with God. Nourished by prayer and above all by love for the Eucharist, [witness] in turn increases holiness in the people who carry it out.

Prayers

others may be added

Bearing witness to the Lord's love, we turn to him with our prayers:

℟. Lord of all joy.

- For those who serve the Church, may they always proclaim the Gospel by the witness of their lives, we pray: ℟.
- For world leaders, that they work to promote the dignity of all people, we pray: ℟.
- For all engaged couples, and those who prepare them for marriage, we pray: ℟.
- For those with chronic illnesses, we pray: ℟.
- For those who are dying, and those who will die today, we pray: ℟.

The Lord is risen and present among us and so we pray as he taught us.

Our Father . . .

God our Father,
like Paul, you called Charles Lwanga to
proclaim your name to all people.
Give us courage to live our faith boldly,
no matter what the cost,
and to find joy in our suffering
for our faith.
Through Christ our Lord.
Amen.

✚ Behold, [God is] alive for ever and ever.

Wednesday, June 4, 2025

✚ All peoples, clap your hands. /
Cry to God with shouts of joy.

Psalm 96

page 380

Reading

John 17:14–19

[Jesus prayed, saying:] "I gave them your word, and the world hated them, because they do not belong to the world any more than I belong to the world. I do not ask that you take them out of the world but that you keep them from the Evil One. They do not belong to the world any more than I belong to the world. Consecrate them in the truth. Your word is truth. As you sent me into the world, so I sent them into the world. And I consecrate myself for them, so that they also may be consecrated in truth."

Reflection

Pope Benedict XVI

To consecrate something or someone means, therefore, to give that thing or person to God as his property, to take it out of the context of what is ours and to insert it in his milieu, so that it no longer belongs to our affairs, but is totally of God. Consecration is thus a taking away from the world and a giving over to the living God. The thing or person no longer belongs to us, or even to itself, but is immersed in God. Such a giving up of something in order to give it over to God, we also call a sacrifice.

Prayers

others may be added

We are called to build up our world in the image and likness of Christ, and so we pray:

℟. **Risen Lord, hear our prayer.**

- For the Church, that she may lead her flock with integrity and truth, we pray: ℟.
- For world leaders, that they promote cultures of encounter among peoples, we pray: ℟.
- For children, that they be cared for and nurtured as they grow, we pray: ℟.
- For those who are dying, and those who will die today, we pray: ℟.

The Lord is risen and present among us and so we pray as he taught us.

Our Father . . .

O Holy God,
you have blessed and sanctified us
by your grace.
Show us how to live in holiness,
through prayer, reconciliation,
forgiveness, service, humility,
and love.
May our example lead others to lives
of holiness and happiness.
Through Christ our Lord.
Amen.

✚ All peoples, clap your hands. /
Cry to God with shouts of joy.

✙ Keep me safe, O God;
you are my hope.

Psalm 121 *page 386*

Reading *John 17:20–26*

Lifting up his eyes to heaven, Jesus prayed saying: "I pray not only for these, but also for those who will believe in me through their word, so that they may all be one, as you, Father, are in me and I in you, that they also may be in us, that the world may believe that you sent me. And I have given them the glory you gave me, so that they may be one, as we are one, I in them and you in me, that they may be brought to perfection as one, that the world may know that you sent me, and that you loved them even as you loved me. Father, they are your gift to me. I wish that where I am they also may be with me, that they may see my glory that you gave me, because you loved me before the foundation of the world. Righteous Father, the world also does not know you, but I know you, and they know that you sent me. I made known to them your name and I will make it known, that the love with which you loved me may be in them and I in them."

Reflection

What a remarkable and intimate prayer Jesus offers to his Father. What kind of relationship do we have with God? Is it like the relationship modeled in the Gospel? Do we know and experience the love between Jesus and his Father within us? Do we believe and know that Jesus is with us just as he was with his disciples? How differently would we live if we really believed that? How different might our world be? Even with the world as divided as it is, the prayer "they may be one" might not seem so outlandish.

Prayers *others may be added*

Called to pray for all people,
we now turn to the Lord:

℟. **Ascended Lord, hear our prayer:**

- For the Church, for an increase of faith, we pray: ℟.
- For world leaders, that they promote peace among peoples, we pray: ℟.
- For parents, that they be given holy Wisdom as they care for their children, we pray: ℟.
- For all who suffer from poverty, we pray: ℟.
- For those who are dying, and those who will die today, we pray: ℟.

The Lord is risen and present among us and so we pray as he taught us.

Our Father . . .

God our Father,
you called St. Boniface to proclaim your Gospel in Germany.
May we bring your Word to all the ends of the earth,
and love our neighbors wherever we find them
Through Christ our Lord.
Amen.

✙ Keep me safe, O God;
you are my hope.

Friday, June 6, 2025

✚ With boldness let us approach the throne of grace, / that we may receive mercy.

Psalm 148

page 390

Reading

John 21:15–19

After Jesus had revealed himself to his disciples and eaten breakfast with them, he said to Simon Peter, "Simon, son of John, do you love me more than these?" Simon Peter answered him, "Yes, Lord, you know that I love you." Jesus said to him, "Feed my lambs." He then said to Simon Peter a second time, "Simon, son of John, do you love me?" Simon Peter answered him, "Yes, Lord, you know that I love you." He said to him, "Tend my sheep." He said to him the third time, "Simon, son of John, do you love me?" Peter was distressed that he had said to him a third time, "Do you love me?" and he said to him, "Lord, you know everything; you know that I love you." Jesus said to him, "Feed my sheep. Amen, amen, I say to you, when you were younger, you used to dress yourself and go where you wanted; but when you grow old, you will stretch out your hands, and someone else will dress you and lead you where you do not want to go." He said this signifying by what kind of death he would glorify God. And when he had said this, he said to him, "Follow me."

Reflection

Pope Francis

Do you love me? The Lord then says: "Feed my sheep." He does not mean just some of the sheep, but all of them, for he loves them all, affectionately referring to them as "mine." The Good Shepherd looks out and wants his flock to be united. . . . All of us are children of God, all brothers and sisters in the Church, all of us making up the Church, all of us. That is how the Lord wants us to be. We are his sheep, his flock, and we can only be so together and as one. Let us overcome all polarization and preserve our communion.

Prayers

others may be added

Showing the Lord our deep and abiding love, we turn to him in prayer:

℟. **Ascended Lord, hear our prayer.**

- For the Church, that we always follow Jesus and feed his sheep, we pray: ℟.
- For world leaders, that they work for an end to poverty, we pray: ℟.
- For greater respect for life, we pray: ℟.
- For all those caught in human trafficking, we pray: ℟.
- For those who are dying, and those who will die today, we pray: ℟.

The Lord is risen and present among us and so we pray as he taught us.

Our Father . . .

Risen Christ,
you called Peter three times to feed
your sheep and to follow you.
Help us to hear your voice,
and give us courage to follow you
when you call us.
You who live and reign for ever
and ever.
Amen.

✚ With boldness let us approach the throne of grace, / that we may receive mercy.

✤ The Holy Spirit will glorify me, /
for he will take what is mine
and declare it to [God].

Psalm 46 *page 372*

Reading *John 21:20–25*

Peter turned and saw the disciple following whom Jesus loved, the one who had also reclined upon his chest during the supper and had said, "Master, who is the one who will betray you?" When Peter saw him, he said to Jesus, "Lord, what about him?" Jesus said to him, "What if I want him to remain until I come? What concern is it of yours? You follow me." So the word spread among the brothers that that disciple would not die. But Jesus had not told him that he would not die, just "What if I want him to remain until I come? What concern is it of yours?"

It is this disciple who testifies to these things and has written them, and we know that his testimony is true. There are also many other things that Jesus did, but if these were to be described individually, I do not think the whole world would contain the books that would be written.

Reflection *Pope Paul VI*

Evangelizing is in fact the grace and vocation proper to the Church, her deepest identity. She exists in order to evangelize, that is to say, in order to preach and teach, to be the channel of the gift of grace, to reconcile sinners with God, and to perpetuate Christ's sacrifice in the Mass, which is the memorial of his death and glorious resurrection.

Prayers *others may be added*

Our concern for others is rooted
in our love for God, and so we pray:

℟. **Ascended Lord, hear our prayer.**

- For the Church, that we always trust and follow Jesus, we pray: ℟.
- For honesty and integrity among world leaders, we pray: ℟.
- For greater dignity for workers, we pray: ℟.
- For those who are lonely, we pray: ℟.
- For those who are dying, and those who will die today, we pray: ℟.

The Lord is risen and present among us and so we pray as he taught us.

Our Father . . .

Generous God,
your grace is everywhere.
May we say "yes" to your call
and follow you with authenticity,
not for reward or recognition.
We eagerly await the fruit of our
cooperation with your work.
Through Christ our Lord.
Amen.

✤ The Holy Spirit will glorify me, /
for he will take what is mine
and declare it to [God].

✤ The love of God has been poured into our hearts.

Psalm 104 *page 383*

Reading *John 14:15–16, 23B–26*

Jesus said to his disciples: If you love me, you will keep my commandments. And I will ask the Father, and he will give you another Advocate to be with you always.

"Whoever loves me will keep my word, and my Father will love him, and we will come to him and make our dwelling with him. Those who do not love me do not keep my words; yet the word you hear is not mine but that of the Father who sent me.

"I have told you this while I am with you. The Advocate, the Holy Spirit whom the Father will send in my name, will teach you everything and remind you of all that I told you."

Reflection *Pope Francis*

The Spirit points out to us the starting point of the spiritual life. What is it? Jesus speaks of it in the first verse of the Gospel, when he says: "If you love me, you will keep my commandments." If you love me, you will keep. . . . This is the "logic" of the Spirit. We tend to think the exact opposite: if we keep the commandments, we will love Jesus. We tend to think that love comes from our keeping, our fidelity and our devotion. Yet the Spirit reminds us that without love as our basis, all the rest is in vain. And that love comes not so much from our abilities, but as his gift. He teaches us to love and we have to ask for this gift. The Spirit of love pours love into our hearts, he makes us feel loved and he teaches us how to love. He is the "motor" of our spiritual lives.

Prayers *others may be added*

In love for God, we keep his command, and offer our prayers for the world:

℟. **Ascended Lord, hear our prayer.**

- For the Church, that she will trust in the promise of the Spirit, we pray: ℟.
- For world leaders, that they will be guided by the Spirit of right judgment, we pray: ℟.
- For a spirit of peace in our families, we pray: ℟.
- For the grace to know the gifts and fruits of the Spirit in our lives, we pray: ℟.
- For those who are dying, and those who will die today, we pray: ℟.

The Lord is risen and present among us and so we pray as he taught us.

Our Father . . .

Risen Lord,
may the mystery of your truth and love
continue to be
evident and compelling to people
in every walk of life.
As we find you in our unique ways,
may we also find one another through
what we hold in common.
Give us ears to listen and be attentive
to your work in our lives,
and help us always to live with the
knowledge of your gifts in our world.
Who live and reign for ever and ever.
Amen.

✤ The love of God has been poured into our hearts.

✤ Taste and see the goodness of the Lord.

Psalm 34

page 370

Reading

Acts 1:12–14

After Jesus had been taken up into heaven, the Apostles returned to Jerusalem from the mount called Olivet, which is near Jerusalem, a sabbath day's journey away. When they entered the city they went to the upper room where they were staying, Peter and John and James and Andrew, Philip and Thomas, Bartholomew and Matthew, James son of Alphaeus, Simon the Zealot, and Judas son of James. All these devoted themselves with one accord to prayer, together with some women, and Mary the mother of Jesus, and his brothers.

Reflection

Imagine the group of people gathered in the upper room after Jesus' ascension entrusted to Mary's motherly care and devoting themselves with one accord to prayer. Throughout the Gospel accounts, Mary reflects in her heart. Her response to the miraculous works of God is contemplation. What must the small group—the Twelve, the women, and Jesus' earthly family—have been thinking and feeling? How might Mary's contemplation have served as a model response for them? How might it serve as a response to God's work today?

Prayers

others may be added

With Mary and all the saints
in heaven, we offer to the Lord
our prayers:

℟. **Lord, graciously hear us.**

- That we, as the Church, may devote ourselves to prayer with one accord, we pray: ℟.
- That all the living may experience peace, we pray: ℟.
- That all in need of love and protection may be held in the love of the Blessed Mother, we pray: ℟.
- That our community may bear Christ's light in the world, we pray: ℟.

Let us offer together the prayer
that Jesus taught us.

Our Father . . .

Lord Jesus,
you gave us your Blessed Mother
as our own.
Help us to see your work in the world
and to reflect on it in our hearts.
Who live and reign for ever and ever.
Amen.

✤ Taste and see the goodness of the Lord.

Tuesday, June 10, 2025

✤ Lord, let your face shine on me.

Psalm 27

page 368

Reading

Matthew 5:13–16

Jesus said to his disciples: "You are the salt of the earth. But if salt loses its taste, with what can it be seasoned? It is no longer good for anything but to be thrown out and trampled underfoot. You are the light of the world. A city set on a mountain cannot be hidden. Nor do they light a lamp and then put it under a bushel basket; it is set on a lampstand, where it gives light to all in the house. Just so, your light must shine before others, that they may see your good deeds and glorify your heavenly Father."

Reflection

Human innovation has been able to solve so many problems! A world of perfect peace and justice must be just around the corner, right? Yet, wherever we look, we see that many are left behind this narrative of constant progress and that new problems keep emerging. All Christians are called to shine Christ's light in the dark places—to bring hope where there is none. Human effort alone cannot create perfect peace or justice—only God can. In the Mass, we receive the perfect peace of Christ and share it with one another. Transformed, we go in peace, ready to be Christ's light for all people.

Prayers

others may be added

Lord, you call us to be salt of the earth and light for the world. Give us, we pray, all that we need:

℟. **Lord, hear our prayer.**

- For the Church, that she may carry Christ's light faithfully through every age, we pray: ℟.
- For all places where the world's darkness seems unconquerable, we pray: ℟.
- For the hopeless and those who have no one to pray for them, we pray: ℟.
- For an increase in faith, hope, and charity, we pray: ℟.

Let us offer together the prayer that Jesus taught us.

Our Father . . .

Loving Father,
you sent your Son into the world
as a light shining in the darkness,
never to be overcome.
Help us to carry your light,
and to witness to your presence
until your light fills the earth as water
fills the sea.
Through Christ our Lord.
Amen.

✤ Lord, let your face shine on me.

✤ Holy is the Lord our God.

Psalm 148 *page 390*

Reading *Acts 12:21b–26; 13:1–3*

In those days a great number who believed turned to the Lord. The news about them reached the ears of the Church in Jerusalem, and they sent Barnabas to go to Antioch. When he arrived and saw the grace of God, he rejoiced and encouraged them all to remain faithful to the Lord in firmness of heart, for he was a good man, filled with the Holy Spirit and faith. And a large number of people was added to the Lord. Then he went to Tarsus to look for Saul, and when he had found him he brought him to Antioch. For a whole year they met with the Church and taught a large number of people, and it was in Antioch that the disciples were first called Christians.

Now there were in the Church at Antioch prophets and teachers: Barnabas, Symeon who was called Niger, Lucius of Cyrene, Manaen who was a close friend of Herod the tetrarch, and Saul. While they were worshiping the Lord and fasting, the Holy Spirit said, "Set apart for me Barnabas and Saul for the work to which I have called them." Then, completing their fasting and prayer, they laid hands on them and sent them off.

Reflection

Through the guidance of the spirit, St. Barnabas sees God's grace operative in the world and rejoices. It can be difficult to discern God's presence and action. There is so much suffering. With the eyes of faith, it is possible to take that suffering seriously and at the same time to see God's work and to respond with joy. This joy is not an end in itself. Rejoicing, St. Barnabas goes on to encourage others, to help them to see the presence and action of God in their lives. What is God doing in your life right now? How might you respond to the gift of God's love?

Prayers *others may be added*

Rejoicing in the gifts the Lord
has given us, we bring before him
our needs:

℟. **Send us your Spirit.**

- For the encouragement of the Church and all who serve her, we pray: ℟.
- For political leaders, that they may be faithful to the common good, we pray: ℟.
- For the hungry, that they may be filled with good things, we pray: ℟.
- For our community, that they may rejoice as they witness God's grace, we pray: ℟.

Let us offer together the prayer
that Jesus taught us.

Our Father . . .

Lord Jesus,
you called your servant Barnabas
and sent the gift of the Holy Spirit
upon him.
Help us walk in your ways,
respond to your call,
and see your grace wherever
we are sent.
Who live and reign for ever and ever.
Amen.

✤ Holy is the Lord our God.

Weekday

Thursday, June 12, 2025

✚ The glory of the Lord will dwell
in our land.

Psalm 105 *page 383*

Reading *Matthew 5:20–26*

Jesus said to his disciples: "I tell you, unless your righteousness surpasses that of the scribes and Pharisees, you will not enter into the Kingdom of heaven.

"You have heard that it was said to your ancestors, / *You shall not kill; and whoever kills will be liable to judgment.* / But I say to you, whoever is angry with his brother will be liable to judgment, and whoever says to his brother, *Raqa*, will be answerable to the Sanhedrin, and whoever says, 'You fool,' will be liable to fiery Gehenna. Therefore, if you bring your gift to the altar, and there recall that your brother has anything against you, leave your gift there at the altar, go first and be reconciled with your brother, and then come and offer your gift. Settle with your opponent quickly while on the way to court. Otherwise your opponent will hand you over to the judge, and the judge will hand you over to the guard, and you will be thrown into prison. Amen, I say to you, you will not be released until you have paid the last penny."

Reflection

Conflict is part of life. Misunderstandings escalate quickly. People hurt each other. Jesus teaches conflict resolution that, while difficult, offers the gift of peace. Because the origin of hatred and violence is within, Jesus proclaims that one's inner attitude toward others must be oriented toward peace. He calls Christians to be the first to seek reconciliation, acknowledge our role in conflicts, and act as peacemakers. How can you bring peace into your challenging relationships? Are you in need of a change of heart?

Prayers *others may be added*

We bring our needs before God, the source of all peace, as we pray:

℟. **Lord, hear our prayer.**

- For the Church and her peacemaking across the world, we pray: ℟.
- For world leaders, that they may seek peace as the highest value, we pray: ℟.
- For all who live in conflict zones and those displaced by war, we pray: ℟.
- For peace in our hearts and our homes, we pray: ℟.

Let us offer together the prayer
that Jesus taught us.

Our Father . . .

Lord Jesus,
you order our days in your peace.
Be near us as we share this peace
with everyone we encounter
so that all may be one, united in you.
Who live and reign for ever and ever.
Amen.

✚ The glory of the Lord will dwell
in our land.

✤ To you, Lord, I will offer a sacrifice of praise.

Psalm 51 *page 373*

Reading *2 Corinthians 4:7–15*

Brothers and sisters: We hold this treasure in earthen vessels, that the surpassing power may be of God and not from us. We are afflicted in every way, but not constrained; perplexed, but not driven to despair; persecuted, but not abandoned; struck down, but not destroyed; always carrying about in the Body the dying of Jesus, so that the life of Jesus may also be manifested in our body. For we who live are constantly being given up to death for the sake of Jesus, so that the life of Jesus may be manifested in our mortal flesh.

So death is at work in us, but life in you. Since, then, we have the same spirit of faith, according to what is written, "I believed, therefore I spoke," we too believe and therefore speak, knowing that the one who raised the Lord Jesus will raise us also with Jesus and place us with you in his presence. Everything indeed is for you, so that the grace bestowed in abundance on more and more people may cause the thanksgiving to overflow for the glory of God.

Reflection

Baptized into Christ Jesus, each Christian bears his Spirit. This is true despite all our limitations and failings. When we turn away from our most selfish and least compassionate impulses, when we turn toward self-giving love in imitation of Jesus, we allow Christ's life within us to flourish. This is our hope: that we might go where Christ leads us, to eternal life with him in heaven. What must you let go of in order for Christ's life to flourish in you?

Prayers *others may be added*

Acknowledging that all that we have and all that we are comes from you, Lord, we bring our needs before you as we pray:

℟. Lord, hear our prayer.

- For the Body of Christ, we pray: ℟.
- For justice and mercy in our world, we pray: ℟.
- For all who are hungry in our world of abundance, we pray: ℟.
- For all people, that they might be ever more closely conformed to Christ Jesus, we pray: ℟.

Let us offer together the prayer
that Jesus taught us.

Our Father . . .

Lord Jesus,
you offer your people the gift
of your life.
Help us turn toward you
and conform our lives to yours
that we might offer our own lives
as a sacrifice of love.
Who live and reign for ever and ever.
Amen.

✤ To you, Lord, I will offer a sacrifice of praise.

Saturday, June 14, 2025

✣ The Lord is kind and merciful.

Psalm 33
page 369

Reading
Matthew 5:33–37

Jesus said to his disciples: "You have heard that it was said to your ancestors, / *Do not take a false oath, / but make good to the Lord all that you vow.* / But I say to you, do not swear at all; not by heaven, for it is God's throne; nor by the earth, for it is his footstool; nor by Jerusalem, for it is the city of the great King. Do not swear by your head, for you cannot make a single hair white or black. Let your 'Yes' mean 'Yes,' and your 'No' mean 'No.' Anything more is from the Evil One."

Reflection

Jesus, fully human and fully divine, offers us a map for what it looks like to be fully and authentically human. He says that our yes should mean yes, and our no, no. These words emphasize the importance of honesty. They also call his followers to something more. Perhaps you have had the experience of "going along to get along" when something inside you wants to do just the opposite. The still, small voice speaking within us is Jesus calling us to integrity.

Prayers
others may be added

Confident in God's generosity
and goodness, we bring our hopes
and needs before God as we pray:

℟. **Lord, graciously hear us.**

- For the Church, that she may proclaim the truth with love, we pray: ℟.
- For our leaders, that they will guide society with integrity, we pray: ℟.
- For people who experience dehumanization and prejudice, we pray: ℟.
- For all peoples, that they might be open to the guidance of our conscience, we pray: ℟.

Let us offer together the prayer
that Jesus taught us.

Our Father . . .

Lord Jesus,
you are the Way, the Truth, and the Life.
Help us walk in your ways and
proclaim your truth until you
come again.
Who live and reign for ever and ever.
Amen.

✣ The Lord is kind and merciful.

✚ Blest be God the Father, / and the Only Begotten Son of God, / and also the Holy Spirit, / for he has shown us his merciful love.

Psalm 122 *page 387*

Reading *John 16:12–15*

Jesus said to his disciples: "I have much more to tell you, but you cannot bear it now. But when he comes, the Spirit of truth, he will guide you to all truth. He will not speak on his own, but he will speak what he hears, and will declare to you the things that are coming. He will glorify me, because he will take from what is mine and declare it to you. Everything that the Father has is mine; for this reason I told you that he will take from what is mine and declare it to you."

Reflection

Jesus proclaims a great mystery: his unity with the Father and the Spirit. This mystery can never be fully comprehended, and yet we are invited to grow in understanding; Jesus will send the Spirit to aid us. This understanding is not purely intellectual. Through Jesus, we are invited to participate in the very life of this mystery. You are known and loved by the mystery that is the ground of the universe! We might wonder what makes God mindful of us. How can it be? How might we respond to this gift of God's everlasting love?

Prayersw *others may be added*

Acknowledging that every good thing comes from you, O, Lord, we humbly bring our needs before you as we pray:

℟. Send us your Spirit, O Lord.

- For the Church, guided always by the work of the Spirit, we pray: ℟.
- For our leaders, that they may be granted wisdom, we pray: ℟.
- For those on the margins of our society, that they may be treated with dignity, respect, and honor, we pray: ℟.
- That we may be filled with wisdom so as to see as God does, we pray: ℟.

Let us offer together the prayer that Jesus taught us.

Our Father . . .

O Wisdom,
from the beginning
your hand has guided the work
of creation.
The greatness of your works is ever
before us.
In your kindness, send your Spirit
upon us.
Make us new creations.
Help us to love like you.
Through Christ our Lord.
Amen.

✚ Blest be God the Father, / and the Only Begotten Son of God, / and also the Holy Spirit, / for he has shown us his merciful love.

Monday, June 16, 2025

✤ The Lord has made known
his salvation.

Psalm 24 *page 367*

Reading *Matthew 5:38–42*

Jesus said to his disciples: "You have heard that it was said, / *An eye for an eye and a tooth for a tooth.* / But I say to you, offer no resistance to one who is evil. When someone strikes you on your right cheek, turn the other one to him as well. If anyone wants to go to law with you over your tunic, hand him your cloak as well. Should anyone press you into service for one mile, go with him for two miles. Give to the one who asks of you, and do not turn your back on one who wants to borrow."

Reflection

People across time and culture have wondered about what it means to live in right relationship to other people, God, and the world around us. Jesus proposes a standard that goes beyond traditional notions of justice in conflict resolution. He calls for generosity in peacemaking that exceeds what is owed. Indeed, he calls upon his disciples to offer no resistance to one who is evil. The contemporary world is marked by division and conflict, in society, politics, and the Church. How might we live out Jesus' ethic of generous peacemaking and nonresistance today?

Prayers *others may be added*

Giving to the one who asks of us,
we offer our prayers to God:

℟. **Lord, hear our prayer.**

- For the Church, sign of Christ's peace, we pray: ℟.
- For a more just and peaceful world, we pray: ℟.
- For all who are affected by violence and conflict, we pray: ℟.
- For us, that our days may be ordered in the peace of Christ, we pray: ℟.

Let us offer together the prayer
that Jesus taught us.

Our Father . . .

Loving God,
you created human beings
that we might know, love, and serve you.
Grant us your peace,
that we might be peacemakers
for a world desperately in need.
Through Christ our Lord.
Amen.

✤ The Lord has made known
his salvation.

✤ Praise the Lord, my soul!

Psalm 27

page 368

Reading

Matthew 5:43–48

Jesus said to his disciples: "You have heard that it was said, / *You shall love your neighbor and hate your enemy.* / But I say to you, love your enemies, and pray for those who persecute you, that you may be children of your heavenly Father, for he makes his sun rise on the bad and the good, and causes rain to fall on the just and the unjust. For if you love those who love you, what recompense will you have? Do not the tax collectors do the same? And if you greet your brothers and sisters only, what is unusual about that? Do not the pagans do the same? So be perfect, just as your heavenly Father is perfect."

Reflection

Nobody's perfect. When we expect perfection from ourselves or the people we love, we set ourselves up for disappointment and heartache. Why would Jesus ask us to be perfect? Perhaps the answer lies in the last part of his statement: "As your heavenly Father is perfect." The blessings we receive cannot be earned; they are all pure gift. God calls us to love abundantly, regardless of whether the person seems to "deserve it." What might that look like as you go about your day today?

Prayers

others may be added

O Lord, we bring our hopes and needs before you. Trusting in your goodness and love, we pray:

℟. Lord, hear us.

- For the Church, font of abundant mercy, we pray: ℟.
- For our political leaders, that they may be guided by the ethic of love, we pray: ℟.
- For anyone who has no one to pray for them, we pray: ℟.
- For all people, that they may change the world with your love, we pray: ℟.

Let us offer together the prayer
that Jesus taught us.

Our Father . . .

God our Father,
you send your blessings upon us—
gifts that are freely given.
Give us hearts that love like you do
so that we may transform the world
by loving abundantly even those who
seem least worthy of our love.
Through Christ our Lord.
Amen.

✤ Praise the Lord, my soul!

✤ Blessed be the [one] who fears the Lord.

Psalm 30

page 369

Reading

Matthew 6:1–6

Jesus said to his disciples: "Take care not to perform righteous deeds in order that people may see them; otherwise, you will have no recompense from your heavenly Father. When you give alms, do not blow a trumpet before you, as the hypocrites do in the synagogues and in the streets to win the praise of others. Amen, I say to you, they have received their reward. But when you give alms, do not let your left hand know what your right is doing, so that your almsgiving may be secret. And your Father who sees in secret will repay you.

"When you pray, do not be like the hypocrites, who love to stand and pray in the synagogues and on street corners so that others may see them. Amen, I say to you, they have received their reward. But when you pray, go to your inner room, close the door, and pray to your Father in secret. And your Father who sees in secret will repay you."

Reflection

Jesus warns us about doing good in order to seek others' approval, whether in the form of applause or little red hearts. Human beings tend to want to hide embarrassments and mistakes while promoting the positive parts of life. Social media have magnified the problem. Comparing our real, complicated, messy lives to the curated versions of other people's lives causes mental health to decline, especially for young people. When we do good for its own sake and in response to God's love for us, we avoid the trap of seeking constant recognition and instead live according to the unique call God has for each beloved child.

Prayers

others may be added

We bring our needs before you, O Lord, trusting that you know us better than we know ourselves:

℟. Lord, hear our prayer.

- For the Church, speaking the truth in charity, we pray: ℟.
- For political leaders, that they have the courage to lead with compassion, we pray: ℟.
- For the hungry and unhoused, we pray: ℟.
- For all peoples, that they may grow in faith, hope, and love, we pray: ℟.

Let us offer together the prayer that Jesus taught us.

Our Father . . .

Father of our Lord Jesus Christ,
you give us every good gift.
Help us do your will.
Guide us as we follow Jesus
and do our best to echo his words:
thy will be done.
Who lives and reigns for ever and ever.
Amen.

✤ Blessed be the [one] who fears the Lord.

✤ Your works, O Lord,
are justice and truth.

Psalm 51 *page 373*

Reading *Matthew 6:7–15*

Jesus said to his disciples: "In praying, do not babble like the pagans, who think that they will be heard because of their many words. Do not be like them.
Your Father knows what you need before you ask him.

"This is how you are to pray: 'Our Father who art in heaven, hallowed be thy name, thy Kingdom come, thy will be done, on earth as it is in heaven. Give us this day our daily bread; and forgive us our trespasses, as we forgive those who trespass against us; and lead us not into temptation, but deliver us from evil.'

"If you forgive others their transgressions, your heavenly Father will forgive you. But if you do not forgive others, neither will your Father forgive your transgressions."

Reflection

When Jesus' disciples asked him how they were to pray, he answered by giving them the Our Father, or the Lord's Prayer. It was completely new to their ears. What must it have been like, to be there, hearing it for the first time, learning to address God as "Father"? How many people have prayed it in the almost two thousand years since? How many times is it prayed every day, all over the world? Meditate on the words as you pray them slowly. What do you notice? What stands out to you? Jesus taught us to pray with these words. These are words that help us to follow in the footsteps of the Lord.

Prayers *others may be added*

Let us bring our prayers before God with confidence that he knows what we need before we ask:

℟. Lord, hear our prayer.

- For the universal Church, we pray: ℟.
- For the world, that it will be filled with the light of God's love, we pray: ℟.
- For those who lack daily bread, we pray: ℟.
- For us, that we might confidently proclaim with the Lord, "thy will be done," we pray: ℟.

Let us offer together the prayer
that Jesus taught us.

Our Father . . .

Loving God,
you sent your son into the world
to call all people to yourself.
Help us walk in your paths.
Conform our hearts to yours.
Help us do your will.
Through Christ our Lord.
Amen.

✤ Your works, O Lord,
are justice and truth.

Weekday

Friday, June 20, 2025

✤ From all their distress God rescues the just.

Psalm 34

page 370

Reading

Matthew 6:19–23

Jesus said to his disciples: "Do not store up for yourselves treasures on earth, where moth and decay destroy, and thieves break in and steal. But store up treasures in heaven, where neither moth nor decay destroys, nor thieves break in and steal. For where your treasure is, there also will your heart be.

"The lamp of the body is the eye. If your eye is sound, your whole body will be filled with light; but if your eye is bad, your whole body will be in darkness. And if the light in you is darkness, how great will the darkness be."

Reflection

Jesus uses the images of moths and thieves to point to a universal truth: nothing that exists on the earth is permanent. Things wear out and break down. Friendships that we thought would last a lifetime end. Children grow up and leave us lonely. People we love die. The only constant in human life is change. Jesus tells his disciples to store up treasure in heaven. We know we cannot take earthly wealth with us when we die. But we can live our lives so that our love for others, our good works, and our virtue will endure and will be our treasure in the life to come.

Prayers

others may be added

With confidence in your goodness,
O Lord, we bring before you our needs as we pray:

℟. **Lord, graciously hear us.**

- For the Church and her leaders, that they may guide the faithful to what is truly valuable, we pray: ℟.
- For greater respect and care for the earth, we pray: ℟.
- For all who have died and all who are grieving, we pray: ℟.
- For us, that we may see the world as God sees it, we pray: ℟.

Let us offer together the prayer
that Jesus taught us.

Our Father . . .

God the Father,
you created the universe—
the vastness of space and
the tiniest atoms.
You are the only constant.
Give us all that we need to love and
serve you and one another
that we might one day share in your
eternal life.
Through Christ our Lord.
Amen.

✤ From all their distress God rescues the just.

✤ The Lord is kind and merciful.

Psalm 23 *page 367*

Reading *Matthew 6:25–34*

Jesus said to his disciples: "Therefore I tell you, do not worry about your life, what you will eat or drink, or about your body, what you will wear. Is not life more than food and the body more than clothing? Look at the birds in the sky; they do not sow or reap, they gather nothing into barns, yet your heavenly Father feeds them. Are not you more important than they? Can any of you by worrying add a single moment to your life-span? Why are you anxious about clothes? Learn from the way the wild flowers grow. They do not work or spin. But I tell you that not even Solomon in all his splendor was clothed like one of them. If God so clothes the grass of the field, which grows today and is thrown into the oven tomorrow, will he not much more provide for you, O you of little faith? So do not worry and say, 'What are we to eat?' or 'What are we to drink?' or 'What are we to wear?' All these things the pagans seek. Your heavenly Father knows that you need them all. But seek first the Kingdom of God and his righteousness, and all these things will be given you besides. Do not worry about tomorrow; tomorrow will take care of itself. Sufficient for a day is its own evil."

Reflection

As Jesus continues to preach the Sermon on the Mount, he provides his disciples instructions about how they should live. He proclaims to them God's care for the birds and the wildflowers, illustrating the fruitlessness of worry. Jesus tells them instead to put the kingdom of God first. What can that mean in our contemporary, anxiety-prone world? When faced with important decisions, sometimes we have to decide between a choice motivated by fear and one motivated by love. Choosing love, even when we are afraid or anxious, helps us to keep our eyes focused on the kingdom.

Prayers *others may be added*

With confidence, we bring our needs
to God, the font of all blessing:

℟. **Send us your Spirit, O Lord.**

- For the Church, confident in Christ's promise of the Spirit, we pray: ℟.
- For our leaders, that they may create societies where it is easier to be good, we pray: ℟.
- For all whose worries are many, that they may find rest, we pray: ℟.
- For us, that our hearts may not be troubled, we pray: ℟.

Let us offer together the prayer
that Jesus taught us.

Our Father . . .

Lord Jesus,
help us listen for the Spirit's guidance
that we might not worry
but rather go with confidence
to proclaim you to the ends of the earth
until you come again.
Who live and reign for ever and ever.
Amen.

✤ The Lord is kind and merciful.

✚ He fed them with the finest wheat / and satisfied them with honey from the rock.

Psalm 46

page 372

Reading

Luke 9:11b–17

Jesus spoke to the crowds about the kingdom of God, and he healed those who needed to be cured. As the day was drawing to a close, the Twelve approached him and said, "Dismiss the crowd so that they can go to the surrounding villages and farms and find lodging and provisions; for we are in a deserted place here." He said to them, "Give them some food yourselves." They replied, "Five loaves and two fish are all we have, unless we ourselves go and buy food for all these people." Now the men there numbered about five thousand. Then he said to his disciples, "Have them sit down in groups of about fifty." They did so and made them all sit down. Then taking the five loaves and the two fish, and looking up to heaven, he said the blessing over them, broke them, and gave them to the disciples to set before the crowd. They all ate and were satisfied. And when the leftover fragments were picked up, they filled twelve wicker baskets.

Reflection

Jesus feeds five thousand people with five loaves and two fish. The story is very familiar, and therefore we might fail to appreciate the scale of this miracle. People come to Jesus and he feeds them. He gives them all that they need. The Eucharist is the source and summit of our faith. Jesus offers his life as a sacrifice for the life of the world. We receive Christ's Body, Blood, Soul, and Divinity in the Eucharist. We share in the very life of God. We conform our lives to Christ's, offering our lives in self-giving love as we follow in his footsteps.

Prayers

others may be added

With confidence, we bring our needs before God, as we pray:

℟. **Lord, hear our prayer.**

- That the Church, the Body of Christ, will carry Christ's love through the world, we pray: ℟.
- That the world's divisions may be healed, we pray: ℟.
- That all who hunger may be satisfied, we pray: ℟.
- That we may be strengthened to love self-sacrificially in imitation of Jesus, we pray: ℟.

Let us offer together the prayer that Jesus taught us.

Our Father . . .

Risen Christ,
you offer us the gift of yourself
in every Mass.
Make our hearts ready to accept
your gift
and respond to it with our whole being,
bearing your love to the world.
Who live and reign for ever and ever.
Amen.

✚ He fed them with the finest wheat / and satisfied them with honey from the rock.

✤ Blessed the people the Lord has chosen to be his own.

Psalm 47

page 372

Reading

Matthew 7:1–5

Jesus said to his disciples: "Stop judging, that you may not be judged. For as you judge, so will you be judged, and the measure with which you measure will be measured out to you. Why do you notice the splinter in your brother's eye, but do not perceive the wooden beam in your own eye? How can you say to your brother, 'Let me remove that splinter from your eye,' while the wooden beam is in your eye? You hypocrite, remove the wooden beam from your eye first; then you will see clearly to remove the splinter from your brother's eye."

Reflection

Jesus offers a simple teaching about judgment: don't do it. The world is full of division, and just like the people in Jesus' day, we make assumptions, judge, and reduce people to actions or appearances. We sort people into categories: this person is acceptable, that one does not deserve my love, concern, or notice. Jesus invites his followers to live in a countercultural way: focus on their own faults and failings. We cannot change other people; we can only change ourselves. Focusing on our own struggles also helps us grow in love and compassion for other people.

Prayers

others may be added

O Lord, you know the needs of our hearts. Hear the prayers we bring humbly before you, as we pray:

℟. **Lord, graciously hear us.**

- For the Church, that she may be a place of welcome for all people, we pray: ℟.
- For political leaders, that they may use wisdom and discernment rather than judgment, we pray: ℟.
- For all who face persecution, hatred, and violence, we pray: ℟.
- For open hearts and minds, we pray: ℟.

Let us offer together the prayer that Jesus taught us.

Our Father . . .

Father,
you offer your love and forgiveness
abundantly.
Make us mindful of your care for us
that we may see as you see,
love as you love,
and act with mercy and justice.
Through Christ our Lord.
Amen.

✤ Blessed the people the Lord has chosen to be his own.

✣ [The one] who does justice will live in the presence of the Lord.

Psalm 71

page 376

Reading

Luke 1:57–66, 80

When the time arrived for Elizabeth to have her child she gave birth to a son. Her neighbors and relatives heard that the Lord had shown his great mercy toward her, and they rejoiced with her. When they came on the eighth day to circumcise the child, they were going to call him Zechariah after his father, but his mother said in reply, "No. He will be called John." But they answered her, "There is no one among your relatives who has this name." So they made signs, asking his father what he wished him to be called. He asked for a tablet and wrote, "John is his name," and all were amazed. Immediately his mouth was opened, his tongue freed, and he spoke blessing God. Then fear came upon all their neighbors, and all these matters were discussed throughout the hill country of Judea. All who heard these things took them to heart, saying, "What, then, will this child be?" For surely the hand of the Lord was with him. The child grew and became strong in spirit, and he was in the desert until the day of his manifestation to Israel.

Reflection

The birth of John the Baptist is one of several miraculous births in the Scripture accounts. Zechariah and Elizabeth had never been able to have children and, having grown old, no longer expected that they might become parents. God blessed them with new life when it seemed impossible. The people of Israel also struggled in a time which seemed hopeless. They struggled under an oppressive political occupation that made them long even more for the promised Messiah. John's miraculous birth foreshadowed that Messiah, a sign of hope, of new life that was beyond what anyone could imagine.

Prayers

others may be added

O Lord, with confidence in your loving care for us, we bring before you our needs:

℟. **Lord, hear our prayer**

- For the Church as she carries hope through a world in need, we pray: ℟.
- For solutions to the most intractable problems of our world, we pray: ℟.
- For people struggling with infertility, we pray: ℟.
- For an increase in hope, we pray: ℟.O

Let us offer together the prayer that Jesus taught us.

Our Father . . .

O Father,
you brought the gift of John the Baptist
to Elizabeth and Zechariah.
You called John the Baptist to go into
the world and proclaim hope.
Nothing is impossible for you.
Grant our prayers and give us
the strength we need
to prepare the way of the Lord
until he comes again.
Who lives and reigns for ever and ever.
Amen.

✣ [The one] who does justice will live in the presence of the Lord.

✤ The Lord remembers his covenant for ever.

Psalm 62 *page 374*

Reading *Genesis 15: 1–6*

The word of the LORD came to Abram in a vision: / "Fear not, Abram! / I am your shield; / I will make your reward very great." /

But Abram said, "O Lord GOD, what good will your gifts be, if I keep on being childless and have as my heir the steward of my house, Eliezer?" Abram continued, "See, you have given me no offspring, and so one of my servants will be my heir." Then the word of the LORD came to him: "No, that one shall not be your heir; your own issue shall be your heir." He took him outside and said: "Look up at the sky and count the stars, if you can. Just so," he added, "shall your descendants be." Abram put his faith in the LORD, who credited it to him as an act of righteousness.

Reflection

What does it mean to have faith? Abram turns to God in his yearning for a child. God promises something beyond what Abram could have imagined: "Look up at the sky and count the stars, if you can. Just so . . . shall your descendants be." God promises Abram the land and descendants. Abram believes. The world is filled with groundless optimism, but God promises that whatever we are going through, he will be with us. He knows the deepest needs of our heart. We are his.

Prayers *others may be added*

Like Abraham, our father in faith,
we put our faith in God and turn
to him in prayer:

℟. **Lord, hear our prayer.**

- For all the faithful, that we may trust in the promises of Christ, we pray: ℟.
- For world leaders, that they may create a society where it is easier for people to be good, we pray: ℟.
- For all who are suffering in mind, body, or spirit, that they may receive consolation and peace, we pray: ℟.
- For us, that we might grow in faith, we pray: ℟.

Let us offer together the prayer
that Jesus taught us.

Our Father . . .

God of Abraham,
you keep your promises.
Help us to remember your mercy
and trust in you until you come again.
Through Christ our Lord.
Amen.

✤ The Lord remembers his covenant for ever.

Thursday, June 26, 2025

✚ Give thanks to the Lord,
for he is good.

Psalm 63

page 375

Reading

Matthew 7:21–29

Jesus said to his disciples: "Not everyone who says to me, 'Lord, Lord,' will enter the Kingdom of heaven, but only the one who does the will of my Father in heaven. Many will say to me on that day, 'Lord, Lord, did we not prophesy in your name? Did we not drive out demons in your name? Did we not do mighty deeds in your name?' Then I will declare to them solemnly, 'I never knew you. Depart from me, you evildoers.'

"Everyone who listens to these words of mine and acts on them will be like a wise man who built his house on rock. The rain fell, the floods came, and the winds blew and buffeted the house. But it did not collapse; it had been set solidly on rock. And everyone who listens to these words of mine but does not act on them will be like a fool who built his house on sand. The rain fell, the floods came, and the winds blew and buffeted the house. And it collapsed and was completely ruined."

When Jesus finished these words, the crowds were astonished at his teaching, for he taught them as one having authority, and not as their scribes.

Reflection

Jesus invites us to consider the foundation on which we are building our life. Many things that are good or morally neutral become problematic when they are placed at the center of one's life. Perhaps we think wealth, fame, or power will provide us with what it takes to withstand the storms of life or even to prevent the storms from happening in the first place. No person escapes suffering. When the storms come, the love of God is the only foundation sturdy enough to support us.

Prayers

others may be added

With confidence, we bring our hopes and needs before God as we pray:

℟. **Lord, graciously hear us.**

✦ For the Church, the sign of Christ's presence, we pray: ℟.

✦ For peace and justice in our world, we pray: ℟.

✦ For all people enduring the storms of life, that God may give them strength and comfort, we pray: ℟.

✦ For us, that we may image God's love for everyone we meet, especially those most in need, we pray: ℟.

Let us offer together the prayer
that Jesus taught us.

Our Father . . .

Loving God,
you have called all people to yourself.
Be with us as we withstand the storms
of life.
Show your face to us and be gracious.
Hep us to recognize those in our midst
in need
that we might carry your love to them.
Through Christ our Lord.
Amen.

✚ Give thanks to the Lord,
for he is good.

✣ The Lord is my shepherd;
there is nothing I shall want.

Psalm 67

page 375

Reading

Luke 15:3–7

Jesus addressed this parable to the Pharisees and scribes: "What man among you having a hundred sheep and losing one of them would not leave the ninety-nine in the desert and go after the lost one until he finds it? And when he does find it, he sets it on his shoulders with great joy and, upon his arrival home, he calls together his friends and neighbors and says to them, 'Rejoice with me because I have found my lost sheep.' I tell you, in just the same way there will be more joy in heaven over one sinner who repents than over ninety-nine righteous people who have no need of repentance."

Reflection

In the parable of the lost sheep, Jesus invites his disciples to contemplate their own belovedness. Never tiring of looking, the Good Shepherd seeks the lost until that one sheep is found. He places the lost one on his shoulders and carries it home, rejoicing. He celebrates. Jesus makes it explicit: this is the way God pursues each one of us. We are each loved as though there are no others. We are sought relentlessly by the one who loves us with an everlasting love.

Prayers

others may be added

With confidence in God's everlasting love, we ofer our needs as we pray:

℟. Lord, hear our prayer.

- For the Church, rejoicing in all who turn to her, we pray: ℟.
- For a greater respect for human rights and human dignity around the world, we pray: ℟.
- For those who are lost and struggling, we pray: ℟.
- For all people, that they might love as Jesus does, we pray: ℟.

Let us offer together the prayer
that Jesus taught us.

Our Father . . .

Good Shepherd,
you seek the lost in every generation,
placing them on your shoulders
and rejoicing.
Help us to turn to you in our difficulties;
to love like you and rejoice in the
belovedness of each human person.
Who live and reign for ever and ever.
Amen.

✣ The Lord is my shepherd;
there is nothing I shall want.

✚ The Lord has remembered
his mercy.

Psalm 84

page 378

Reading

Luke 2:41–51

Each year Jesus' parents went to Jerusalem for the feast of Passover, and when he was twelve years old, they went up according to festival custom. After they had completed its days, as they were returning, the boy Jesus remained behind in Jerusalem, but his parents did not know it. Thinking that he was in the caravan, they journeyed for a day and looked for him among their relatives and acquaintances, but not finding him, they returned to Jerusalem to look for him. After three days they found him in the temple, sitting in the midst of the teachers, listening to them and asking them questions, and all who heard him were astounded at his understanding and his answers. When his parents saw him, they were astonished, and his mother said to him, "Son, why have you done this to us? Your father and I have been looking for you with great anxiety." And he said to them, "Why were you looking for me? Did you not know that I must be in my Father's house?" But they did not understand what he said to them. He went down with them and came to Nazareth, and was obedient to them; and his mother kept all these things in her heart.

Reflection

Mary, throughout her life, is a model of contemplation. She reflects in her heart, a heart that will know great suffering because of her yes to God. Many people believe that God rewards those who have been faithful with material goods and protection from suffering. Mary, most blessed among women, reveals that this is a false belief. Mary loves purely because in her confusion and even in her suffering, she turns to God. She reflects in her heart. As her children, we are called to follow her example. Let us turn to God in contemplation, that we might love with hearts like hers.

Prayers

others may be added

Turning to God in our need, we pray:

℟. **Lord, hear graciously hear us.**

- For the Church throughout the world, we pray: ℟.
- That our leaders may be guided by reflection and discernment, we pray: ℟.
- For people who lack the basic necessities of life, we pray: ℟.
- For all people, that they may love purely and fully despite their struggles and sufferings, we pray: ℟.

Let us offer together the prayer
that Jesus taught us.

Our Father . . .

Lord God,
Help us to reflect like Mary
that we might know the work we are
to do in the world
and have the strength to live out
your call.
Through Christ our Lord.
Amen.

✚ The Lord has remembered
his mercy.

✣ Peter the Apostle, and Paul the teacher of the Gentiles, / these have taught us your law, O Lord.

Psalm 27

page 368

Reading

Matthew 16:13–19

When Jesus went into the region of Caesarea Philippi he asked his disciples, "Who do people say that the Son of Man is?" They replied, "Some say John the Baptist, others Elijah, still others Jeremiah or one of the prophets." He said to them; "But who do you say that I am?" Simon Peter said in reply, "You are the Christ, the Son of the living God." Jesus said to him in reply, "Blessed are you, Simon son of Jonah. For flesh and blood has not revealed this to you, but my heavenly Father. And so I say to you, you are Peter, and upon this rock I will build my Church, and the gates of the netherworld shall not prevail against it. I will give you the keys to the Kingdom of heaven. Whatever you bind on earth shall be bound in heaven; and whatever you loose on earth shall be loosed in heaven."

Reflection

Jesus asks his friends a question that is as essential today as it was two thousand years ago: who do you say that I am? Peter answers him: "You are the Christ, the Son of the living God." Peter is given the gift of seeing Jesus as he is. He receives this gift—the revelation of Jesus' identity—at the same time he receives his call from God—the response to that gift. Each one of us is given the grace to recognize Jesus. How might we prepare to meet him in the Eucharist and in the vulnerable in our midst?

Prayers

others may be added

In communion with all the saints,
we bring our needs before God:

℟. Lord, hear our prayer.

- For the Church's prophetic leadership, especially the pope, the successor of Peter, we pray: ℟.
- For the world to grow in peace and justice, we pray: ℟.
- For people who are incarcerated and families separated by incarceration, we pray: ℟.
- For those who face discrimination or persecution for their faith, we pray: ℟.
- For the courage to live out God's call, we pray: ℟.

Let us offer together the prayer
that Jesus taught us.

Our Father . . .

God of all blessings,
you sent your Spirit upon Sts. Peter
and Paul
that they might serve your people
with fidelity
and in imitation of the Master.
Grant us the same Spirit,
that we might know, love, and serve you
and show others the way to your love.
Through Christ our Lord.
Amen.

✣ Peter the Apostle, and Paul the teacher of the Gentiles, / these have taught us your law, O Lord.

Monday, June 30, 2025

✣ The Lord is kind and merciful.

Psalm 91 *page 379*

Reading *Matthew 8:18–22*

When Jesus saw a crowd around him, he gave orders to cross to the other shore. A scribe approached and said to him, "Teacher, I will follow you wherever you go." Jesus answered him, "Foxes have dens and birds of the sky have nests, but the Son of Man has nowhere to rest his head." Another of his disciples said to him, "Lord, let me go first and bury my father." But Jesus answered him, "Follow me, and let the dead bury their dead."

Reflection

Sometimes Jesus' desire that we follow him can be difficult to understand. The scribe wants to follow Jesus but he also wants to take care of a very human obligation: burying his father. We know that burying the dead is a good thing to do, a work of mercy. What can Jesus mean? We might find a clue in the call narratives of those who would become the Twelve. We hear that they drop everything to follow him. They come "right then." It is very human to make excuses for why we cannot respond with urgency to God's call in our lives. Jesus asks us to respond "right then." What is he asking of you today?

Prayers *others may be added*

Let us bring our prayers before God:

℟. Lord, hear us.

- For the Church, the People of God, we pray: ℟.
- For world leaders, that they may create cultures of life, we pray: ℟.
- For those who have died and those who grieve them, we pray: ℟.
- For a wholehearted response to God's call, we pray: ℟.

Let us offer together the prayer
that Jesus taught us.

Our Father . . .

Loving God,
you call all people to yourself
so that one day there might be one flock
and one Shepherd.
Make us attentive to your call
and courageous to respond with
urgency to a world in need.
Through Christ our Lord.
Amen.

✣ The Lord is kind and merciful.

✤ O Lord, your mercy
is before my eyes.

Psalm 95

page 380

Reading

Matthew 8:23–27

As Jesus got into a boat, his disciples followed him. Suddenly a violent storm came up on the sea, so that the boat was being swamped by waves; but he was asleep. They came and woke him, saying, "Lord, save us! We are perishing!" He said to them, "Why are you terrified, O you of little faith?" Then he got up, rebuked the winds and the sea, and there was great calm. The men were amazed and said, "What sort of man is this, whom even the winds and the sea obey?"

Reflection

People loved to be close to Jesus. They were drawn to him, though they could not quite understand why. We can see this in his disciples' constant question: Who are you? What must they have been thinking and feeling as the storm tossed their boat while Jesus slept? In their fear they awakened Jesus because they felt sure he could help. Yet when he quieted the storm, they were astonished. We know that Jesus tells us: do not be afraid. Many of us struggle, like the disciples in the boat. We believe that Jesus is the source of our peace, but we cling to other sources of security. How might you find Christ's peace in the midst of your struggles?

Prayers

others may be added

We bring our prayers before God, the source of every good thing, as we pray:

℟. **Grant us your peace.**

- For unity in the Church, we pray: ℟.
- For the healing of political divisions, we pray: ℟.
- For those whose homes and livelihoods are harmed by extreme weather, we pray: ℟.
- For trust in Christ, the source of all peace, we pray: ℟.

Let us offer together the prayer
that Jesus taught us.

Our Father . . .

Lord Jesus,
you have told us we need not fear,
for you will be with us until the end
of the age.
Hear the prayers of your faithful
and grant us peace in our days.
Who live and reign for ever and ever.
Amen.

✤ O Lord, your mercy
is before my eyes.

Wednesday, July 2, 2025

✤ The Lord hears the cry of the poor.

Psalm 98

page 381

Reading

Genesis 21:5; 8–10

Abraham was a hundred years old when his son Isaac was born to him. Isaac grew, and on the day of the child's weaning Abraham held a great feast.

Sarah noticed the son whom Hagar the Egyptian had borne to Abraham playing with her son Isaac; so she demanded of Abraham: "Drive out that slave and her son! No son of that slave is going to share the inheritance with my son Isaac!"

Reflection

God's promise has been fulfilled. Isaac is born. Sarah worries about the sturdiness of God's promise. She wants to protect her baby, especially after waiting for him for such a long time. Sarah responds to her fear in a cruel way: she demands that Hagar and Ishmael be sent away. With God, promises are abundant. God promises Abraham that he will care for Ishmael because he is part of the covenant. Where fear sought to exclude, God's abundant love and faithfulness expanded.

Prayers

others may be added

Trusting in God's providence, we offer to him our prayers as we pray:

℟. **Lord, hear us.**

- For a welcoming Church, we pray: ℟.
- For an increase in respect for human life and dignity throughout the world, we pray: ℟.
- For all people who are marginalized or excluded, we pray: ℟.
- For the gift of counsel to make decisions guided by God's abundant love, we pray: ℟.

Let us offer together the prayer that Jesus taught us.

Our Father . . .

God of promises,
you guided Hagar through
the wilderness
to a place where she could draw water
for her son.
Guide us on the way;
show us everything we need
that we might faithfully live out
our call as your people.
Through Christ our Lord.
Amen.

✤ The Lord hears the cry of the poor.

✠ You are my God, I confess you; /
. . . I exalt you; / . . . I will thank you.

Psalm 103

page 382

Reading

John 20:24–29

Thomas, called Didymus, one of the Twelve, was not with them when Jesus came. So the other disciples said to him, "We have seen the Lord." But Thomas said to them, "Unless I see the mark of the nails in his hands and put my finger into the nailmarks and put my hand into his side, I will not believe." Now a week later his disciples were again inside and Thomas was with them. Jesus came, although the doors were locked, and stood in their midst and said, "Peace be with you." Then he said to Thomas, "Put your finger here and see my hands, and bring your hand and put it into my side, and do not be unbelieving, but believe." Thomas answered and said to him, "My Lord and my God!" Jesus said to him, "Have you come to believe because you have seen me? Blessed are those who have not seen and have believed."

Reflection

St. Thomas is remembered for questioning the witness of the other disciples. His doubt is normal. The others had seen Jesus with their own eyes. We might choose to remember Thomas for his proclamation of faith: "My Lord and my God!" Thomas' witness testifies to the truth of the resurrection. Empowered by encounter, he goes out to all the world. Like Thomas, our faith is centered on encountering the risen Christ—in the Eucharist at every Mass. Through the experience of the risen Lord, we are transformed and become witnesses to the Good News of the resurrection.

Prayers

others may be added

O God, you know the needs of our hearts. Hear the prayers of your people as we pray:

℟. **Send us your Spirit, O Lord.**

- For the Church as she proclaims the risen Christ, we pray: ℟.
- For peace in our world, we pray: ℟.
- For all who lack the basic necessities of life, we pray: ℟.
- For an increase in faith, that we may become strengthened in our witness to the resurrection, we pray: ℟.

Let us offer together the prayer
that Jesus taught us.

Our Father . . .

Lord Jesus,
you come to meet us,
just as you appeared to St. Thomas.
Transform our hearts
so that we may give witness
to your resurrection
until you come again.
Who live and reign for ever and ever.
Amen.

✠ You are my God, I confess you; /
. . . I exalt you; / . . . I will thank you.

Friday, July 4, 2025

✤ Give thanks to the Lord,
for he is good.

Psalm 115 *page 385*

Reading *Matthew 9:1–8*

Today's reading is from the Mass for Independence Day.

Jesus entered a boat, made the crossing, and came into his own town. And there people brought to him a paralytic, lying on a stretcher. When Jesus saw their faith, he said to the paralytic, "Courage, child, your sins are forgiven." At that, some of the scribes said to themselves, "This man is blaspheming." Jesus knew what the scribes were thinking, and said, "Why do you harbor evil thoughts? Which is easier, to say, 'Your sins are forgiven,' or to say, 'Rise and walk'? But that you may know that the Son of Man has authority on earth to forgive sins"—he then said to the paralytic, "Rise, pick up your stretcher, and go home." He rose and went home. When the crowds saw this they were struck with awe and glorified God who had given such authority to men.

Reflection

Jesus was an amazing ethical teacher. It was one dimension of his ministry to proclaim the Kingdom. Healing was another. Jesus offered real healing to people who were suffering in body, mind, and spirit. We see that our country and world are in need of healing. We turn to Jesus, who heals all divisions, that he might offer us new life and new freedom so that we might fulfill our nation's promise of liberty and justice for all.

Prayers *others may be added*

With hope for our country and our world, we bring our needs before God as we pray:

℟. Lord, hear our prayer.

- For Church leaders, that they may be guided by God's justice, we pray: ℟.
- For healing of the world's divisions, we pray: ℟.
- For the hungry, unhoused, and marginalized in our society, we pray: ℟.
- For peace and justice, we pray: ℟.

Let us offer together the prayer that Jesus taught us.

Our Father . . .

Loving God,
you offer all people true freedom
as your children.
Guide us as we use the gift of freedom
so that we may serve you
and bring your peace and justice
to the world.
Through Christ our Lord.
Amen.

✤ Give thanks to the Lord,
for he is good.

✚ Praise the Lord for the Lord is good!

Psalm 121

page 386

Reading

Matthew 9:14–17

The disciples of John approached Jesus and said, "Why do we and the Pharisees fast much, but your disciples do not fast?" Jesus answered them, "Can the wedding guests mourn as long as the bridegroom is with them? The days will come when the bridegroom is taken away from them, and then they will fast. No one patches an old cloak with a piece of unshrunken cloth, for its fullness pulls away from the cloak and the tear gets worse. People do not put new wine into old wineskins. Otherwise the skins burst, the wine spills out, and the skins are ruined. Rather, they pour new wine into fresh wineskins, and both are preserved."

Reflection

A small subset of the Jewish people lived out an extreme interpretation of the Law of Moses. They believed this interpretation was the only way to serve God. It set them apart from other people and some became self-satisfied and arrogant, thinking themselves worthy of God's care and protection. We know Jesus upended this system. Yet we can be just as judgmental, self-satisfied, and arrogant about our own religious practices. Nothing we can do will make God love us more than God already does. This radical belovedness is an essential part of the ministry of Jesus. This new wine resists all attempts to contain it in old wineskins that suggest some are more worthy than others. Each person is God's beloved child.

Prayers

others may be added

Knowing God's love and care for us,
we offer to him our needs:

℟. **Lord, graciously hear us.**

- For the Church, that she may be a place of welcome to all people, we pray: ℟.
- For peace in our world, we pray: ℟.
- For all who live at the margins of society, we pray: ℟.
- For all people, that they may resist the impulse to judge and instead see Christ revealed in each human person, we pray: ℟.

Let us offer together the prayer
that Jesus taught us.

Our Father . . .

Loving God,
you created us in love
and call all people to yourself.
Give us everything we need
to love and serve you.
Help us to see your face in everyone
we meet.
Through Christ our Lord.
Amen.

✚ Praise the Lord for the Lord is good!

Sunday, July 6, 2025

✣ Your right hand is filled
with saving justice.

Psalm 24

page 367

Reading

Luke 10: 1–9

At that time the Lord appointed seventy-two others whom he sent ahead of him in pairs to every town and place he intended to visit. He said to them, "The harvest is abundant but the laborers are few; so ask the master of the harvest to send out laborers for his harvest. Go on your way; behold, I am sending you like lambs among wolves. Carry no money bag, no sack, no sandals; and greet no one along the way. Into whatever house you enter, first say, 'Peace to this household.' If a peaceful person lives there, your peace will rest on him; but if not, it will return to you. Stay in the same house and eat and drink what is offered to you, for the laborer deserves his payment. Do not move about from one house to another. Whatever town you enter and they welcome you, eat what is set before you, cure the sick in it and say to them, 'The kingdom of God is at hand for you.' "

Reflection

Jesus sends out seventy-two disciples to proclaim the Kingdom of God and heal people. The disciples are amazed at the miracles they are able to do. Jesus cautions them not to get carried away. Most of us are not able to perform miracles, but we do what we can for others. Jesus says: remember that these actions themselves are not the true source of your joy. Your joy does not come from what you do. Joy comes from hope in everlasting life. This inner disposition keeps us focused on what is truly important and gives us what we need to serve God and our neighbor every day.

Prayers

others may be added

Responding to the call to serve the Lord, we offer to him our prayers:

℟. Lord, hear our prayer.

- For the Church, guiding us toward heaven, we pray: ℟.
- For hope in the face of the world's most pressing difficulties, we pray: ℟.
- For the sick, we pray: ℟.
- For humility and hope, we pray: ℟.

Let us offer together the prayer
that Jesus taught us.

Our Father . . .

Lord Jesus,
you teach us how to live.
Help us to discern the right path.
Show us how to serve God
and one another
as you guide us to eternal life.
Who live and reign for ever and ever.
Amen.

✣ Your right hand is filled
with saving justice.

✤ In you, my God, I place my trust.

Psalm 23 *page 367*

Reading *Matthew 9:18–26*

While Jesus was speaking, an official came forward, knelt down before him, and said, "My daughter has just died. But come, lay your hand on her, and she will live." Jesus rose and followed him, and so did his disciples. A woman suffering hemorrhages for twelve years came up behind him and touched the tassel on his cloak. She said to herself, "If only I can touch his cloak, I shall be cured." Jesus turned around and saw her, and said, "Courage, daughter! Your faith has saved you." And from that hour the woman was cured.

When Jesus arrived at the official's house and saw the flute players and the crowd who were making a commotion, he said, "Go away! The girl is not dead but sleeping." And they ridiculed him. When the crowd was put out, he came and took her by the hand, and the little girl arose. And news of this spread throughout all that land.

Reflection

People wanted to be near Jesus. Crowds followed him. We can imagine that in a world without modern medicine, people would be desperate to alleviate their suffering and the suffering of the people they loved. The healing Jesus offered also showed them that in the kingdom of God physical infirmity and even death is conquered forever. Because we do not yet experience the kingdom's fulfillment, we live in hope.

Prayers *others may be added*

Believing in the healing mercy of God, we offer to him our prayers:

℟. **Lord, hear our prayer.**

- For healing in the Church, we pray: ℟.
- For world leaders, that they may prioritize the health and safety of their people, we pray: ℟.
- For the sick, we pray: ℟.
- For an increase in hope, we pray: ℟.

Let us offer together the prayer that Jesus taught us.

Our Father . . .

Lord Jesus,
you brought healing to the people
you encountered as you walked
this earth.
Heal the world of its divisions
and people of their ills
so that all may be one.
Who live and reign for ever and ever.
Amen.

✤ In you, my God, I place my trust.

Tuesday, July 8, 2025

✚ In justice, I shall behold your face,
O Lord.

Psalm 34 *page 370*

Reading *Matthew 9:32–38*

A demoniac who could not speak was brought to Jesus, and when the demon was driven out the mute man spoke. The crowds were amazed and said, "Nothing like this has ever been seen in Israel." But the Pharisees said, "He drives out demons by the prince of demons."

Jesus went around to all the towns and villages, teaching in their synagogues, proclaiming the Gospel of the Kingdom, and curing every disease and illness. At the sight of the crowds, his heart was moved with pity for them because they were troubled and abandoned, like sheep without a shepherd. Then he said to his disciples, "The harvest is abundant but the laborers are few; so ask the master of the harvest to send out laborers for his harvest."

Reflection

Although most Catholics know that Jesus was both fully human and fully divine, the moments in the Gospel when he is moved by very human emotions are uniquely compelling. His emotions are reminders that Jesus was not God dressed up in a human suit. He sees the people, troubled and lacking guidance, and his heart is moved with pity. When we struggle, we might imagine that Jesus feels frustrated with our behavior. Yet we see instead that Jesus is merciful and compassionate toward us. We are loved and cared for no matter what we are facing.

Prayers *others may be added*

The Lord hears the cry of the poor
and so we pray:

℟. Lord, hear our prayer.

- For the Church, that through the guidance of the Holy Spirit she may be a refuge for all people, we pray: ℟.
- For unity and communion in our world today, we pray: ℟.
- For those facing uncertainty and confusion, we pray: ℟.
- For all people, that in moments of difficulty, they may turn to the Shepherd, who never stops seeking us, we pray: ℟.

Let us offer together the prayer
that Jesus taught us.

Our Father . . .

Loving Father,
you sent your Son into the world
so that we might share in the divine life
with you.
Shepherd us through this life
so we may serve you with
our whole hearts.
Through Christ our Lord.
Amen.

✚ In justice, I shall behold your face,
O Lord.

✤ Lord, let your mercy be on us,
as we place our trust in you.

Psalm 138

page 388

Reading

Matthew 10:1–7

Jesus summoned his Twelve disciples and gave them authority over unclean spirits to drive them out and to cure every disease and every illness. The names of the Twelve Apostles are these: first, Simon called Peter, and his brother Andrew; James, the son of Zebedee, and his brother John; Philip and Bartholomew, Thomas and Matthew the tax collector; James, the son of Alphaeus, and Thaddeus; Simon the Cananean, and Judas Iscariot who betrayed Jesus.

Jesus sent out these Twelve after instructing them thus, "Do not go into pagan territory or enter a Samaritan town. Go rather to the lost sheep of the house of Israel. As you go, make this proclamation: 'The Kingdom of heaven is at hand.'"

Reflection

Jesus commissions the Twelve to go out to the people of Israel healing the sick, driving out unclean spirits, and proclaiming the kingdom of God. And he calls each Christian to participate in his ministry. Some, like the Twelve, are ordained to serve the people of God. All the baptized are called to proclaim the kingdom of God and to serve others. Our call may change over the course of our life. Is Jesus calling you to something new? Imagine yourself among the Twelve, hearing his words: "Make this proclamation: 'The kingdom of heaven is at hand.'"

Prayers

others may be added

We bring our needs before God
as we pray:

℟. Lord, hear our prayer.

- For all bishops, priests, and deacons, we pray: ℟.
- For healing of the world's divisions, we pray: ℟.
- For everyone who is ill in mind, body, or spirit, we pray: ℟.
- For an increase in faith, hope, and love, we pray: ℟.

Let us offer together the prayer
that Jesus taught us.

Our Father . . .

Lord Jesus,
you sent your disciples into the world
to proclaim the kingdom of God
and to bring hope to all they encountered.
Hear our prayers and make us people of hope,
Who live and reign for ever and ever.
Amen.

✤ Lord, let your mercy be on us,
as we place our trust in you.

Thursday, July 10, 2025

✠ Remember the marvels the Lord has done.

Psalm 130

page 388

Reading

Matthew 10:7–15

Jesus said to his Apostles: "As you go, make this proclamation: 'The Kingdom of heaven is at hand.' Cure the sick, raise the dead, cleanse the lepers, drive out demons. Without cost you have received; without cost you are to give. Do not take gold or silver or copper for your belts; no sack for the journey, or a second tunic, or sandals, or walking stick. The laborer deserves his keep. Whatever town or village you enter, look for a worthy person in it, and stay there until you leave. As you enter a house, wish it peace. If the house is worthy, let your peace come upon it; if not, let your peace return to you. Whoever will not receive you or listen to your words—go outside that house or town and shake the dust from your feet. Amen, I say to you, it will be more tolerable for the land of Sodom and Gomorrah on the day of judgment than for that town."

Reflection

When the disciples set out without money or baggage they become totally dependent on God for everything they need. Paradoxically, the disciples are completely free, possibly for the first time. The disciples have received without cost and they are to give freely. They offer peace to everyone, leaving the question of each one's worthiness to God alone. We often think about independence as the source of freedom, especially political and financial independence. But true freedom comes only from God. Recognizing that we have no control over anything that happens outside of us, we stop trying to control the external world and turn to God as the ground of our hope.

Prayers

others may be added

We bring our needs before God
as we pray:

℟. **Lord, hear our prayer.**

- That the Holy Spirit will work through the Church, we pray: ℟.
- That the peace of Christ may fill the world, we pray: ℟.
- That those who are hungry or unhoused will have their basic needs met, we pray: ℟.
- That our faith will be increased and we may listen to God's guidance, we pray: ℟.

Let us offer together the prayer
that Jesus taught us.

Our Father . . .

Lord Jesus,
you invited the Twelve to trust
in the Father's goodness.
Help us to grow in faith that we may
serve you likewise.
Who live and reign for ever and ever.
Amen.

✠ Remember the marvels the Lord has done.

✣ The salvation of the just comes from the Lord.

Psalm 51 *page 373*

Reading *Matthew 10:16–23*

Jesus said to his Apostles: "Behold, I am sending you like sheep in the midst of wolves; so be shrewd as serpents and simple as doves. But beware of men, for they will hand you over to courts and scourge you in their synagogues, and you will be led before governors and kings for my sake as a witness before them and the pagans. When they hand you over, do not worry about how you are to speak or what you are to say. You will be given at that moment what you are to say. For it will not be you who speak but the Spirit of your Father speaking through you. Brother will hand over brother to death, and the father his child; children will rise up against parents and have them put to death. You will be hated by all because of my name, but whoever endures to the end will be saved. When they persecute you in one town, flee to another. Amen, I say to you, you will not finish the towns of Israel before the Son of Man comes."

Reflection

Jesus sends out his friends to spread the Good News with trust in God's care for them. This is not naivete. Jesus' instructions display a profound awareness of the difficulties that await them. The kingdom of God proclaimed by the prophets, a kindgom marked by peace, justice, beauty, truth, and love, faces opposition in our world. The kingdom of God is both present and not yet fully realized. What can we do as we await its fulfillment? How can we stand for the kingdom in a world hostile to its values?

Prayers *others may be added*

Called to take care of the lost,
we offer to the Lord our prayers:

℟. **Send us your Spirit, O Lord.**

- For the Church, as she proclaims the Gospel faithfully, we pray: ℟.
- For justice, peace, love, and compassion to fill the earth, we pray: ℟.
- For those facing religious persecution, we pray: ℟.
- For courage, that we may stand up for the truth, we pray: ℟.

Let us offer together the prayer
that Jesus taught us.

Our Father . . .

O Father,
you have filled the hungry
with good things
and you are mindful of our needs.
Grant us peace
and trust as we work to bring forth
the kingdom.
Through Christ our Lord.
Amen.

✣ The salvation of the just comes from the Lord.

Saturday, July 12, 2025

✤ Be glad you lowly ones;
may your hearts be glad!

Psalm 27 *page 368*

Reading *Matthew 10:24–33*

Jesus said to his Apostles: "No disciple is above his teacher, no slave above his master. It is enough for the disciple that he become like his teacher, for the slave that he become like his master. If they have called the master of the house Beelzebul, how much more those of his household!

"Therefore do not be afraid of them. Nothing is concealed that will not be revealed, nor secret that will not be known. What I say to you in the darkness, speak in the light; what you hear whispered, proclaim on the housetops. And do not be afraid of those who kill the body but cannot kill the soul; rather, be afraid of the one who can destroy both soul and body in Gehenna. Are not two sparrows sold for a small coin? Yet not one of them falls to the ground without your Father's knowledge. Even all the hairs of your head are counted. So do not be afraid; you are worth more than many sparrows. Everyone who acknowledges me before others I will acknowledge before my heavenly Father. But whoever denies me before others, I will deny before my heavenly Father."

Reflection

Anxiety and worry are prevalent in the world today. It is easy to see why: violence, poverty, and addiction are constantly in the news. People who live under conditions of uncertainty and stress can develop physical ailments and even have difficulty making important decisions because their brains are busy trying to survive. Jesus invites us to understand: You are beloved, whatever your external circumstances. The hairs of your head are counted. Rest in that belovedness. You need not do anything to earn the love of God.

Prayers *others may be added*

With confidence, we bring our hopes and needs before God as we pray:

℟. **Lord, hear our prayer.**

- For the Church, the Bride of Christ, we pray: ℟.
- For our leaders, that they may create conditions for people to live in peace, we pray: ℟.
- For all who struggle with depression and anxiety, we pray: ℟.
- For rest in God's love for us, we pray: ℟.

Let us offer together the prayer that Jesus taught us.

Our Father . . .

Father,
your love and care for us knows
no limits.
Help us to listen to your words when
you say:
Do not be afraid.
May we follow you with our
whole heart.
Through Christ our Lord.
Amen.

✤ Be glad you lowly ones;
may your hearts be glad!

✤ I shall be filled with the vision
of your glory.

Psalm 122

page 387

Reading

Luke 10:29–37

[The scholar of the Law] said to Jesus, "And who is my neighbor?" Jesus replied, "A man fell victim to robbers as he went down from Jerusalem to Jericho. They stripped and beat him and went off leaving him half-dead. A priest happened to be going down that road, but when he saw him, he passed by on the opposite side. Likewise a Levite came to the place, and when he saw him, he passed by on the opposite side. But a Samaritan traveler who came upon him was moved with compassion at the sight. He approached the victim, poured oil and wine over his wounds and bandaged them. Then he lifted him up on his own animal, took him to an inn, and cared for him. The next day he took out two silver coins and gave them to the innkeeper with the instruction, 'Take care of him. If you spend more than what I have given you, I shall repay you on my way back.' Which of these three, in your opinion, was neighbor to the robbers' victim?" He answered, "The one who treated him with mercy." Jesus said to him, "Go and do likewise."

Reflection

Who is my neighbor? The question that prompts the famous parable of the good Samaritan can often be lost on us in our divided society and, sadly, even in our Church. Remembering that Jews and Samaritans would not eat together or share objects in common may help us to envision the people in our society Jesus might have called "good" if he were addressing the parable to us. Who might I refuse to eat with? Who would I not want to touch? Why? Each human being is a beloved child of God. Our call to love is not limited to those who love us. We must see as Jesus sees and love as Jesus loves.

Prayers

others may be added

With hope, we bring our needs before God who first loved us, as we pray

℟. **Lord, hear our prayer.**

- For unity among the people of God, we pray: ℟.
- For peace and reconciliation in the world's conflict zones, we pray: ℟.
- For victims of violence and those who care for them, we pray: ℟.
- That we might love like Jesus, we pray: ℟.

Let us offer together the prayer that Jesus taught us.

Our Father . . .

Loving God,
you teach us that the greatest path
is the one that is guided by love.
Help us love when it is difficult.
Give us the gift of seeing each person
as your beloved child.
Through Christ our Lord.
Amen.

✤ I shall be filled with the vision
of your glory.

Memorial of St. Kateri Tekakwitha, Virgin

Monday, July 14, 2025

✤ Our help is in the name of the Lord.

Psalm 24 *page 367*

Reading *Exodus 1:8–14, 22*

A new king, who knew nothing of Joseph, came to power in Egypt. He said to his subjects, "Look how numerous and powerful the people of the children of Israel are growing, more so than we ourselves! Come, let us deal shrewdly with them to stop their increase; otherwise, in time of war they too may join our enemies to fight against us, and so leave our country."

Accordingly, taskmasters were set over the children of Israel to oppress them with forced labor. Thus they had to build for Pharaoh the supply cities of Pithom and Raamses. Yet the more they were oppressed, the more they multiplied and spread. The Egyptians, then, dreaded the children of Israel and reduced them to cruel slavery, making life bitter for them with hard work in mortar and brick and all kinds of field work—the whole cruel fate of slaves.

Pharaoh then commanded all his subjects, "Throw into the river every boy that is born to the Hebrews, but you may let all the girls live."

Reflection

What must it have been like for the people of Israel when the new pharaoh came to power? The Egyptians felt threatened by the increased population that might upset the balance of power. Tragically, regime change can come with violent oppression in the contemporary world as well. As you reflect on the experience of the Israelites in Egypt—forced labor, cruel slavery, and victims of genocide—consider who in our world faces this type of oppression. How might you look upon these people as your neighbor?

Prayers *others may be added*

We bring our hopes and needs before God, as we pray:

℟. Lord, hear our prayer.

- For a Church that speaks the truth of God, we pray: ℟.
- For world leaders, that they may protect and promote human rights, especially among minority groups, we pray: ℟.
- For all the oppressed and those forced to flee from oppression, that they may experience true freedom, we pray: ℟.
- For growth in love and compassion, we pray: ℟.

Let us offer together the prayer that Jesus taught us.

Our Father . . .

O God,
you guide your people in every age,
walking with us from slavery
to freedom.
Be with us as we carry the light
of your presence
to the world's darkest places.
Through Christ our Lord.
Amen.

✤ Our help is in the name of the Lord.

✤ Turn to the Lord in your need,
and you will live.

Psalm 27

page 368

Reading

Exodus 2:5–10

Pharaoh's daughter came down to the river to bathe, while her maids walked along the river bank. Noticing the basket among the reeds, she sent her handmaid to fetch it. On opening it, she looked, and lo, there was a baby boy, crying! She was moved with pity for him and said, "It is one of the Hebrews' children." Then his sister asked Pharaoh's daughter, "Shall I go and call one of the Hebrew women to nurse the child for you?" "Yes, do so," she answered. So the maiden went and called the child's own mother. Pharaoh's daughter said to her, "Take this child and nurse it for me, and I will repay you." The woman therefore took the child and nursed it. When the child grew, she brought him to Pharaoh's daughter, who adopted him as her son and called him Moses; for she said, "I drew him out of the water."

Reflection

The women whose story begins the Book of Exodus have much courage. The law says Hebrew baby boys must be murdered at birth, but the midwives defy it. Moses' mother hides him. She does not throw him into the river as authority demands but makes for him a little ark to float in. Pharaoh's daughter finds him and even though she knows he is a Hebrew baby she adopts him rather than comply with the law. Moses' sister arranges for the baby's mother to be paid to be his wet nurse. Moses' life begins with a series of women standing up for his life. What a beautiful example of women standing together on the side of the most vulnerable and protecting human life!

Prayers

others may be added

Called to protect all life, we turn
to the Lord with our needs:

℟. **Lord, hear our prayer.**

- For the Church's pro-life witness,
we pray: ℟.
- For our leaders, that they will protect
society's most vulnerable members,
we pray: ℟.
- For women who are facing unplanned
pregnancies, we pray: ℟.
- For all to grow in love and service,
especially the most vulnerable,
we pray: ℟.

Let us offer together the prayer
that Jesus taught us.

Our Father . . .

Loving God,
you prepared Moses
from his youngest days
that he might lead the people
from slavery to freedom.
Protect all vulnerable children
from harm.
Be with us as we walk in freedom
and journey to eternal life.
Through Christ our Lord.
Amen.

✤ Turn to the Lord in your need,
and you will live.

Weekday

Wednesday, July 16, 2025

✤ The Lord is kind and merciful.

Psalm 30

page 369

Reading

Exodus 3:1–6, 9–10

Moses was tending the flock of his father-in-law Jethro, the priest of Midian. Leading the flock across the desert, he came to Horeb, the mountain of God. There an angel of the LORD appeared to him in fire flaming out of a bush. As he looked on, he was surprised to see that the bush, though on fire, was not consumed. So Moses decided, "I must go over to look at this remarkable sight, and see why the bush is not burned."

When the LORD saw him coming over to look at it more closely, God called out to him from the bush, "Moses! Moses!" He answered, "Here I am." God said, "Come no nearer! Remove the sandals from your feet, for the place where you stand is holy ground. I am the God of your father," he continued, "the God of Abraham, the God of Isaac, the God of Jacob. The cry of the children of Israel has reached me, and I have truly noted that the Egyptians are oppressing them. Come, now! I will send you to Pharaoh to lead my people, the children of Israel, out of Egypt."

Reflection

"Remove the sandals from your feet, for the place where you stand is holy ground!" Imagine Moses, caring for his father-in-law's sheep, having what was probably a typical day. He sees a fire that burns but does not consume, and then hears a voice calling out to him. What must that have been like? He is called out of his ordinary life to an extraordinary mission: to lead the people of Israel from slavery and to be a great prophet. His mission begins with an act of reverence and humility. God calls ordinary people to do extraordinary things with reverence and humility.

Prayers

others may be added

With wonder at your care for us,
we turn to you, O Lord, as we pray:

℟. **Lord, hear our prayer.**

- For the Church, that she may be strengthened in her witness to the God of Abraham, Isaac, and Jacob, we pray: ℟.
- For religious freedom across the globe, we pray: ℟.
- For victims of violence and oppression, we pray: ℟.
- For an increase in respect toward life and human dignity, we pray: ℟.

Let us offer together the prayer
that Jesus taught us.

Our Father . . .

Loving Father,
you revealed yourself to Moses
in the burning bush.
Show us your face throughout
the journey of our lives,
that we may remember to remove
our shoes
as we walk on the holy ground you have
created for us.
Through Christ our Lord.
Amen.

✤ The Lord is kind and merciful.

✚ The Lord remembers his covenant for ever.

Psalm 51

page 373

Reading

Exodus 3:13–15

Moses, hearing the voice of the LORD from the burning bush, said to him, "When I go to the children of Israel and say to them, 'The God of your fathers has sent me to you,' if they ask me, 'What is his name?' what am I to tell them?" God replied, "I am who am." Then he added, "This is what you shall tell the children of Israel: I AM sent me to you."

God spoke further to Moses, "Thus shall you say to the children of Israel: The LORD, the God of your fathers, the God of Abraham, the God of Isaac, the God of Jacob, has sent me to you."

Reflection

Having received God's call, Moses asks a practical question: Who should I say has sent me? In this moment, God reveals the divine name to Moses. The name is a bit of a puzzle, like the Mystery it describes. Often translated as "I am," or "I am who am," it has a sense of eternal beingness. It is the holiest name for God and is not pronounced by most Jewish people out of respect for its transcendence. People often use the word *god* very casually. The name that is revered and unable to be fully comprehended reminds us that God is ultimately a mystery whom we can encounter but never grasp.

Prayers

others may be added

Hear the prayers of your people, Lord, as we pray: .

℟. Lord, hear our prayer.

- That the baptized may seek the knowledge of God with both mind and heart, we pray: ℟.
- That those who carry heavy burdens of disease, hunger, and oppression may know justice and peace, we pray: ℟.
- That all who teach the faith may be filled with wisdom and understanding, we pray: ℟.
- That those who have died may find rest in God, we pray: ℟.

Let us offer together the prayer that Jesus taught us.

Our Father . . .

Father,
in your care for your people,
you called Moses to lead them from
slavery to freedom.
Hear our own cries for justice
and compassion.
Change our hearts that we might be
ready to answer your call.
Through Christ our Lord.
Amen.

✚ The Lord remembers his covenant for ever.

Friday, July 18, 2025

✤ I will take the cup of salvation,
and call on the name of the Lord.

Psalm 34 *page 370*

Reading *Exodus 12:11–14*

"This is how you are to eat [the lamb]: with your loins girt, sandals on your feet and your staff in hand, you shall eat like those who are in flight. It is the Passover of the LORD. For on this same night I will go through Egypt, striking down every first born of the land, both man and beasts, and executing judgment on all the gods of Egypt—I, the LORD! But the blood will mark the houses where you are. Seeing the blood, I will pass over you; thus, when I strike the land of Egypt, no destructive blow will come upon you.

"This day shall be a memorial feast for you, which all your generations shall celebrate with pilgrimage to the LORD, as a perpetual institution."

Reflection

The Exodus is the defining moment for the Jewish people. It is celebrated today just as it has been for thousands of years. The Jewish people were oppressed, enslaved, and victims of genocide. God delivered them. God made them free. The Passover makes this moment present for the generations so that they too might experience God's saving care for the people. The Last Supper was a Passover meal, a moment that becomes present for us during every Mass. We are invited to experience God's saving love. We are given a gift: the freedom of the children of God

Prayers *others may be added*

O Lord, come to the aid of a world in need. Hear us, as we pray:

℟. Lord, hear our prayer.

- For the Church's Eucharistic mission, we pray: ℟.
- For an end to political oppression, we pray: ℟.
- For refugees, we pray: ℟.
- For growth in gratitude, we pray: ℟.
- For the service of God and neighbor, we pray: ℟.

Let us offer together the prayer
that Jesus taught us.

Our Father . . .

God of the covenant,
you led the Hebrew people out of
slavery in Egypt.
Free us from whatever separates us
from your love
so that we may know, love, and serve
you with all our hearts.
Through Christ our Lord.
Amen.

✤ I will take the cup of salvation,
and call on the name of the Lord.

✚ His mercy endures for ever.

Psalm 23 *page 367*

Reading *Exodus 12:37–42*

The children of Israel set out from Rameses for Succoth, about six hundred thousand men on foot, not counting the little ones. A crowd of mixed ancestry also went up with them, besides their livestock, very numerous flocks and herds. Since the dough they had brought out of Egypt was not leavened, they baked it into unleavened loaves. They had rushed out of Egypt and had no opportunity even to prepare food for the journey.

The time the children of Israel had stayed in Egypt was four hundred and thirty years. At the end of four hundred and thirty years, all the hosts of the LORD left the land of Egypt on this very date. This was a night of vigil for the LORD, as he led them out of the land of Egypt; so on this same night all the children of Israel must keep a vigil for the LORD throughout their generations.

Reflection

What would you do if you had to leave your home very quickly? The Jewish people were in such a rush that they did not have time to prepare food—even knowing that they were traveling into the desert and away from the rich Nile valley. They did not have time to let their bread rise, and so they baked it without leaven. Consider the urgency of their need. When we receive the Eucharist, the unleavened bread transformed into the Body of Christ, do we experience anything similar? How do we experience God responding to our deepest needs?

Prayers *others may be added*

Let us bring our needs before our God, who listens to the cries of his people:

℟. **Lord, hear our prayer.**

- For the Church, the People of God, we pray: ℟.
- For peace in our world and an end to violence and oppression, we pray: ℟.
- For all who are hungry, that they may receive an abundance of good food, we pray: ℟.
- For all peoples, that they may conform their lives ever more closely to Christ, we pray: ℟.

Let us offer together the prayer
that Jesus taught us.

Our Father . . .

God of the hungry,
you have given your people an
abundance of gifts,
calling them out of slavery and into
the freedom of the children of God.
Make us free from all that is binding
so that we may love and serve you.
Through Christ our Lord.
Amen.

✚ His mercy endures for ever.

Sunday, July 20, 2025

✤ The Lord sustains my soul.

Psalm 46

page 372

Reading

Luke 10:38–42

Jesus entered a village where a woman whose name was Martha welcomed him. She had a sister named Mary who sat beside the Lord at his feet listening to him speak. Martha, burdened with much serving, came to him and said, "Lord, do you not care that my sister has left me by myself to do the serving? Tell her to help me." The Lord said to her in reply, "Martha, Martha, you are anxious and worried about many things. There is need of only one thing. Mary has chosen the better part and it will not be taken from her."

Reflection

Martha and Mary welcomed Jesus into their home many times. Mary spends the time enjoying being with Jesus. Martha becomes frustrated in a relatable way. She is aware that she has taken on all the burdens of hosting. Yet Jesus—the same Jesus who says that the greatest is the one who serves—does not take her side. Could he be saying that service and hospitality have no value? No. He tells Martha that her anxiety and worry over practical concerns are unneeded. Martha can be free. She can be in the moment, enjoying the gift of Jesus' presence.

Prayers

others may be added

Confident in God's care for us,
we turn to him in prayer:

℟. Lord, graciously hear us.

- For the Church, contemplative and humbly serving, we pray: ℟.
- For an increased respect for human dignity across the world, we pray: ℟.
- For anyone lacking life's basic necessities, that they might receive hospitality and care, we pray: ℟.
- That we might grow in contemplation of your goodness, we pray: ℟.

Let us offer together the prayer
that Jesus taught us.

Our Father . . .

Lord Jesus,
you teach us that contemplation
  is the better part.
Help us to release our worries.
Guide us along the path of discipleship
as we reflect on things in our hearts.
Who live and reign for ever and ever.
Amen.

✤ The Lord sustains my soul.

✚ Let us sing to the Lord; he has covered himself in glory.

Psalm 47

page 372

Reading

Exodus 14:15–18

Then the LORD said to Moses, "Why are you crying out to me? Tell the children of Israel to go forward. And you, lift up your staff and, with hand outstretched over the sea, split the sea in two, that the children of Israel may pass through it on dry land. But I will make the Egyptians so obstinate that they will go in after them. Then I will receive glory through Pharaoh and all his army, his chariots and charioteers. The Egyptians shall know that I am the LORD, when I receive glory through Pharaoh and his chariots and charioteers."

Reflection

God has heard the cry of the Israelites in Egypt, but their struggle is not over. The Egyptian army pursues the Jewish people out of Egypt, and the Red Sea bars their path. They are trapped. In an impossible predicament, they look for someone to blame: Moses. Moses tells them not to fear! These words, spoken in what must have been a moment of pure terror, seem absurd. Yet they had no need to fear. God was fighting for them, opening a way where there was no way. God is there with them in their time of need. They need not fear because they are not alone.

Prayers

others may be added

We turn to you, O, Lord, in our need, as we pray:

℟. Lord, hear our prayer..

- For Church leaders, that they may be unafraid in the face of difficulties, we pray: ℟.
- For government leaders, that they may hold peace and justice in esteem, we pray: ℟.
- For all who live in fear of violence, we pray: ℟.
- For us, that we we might grow in faith, confident in God's abiding presence, we pray: ℟.

Let us offer together the prayer that Jesus taught us.

Our Father . . .

Loving God,
you brought the Israelites safely
through the Red Sea,
giving the gift of freedom,
and protecting them with
your presence.
Open a path of freedom from our fears.
Abide with us that we might live
in your presence.
Through Christ our Lord.
Amen.

✚ Let us sing to the Lord; he has covered himself in glory.

Tuesday, July 22, 2025

✚ Let us sing to the Lord.

Psalm 71

page 376

Reading

John 20:1–2

On the first day of the week, Mary Magdalene came to the tomb early in the morning, while it was still dark, and saw the stone removed from the tomb. So she ran and went to Simon Peter and to the other disciple whom Jesus loved, and told them, "They have taken the Lord from the tomb, and we don't know where they put him."

Reflection

Mary Magdalene does not recognize the risen Christ until he says her name: Mary. What must she have been feeling when Jesus spoke to her? How did that one word change everything? Mary Magdalene recognized his voice and followed him. She became the apostle to the apostles: the first to encounter the risen Christ and proclaim the Good News of the resurrection. Every disciple of the Lord seeks him. Like Mary Magdalene, we might not know whom we are looking for, but when we recognize Jesus, we are transformed, going out, as Mary Magdalene did, to proclaim him.

Prayers

others may be added

With St. Mary Magdalene, we seek you, O Lord. Hear us, as we pray:

℟. Lord, hear our prayer.

- For the missionary Church, proclaiming the Good News, we pray: ℟.
- For peace among the nations, we pray: ℟.
- For all who grieve, that they might be consoled, we pray: ℟.
- For us, that we might become more attentive to your call and respond joyfully, we pray: ℟.

Let us offer together the prayer that Jesus taught us.

Our Father . . .

Loving God,
you called Mary Magdalene to announce
the resurrection.
Hear the prayers of your family
and make us witnesses of
the Good News,
so that your light might fill the world
as water fills the sea.
Through Christ our Lord.
Amen.

✚ Let us sing to the Lord.

✤ The Lord gave them bread
from heaven.

Psalm 62

page 374

Reading

Exodus 16: 4–5

Then the LORD said to Moses, "I will now rain down bread from heaven for you. Each day the people are to go out and gather their daily portion; thus will I test them, to see whether they follow my instructions or not. On the sixth day, however, when they prepare what they bring in, let it be twice as much as they gather on the other days."

Reflection

The bread from heaven is a gift from God to sustain the Israelites on their journey in the desert. God has made them free, yet the people do not trust God, crying out that they would have preferred abundance and slavery to uncertainty and freedom. The manna is a school of trust for the people. Day by day, the people accept the gift, trusting in God's continued care for them. This daily bread provides everything that they need. There is no need to squirrel things away. God provides for the people.

Prayers

others may be added

With trust, we turn to you, O Lord,
as we pray

℟. **Lord, save your people.**

- For the Church, confident in God's providence, we pray: ℟.
- For world leaders, that they may promote the common good, we pray: ℟.
- For all who are hungry, we pray: ℟.
- For an increase in faith, we pray: ℟.

Let us offer together the prayer
that Jesus taught us.

Our Father . . .

Risen Lord,
you gave the gift of bread from heaven
to your people
as they wandered the desert from
slavery to freedom.
Give us the grace to trust in your
providence
and help us to receive with reverence
the Bread of Heaven, the Body and
Blood of Christ.
Who lives and reigns for ever and ever.
Amen.

✤ The Lord gave them bread
from heaven.

Thursday, July 24, 2025

✤ Glory and praise for ever!

Psalm 63

page 375

Reading

Matthew 13:10–13

The disciples approached Jesus and said, "Why do you speak to the crowd in parables?" He said to them in reply, "Because knowledge of the mysteries of the Kingdom of heaven has been granted to you, but to them it has not been granted. To anyone who has, more will be given and he will grow rich; from anyone who has not, even what he has will be taken away. This is why I speak to them in parables, because / *they look but do not see and hear but do not listen or understand.*

Reflection

When we wonder about the big questions in life, we might want shortcuts to finding peace, happiness, and fulfillment. Teachers who tell us there are quick and easy ways to a life well-lived appeal to us, even if their words do not ultimately satisfy. Jesus' disciples seem to have hoped he might be more direct with his instruction. Jesus says: these parables, which use something familiar to ponder something unknowable, are things to experience and reflect upon. A direct statement can be assimilated or discarded. The parables grow with us, helping us to greater understanding about the Mystery that is at the center of all reality.

Prayers

others may be added

O Lord, you know us better than we know ourselves. Look with favor on us as we pray:

℟. Show us your face, O Lord.

- For the Church, wondering together about the Mystery of God, we pray: ℟.
- For wisdom among world leaders, we pray: ℟.
- For those who are poor, marginalized, and hopeless, we pray: ℟.
- For our continuing conversion to Christ, we pray: ℟.

Let us offer together the prayer that Jesus taught us.

Our Father . . .

Lord Jesus,
you invite us to contemplation,
meditating upon the mysteries
of our faith.
Be with us in our wondering,
that we might always grow closer to you
in every word and action.
Who live and reign for ever and ever.
Amen.

✤ Glory and praise for ever!

✤ The Lord will guard us as a shepherd guards his flock.

Psalm 67

page 375

Reading

Matthew 20:20–28

The mother of the sons of Zebedee approached Jesus with her sons and did him homage, wishing to ask him for something. He said to her, "What do you wish?" She answered him, "Command that these two sons of mine sit, one at your right and the other at your left, in your Kingdom." Jesus said in reply, "You do not know what you are asking. Can you drink the chalice that I am going to drink?" They said to him, "We can." He replied, "My chalice you will indeed drink, but to sit at my right and at my left, this is not mine to give but is for those for whom it has been prepared by my Father." When the ten heard this, they became indignant at the two brothers. But Jesus summoned them and said, "You know that the rulers of the Gentiles lord it over them, and the great ones make their authority over them felt. But it shall not be so among you. Rather, whoever wishes to be great among you shall be your servant; whoever wishes to be first among you shall be your slave. Just so, the Son of Man did not come to be served but to serve and to give his life as a ransom for many."

Reflection

What gives a person esteem in our culture? Whom do we admire? What do we find impressive? People spend a lot of time and energy managing their reputations and seeking after status. At the end of our lives, will we be satisfied by this type of striving? Jesus says that one who is first is the one who makes him (or her) self the slave of all. This is how we imitate Jesus, who came "not to be served, but to serve."

Prayers

others may be added

Let us bring our needs before God, the one who loves us with everlasting love, as we pray:

℟. **Lord, hear our prayer..**

- For the Church, humbly serving in imitation of the Lord, we pray: ℟.
- For world leaders, that they may embrace their role as servant, we pray: ℟.
- For all whose freedom is restricted by authoritarian regimes, we pray: ℟.
- For growth in our service of others, we pray: ℟.

Let us offer together the prayer that Jesus taught us.

Our Father . . .

Lord Jesus,
you teach us to love as you love
and to offer our lives as a gift.
Give us the gift of your presence
that we might learn to love as you do.
Who live and reign for ever and ever.
Amen.

✤ The Lord will guard us as a shepherd guards his flock.

Memorial of Sts. Joachim and Anne,
Parents of the Blessed Virgin Mary
Saturday, July 26, 2025

✣ Offer to God a sacrifice of praise.

Psalm 84 *page 378*

Reading *Matthew 13:16–17*

Jesus said to his disciples: "Blessed are your eyes, because they see, and your ears, because they hear. Amen, I say to you, many prophets and righteous people longed to see what you see but did not see it, and to hear what you hear but did not hear it."

Reflection

Jesus reminds us that the gift of faith is not ours due to merit but rather faith is pure gift. God always loves us first. God gives us the gift of being able to hear and understand the Word proclaimed. We can be tempted to think of ourselves as superior to unbelievers. To do so is to forget the tremendous gift we have received from God: encountering Jesus and believing. Rather than judging those who do not believe, we can thank God for the gift of self-revelation that has come to us: Jesus.

Prayers *others may be added*

O Lord, who loved us first, we turn to you in our need as we pray:

℟. **Lord, hear our prayer. .**

- For the Church's mission of evangelization, we pray: ℟.
- For peace and justice to be the highest value for all nations, we pray: ℟.
- For all who are ill in mind, body, or spirit, we pray: ℟.
- For an increase in faith, we pray: ℟.

Let us offer together the prayer that Jesus taught us.

Our Father . . .

Risen Lord,
you give us the gift of yourself
in the Eucharist.
Transform our hearts that we may
carry your hope to a world in need.
Who live and reign for ever and ever.
Amen.

✣ Offer to God a sacrifice of praise.

✚ God . . . unites those who dwell in his house.

Psalm 85 *page 379*

Reading *Luke 11:9–13*

[Jesus said:] “And I tell you, ask and you will receive; seek and you will find; knock and the door will be opened to you. For everyone who asks, receives; and the one who seeks, finds; and to the one who knocks, the door will be opened. What father among you would hand his son a snake when he asks for a fish? Or hand him a scorpion when he asks for an egg? If you then, who are wicked, know how to give good gifts to your children, how much more will the Father in heaven give the Holy Spirit to those who ask him?”

Reflection

Sometimes we turn to God from a place of our deepest longing and become frustrated when we do not receive an immediate response, especially the response we think we ought to receive. Jesus encourages us to have trust in providence grounded in God’s goodness and love. Moreover, he encourages us to be persistent in prayer, giving over our greatest concerns to God, the giver of every great gift. This is not easy. We want what we want when we want it. Entrusting ourselves to God, who knows us better than we know ourselves, is a moment of surrender, trusting that God is able to transform whatever we are struggling with through the gift of God’s own presence with us.

Prayers *others may be added*

Hear us, Lord. We knock on your door with our hopes and needs as we pray:

℟. Lord, hear our prayer.

- For the Church, the People of God, we pray: ℟.
- For the peace of Christ to spread through all the world and heal the most intractable conflicts, we pray: ℟.
- For all people whose basic needs are not met, we pray: ℟.
- For persistence in prayer, we pray: ℟.

Let us offer together the prayer that Jesus taught us.

Our Father . . .

Father of encouragement,
your care for us surpasses our understanding.
Your love provides us with every great gift.
Help us to turn to you in our need and express our gratitude,
for all things are possible with you.
Through Christ our Lord.
Amen.

✚ God . . . unites those who dwell in his house.

Monday, July 28, 2025

✠ Give thanks to the Lord,
for he is good.

Psalm 91 *page 379*

Reading *Matthew 13:31–35*

Jesus proposed a parable to the crowds. “The Kingdom of heaven is like a mustard seed that a person took and sowed in a field. It is the smallest of all the seeds, yet when full-grown it is the largest of plants. It becomes a large bush, and the *birds of the sky come and dwell in its branches.*”

He spoke to them another parable. “The Kingdom of heaven is like yeast that a woman took and mixed with three measures of wheat flour until the whole batch was leavened.”

All these things Jesus spoke to the crowds in parables. He spoke to them only in parables, to fulfill what had been said through the prophet: / *I will open my mouth in parables, / I will announce what has lain hidden from the foundation of the world.*

Reflection

People love to understand how things work. Sometimes, a deepened understanding of “how” can decrease our awe. Yet, no matter how well we understand the mechanisms of seeds, watching a sprout emerge from a seed coat and a root drop into the soil is always a wonder. Watching dough rise always feels a little like magic. Jesus’ parables of growth and transformation, teaching about the kingdom of God through comparison with things familiar to us, are captivating in their simplicity and profundity, much like mustard seeds and yeast themselves. Jesus says this is what the kingdom of God is like.

Prayers *others may be added*

Sowing the seeds of faith, we turn to the Lord with the needs of our world:

℟. Be with us, O Lord.

- For the Church, proclaiming God’s power and love, we pray: ℟.
- For justice and mercy to govern our world, we pray: ℟.
- For the most vulnerable among us, especially those who are poor, those who aer sick, and the unborn, we pray: ℟.
- For all peoples, that they might experience the transformative power of God, we pray: ℟.

Let us offer together the prayer
that Jesus taught us.

Our Father . . .

Father,
you give us an abundance of gifts,
showing your power in the tiniest seeds
and the rising of dough.
Help us to recognize your kingdom at
hand wherever it may be found.
Through Christ our Lord.
Amen.

✠ Give thanks to the Lord,
for he is good.

✤ The Lord is kind and merciful.

Psalm 95

page 380

Reading

John 11:19–27

Many of the Jews had come to Martha and Mary to comfort them about their brother [Lazarus, who had died]. When Martha heard that Jesus was coming, she went to meet him; but Mary sat at home. Martha said to Jesus, "Lord, if you had been here, my brother would not have died. But even now I know that whatever you ask of God, God will give you." Jesus said to her, "Your brother will rise." Martha said to him, "I know he will rise, in the resurrection on the last day." Jesus told her, "I am the resurrection and the life; whoever believes in me, even if he dies, will live, and anyone who lives and believes in me will never die. Do you believe this?" She said to him, "Yes, Lord. I have come to believe that you are the Christ, the Son of God, the one who is coming into the world."

Reflection

Martha does not hide from Jesus the distress she is feeling. Many of us feel like we have to suppress powerful emotions to make the people around us feel more comfortable. Jesus does not require that of Martha or of anyone. Martha's faith is sturdy, and yet she is profoundly sorrowful, and even disappointed. Many of us have felt this way when we are grieving. Why didn't we receive a miracle? Jesus brings about a transformation that exceeds anything Martha could have expected. But Jesus also allows her to grieve and he grieves too, weeping for Lazarus. He enters into that place of separation and darkness with us and in so doing, he transforms it.

Prayers

others may be added

In hope, we turn to you, O God,
as we pray:

℟. **Lord, hear our prayer.**

- That all the baptized may give witness to the resurrection with their lives, we pray: ℟.
- That world leaders govern with greater respect for human rights and human dignity, we pray: ℟.
- That everyone who is grieving may receive consolation, we pray: ℟.
- That we may grow in hope, we pray: ℟.

Let us offer together the prayer
that Jesus taught us.

Our Father . . .

Lord Jesus,
you are the resurrection and the life,
the ground of all our hope.
Come into the darkest places of a world
in need and into our hearts,
so that, enlightened, we may carry
your light to all people.
Who live and reign for ever and ever.
Amen.

✤ The Lord is kind and merciful.

Wednesday, July 30, 2025

✤ Holy is the Lord our God.

Psalm 98

page 381

Reading

Matthew 13: 44–46

Jesus said to his disciples: "The Kingdom of heaven is like a treasure buried in a field, which a person finds and hides again, and out of joy goes and sells all that he has and buys that field. Again, the Kingdom of heaven is like a merchant searching for fine pearls. When he finds a pearl of great price, he goes and sells all that he has and buys it."

Reflection

There is something hidden about the kingdom, as we see in these two brief parables. It is a treasure buried in a field—that a person hides again and purchases, almost by stealth. It is a pearl, hidden until the diver brings it to light, with great danger and risk. The kingdom is also all-encompassing—it will cost us everything we own to take hold of it. What do they feel, those who find this treasure, and joyfully sacrifice all they have to obtain it? In the words of the hymn of St. Bernard of Clairvaux, "To those who ask how kind thou art, / How good to those who seek! / But what to those who find? Ah, this / Nor tongue nor pen can show; / The love of Jesus, what it is / None but his loved ones know" (translated by E. Caswall; public domain). Yes, the kingdom is a treasure and a mystery.

Prayers

others may be added

We come before you, O Lord,
with our prayers:

℟. **Lord, hear our prayer.**

- For the ordained and lay ministers who proclaim the Good News, we pray: ℟.
- For an end to war and conflict in our world, we pray: ℟.
- For those who endure religious persecution, we pray: ℟.
- For us, that we might never count the cost of the Good News, we pray: ℟.

Let us offer together the prayer
that Jesus taught us.

Our Father . . .

Lord Jesus,
you offer us the gift of parables
that we might enter ever more into
your mysteries.
Help us to love without counting
the cost,
and to appreciate the gift of yourself,
you, who are the greatest of
all treasures.
Who live and reign for ever and ever.
Amen.

✤ Holy is the Lord our God.

✚ How lovely is your dwelling place,
O Lord.

Psalm 103 *page 382*

Reading *Matthew 13:47–53*

Jesus said to the disciples: "The Kingdom of heaven is like a net thrown into the sea, which collects fish of every kind. When it is full they haul it ashore and sit down to put what is good into buckets. What is bad they throw away. Thus it will be at the end of the age. The angels will go out and separate the wicked from the righteous and throw them into the fiery furnace, where there will be wailing and grinding of teeth."

"Do you understand all these things?" They answered, "Yes." And he replied, "Then every scribe who has been instructed in the Kingdom of heaven is like the head of a household who brings from his storeroom both the new and the old." When Jesus finished these parables, he went away from there.

Reflection

Good people become ill and die young. Others harm people and thrive. People have longed for divine justice to redress what the world deals out seemingly at random. Yet modern people feel squeamish about discussing God's judgment at the end of time. It may be a good thing. Only God knows the heart. No one is perfect and our value is not based on the worst thing we have ever done. We need not judge others' worthiness. The net collects many types of fish. The sorting is for hands other than ours. We do what we can with the circumstances we are given. We ask God for mercy when we fail. We do our best to live out the greatest commandment: love.

Prayers *others may be added*

With confidence in God's care for us
let us bring our needs before him:

℟. Lord, hear our prayer.

✦ For the missionary Church,
we pray: ℟.

✦ For world leaders to govern with
justice, we pray: ℟.

✦ For those who are sick, their
caregivers, and the people who love
them, we pray: ℟.

✦ For an openness to respond to God's
call in our lives, we pray: ℟.

Let us offer together the prayer
that Jesus taught us.

Our Father . . .

Lord Jesus,
you cast a wide net,
calling all people to yourself
that we may be one.
Change our hearts
that we may live in the freedom
of the children of God
Loving as you love
and serving as you serve.
Who live and reign for ever and ever.
Amen.

✚ How lovely is your dwelling place,
O Lord.

Memorial of St. Alphonsus Liguori,
Bishop and Doctor of the Church
Friday, August 1, 2025

✚ Sing with joy to God our help.

Psalm 115 *page 385*

Reading *Matthew 13:54–58*

Jesus came to his native place and taught the people in their synagogue. They were astonished and said, "Where did this man get such wisdom and mighty deeds? Is he not the carpenter's son? Is not his mother named Mary and his brothers James, Joseph, Simon, and Judas? Are not his sisters all with us? Where did this man get all this?" And they took offense at him. But Jesus said to them, "A prophet is not without honor except in his native place and in his own house." And he did not work many mighty deeds there because of their lack of faith.

Reflection

Many people have wondered about Jesus' life between the time he was lost in the temple and the beginning of his public ministry. These events are not recorded for us in Scripture. It was obviously difficult for the people who knew him as a child and a young man to align their perception of him with his preaching, teaching, and healing. Our previous experiences can make it difficult to see the truth even when it is right before our eyes. What might it have been like for the people around Jesus if they had let curiosity guide them? How might that curiosity have opened them up to encounter the Son of God?

Prayers *others may be added*

O Lord, we turn to you as we pray:

℟. **Open our hearts, Lord.**

- For the Holy Spirit's guidance in the Church, we pray: ℟.
- For the promotion of human rights and dignity across the world, we pray: ℟.
- For all those who lack food, shelter, and clean water, we pray: ℟.
- For all peoples, that we might see your face in our neighbor in need, we pray: ℟.

Let us offer together the prayer that Jesus taught us.

Our Father . . .

O Lord,
you came into the world
to share your life with us.
Help us to recognize you
in the people we meet,
especially those who are
most vulnerable
and in need of care,
that we may be your hands
and feet in the world.
Through Christ our Lord.
Amen.

✚ Sing with joy to God our help.

✚ O God, let all the nations praise you!

Psalm 121 *page 386*

Reading *Matthew 14:6–10*

[A]t a birthday celebration for Herod, the daughter of Herodias performed a dance before the guests and delighted Herod so much that he swore to give her whatever she might ask for. Prompted by her mother, she said, "Give me here on a platter the head of John the Baptist." The king was distressed, but because of his oaths and the guests who were present, he ordered that it be given, and he had John beheaded in the prison.

Reflection

Truth, and the world's hostility to it, is a theme throughout the Gospel accounts. The world's powerful are often surrounded by people who tell them only what they want to hear, causing them to land far afield of the goodness, truth, and beauty that mark life with God. John the Baptist spoke the truth, even when it put his life in danger. Eventually, he was put to death because of it. Jesus says he is the Way, the Truth, and the Life. He teaches that the truth will set us free. What truths need to be spoken in your life? How might you choose to live more fully in the truth?

Prayers *others may be added*

We bring before God our hopes and needs, as we pray:

℟. Lord, hear our prayer.

- For the Church as she challenges the values of our world, we pray: ℟.
- For political leaders to look with clear eyes on the problems of a world in need, we pray: ℟.
- For those who are ill or elderly, the unborn, those who are poor, and all whose human dignity is challenged in our world, we pray: ℟.
- For courage to speak the truth and for eyes free of self-deception, we pray: ℟.

Let us offer together the prayer
that Jesus taught us.

Our Father . . .

Lord Jesus,
you are the Way, the Truth, and the Life.
Guide us along your path,
that we may know, love, and serve you.
Who live and reign for ever and ever.
Amen.

✚ O God, let all the nations praise you!

✤ You are my rescuer, my help.

Psalm 24

page 367

Reading

Luke 12:16–21

Then [Jesus] told [the crowd] a parable. "There was a rich man whose land produced a bountiful harvest. He asked himself, 'What shall I do, for I do not have space to store my harvest?' And he said, 'This is what I shall do: I shall tear down my barns and build larger ones. There I shall store all my grain and other goods and I shall say to myself, "Now as for you, you have so many good things stored up for many years, rest, eat, drink, be merry!"' But God said to him, 'You fool, this night your life will be demanded of you; and the things you have prepared, to whom will they belong?' Thus will it be for all who store up treasure for themselves but are not rich in what matters to God."

Reflection

The harvest is so abundant that the man cannot even store it. What might the equivalent be today? Is it wrong to plan for the future? The rich fool builds more barns. He does not share. He plans. He tries to control. People today face similar difficulties. What is enough? How might we live in a society of abundance? How can wealth protect us from difficulty? As children of God, our identity comes from relationships, not from external circumstance. When we rest in this identity, we relinquish some of our need to control the uncontrollable.

Prayers

others may be added

With trust in your care for us, O Lord,
we bring before you our needs:

℟. **Lord, hear our prayer.**

- That the Church be strengthened in her mission to the world's poor, we pray: ℟.
- That world leaders seek to eradicate extreme poverty, we pray: ℟.
- That all who lack life's basic necessities may find strength in their struggles, we pray: ℟.
- That we might increase in faith, we pray: ℟.

Let us offer together the prayer
that Jesus taught us.

Our Father . . .

Lord Jesus,
you invite us to trust in God's love for us.
Help us to rest in our belovedness
and to extend your love to all
who need it.
Who live and reign for ever and ever.
Amen.

✤ You are my rescuer, my help.

✤ Sing with joy to God our help!

Psalm 34 *page 370*

Reading *Matthew 14:13–21*

When Jesus heard of the death of John the Baptist, he withdrew in a boat to a deserted place by himself. The crowds heard of this and followed him on foot from their towns. When he disembarked and saw the vast crowd, his heart was moved with pity for them, and he cured their sick. When it was evening, the disciples approached him and said, "This is a deserted place and it is already late; dismiss the crowds so that they can go to the villages and buy food for themselves." He said to them, "There is no need for them to go away; give them some food yourselves." But they said to him, "Five loaves and two fish are all we have here." Then he said, "Bring them here to me," and he ordered the crowds to sit down on the grass. Taking the five loaves and the two fish, and looking up to heaven, he said the blessing, broke the loaves, and gave them to the disciples, who in turn gave them to the crowds. They all ate and were satisfied, and they picked up the fragments left over—twelve wicker baskets full. Those who ate were about five thousand men, not counting women and children.

Reflection

After all of the people—thousands of people!—had eaten the food that Jesus had broken and shared, there were twelve wicker baskets filled with leftovers. Whenever we pray the Lord's Prayer, we say the words: "Give us this day our daily bread." We ask God for what we need for today. God offers us more—twelve baskets of leftovers. Too often, we fail to notice God's abundant blessings. How might we be more attentive to the gifts of God? How might we respond to God's care for us?

Prayers *others may be added*

With gratitude, we turn to the Lord
in hope as we pray:

℟. **Lord, hear our prayer.**

- For a greater devotion to the Eucharist among the faithful, we pray: ℟.
- For wisdom among world leaders, we pray: ℟.
- For the hungry, we pray: ℟.
- For an increase in gratitude for the gifts of God, we pray: ℟.

Let us offer together the prayer
that Jesus taught us.

Our Father . . .

Risen Lord,
you feed your people with
your own Body.
Transform our hearts and minds,
that we might be ever more like you,
ready to love and serve.
Who live and reign for ever and ever.
Amen.

✤ Sing with joy to God our help!

Tuesday, August 5, 2025

✤ Be merciful, O Lord,
for we have sinned.

Psalm 23 *page 367*

Reading *Matthew 14:22–33*

Jesus made the disciples get into a boat and precede him to the other side of the sea, while he dismissed the crowds. After doing so, he went up on the mountain by himself to pray. When it was evening he was there alone. Meanwhile the boat, already a few miles offshore, was being tossed about by the waves, for the wind was against it. During the fourth watch of the night, he came toward them, walking on the sea. When the disciples saw him walking on the sea they were terrified. "It is a ghost," they said, and they cried out in fear. At once Jesus spoke to them, "Take courage, it is I; do not be afraid." Peter said to him in reply, "Lord, if it is you, command me to come to you on the water." He said, "Come." Peter got out of the boat and began to walk on the water toward Jesus. But when he saw how strong the wind was he became frightened; and, beginning to sink, he cried out, "Lord, save me!" Immediately Jesus stretched out his hand and caught him, and said to him, "O you of little faith, why did you doubt?" After they got into the boat, the wind died down. Those who were in the boat did him homage, saying, "Truly, you are the Son of God."

Reflection

Jesus did so many things that astonished people, even his closest friends and disciples. What must it have been like for Peter to see Jesus walking across the wind-tossed water to their boat? He wanted to go to Jesus. Peter both trusted and was frightened. Sinking, he called out for Jesus, who grabbed him. Sometimes we feel guilty for doubting or feeling discouraged. Those feelings are just part of being human. When we call out to Jesus, he will hold us up. He hears us in our moments of deepest need.

Prayers *others may be added*

We cry out to you, Lord, as we pray

℟. **Lord, hear our prayer.**

- For the Holy Father, the successor of St. Peter, that he may guide all people on the path to holiness, we pray: ℟.
- For a more just and peaceful world, we pray: ℟.
- For those who are poor, sick, and marginalized, we pray: ℟.
- For an increase in faith, hope, and charity, we pray: ℟.

Let us offer together the prayer
that Jesus taught us.

Our Father . . .

Lord Jesus,
you call us to be your disciples.
Guide us on our path to holiness.
Hear us when we cry out to you
Who live and reign for ever and ever.
Amen.

✤ Be merciful, O Lord,
for we have sinned.

✠ When Christ appears,
we shall be like him.

Psalm 122

page 387

Reading

Luke 9:28B–36

Jesus took Peter, John, and James and went up a mountain to pray. While he was praying his face changed in appearance and his clothing became dazzling white. And behold, two men were conversing with him, Moses and Elijah, who appeared in glory and spoke of his exodus that he was going to accomplish in Jerusalem. Peter and his companions had been overcome by sleep, but becoming fully awake, they saw his glory and the two men standing with him. As they were about to part from him, Peter said to Jesus, "Master, it is good that we are here; let us make three tents, one for you, one for Moses, and one for Elijah." But he did not know what he was saying. While he was still speaking, a cloud came and cast a shadow over them, and they became frightened when they entered the cloud. Then from the cloud came a voice that said, "This is my chosen Son; listen to him." After the voice had spoken, Jesus was found alone. They fell silent and did not at that time tell anyone what they had seen.

Reflection

Peter, James, and John are offered a glimpse of the resurrection, a moment of hope. Jesus had predicted his passion, but they did not understand. How could they? Later, when things looked darkest, the memory of the transfiguration gave them something to hold onto. We may never be given the gift of seeing Moses, Elijah, and Jesus during this life, but we are given moments of consolation and peace that sustain us through our crosses. When we see clearly what God is doing in the world and meditate upon it, we know there is a foundation for our hope.

Prayers

others may be added

Confident in your love and protection,
Father, we bring our needs before you:

℟. Lord, hear our prayer.

- For a hope-filled Church, we pray: ℟.
- For increased care for and stewardship of the environment, we pray: ℟.
- For victims of violence and persecution, we pray: ℟.
- For greater openness to the work of the Spirit in our lives, we pray: ℟.

Let us offer together the prayer
that Jesus taught us.

Our Father . . .

Risen Lord,
you give us glimpses of that which
we hope for,
as you showed your disciples your glory.
Make our hope firm
that we might await you in joy and peace
until you come again.
Who live and reign for ever and ever.
Amen.

✠ When Christ appears,
we shall be like him.

Thursday, August 7, 2025

✚ If today you hear his voice,
harden not your hearts.

Psalm 34 *page 370*

Reading *Matthew 16:13b–19*

[Jesus asked], "Who do people say that the Son of Man is?" They replied, "Some say John the Baptist, others Elijah, still others Jeremiah or one of the prophets." He said to them, "But who do you say that I am?" Simon Peter said in reply, "You are the Christ, the Son of the living God." Jesus said to him in reply, "Blessed are you, Simon son of Jonah. For flesh and blood has not revealed this to you, but my heavenly Father. And so I say to you, you are Peter, and upon this rock I will build my Church, and the gates of the netherworld shall not prevail against it. I will give you the keys to the Kingdom of heaven. Whatever you bind on earth shall be bound in heaven; and whatever you loose on earth shall be loosed in heaven."

Reflection

This Gospel passage is all about identity. Everyone wants to know who Jesus is. Is he one of the ancient prophets, come back to Israel? Is he John the Baptist, raised from the dead? Jesus asks his disciples, "But who do you say that I am?" It is not enough to listen to the explanations of others as to the identity of Christ. The only way to know Christ is through personal encounter with him. Peter, inspired by the Holy Spirit, knows who Jesus is—the very Son of God. In knowing Jesus, Peter learns his own true identity: "You are Peter, and upon this rock I will build my Church." The more we come to know Jesus, the more we come to know ourselves, in all our potential and all our weakness.

Prayers *others may be added*

Lord, you know our hearts. Let us turn to you now in prayer:

℟. **Lord, hear our prayer**

- For the Church as she continues to speak the truth in a sometimes hostile world, we pray: ℟.
- For world leaders, that they may be guided by their consciences to pursue the common good, we pray: ℟.
- For those who are poor, or marginalized, or oppressed, we pray: ℟.
- For an increase in charity, we pray: ℟.

Let us offer together the prayer
that Jesus taught us.

Our Father . . .

Lord Jesus,
you are the Christ, Son of the living God.
Teach us to see you in the faces of our
sisters and brothers.
When we meet, let us ask ourselves,
"Who is this person, if not Christ
Himself?"
When we are asked who you are,
let us answer by sharing all we have:
our faith, our hope, our charity, our love.
You who live and reign for ever
and ever.
Amen.

✚ If today you hear his voice,
harden not your hearts.

✠ I remember the deeds of the Lord.

Psalm 13

page 365

Reading

Matthew 16:24–28

Jesus said to his disciples, "Whoever wishes to come after me must deny himself, take up his cross, and follow me. For whoever wishes to save his life will lose it, but whoever loses his life for my sake will find it. What profit would there be for one to gain the whole world and forfeit his life? Or what can one give in exchange for his life? For the Son of Man will come with his angels in his Father's glory, and then he will repay each according to his conduct. Amen, I say to you, there are some standing here who will not taste death until they see the Son of Man coming in his Kingdom."

Reflection

In the face of many of our life's crosses, especially those involving personal suffering, our first impulse is to resist, deny, and escape. Unfortunately, this strategy does not, generally, bring resolution or peace, externally or internally. Jesus offers us a model: Surrender. Take up your cross. Follow him, uniting your suffering to his. Invite God to transform it. No matter what we are going through, God is with us, not removing our suffering with a magic wand, but making it meaningful. Bringing new life

Prayers

others may be added

Bringing our needs before the God
who first loved us, we pray:

℟. **Lord, hear our prayer.**

- That all the baptized may walk the path of self-sacrificing love with courage, we pray: ℟.
- That political leaders may embrace the role of servant, we pray: ℟.
- That all people carrying the crosses of poverty, illness, and marginalization may be given peace, we pray: ℟.
- That the God of life might transform our tears into joy, we pray: ℟.

Let us offer together the prayer
that Jesus taught us.

Our Father . . .

Lord Jesus,
you came into the world
to show us the path of
self-sacrificing love
even unto death on the cross.
Give us the strength to carry crosses,
whatever they may be,
with compassion, mercy, and kindness.
Who live and reign for ever and ever.
Amen.

✠ I remember the deeds of the Lord.

Weekday

Saturday, August 9, 2025

✤ I love you Lord, my strength.

Psalm 30

page 369

Reading

Matthew 17:14–20

A man came up to Jesus, knelt down before him, and said, "Lord, have pity on my son, who is a lunatic and suffers severely; often he falls into fire, and often into water. I brought him to your disciples, but they could not cure him." Jesus said in reply, "O faithless and perverse generation, how long will I be with you? How long will I endure you? Bring the boy here to me." Jesus rebuked him and the demon came out of him, and from that hour the boy was cured. Then the disciples approached Jesus in private and said, "Why could we not drive it out?" He said to them, "Because of your little faith. Amen, I say to you, if you have faith the size of a mustard seed, you will say to this mountain, 'Move from here to there,' and it will move. Nothing will be impossible for you."

Reflection

Many of us have faced the devastation of unanswered prayers. Sometimes the miracle does not come. The father in the story is a model for us. He continues to turn to Jesus, even when he does not receive healing for his son. This is the mountain-moving moment. His son is healed. What if he had not been? Jesus would not have left him. Turning toward Jesus opens possibilities, even in the face of profound disappointment. Jesus, God with us, invites us to remain in his love, to believe that suffering can be transformed.

Prayers

others may be added

O Lord, our faith is small, but we turn to you in hope as we pray:

℟. Lord, graciously hear us.

- For the Church, that she may be a place of welcome for all people, especially those on the margins of society, we pray: ℟.
- For world leaders, that they seek to promote the common good, we pray: ℟.
- For the sick, especially those struggling with mental illness, that they might find healing and peace, we pray: ℟.
- For an increase in faith, we pray: ℟.

Let us offer together the prayer that Jesus taught us.

Our Father . . .

Lord Jesus,
you taught us that faith the size of
a mustard seed is sufficient,
for it brings about most
astounding things.
Increase our faith so that we might
know and love you with all our hearts
and bring healing to a broken and
divided world.
Who live and reign for ever and ever.
Amen.

✤ I love you Lord, my strength.

✚ O God / . . . forget not the cries
of those who seek you.

Psalm 122

page 387

Reading

Luke 12:32–34

Jesus said to his disciples: "Do not be afraid any longer, little flock, for your Father is pleased to give you the kingdom. Sell your belongings and give alms. Provide money bags for yourselves that do not wear out, an inexhaustible treasure in heaven that no thief can reach nor moth destroy. For where your treasure is, there also will your heart be."

Reflection

Jesus tells his disciples: "Where your treasure is, there also will your heart be." The things we most highly value on earth are not wrong or bad, just impermanent. The only constant in earthly life is change. Children may be our treasure, but—if we are lucky—they will become adults who no longer need the kind of active care from which our lives can derive meaning. The inexhaustible treasure, the money bag that will never wear out, comes when we pursue the love of God and neighbor that Jesus commands.

Prayers

others may be added

O Lord, you invite us to a life of service. Hear us as we ask for what we need to live out your call:

℟. **Lord, hear us.**

- For the Church, that she may faithfully guide her children to heaven, we pray: ℟.
- For all people, that they may grow in virtue and serve their fellow human beings and the common good, we pray: ℟.
- For those who are sick, or poor, or marginalized, we pray: ℟.
- For us, that we may receive the gift of wisdom to see as God sees and meet the needs of the world with the compassion of Jesus, we pray: ℟.

Let us offer together the prayer that Jesus taught us.

Our Father . . .

Loving Father,
You call all people to yourself
in every age,
desiring to live in love with each
of your children.
Look upon us kindly
as we come to do your will
that we might have life with you,
the treasure that no one can take away
from us.
Through Christ our Lord.
Amen.

✚ O God / . . . forget not the cries
of those who seek you.

✥ Praise the Lord, Jerusalem.

Psalm 24

page 367

Reading

Deuteronomy 10:20–22

Moses said to the people: "The LORD, your God, shall you fear, and him shall you serve; hold fast to him and swear by his name. He is your glory, he, your God, who has done for you those great and terrible things which your own eyes have seen. Your ancestors went down to Egypt seventy strong, and now the LORD, your God, has made you as numerous as the stars of the sky."

Reflection

At times the practice of faith is reduced to an ethical enterprise or a divine to-do list that, when perfectly executed, yields God's favor and worldly blessings. In reality, the reverse is true. God's love is first, primary, and unconditional. Whatever we do—whether it is worship or the caring for the vulnerable to which Moses calls the people—is a response to God's love. It is gratitude for the gift, given freely, of the Creator of the Universe.

Prayers

others may be added

O Lord, your love for us is everlasting.
Hear us as we pray:

℟. **Lord, hear our prayer.**

- For the Church, that she may remember God's love and faithfulness, we pray: ℟.
- For an increased respect for human rights and human dignity, we pray: ℟.
- For migrants and refugees, we pray: ℟.
- For us, that we might grow in gratitude for the gifts of God, we pray: ℟.

Let us offer together the prayer
that Jesus taught us.

Our Father . . .

Father,
you have chosen us to be your people
and have given us an abundance
of gifts.
Accept our worship, our love, our
gratitude, and our good works,
that as we await your Son's return,
we may cooperate with you to bring
forth your kingdom on earth.
Through Christ our Lord.
Amen.

✥ Praise the Lord, Jerusalem.

✤ The portion of the Lord is his people.

Psalm 27 *page 368*

Reading *Matthew 18:1–5*

The disciples approached Jesus and said, "Who is the greatest in the Kingdom of heaven?" He called a child over, placed it in their midst, and said, "Amen, I say to you, unless you turn and become like children, you will not enter the Kingdom of heaven. Whoever becomes humble like this child is the greatest in the Kingdom of heaven. And whoever receives one child such as this in my name receives me."

Prayers *Pope Fracis*

Whoever becomes like a little child, Jesus tells us, "is the greatest in the kingdom of heaven" (Mt 18:4). The true greatness of man consists in making himself small before God. For God is not known through grand ideas and extensive study, but rather through the littleness of a humble and trusting heart. To be great before the Most High does not require the accumulation of honour and prestige or earthly goods and success, but rather a complete self-emptying. A child has nothing to give and everything to receive. A child is vulnerable, and depends on his or her father and mother. The one who becomes like a little child is poor in self but rich in God.

Prayers *others may be added*

We turn to you, O Lord, bringing before you our hopes as we pray:

℟. Lord, hear our prayer.

- For the Church's prophetic witness, we pray: ℟.
- For the promotion of the common good, we pray: ℟.
- For those who are poor and all who lack the basic necessities of life, we pray: ℟.
- For us, that we might grow in love of God and neighbor, we pray: ℟.

Let us offer together the prayer that Jesus taught us.

Our Father . . .

O Lord,
your word is sweet in our mouth.
Help us to proclaim you to all people,
that they may know you, love you,
and serve you.
Who live and reign for ever and ever.
Amen.

✤ The portion of the Lord is his people.

Wednesday, August 13, 2025

✤ Blessed be God who filled my soul with fire!

Psalm 30

page 369

Reading

Deuteronomy 34:4–8

The LORD then said to [Moses], "This is the land which I swore to Abraham, Isaac, and Jacob that I would give to their descendants. I have let you feast your eyes upon it, but you shall not cross over." So there, in the land of Moab, Moses, the servant of the LORD, died as the LORD had said; and he was buried in the ravine opposite Beth-peor in the land of Moab, but to this day no one knows the place of his burial. Moses was one hundred and twenty years old when he died, yet his eyes were undimmed and his vigor unabated. For thirty days the children of Israel wept for Moses in the plains of Moab, till they had completed the period of grief and mourning for Moses.

Reflection

Moses views the Promised Land, the fruit of his life's work, but he never experiences it. Dr. Martin Luther King Jr. famously reflected on his work for justice as an experience of going to the mountaintop. He understood what God was doing in the world and in his own life by looking to the Scriptures and seeing how God had acted in history. When we are not sure how God is acting in our lives or in the world, we can look to the Scriptures to discern: How has God acted in salvation history? What do we see that is similar in our world today? This is a vital tool for understanding what God is calling us to do, our own vocation of love and service.

Prayers

others may be added

Let us bring our hopes and needs before God as we pray:

℟. Lord, hear our prayer.

- For an openness to the Holy Spirit in the Church, we pray: ℟.
- For an end to environmental degradation, we pray: ℟.
- For anyone who lives under oppression, that they might find freedom, we pray: ℟.
- For us, that we might see God's promises come to fulfillment in Christ Jesus, we pray: ℟.

Let us offer together the prayer that Jesus taught us.

Our Father . . .

God of the covenant,
you are the keeper of promises.
You promise that the coming kingdom
will be marked by peace, justice,
and mercy.
Guide us as we walk humbly
in your ways
hoping always in your Word.
Through Christ our Lord.
Amen.

✤ Blessed be God who filled my soul with fire!

✠ Do not forget the works of the Lord!

Psalm 51

page 373

Reading

Matthew 18:21–22

Peter approached Jesus and asked him, "Lord, if my brother sins against me, how often must I forgive him? As many as seven times?" Jesus answered, "I say to you, not seven times but seventy-seven times."

Reflection

Each one of us falls short of our moral ideals. When we fail, and especially when our failures are failures of love, we are aware of mitigating circumstances and consider the mistake within the context of our broader life. This helps us resolve to do better and forgive ourselves. Yet we rarely extend this same grace to others. Jesus invites us to offer the same grace and forgiveness we extend to ourselves and that God extends to us—an infinite amount—to other people. God sees us as beloved children, not as the sum of our choices. We are called to see each person as God's beloved child and to forgive perfectly, as God does.

Prayers

others may be added

Knowing our finitude and limitations, we bring our needs before the Lord:

℟. Lord, graciously hear us.

- For the Church, holy and always in need of purification, we pray: ℟.
- For an end to all war and violence, we pray: ℟.
- For those who are poor, or marginalized, or sick, we pray: ℟.
- For us, that we all might experience pardon and peace, we pray: ℟.

Let us offer together the prayer that Jesus taught us.

Our Father . . .

Loving Father,
you forgive us our debts
as we forgive our debtors.
Give us a spirit of generosity
and gratitude
that we might love like you do.
Through Christ our Lord.
Amen.

✠ Do not forget the works of the Lord!

✤ Glorious things are spoken of you, O Mary.

Psalm 34

page 370

Reading

Luke 1:41–45

When Elizabeth heard Mary's greeting, the infant leaped in her womb, and Elizabeth, filled with the Holy Spirit, cried out in a loud voice and said, "Blessed are you among women, and blessed is the fruit of your womb. And how does this happen to me, that the mother of my Lord should come to me? For at the moment the sound of your greeting reached my ears, the infant in my womb leaped for joy. Blessed are you who believed that what was spoken to you by the Lord would be fulfilled."

Reflection

Elizabeth tells Mary that she is blessed because she "believed that what was spoken to [her] by the Lord would be fulfilled." Mary's response is the prayer that we know as the Magnificat, a song of praise that tells of God's care for and goodness to the oppressed and God's fulfillment of promises to the people of Israel. God has promised something to us: that we might have eternal life in heaven with Mary and all the saints. With Mary, we might proclaim: "My soul proclaims the greatness of the Lord!"

Prayers

others may be added

O Lord, hear the cry of your people as we pray:

℟. **Remember your mercy, O Lord.**

- For the Church's ministry to the poor, we pray: ℟.
- For an end to all division in our world and peace in our days, we pray: ℟.
- For those who are hungry, that they may be filled with good things, we pray: ℟.
- For us, that we may be guided by the Blessed Virgin Mary, our mother and our model, we pray: ℟.

Let us offer together the prayer
that Jesus taught us.

Our Father . . .

Father,
you call all people to yourself.
You care for us in our need
and keep your promises.
Lead us on your path that we might experience
the fulfillment of the promise of the resurrection.
Through Christ our Lord.
Amen.

✤ Glorious things are spoken of you, O Mary.

✤ You are my inheritance, O Lord.

Psalm 23 *page 367*

Reading *Matthew 19:13–15*

Children were brought to Jesus that he might lay his hands on them and pray. The disciples rebuked them, but Jesus said, "Let the children come to me, and do not prevent them; for the Kingdom of heaven belongs to such as these." After he placed his hands on them, he went away.

Reflection

Adults' motivations are complex. Children, especially young children, are more likely to be guided by one thing alone: their inner wisdom. Maybe you have seen a parent ask a reluctant child to greet an unfamiliar adult. Maybe the child offered a small wave in return. A little child would only approach Jesus because something inside of her said, "Go!" Jesus says the kingdom belongs to such as these, people who hear his voice and recognize it, who come when he calls. He invites us to this kind of response: to hear his voice, recognize it, and follow.

Prayers *others may be added*

Lord, you call all people to yourself. Hear these prayers we bring before you:

℟. **Lord, hear our prayer.**

- For the Church's prophetic witness to a consistent ethic of life, we pray: ℟.
- For an end to violent conflict and oppression, we pray: ℟.
- For children, born and unborn, that these vulnerable members of society be cared for with tenderness, we pray: ℟.
- For us, that we might be more attentive to the call of the Lord Jesus, we pray: ℟.

Let us offer together the prayer that Jesus taught us.

Our Father . . .

Loving Father,
you have called us by name
and made us your children.
Hear the prayers we have humbly
brought before you
and make us childlike in our trust
of your care and protection.
Through Christ our Lord.
Amen.

✤ You are my inheritance, O Lord.

✤ One day within your courts /
is better than a thousand elsewhere.

Psalm 46 *page 372*

Reading *Luke 12:49–53*

Jesus said to his disciples: "I have come to set the earth on fire, and how I wish it were already blazing! There is a baptism with which I must be baptized, and how great is my anguish until it is accomplished! Do you think that I have come to establish peace on the earth? No, I tell you, but rather division. From now on a household of five will be divided, three against two and two against three; a father will be divided against his son and a son against his father, a mother against her daughter and a daughter against her mother, a mother-in-law against her daughter-in-law and a daughter-in-law against her mother-in-law."

Reflection

Although the Way of Jesus is easy and his burden light, the values of the Gospel and the values of the world are often opposed. Consider Thanksgiving dinner. People who love each other but who disagree on important issues are not able to be at peace with one another, even for just one meal. Alternatively, they create a false peace of smiling faces and simmering resentment. Though Jesus offered his peace, he knew human nature. He challenges us to make peace while continuing to be who we are—neither falsely conciliatory nor manipulative—and to trust in God's ability to heal the world's divisions.

Prayers *others may be added*

Confident that that the Lord hears us,
we offer to him our petitions:

℟. Lord, hear our prayer

- For authentic dialogue in the Church, we pray: ℟.
- For resolution of the world's most intractable conflicts, we pray: ℟.
- For refugees fleeing violence and persecution, we pray: ℟.
- For growth in love of God and neighbor, we pray: ℟.

Let us offer together the prayer
that Jesus taught us.

Our Father . . .

Lord Jesus,
you offer the world the gift of your peace.
Make us peacemakers,
seeking to heal the world,
that we might prepare the way
for you to come again.
Who live and reign for ever and ever.
Amen.

✤ One day within your courts /
is better than a thousand elsewhere.

✚ Remember us, O Lord,
as you favor your people.

Psalm 47

page 372

Reading

Matthew 19:16–22

A young man approached Jesus and said, "Teacher, what good must I do to gain eternal life?" He answered him, "Why do you ask me about the good? There is only One who is good. If you wish to enter into life, keep the commandments." He asked him, "Which ones?" And Jesus replied, / "*You shall not kill; / you shall not commit adultery; / you shall not steal; / you shall not bear false witness; / honor your father and your mother; / and you shall love your neighbor as yourself.*" / The young man said to him, "All of these I have observed. What do I still lack?" Jesus said to him, "If you wish to be perfect, go, sell what you have and give to the poor, and you will have treasure in heaven. Then come, follow me." When the young man heard this statement, he went away sad, for he had many possessions.

Reflection

The rich young man went away sad because he had many possessions. Most of us are very attached to our personal belongings. Even if we live very modestly, we probably own more than wealthy people in the time of Jesus. Many people have been fascinated by saints like Francis of Assisi, who took the Gospel call to poverty literally—with good reason. We suspect that our attachment to "stuff" imperils our ability to follow Jesus. How might you embrace the Gospel imperative to care for the poor? How might you change your relationship to your personal belongings to live this out?

Prayers

others may be added

Knowing God's care for us, we bring to him our prayers:

℟. **Lord, hear our prayer.**

- For the Church's mission to proclaim the Good News to the poor, we pray: ℟.
- For an end to extreme poverty across the globe, we pray: ℟.
- For all people who lack the basic necessities of life, we pray: ℟.
- For compassion given to all who suffer, we pray: ℟.

Let us offer together the prayer that Jesus taught us.

Our Father . . .

Loving God,
you write your law upon our hearts.
Transform our hearts that we might
turn away from selfishness
and toward self-sacrificing love
in imitation of Jesus.
Give us the courage to say,
"Here I am, Lord,"
to whatever your will for us.
Through Christ our Lord.
Amen.

✚ Remember us, O Lord,
as you favor your people.

Tuesday, August 19, 2025

✚ The Lord speaks of peace
to his people.

Psalm 71

page 376

Reading

Matthew 19:28–30

Jesus said to [the disciples], "Amen, I say to you that you who have followed me, in the new age, when the Son of Man is seated on his throne of glory, will yourselves sit on twelve thrones, judging the twelve tribes of Israel. And everyone who has given up houses or brothers or sisters or father or mother or children or lands for the sake of my name will receive a hundred times more, and will inherit eternal life. But many who are first will be last, and the last will be first."

Reflection

Jesus calls his disciples to an ever-deepening commitment to love as he loves. Yet they are human, like all of us. No matter what we do, we cannot save ourselves. We cannot earn admittance to the kingdom of heaven no matter how hard we try. If left up to our own devices, none of us will be saved. But with God, all things are possible. We are able to live out the ethics of the Gospel because we are God's beloved children. We do our best to live out our Gospel call, always aware of our sinfulness and our finitude and asking for God's help.

Prayers

others may be added

Let us turn to the Lord in prayer:

℟. **Lord, graciously hear us.**

- For the pope, the successor of St. Peter, as he guides the faithful to heaven, we pray: ℟.
- For an end to war and violent conflict, we pray: ℟.
- For anyone who feels hopeless, we pray: ℟.
- For each one of us as we journey on our path to holiness, we pray: ℟.

Let us offer together the prayer
that Jesus taught us.

Our Father . . .

Loving Father,
you have called us to be in right
relationship with you.
Make us worthy of this precious gift.
Open our eyes and our hearts
to our neighbor
that all may be one.
Through Christ our Lord.
Amen.

✚ The Lord speaks of peace
to his people.

✤ Lord, in your strength the king is glad.

Psalm 62

page 374

Reading

Matthew 20:8–16

When it was evening the owner of the vineyard said to his foreman, "Summon the laborers and give them their pay, beginning with the last and ending with the first." When those who had started about five o'clock came, each received the usual daily wage. So when the first came, they thought that they would receive more, but each of them also got the usual wage. And on receiving it they grumbled against the landowner, saying, "These last ones worked only one hour, and you have made them equal to us, who bore the day's burden and the heat." He said to one of them in reply, "My friend, I am not cheating you. Did you not agree with me for the usual daily wage? Take what is yours and go. What if I wish to give this last one the same as you? Or am I not free to do as I wish with my own money? Are you envious because I am generous?" Thus, the last will be first, and the first will be last."

Reflection

All of the workers receive what they were promised. Why, then, is this parwable so difficult? We might recognize ourselves in the workers who spent the whole day in the heat. When something bad happens in our lives, do we give God praise and thanksgiving for the many good gifts we have received? Or do we remind God how much more deserving we are than our neighbor, the one whose life seems unjustly charmed? We do not earn blessings. And the greatest blessing—sharing in the divine life in heaven—is one that we hope to share with all people, sinners like us, but beloved of God.

Prayers

others may be added

With confidence, we bring our needs before God as we pray:

℟. Lord, hear our prayer.

- For the Church, the People of God, we pray: ℟.
- For an increased commitment to economic justice within and among the nations, we pray: ℟.
- For the most vulnerable in our society, especially those who are poor, or sick, or elderly, and the unborn, we pray: ℟.
- For growth in love of God and one another, we pray: ℟.

Let us offer together the prayer that Jesus taught us.

Our Father . . .

Father,
you keep your promises to your people.
Help us to grow in love and service
that we might rejoice fully in your love
for every human person.
Through Christ our Lord.
Amen.

✤ Lord, in your strength the king is glad.

Thursday, August 21, 2025

✚ Here I am Lord; I come
to do your will.

Psalm 63

page 375

Reading

Matthew 22:1b–9

[Jesus said:] "The Kingdom of heaven may be likened to a king who gave a wedding feast for his son. He dispatched his servants to summon the invited guests to the feast, but they refused to come. A second time he sent other servants, saying, 'Tell those invited: "Behold, I have prepared my banquet, my calves and fattened cattle are killed, and everything is ready; come to the feast."' Some ignored the invitation and went away, one to his farm, another to his business. The rest laid hold of his servants, mistreated them, and killed them. The king was enraged and sent his troops, destroyed those murderers, and burned their city. Then the king said to his servants, 'The feast is ready, but those who were invited were not worthy to come. Go out, therefore, into the main roads and invite to the feast whomever you find.'"

Reflection

During these days we have heard many parables about the kingdom of heaven. One thing they all have in common is a complete reversal of human expectations. A great king sends out invitations to the wedding feast of his son. Instead of responding to his invitation, the people ignore him, are too busy to come, or even attack the messengers who bring the invitation! So instead, the king sends word to the highways and byways, and brings in all sorts of people, "bad and good alike," to sit at the wedding feast. We too are receiving an invitation from the King, to a marvelous feast: Eucharist, the wedding-supper of the Lamb. Are we too busy with other things to respond?

Prayers

others may be added

Let us bring our needs before you,
O Lord, as we pray:

℟. Open our hearts, Lord.

- For the healing of all divisions in the Church, we pray: ℟.
- For a greater respect for human rights and human dignity across the world, we pray: ℟.
- For all people who experience discrimination, hatred, and prejudice, we pray: ℟.
- For the compassion to tend to the needs of the world, we pray: ℟.

Let us offer together the prayer
that Jesus taught us.

Our Father . . .

Lord Jesus,
you show us what it means
to love perfectly
in the midst of the world's suffering.
Make our hearts love like yours
that we may be your love to a world
in need.
Who live and reign for ever and ever.
Amen.

✚ Here I am Lord; I come
to do your will.

✚ Praise the Lord, my soul!

Psalm 67

page 375

Reading

Matthew 22:34–40

When the Pharisees heard that Jesus had silenced the Sadducees, they gathered together, and one of them, a scholar of the law, tested him by asking, "Teacher, which commandment in the law is the greatest?" He said to him, "You shall love the Lord, your God, with all your heart, with all your soul, and with all your mind. This is the greatest and the first commandment. The second is like it: You shall love your neighbor as yourself. The whole law and the prophets depend on these two commandments."

Reflection

What does it mean to love your neighbor as yourself? Jesus does not ask anyone to be a doormat. He says love your neighbor as yourself, which means you must also love yourself. Sometimes, you might need to fulfill an obligation to work, yourself, or your family rather than jumping to help everyone who asks for your assistance. But it is easy to turn our obligations into excuses. A key part of loving your neighbor as yourself is offering the gift of your presence, even when you are busy or in a hurry or you do not feel especially loving. Jesus was fully present with the people around him and offers the gift of his presence to us today. Likewise, we can share our own presence with people, loving them not for what they do but because of who they are: beloved children of God.

Prayers

others may be added

We turn to you, O Lord, always
aware of your love and compassion
as we pray:

℟. **Lord, hear our prayer.**

- For an increase in devotion to the Eucharist, we pray: ℟.
- That the world's leaders may pursue the common good, we pray: ℟.
- For those who are sick, those who have suffered injuries, and refugees, we pray: ℟.
- For hearts conformed to Christ, we pray: ℟.

Let us offer together the prayer
that Jesus taught us.

Our Father . . .

Lord Jesus,
you show us what it means to love.
Guide us away from selfishness
and toward your path of sacrificial love.
Who live and reign for ever and ever.
Amen.

✚ Praise the Lord, my soul!

Saturday, August 23, 2025

✚ The Lord blesses those
who fear him.

Psalm 84

page 378

Reading

Matthew 23:1–12

Jesus spoke to the crowds and to his disciples, saying, "The scribes and the Pharisees have taken their seat on the chair of Moses. Therefore, do and observe all things whatsoever they tell you, but do not follow their example. For they preach but they do not practice. They tie up heavy burdens hard to carry and lay them on people's shoulders, but they will not lift a finger to move them. All their works are performed to be seen. They widen their phylacteries and lengthen their tassels. They love places of honor at banquets, seats of honor in synagogues, greetings in marketplaces, and the salutation 'Rabbi.' As for you, do not be called 'Rabbi.' You have but one teacher, and you are all brothers. Call no one on earth your father; you have but one Father in heaven. Do not be called 'Master'; you have but one master, the Christ. The greatest among you must be your servant. Whoever exalts himself will be humbled; but whoever humbles himself will be exalted."

Reflection

Jesus has harsh words for the scribes and Pharisees. These were the good religious people! As "good Catholics," are there times when we place heavy burdens on others? As we seek to walk our path of discipleship, are we ever practicing in a disingenuous or performative way? The way we present our faith—especially on social media—can be a way of exalting ourselves. As always, the key is probably not to think less of ourselves but to think about ourselves less. We are not God. Everyone around us is, like us, God's beloved. We have no need to exalt ourselves because there is nothing we can do that would make God love us more than God already does.

Prayers

others may be added

Lord, you know the needs of our
hearts. Hear us as we pray:

Lord, hear our prayer.

- For Church leaders, that they might guide God's people with humility, we pray: ℟.
- For peace in our world, we pray: ℟.
- For the poor and the marginalized, we pray: ℟.
- For just, loving, merciful, and humble actions, we pray: ℟.

Let us offer together the prayer
that Jesus taught us.

Our Father . . .

Father,
you made us to know, love,
and serve you,
and to share in your divine life
in heaven.
Help us to realize that this is enough,
that we need not earn your love
but only receive it
and respond with gratitude.
Through Christ our Lord.
Amen.

✚ The Lord blesses those
who fear him.

✤ Turn your ear, O Lord,
and answer me.

Psalm 46 *page 372*

Reading *Luke 13:22–30*

Jesus passed through towns and villages, teaching as he went and making his way to Jerusalem. Someone asked him, "Lord, will only a few people be saved?" He answered them, "Strive to enter through the narrow gate, for many, I tell you, will attempt to enter but will not be strong enough. After the master of the house has arisen and locked the door, then will you stand outside knocking and saying, 'Lord, open the door for us.' He will say to you in reply, 'I do not know where you are from.' And you will say, 'We ate and drank in your company and you taught in our streets.' Then he will say to you, 'I do not know where you are from. Depart from me, all you evildoers!' And there will be wailing and grinding of teeth when you see Abraham, Isaac, and Jacob and all the prophets in the kingdom of God and you yourselves cast out. And people will come from the east and the west and from the north and the south and will recline at table in the kingdom of God. For behold, some are last who will be first, and some are first who will be last."

Reflection

When we contemplate the narrow gate, we might consider how difficult it is to do the right thing. Despite our best intentions, we fail again and again as we attempt to follow Jesus. Luckily, Jesus tells us we need only ask for God's help in order to receive it. God is always ready to offer forgiveness and mercy, but sometimes we are not ready to receive it. When we receive sacramental grace in reconciliation, it helps us to live in a new way, the way we want to live. As we attempt to walk the narrow path of holiness, we can celebrate our resolve to sin no more with great joy, knowing we do not do this alone.

Prayers *others may be added*

Reliant on God for that we need,
we come before him as we pray:

℟. Lord, graciously hear us.

- For a spirit of hospitality in the Church, we pray: ℟.
- For an end to extreme poverty in our world, we pray: ℟.
- For all those who suffer religious persecution, we pray: ℟.
- For wisdom and discernment on our path of discipleship, we pray: ℟.

Let us offer together the prayer
that Jesus taught us.

Our Father . . .

Lord Jesus,
you have called us to follow you.
Help us to know your will
and to conform ours to it with great joy.
Who live and reign for ever and ever.
Amen.

✤ Turn your ear, O Lord,
and answer me.

Monday, August 25, 2025

✤ The Lord takes delight in his people.

Psalm 47 *page 372*

Reading *Matthew 23:13*

Jesus said to the crowds and to his disciples: "Woe to you, scribes and Pharisees, you hypocrites. You lock the Kingdom of heaven before men. You do not enter yourselves, nor do you allow entrance to those trying to enter."

Reflection

The Pharisees and scribes were the righteous people, the religious people, keepers of every commandment, every job and title of the law. But it is for these "good guys" that Jesus reserves his harshest condemnation, for they have turned the love of God and the practice of religion into something complicated and strange, difficult if not impossible. Their elaborate arguments are designed to justify themselves and exclude others from God's favor. Three times Jesus repeats that they are "blind," for they have made the law an empty formula and are no longer able to see the reality of God who lies within and yet beyond all the forms of the law. It is a good reminder for us as well, that our faith is more about opening doors than closing them. It is more about grace, truth, and love than it is about rules and prohibitions.

Prayers *others may be added*

Hear our pleas, O Lord, as we pay:

℟. **Lord, hear our prayer.**

- For the Church, that she may be a light to all people, we pray: ℟.
- For world leaders, that they may promote the common good, we pray: ℟.
- For victims of religious, political, or racially-based violence, we pray: ℟.
- For us, that we may respond wholeheartedly to God's call in our lives, we pray: ℟.

Let us offer together the prayer
that Jesus taught us.

Our Father . . .

Father,
you have called us by name
and have invited us to live in your love.
Bring our good purposes to fulfillment
that all may glorify you.
Through Christ our Lord.
Amen.

✤ The Lord takes delight in his people.

✚ You have searched me
and you know me, Lord.

Psalm 71

page 376

Reading

1 Thessalonians 2:1–8

"You yourselves know, brothers and sisters, that our reception among you was not without effect. Rather, after we had suffered and been insolently treated, as you know, in Philippi, we drew courage through our God to speak to you the Gospel of God with much struggle. Our exhortation was not from delusion or impure motives, nor did it work through deception. But as we were judged worthy by God to be entrusted with the Gospel, that is how we speak, not as trying to please men, but rather God, who judges our hearts. Nor, indeed, did we ever appear with flattering speech, as you know, or with a pretext for greed—God is witness—nor did we seek praise from men, either from you or from others, although we were able to impose our weight as Apostles of Christ. Rather, we were gentle among you, as a nursing mother cares for her children. With such affection for you, we were determined to share with you not only the Gospel of God, but our very selves as well, so dearly beloved had you become to us."

Reflection

St. Paul describes himself and the other leaders in the early Church as nursing mothers. The image of feeding someone with one's own body connotes intimacy and tenderness as well as the self-sacrifcial love of Christ in the Eucharist. Little babies are completely reliant on others to care for them. When we think of the mother of a newborn, we think of how fully she devotes herself to that child's care, not because she has to but because she is overflowing with love. That is the love God has for you!

Prayers

others may be added

O Lord, you have loved us with
an everlasting love. Hear the prayers
of your family, as we pray:

℟. **Lord, hear our prayer.**

- That all divisions in the Church may cease, we pray: ℟.
- That there will be an increased respect for life and human dignity, we pray: ℟.
- That the most vulnerable in our society may receive protection, we pray: ℟.
- That we may always seek to please God, we pray: ℟.

Let us offer together the prayer
that Jesus taught us.

Our Father . . .

Lord Jesus,
you love and care for us
with tender mercy and compassion.
Help us to love as you love,
to be your hands and feet in the world
until you come again.
Who live and reign for ever and ever.
Amen.

✚ You have searched me
and you know me, Lord.

✣ You have searched me
and you know me, Lord.

Psalm 62 *page 374*

Reading *Matthew 23:27–32*

Jesus said, "Woe to you, scribes and Pharisees, you hypocrites. You are like whitewashed tombs, which appear beautiful on the outside, but inside are full of dead men's bones and every kind of filth Even so, on the outside you appear righteous, but inside you are filled with hypocrisy and evildoing.

"Woe to you, scribes and Pharisees, you hypocrites. You build the tombs of the prophets and adorn the memorials of the righteous, and you say, 'If we had lived in the days of our ancestors, we would not have joined them in shedding the prophets' blood.' Thus you bear witness against yourselves that you are the children of those who murdered the prophets; now fill up what your ancestors measured out!"

Reflection

In the time of Jesus, one approach to Jewish law involved a rigid adherence to a particular interpretation of the law of Moses. We know that particular ritual practices can help us grow closer to God because they help us to be mindful of him and conformed to his will. But like the Pharisees, we are capable of making the external realities ends in and of themselves. We might become highly judgmental of other people, or we might seek admiration for our right actions and right opinions rather than seeking to live from the inside out, guided by an ethics of love. Instead, we are called to live humble lives and to point others to the self-sacrificing love of Christ.

Prayers *others may be added*

With trust in God's care for us,
we bring you our needs as we pray:

℟. **Lord, hear our prayer.**

- For the Church's leaders to be guided by the Holy Spirit and to act with integrity, we pray: ℟.
- For governments to promote the common good, we pray: ℟.
- For all who feel excluded from the Church, we pray: ℟.
- For us, that we may be less judgmental and more loving, we pray: ℟.

Let us offer together the prayer
that Jesus taught us.

Our Father . . .

Lord Jesus,
you call us to live as humble servants.
Help us to love people as they are
and to point them to you.
Who live and reign for ever and ever.
Amen.

✣ You have searched me
and you know me, Lord.

✣ Fill us with your love, O Lord.

Psalm 63 *page 375*

Reading *Matthew 24:42–51*

Jesus said to his disciples: "Stay awake! For you do not know on which day your Lord will come. Be sure of this: if the master of the house had known the hour of night when the thief was coming, he would have stayed awake and not let his house be broken into. So too, you also must be prepared, for at an hour you do not expect, the Son of Man will come.

"Who, then, is the faithful and prudent servant, whom the master has put in charge of his household to distribute to them their food at the proper time? Blessed is that servant whom his master on his arrival finds doing so. Amen, I say to you, he will put him in charge of all his property. But if that wicked servant says to himself, 'My master is long delayed,' and begins to beat his fellow servants, and eat and drink with drunkards, the servant's master will come on an unexpected day and at an unknown hour and will punish him severely and assign him a place with the hypocrites, where there will be wailing and grinding of teeth."

Reflection

From the beginning of the world, God has been working to bring forth a communion of harmony. We cannot know when this work will reach its fulfillment, when Christ will come again in all his glory and God's light will fill the earth as water fills the sea. Jesus calls us to stay awake, to keep watch. We must guard our hearts in order to be ready. We can also think about this as the anticipatory waiting we experience in advance of something very joyful, such as the birth of a baby. God is doing something new. Keep watch! Don't miss a moment!

Prayers *others may be added*

You transform the world with your presence, O Lord. Come into the darkest places with your wonderful light, as we pray

℟. Come, Lord Jesus!

- That all the faithful may walk in the light of the Lord, we pray: ℟.
- That God's light might fill the earth as water fills the sea, we pray: ℟.
- That those who are hungry may be filled with good things, we pray: ℟.
- That we might wait joyfully for your coming , we pray: ℟.

Let us offer together the prayer that Jesus taught us.

Our Father . . .

Lord Jesus,
you call us to stay awake,
and to faithfully keep the watch.
Our world as we know it breaks
our hearts.
Help us to live in hope as we await
your coming.
Who live and reign for ever and ever.
Amen.

✣ Fill us with your love, O Lord.

✚ Rejoice in the Lord, you just!

Psalm 67

page 375

Reading

Mark 6:21b–24

Herod, on his birthday, gave a banquet for his courtiers, his military officers, and the leading men of Galilee. Herodias' own daughter came in and performed a dance that delighted Herod and his guests. The king said to the girl, "Ask of me whatever you wish and I will grant it to you." He even swore many things to her, "I will grant you whatever you ask of me, even to half of my kingdom." She went out and said to her mother, "What shall I ask for?" Her mother replied, "The head of John the Baptist." The girl hurried back to the king's presence and made her request, "I want you to give me at once on a platter the head of John the Baptist."

Reflection

In the middle of Mark's account of the ministry of Jesus comes this account of the death of John the Baptist. The story seems like an interruption in the flow of the Gospel, but its placement is very intentional. The story of John's death anticipates what will happen to Jesus. Herod does not want to kill John, any more than Pilate wants to kill Jesus; but he succumbs to pressure from his wife and from those around him, and he issues the order of condemnation. John is the forerunner; and Jesus is already aware that he will walk the same path.

Prayers

others may be added

Lord, you told us to ask and it will be given us. Answer when we knock, as we pray:

℟. Come, Lord Jesus!

- That the Church might be a light for all people, we pray: ℟.
- For an end to violence, we pray: ℟.
- For all who lack hope or live in hopeless situations, we pray: ℟.
- For us, that we might receive sufficient grace for today, we pray: ℟.

Let us offer together the prayer that Jesus taught us.

Our Father . . .

Gracious and loving God,
whose prophets revealed your plan
of salvation,
as your servant John the Baptist
foretold the coming of your Son,
let us joyfully proclaim the Gospel
to each and to all, every day of our lives.
Through Christ our Lord.
Amen.

✚ Rejoice in the Lord, you just!

✚ The Lord comes to rule the earth with justice.

Psalm 84 *page 378*

Reading *1 Thessalonians 4:9–11*

Brothers and sisters: On the subject of fraternal charity you have no need for anyone to write you, for you yourselves have been taught by God to love one another. Indeed, you do this for all the brothers throughout Macedonia. Nevertheless we urge you, brothers and sisters, to progress even more, and to aspire to live a tranquil life, to mind your own affairs, and to work with your own hands, as we instructed you.

Prayers *Justice in the World*

Our relationship to our neighbor is bound up with our relationship to God. Our response to the love of God, who saved us through Christ, is shown to be effective in our love and service of people. Christian love of neighbor and justice cannot be separated. For love implies an absolute demand for justice, namely a recognition of the dignity and rights of one's neighbors. Justice attains its inner fullness only in love. Because every person is truly a visible image of the invisible God and a sibling of Christ, the Christian finds in every person God himself and God's absolute demand for justice and love.

Prayers *others may be added*

With gratitude for all God's gifts, we turn to you in our need, as we pray:

℟. Lord, hear our prayer.

- For the pope, that he may be a good steward of the People of God, we pray: ℟.
- For our leaders, that they may use the gifts they have been given to promote the common good, we pray: ℟.
- For all who are burdened by poverty, we pray: ℟.
- For an increase in gratitude for the many gifts in our lives, we pray: ℟.

Let us offer together the prayer
that Jesus taught us.

Our Father . . .

Father,
you have given us every good gift.
Help us to use our talents for good works
that we might offer you an abundant
increase.
Through Christ our Lord.
Amen.

✚ The Lord comes to rule the earth with justice.

Sunday, August 31, 2025

✠ Have mercy on me, O Lord.

Psalm 85 *page 379*

Reading *Sirach 3:17-18, 20, 28–29*

My child, conduct your affairs with humility, / and you will be loved more than a giver of gifts. / Humble yourself the more, the greater you are, / and you will find favor with God. / What is too sublime for you, seek not, / into things beyond your strength search not. / The mind of a sage appreciates proverbs, / and an attentive ear is the joy of the wise. / Water quenches a flaming fire, / and alms atone for sins.

Reflection *St. Teresa of Calcutta*

Humility is the mother of all virtues—purity, charity, and obedience. It is in being humble that our love becomes real, devoted, and ardent. If you are humble nothing will touch you, neither praise nor disgrace, because you know what you are. If you are blamed you will not be discouraged. If they call you a saint you will not put yourself on a pedestal.

Prayers *others may be added*

With humble hearts, we offer
to the Lord our prayers:

℟. Lord, hear our prayer.

- That the leaders of the Church may be models of simplicity of life and humility of heart, we pray: ℟.
- That world leaders may govern by humble actions that protect the common good and not selfless gain, we pray: ℟.
- That all Christians may empty themselves for the good of others and not for empty show, we pray: ℟.
- That the humble of heart may be raised to eternal life, we pray: ℟.

Let us offer together the prayer
that Jesus taught us.

Our Father . . .

Loving God,
you are the Holy One;
we are surrounded by your magnificent
creation.
Standing in awe,
let us give our humble thanks.
No gift we bring is greater
than the abundant blessings
you show us.
Let us pray unceasingly,
that we may awaken to all that is sacred.
Our willingness to praise you is our
real gift.
Through Christ our Lord.
Amen.

✠ Have mercy on me, O Lord.

✤ The Lord comes to judge the earth.

Psalm 91
page 379

Reading
Luke 4:17b–20

[Jesus] unrolled the scroll and found the passage where it was written: / *The Spirit of the Lord is upon me, / because he has anointed me / to bring glad tidings to the poor. / He has sent me to proclaim liberty to captives / and recovery of sight to the blind, / to let the oppressed go free, / and to proclaim a year acceptable to the Lord.*

Rolling up the scroll, he handed it back to the attendant and sat down, and the eyes of all in the synagogue looked intently at him.

Reflection

We think we know people until they say or do something that surprises us. Today's Gospel tells the story of Jesus in the synagogue surrounded by his hometown folk. When Jesus stood up to read, the people were astonished, for they had sized him up as simply "Joseph's son." They became so threatened that they tried to kill him. Like the people of Nazareth, we too can be narrow-minded. We often form opinions of others based on their heritage, race, religion, looks, and numerous other external factors. Jesus' words challenge us to part with own perspectives, to accept that the Spirit blows where it will, and to be prepared to be utterly amazed.

Prayers
others may be added

Trusting the Spirit of God, we offer our petitions:

℟. O God, hear us.

- For eyes open to God's presence in unexpected people or places, we pray: ℟.
- For the unemployed and those searching for meaningful work, we pray: ℟.
- For those who labor in harsh conditions, we pray: ℟.
- For the safety of travelers this Labor Day weekend, we pray: ℟.
- For those who are sick and those whose labor on earth is now finished, we pray: ℟.

Let us offer together the prayer that Jesus taught us.

Our Father . . .

God of all times and seasons,
your Spirit anointed Isaiah and
 your Son, our Lord
to proclaim the Good News.
May this same Spirit call us to labor
 for your kingdom,
that we might produce a rich harvest
 of peace and justice.
Through Christ our Lord.
Amen

✤ The Lord comes to judge the earth.

Tuesday, September 2, 2025

✤ I believe I shall see the good things of the Lord in the land of the living.

Psalm 95 *page 380*

Reading *1 Thessalonians 5:1–6, 9–11*

Concerning times and seasons, brothers and sisters, you have no need for anything to be written to you. For you yourselves know very well that the day of the Lord will come like a thief at night. When people are saying, "Peace and security," then sudden disaster comes upon them, like labor pains upon a pregnant woman, and they will not escape.

But you, brothers and sisters, are not in darkness, for that day to overtake you like a thief. For all of you are children of the light and children of the day. We are not of the night or of darkness. Therefore, let us not sleep as the rest do, but let us stay alert and sober. For God did not destine us for wrath, but to gain salvation through our Lord Jesus Christ, who died for us, so that whether we are awake or asleep we may live together with him. Therefore, encourage one another and build one another up, as indeed you do.

Reflection

My mother was always prepared for company. Whenever the house would need tidying, she would say, "Red up this house, because you never know who is coming." "Red up" is a term people from Pittsburgh use for cleaning or straightening up. My mother's proverb taught my brother and me to have our house in order in anticipation of an unexpected visitor. The apostle Paul reminds the people of Thessalonica to keep their moral and spiritual houses in order in anticipation of the day of the Lord. Both mom's saying and St. Paul's letter are reminders to us to always be always at the edge of our seats, ever alert for a divine encounter.

Prayers *others may be added*

With confidence, we bring our prayers to God:

℟. **Peaceful God, hear our prayer.**

- For hearts that recognize what God is doing even now, we pray: ℟.
- For those who live amid the darkness of war and violence, we pray: ℟.
- For greater compassion for those with mental illness or physical disability: we pray: ℟.
- For the dying and those who wait with them, and for those who mourn, we pray: ℟.

Let us offer together the prayer that Jesus taught us.

Our Father . . .

God of love,
you dwell within us.
Open our eyes to see
your presence around us
in every person
and in all circumstances of life.
Through Christ our Lord.
Amen.

✤ I believe I shall see the good things of the Lord in the land of the living.

✤ I trust in the mercy of God for ever.

Psalm 98

page 381

Reading

Luke 4:38–41

After Jesus left the synagogue, he entered the house of Simon. Simon's mother-in-law was afflicted with a severe fever, and they interceded with him about her. He stood over her, rebuked the fever, and it left her. She got up immediately and waited on them.

At sunset, all who had people sick with various diseases brought them to him. He laid his hands on each of them and cured them. And demons also came out from many, shouting, "You are the Son of God." But he rebuked them and did not allow them to speak because they knew that he was the Christ.

Reflection

Jesus was on the move once again. After leaving Nazareth, he went to Capernaum, where he taught in the synagogue, cast out demons, and cured the sick. Unlike the people who drove him out of his hometown of Nazareth, the people of Capernaum did not want him to leave. But Jesus tells them that he must move on. Jesus wasn't interested in sticking around to assess the impact of his work. He was focused on doing God's work—proclaiming the kingdom in as many ways as possible and to as many persons as would welcome his message. May we, who are called to share in the work of Jesus, keep our attention on reaching out to those in need.

Prayers

others may be added

Together, we pray for the whole human family:

℟. **Healing God hear us.**

- For patience and understanding in times of peril, we pray: ℟.
- For communities recovering from natural disasters, we pray: ℟.
- For families estranged or separated by misunderstanding, we pray: ℟.
- For those suffering from cancer, Alzheimer's, and other diseases, we pray: ℟.

Let us offer together the prayer that Jesus taught us.

Our Father . . .

God of mercy,
you are slow to anger and rich
in kindness.
Grant, we pray,
the courage to proclaim the good news
of your love
to those near and far.
Through Christ our Lord.
Amen.

✤ I trust in the mercy of God for ever.

Weekday

Thursday, September 4, 2025

✣ The Lord has made known
his salvation.

Psalm 103 *page 382*

Reading *Luke 5:3b–11*

[Jesus] sat down and taught the crowds from the boat. After he had finished speaking, he said to Simon, "Put out into deep water and lower your nets for a catch." Simon said in reply, "Master, we have worked hard all night and have caught nothing, but at your command I will lower the nets." When they had done this, they caught a great number of fish and their nets were tearing. They signaled to their partners in the other boat to come to help them. They came and filled both boats so that the boats were in danger of sinking. When Simon Peter saw this, he fell at the knees of Jesus and said, "Depart from me, Lord, for I am a sinful man." For astonishment at the catch of fish they had made seized him and all those with him, and likewise James and John, the sons of Zebedee, who were partners of Simon. Jesus said to Simon, "Do not be afraid; from now on you will be catching men." When they brought their boats to the shore, they left everything and followed him.

Reflection

The fishermen in today's Gospel know what it is like to come up empty. After working the sea all night, their nets are barren, leaving them exhausted and, perhaps, feeling like failures. Their encounter with Jesus changes everything. When he encourages them to try again, they end up with more fish than they know what to do with. Jesus wants their daily efforts to bear fruit. Like the disciples, our efforts can seem fruitless and we too grow tired and weary. The Holy Spirit is always at our side, encouraging us to try again so that we might know the hope to which we are called.

Prayers *others may be added*

Confident in God's mercy, we offer
our prayers.

℟. God of abundance, hear our prayer.

- For those who suffer burnout or those discouraged by failure, we pray: ℟.
- For those who serve in the military and for all in harm's way, we pray: ℟.
- For those trapped in addiction or human trafficking, we pray: ℟.
- For hospitality to the immigrant, the newcomer, and the lonely, we pray: ℟.

Let us offer together the prayer
that Jesus taught us.

Our Father . . .

God of new life,
you know our needs before we ask.
Hear these petitions
and those hidden in the depths
of our hearts.
Give us the courage to persevere,
to seek, to knock,
and to ask with great faith
that you will bestow your blessings
on us.
Through Christ our Lord.
Amen.

✣ The Lord has made known
his salvation.

✚ Come with joy into the presence of the Lord.

Psalm 115

page 385

Reading

Colossians 1:15–20

Brothers and sisters: Christ Jesus is the image of the invisible God, the firstborn of all creation. For in him were created all things in heaven and on earth, the visible and the invisible, whether thrones or dominions or principalities or powers; all things were created through him and for him. He is before all things, and in him all things hold together. He is the head of the Body, the Church. He is the beginning, the firstborn from the dead, that in all things he himself might be preeminent. For in him all the fullness was pleased to dwell, and through him to reconcile all things for him, making peace by the Blood of his cross through him, whether those on earth or those in heaven.

Reflection

When you think of Jesus, what image comes to mind? When you think of the risen Christ, what would that look like? Innumerable artists have attempted to depict their idea of what Jesus looked like, but the truth is that no one really knows for sure. In what is believed to be an ancient hymn, St. Paul offers to the Colossians a grand image of Christ as Lord of all. Yet, we know that Jesus humbled himself enough to embody the image of a human being. So, if we want to identify an image of Jesus, we don't have to look very far. In Christ, God has revealed the divine image and we are forever a part of that.

Prayers

others may be added

To God, who is abounding in mercy, we pray:

℟. God of life, hear our prayer.

- For victims of racism and hateful speech , we pray: ℟.
- For children who know only conflict and violence, we pray: ℟.
- For the grace to forgive and to seek forgiveness , we pray: ℟.
- For families and communities in need of reconciliation, we pray: ℟.

Let us offer together the prayer that Jesus taught us.

Our Father . . .

O God,
you make all things new.
Guide us with your wisdom
that we might rely not on our
own strength
but on you alone
who raise the dead to new life.
Through Christ our Lord.
Amen.

✚ Come with joy into the presence of the Lord.

Saturday, September 6, 2025

✚ God himself is my help.

Psalm 121
page 386

Reading
Luke 6:1–5

While Jesus was going through a field of grain on a sabbath, his disciples were picking the heads of grain, rubbing them in their hands, and eating them. Some Pharisees said, "Why are you doing what is unlawful on the sabbath?" Jesus said to them in reply, "Have you not read what David did when he and those who were with him were hungry? How he went into the house of God, took the bread of offering, which only the priests could lawfully eat, ate of it, and shared it with his companions?" Then he said to them, "The Son of Man is lord of the sabbath."

Reflection
Our contemporary society has all but lost the notion of Sabbath rest, but in Jesus' day there were ample debates among teachers of the law about what could and could not be done on the Sabbath. The disciples were hungry so they picked heads of grain, rubbed them in their hands, and ate the kernels. Their action could be construed as work, which was forbidden on the Sabbath. When questioned by the Pharisees, Jesus recalls a precedent from 1 Samuel where human hunger outweighed rigid obedience to the law, (see 21:2–7). Today's Gospel reminds us that God's law never excludes basic human needs, but is meant to give life in abundance.

Prayers
others may be added

We pray now for our needs and
the needs of the whole world:

℟. Saving God, hear us.

- For a deeper understanding of one another's experience and point of view, we pray: ℟.
- For leaders of nations, lawmakers and judges whose decisions carry the weight of life and death, we pray: ℟.
- For those who hunger for daily bread or human dignity, we pray: ℟.
- For those who suffer isolation or the judgment of others, we pray: ℟.

Let us offer together the prayer
that Jesus taught us.

Our Father . . .

Gracious God,
your love frees us from the grip
  of blind obedience.
Fill our hearts with joy
that we might freely share with others
  your life-giving presence.
Through Christ our Lord.
Amen.

✚ God himself is my help.

✣ You are just, O Lord.

Psalm 122

page 387

Reading

Luke 14:25–33

Great crowds were traveling with Jesus, and he turned and addressed them, "If anyone comes to me without hating his father and mother, wife and children, brothers and sisters, and even his own life, he cannot be my disciple. Whoever does not carry his own cross and come after me cannot be my disciple. Which of you wishing to construct a tower does not first sit down and calculate the cost to see if there is enough for its completion? Otherwise, after laying the foundation and finding himself unable to finish the work the onlookers should laugh at him and say, 'This one began to build but did not have the resources to finish.' Or what king marching into battle would not first sit down and decide whether with ten thousand troops he can successfully oppose another king advancing upon him with twenty thousand troops? But if not, while he is still far away, he will send a delegation to ask for peace terms. In the same way, anyone of you who does not renounce all his possessions cannot be my disciple."

Reflection

To follow Jesus is to go all in, to surrender all, and to carry one's cross. When Jesus spoke these words to his disciples he was well aware of the betrayal and death that awaited him. He wanted them to understand that following him would also mean hardship and perhaps even death. Few of us will be asked to leave our loved ones or to renounce all our possessions, but we are being asked to weigh what it means to be a disciple. Like any relationship worth having, being in covenant relationship with Jesus is demanding. The famous Lutheran pastor, Dietrich Bonhoeffer, describes discipleship as a costly grace, "It is costly because it calls for obedience; it is grace because it calls for obedience to Christ. It is costly because it may cost us our lives; it is grace because only thus are we brought to new life."

Prayers

others may be added

We lift our hearts, minds, and spirits in prayer:

℟. Lord, hear our prayer.

- For freedom from whatever prevents us from following Jesus with our whole heart we pray: ℟.
- For those who suffer because of famine, drought, or the effects of climate change, we pray: ℟.
- For those seeking change in their lives, we pray: ℟.

Let us offer together the prayer that Jesus taught us.

Our Father . . .

O God,
in wisdom you created us,
in love you redeemed us,
in hope you sustain us.
Grant, we pray,
the courage to carry our crosses
and to follow your son, Jesus,
Through Christ our Lord.
Amen.

✣ You are just, O Lord.

Memorial of the Nativity
of the Blessed Virgin Mary
Monday, September 8, 2025

✤ In God is my safety and my glory.

Psalm 98

page 381

Reading

Matthew 1:18–21a

[T]his is how the birth of Jesus Christ came about. When his mother Mary was betrothed to Joseph, but before they lived together, she was found with child through the Holy Spirit. Joseph her husband, since he was a righteous man, yet unwilling to expose her to shame, decided to divorce her quietly. Such was his intention when, behold, the angel of the Lord appeared to him in a dream and said, "Joseph, son of David, do not be afraid to take Mary your wife into your home. For it is through the Holy Spirit that this child has been conceived in her. She will bear a son and you are to name him Jesus."

Reflection

According to Jewish belief, the Messiah would be a descendant of both Abraham and David. Matthew traces the lineage of Jesus by beginning with Abraham. Matthew, writing to a Jewish community, wanted to convince the people that Jesus was the intended Messiah and the legal heir of the throne of David through Solomon, Joseph's ancestor. Not everyone in the lineage was a king or patriarch. Many are unknowns, names without faces or stories, and many were known to have led shameful lives. Perhaps that is Matthew's point. God not only remembers the faceless, the forgotten, and the sinner—God includes them in his saving plan. No one is too unimportant or too insignificant for God's purpose.

Prayers

others may be added

Trusting in God's faithful love,
we pray:

℟. **Saving God, hear us.**

- For the Church around the world and for those discerning a religious vocation, we pray: ℟.
- For peace for those who live in fear brought about by war or oppressive governments , we pray: ℟.
- For the unborn and for parents who seek help for an unplanned pregnancy, we pray: ℟.
- For those facing surgery or undergoing extended medical treatment, we pray: ℟.

Let us offer together the prayer
that Jesus taught us.

Our Father . . .

God who saves us,
through the lineage of David
and the womb of Mary,
your Son Jesus took flesh.
Deepen our faith in your promises
that we may never hesitate
to share your faithful love
with all the world.
Through Christ our Lord.
Amen

✤ In God is my safety and my glory.

✚ The Lord is compassionate toward all his works.

Psalm 62

page 374

Reading

Luke 6:12–16

Jesus departed to the mountain to pray, and he spent the night in prayer to God. When day came, he called his disciples to himself, and from them he chose Twelve, whom he also named Apostles: Simon, whom he named Peter, and his brother Andrew, James, John, Philip, Bartholomew, Matthew, Thomas, James the son of Alphaeus, Simon who was called a Zealot, and Judas the son of James, and Judas Iscariot, who became a traitor.

Reflection

Absorbed in prayer before choosing his apostles, Jesus reminds us that prayer and decision-making go hand in hand. When faced with decisions, we need the guidance of the Holy Spirit. St. Peter Claver, a Jesuit whose memorial is today, was a person of prayer whose bold decisions led to an extraordinary life. He left his homeland of Spain in 1610 for Cartagena, Colombia, where he spent the rest of his life caring for slaves crossing the Atlantic from West Africa. Prayer not only helps us to make good decisions, it can lead us to places we might otherwise never have imagined.

Prayers

others may be added

To God who calls us his own people,
we bring our prayers:

℟. Lord, hear us.

- For discernment and courage for all those who seek God's will, we pray: ℟.
- For victims of racism, prejudice, and bigotry, we pray: ℟.
- For an end to poverty and economic disparity, we pray: ℟.
- For those who have asked for our prayers and for those who have no one to pray for them, we pray: ℟.

Let us offer together the prayer
that Jesus taught us.

Our Father . . .

God our hope,
you know our needs
even before we utter a word.
Give us courage and persistence
in prayer
to empty ourselves.
Help us to be mindful of your presence
this day
in ways large and small.
Through Christ our Lord.
Amen.

✚ The Lord is compassionate toward all his works.

Wednesday September 10, 2025

✚ The Lord is compassionate toward all his works.

Psalm 51 *page 373*

Reading *Colossians 3:1–11*

Brothers and sisters: If you were raised with Christ, seek what is above, where Christ is seated at the right hand of God. Think of what is above, not of what is on earth. For you have died, and your life is hidden with Christ in God. When Christ your life appears, then you too will appear with him in glory.

Put to death, then, the parts of you that are earthly: immorality, impurity, passion, evil desire, and the greed that is idolatry. Because of these the wrath of God is coming upon the disobedient. By these you too once conducted yourselves, when you lived in that way. But now you must put them all away: anger, fury, malice, slander, and obscene language out of your mouths. Stop lying to one another, since you have taken off the old self with its practices and have put on the new self, which is being renewed, for knowledge, in the image of its creator. Here there is not Greek and Jew, circumcision and uncircumcision, barbarian, Scythian, slave, free; but Christ is all and in all.

Reflection

Those who have had near-death experiences often share similar stories. At the time of death, they are transported outside of their bodies and arrive at a place with an overwhelming sense of peace and warmth. Perhaps most significant is what happens after they return. They make dramatic life changes. They no longer fear death, living as if death were already behind them. This is what St. Paul is saying to the Colossians. He reminds them that by their baptism they have already died. They are now to live as new people. What if we truly believed we died in baptism? What if we lived as if death were already behind us?

Prayers *others may be added*

Baptized into Christ Jesus, let us pray in a spirit of compassion and hope:

℟. Peaceful God, hear us.

- For the grace to face and to let go of our fears, we pray: ℟.
- For lasting peace in war-torn places in our world, we pray: ℟.
- For those who are hungry and those living on the streets of our cities, we pray: ℟.
- For the broken-hearted, those who mourn, and those who are long-suffering, we pray: ℟.

Let us offer together the prayer that Jesus taught us.

Our Father . . .

God of the poor,
you bless our lives with your goodness.
Give us the grace to be people
of the Beatitudes,
who continue to seek you with sincere
and humble hearts.
Through Christ our Lord.
Amen.

✚ The Lord is compassionate toward all his works.

✤ Let everything that breathes praise the Lord!

Psalm 72 *page 376*

Reading *Luke 6:27–31, 35–36*

Jesus said to his disciples: "To you who hear I say, love your enemies, do good to those who hate you, bless those who curse you, pray for those who mistreat you. To the person who strikes you on one cheek, offer the other one as well, and from the person who takes your cloak, do not withhold even your tunic. Give to everyone who asks of you, and from the one who takes what is yours do not demand it back. Do to others as you would have them do to you. . . . [L]ove your enemies and do good to them, and lend expecting nothing back; then your reward will be great and you will be children of the Most High, for he himself is kind to the ungrateful and the wicked. Be merciful, just as also your Father is merciful."

Reflection

In his 1980 letter, *Mystery and Worship of the Most Holy Eucharist*, Pope St. John Paul II observed that, unlike in the decades before the Second Vatican Council, most of the faithful were now receiving Communion. He questioned whether communicants truly understood what it meant to partake in this sacred meal. The Eucharist, he states, affects how a person treats others. In other words, more is required of those who share Christ's Body and Blood. We are called to love as Christ loves, to do good to our enemies, to bless those who curse us and to pray for those who mistreat us. A tall order to be sure, but living this way is what we say Amen to each time we approach the table of the Lord.

Prayers *others may be added*

To God who is love, we pour out our needs:

℟. **Loving and compassionate God, hear us.**

✦ For freedom from whatever prevents us from showing mercy to others, we pray: ℟.

✦ For those who perished in the attacks on September 11 and for those who continue to mourn their loss, we pray: ℟.

✦ For those who suffer danger from wildfires and other natural disasters , we pray: ℟.

✦ For single parents and families who struggle to provide basic needs for their children, we pray: ℟.

Let us offer together the prayer that Jesus taught us.

Our Father . . .

Good and gracious God,
your love for us is unconditional.
Give us the grace to see others as you see,
through the eyes of mercy, generosity
and compassion.
Through Christ our Lord.
Amen.

✤ Let everything that breathes praise the Lord!

Friday, September 12, 2025

✤ You are my inheritance, O Lord.

Psalm 103 *page 382*

Reading *1 Timothy 1:1–2, 12–14*

Paul, an Apostle of Christ Jesus by command of God our savior and of Christ Jesus our hope, to Timothy, my true child in faith: grace, mercy, and peace from God the Father and Christ Jesus our Lord.

I am grateful to him who has strengthened me, Christ Jesus our Lord, because he considered me trustworthy in appointing me to the ministry. I was once a blasphemer and a persecutor and an arrogant man, but I have been mercifully treated because I acted out of ignorance in my unbelief. Indeed, the grace of our Lord has been abundant, along with the faith and love that are in Christ Jesus.

Reflection *Pope Francis*

Mercy is always a gratuitous act of our heavenly Father, an unconditional and unmerited act of love. Consequently, we cannot risk opposing the full freedom of the love with which God enters into the life of every person. Mercy is this concrete action of love that, by forgiving, transforms and changes our lives. In this way, the divine mystery of mercy is made manifest. God is merciful (see Exodus 34:6); his mercy lasts for ever (see Psalm 136). From generation to generation, it embraces all those who trust in him and it changes them, by bestowing a share in his very life.

Prayers *others may be added*

To God who is always near, we offer our prayers:

℟. Peaceful God, hear our prayer.

✦ For the humility to listen with love and to speak with kindness, we pray: ℟.

✦ For hospitality that extends beyond our comfort zone, we pray: ℟.

✦ For missing persons and those enslaved by human trafficking, we pray: ℟.

✦ For victims of abuse, for those addicted and those in recovery, we pray: ℟.

Let us offer together the prayer that Jesus taught us.

Our Father . . .

Merciful God,
you call us to live in the light
of your love.
Teach us humility that we may be
mindful of our every thought,
word and action this day.
Through Christ our Lord.
Amen.

✤ You are my inheritance, O Lord.

✤ Blessed be the name of the Lord
for ever.

Psalm 34

page 370

Reading

Luke 6:43–49

Jesus said to his disciples: "A good tree does not bear rotten fruit, nor does a rotten tree bear good fruit. For every tree is known by its own fruit. For people do not pick figs from thornbushes, nor do they gather grapes from brambles. A good person out of the store of goodness in his heart produces good, but an evil person out of a store of evil produces evil; for from the fullness of the heart the mouth speaks.

"Why do you call me, 'Lord, Lord,' but not do what I command? I will show you what someone is like who comes to me, listens to my words, and acts on them. That one is like a man building a house, who dug deeply and laid the foundation on rock; when the flood came, the river burst against that house but could not shake it because it had been well built. But the one who listens and does not act is like a person who built a house on the ground without a foundation. When the river burst against it, it collapsed at once and was completely destroyed."

Reflection

In today's Gospel, Jesus says that bearing the spiritual fruit of his word requires listening and acting. So often when we come to God in prayer, we do most of the talking. Likewise, when we pray the Scriptures, we don't always take the time be silent long enough to hear what God is saying to us. In Hebrew, the word for *word* is *dabar*, but it can also mean the action that comes forth from the spoken word. We are called to not only listen, but also to act on God's Word. God's Word is living and dynamic and continues to speak to us in new ways. That Word will bear fruit when it finds a new hearing that prompts us to act out of love.

Prayers

others may be added

Our help comes from the Lord,
whom we now call upon:

℟. Lord, hear us.

- For preachers, readers, and catechists, for all who preach and teach God's word: we pray: ℟.
- For an end to the death penalty and f or healing for all victims of violence, we pray: ℟.
- For migrant workers, clement weather and abundant crops, we pray: ℟.
- For the dying and those who wait with them, for all who mourn their dead, pray: ℟.

Let us offer together the prayer
that Jesus taught us.

Our Father . . .

God, you who sustain us,
your Word is living and active
and will not rest or return
until it accomplishes its purpose.
May we listen with open hearts and
have the courage
to act on the call your word inspires.
Through Christ our Lord.
Amen.

✤ Blessed be the name of the Lord
for ever.

✤ We should glory in the cross
of our Lord Jesus Christ.

Psalm 122

page 387

Reading

John 3:13–17

Jesus said to Nicodemus: "No one has gone up to heaven except the one who has come down from heaven, the Son of Man. And just as Moses lifted up the serpent in the desert, so must the Son of Man be lifted up, so that everyone who believes in him may have eternal life."

For God so loved the world that he gave his only Son, so that everyone who believes in him might not perish but might have eternal life. For God did not send his Son into the world to condemn the world, but that the world might be saved through him.

Reflection

The cross is one of the most ancient symbols of the Christian religion. Crosses appear to be everywhere, hanging from rearview mirrors, standing on faraway hills, adorning necks, ear lobes, fingers, and wrists. Because of this, the central meaning of the cross can be taken for granted. Some see the cross as a sign of suffering, while others view it as a sign of promise. Today's Gospel urges us to recognize the cross as pure love. God sent his only Son who surrendered himself on the cross because God loved the world. This instrument of torture has become the symbol of triumph of life over death. May we, who have been claimed by Christ with the sign of the cross embrace it as an instrument of reconciliation and hope.

Prayers

others may be added

Mindful that we are called to continue Christ's saving mission, we pray:

℟. **God of love, hear us.**

- For the grace to be vulnerable, for patience and humility in times of hardship, we pray: ℟.
- For a deeper understanding between Christians, Muslims, and Jews, we pray: ℟.
- For those who feel forsaken or abandoned, we pray: ℟.
- For those who bear the cross of illness or the burden of anxiety, pray: ℟.

Let us offer together the prayer
that Jesus taught us.

Our Father . . .

Faithful Lord,
by his cross your Son Jesus.
embraced the wounds of a broken
humanity.
May the cross be for us
a source of strength in our weakness
and a source of solidarity with all those
who suffer.
Through Christ our Lord.
Amen

✤ We should glory in the cross
of our Lord Jesus Christ.

✙ Blessed be the Lord, for he has heard my prayer.

Psalm 24

page 367

Reading

John 19:25–27

Standing by the cross of Jesus were his mother and his mother's sister, Mary the wife of Clopas, and Mary Magdalene. When Jesus saw his mother and the disciple there whom he loved he said to his mother, "Woman, behold, your son." Then he said to the disciple, "Behold, your mother." And from that hour the disciple took her into his home.

Reflection

Today is the Memorial of Our Lady of Sorrows. It was formerly called "The Seven Dolors" or "Sorrows" of Mary, and it commemorates seven instances in Scripture that marked times of pain or distress in Mary's life. Today's Gospel, which depicts the crucifixion and death of Jesus, is one of those instances. What mother wouldn't be in agony over the suffering and death of her child? Mary was human, after all, and experienced the myriad of emotions of motherhood. The words of Jesus from the cross giving Mary to the beloved disciple and the disciple to Mary have long been interpreted as symbolic. They establish Mary as the mother of all Christians, represented by the beloved disciple. Mary is now our mother with whom we can relate as Our Lady of Sorrows, but as the Mother of Jesus, she is also the Cause of our Joy.

Prayers

others may be added

With Mary, let us cry out to God with our prayers:

℟. **Compassionate God, hear us.**

- For the grace to bear one another's burdens, we pray: ℟.
- For refugees and for families separated at the borders, we pray: ℟.
- For parents enduring difficult circumstances or experiencing financial distress, we pray: ℟.
- For courage and perseverance for those who face trials, we pray: ℟..

Let us offer together the prayer that Jesus taught us.

Our Father . . .

God of promise,
from the cross, Jesus calls out
to his mother
and to the beloved disciple.
Grant, we pray, the courage
to share in the sufferings
of Christ and of his mother.
Lead us to greater compassion
and understanding
of the wounds that others bear.
Through Christ our Lord.
Amen.

✙ Blessed be the Lord, for he has heard my prayer.

Memorial of Sts. Cornelius, Pope, and Cyprian, Bishop, Martyrs

Tuesday, September 16, 2025

✤ I will walk with blameless heart.

Psalm 27

page 368

Reading

1 Timothy 3:1–7

Beloved, this saying is trustworthy: whoever aspires to the office of bishop desires a noble task. Therefore, a bishop must be irreproachable, married only once, temperate, self-controlled, decent, hospitable, able to teach, not a drunkard, not aggressive, but gentle, not contentious, not a lover of money. He must manage his own household well, keeping his children under control with perfect dignity; for if a man does not know how to manage his own household, how can he take care of the Church of God? He should not be a recent convert, so that he may not become conceited and thus incur the Devil's punishment. He must also have a good reputation among outsiders, so that he may not fall into disgrace, the Devil's trap.

Reflection

In today's reading, St. Paul outlines the qualifications for Church leaders, aware that shepherding the flock is a formidable task. Some two hundred years later, this would prove true in the stories of Sts. Cornelius and Cyprian, whose memorial is today. Cornelius and Cyprian were friends who served as bishops in Rome and in Carthage, respectively. Both served during the persecutions of the emperor Decius, when a controversy arose over whether and how to readmit those who had abandoned the faith. Both refused to cave into the demands of their persecutors, encouraging one another as faithful servants to the end.

Prayers

others may be added

With humility and confidence,
let us give voice to our prayers:

℟. God of strength, hear us.

- For pastoral leaders here and around the world, we pray: ℟.
- For an end to the practices of torture and capital punishment, we pray: ℟.
- For freedom from the temptation toward cowardice in the face of injustice, we pray: ℟.
- For those whose lives are demeaned by the cruelty of others, pray: ℟.

Let us offer together the prayer
that Jesus taught us.

Our Father . . .

God our peace,
you called Sts. Cornelius and Cyprian
to shepherd your flock.
May their faithfulness and dedication
awaken us to prophetic witness,
that we might spread the Gospel
in word and deed
even amid times of testing and trial.
Through Christ our Lord.
Amen.

✤ I will walk with blameless heart.

✤ How great are the works of the Lord!

Psalm 30

page 369

Reading

1 Timothy 3:14–16

Beloved: I am writing you, although I hope to visit you soon. But if I should be delayed, you should know how to behave in the household of God, which is the Church of the living God, the pillar and foundation of truth. Undeniably great is the mystery of devotion,

Who was manifested in the flesh, / vindicated in the spirit, / seen by angels, / proclaimed to the Gentiles, / believed in throughout the world, / taken up in glory.

Reflection

When you hear the word *church*, what first comes to mind, an image of building or an image of a community? The word for *church* in Greek is *ekklesia* and means the people of God. In the century following the death of Christ, the new community of believers didn't have church buildings in which to worship so they gathered in homes. They knew t*hemselves* as the ekklesia, or as God's chosen people. Only later did the term *church* take on the meaning of a building. May we see ourselves anew this day as the Body of Christ on earth, called to be the hands and feet of Jesus for the life of the world.

Prayers

others may be added

In hope and with joy, we lift our hearts in prayer:

℟. God of grace, hear us.

- For the grace to live out the call of our baptism, we pray: ℟.
- For an end to the violence that afflicts our streets, neighborhoods, and towns, we pray: ℟.
- For those who feel alienated or unwelcome in our Church, we pray: ℟.
- For those who are sick, those who care for the elderly, and those who live with a physical disability, we pray: ℟.

Let us offer together the prayer that Jesus taught us.

Our Father . . .

O God,
in Christ you have called a people
to yourself.
Grant, we pray, the grace
to be your presence on earth,
to believe, to love, and to serve.
Through Christ our Lord.
Amen.

✤ How great are the works of the Lord!

Thursday, September 18, 2025

✤ How great are the works of the Lord!

Psalm 51 *page 373*

Reading *Luke 7:37–38, 48–50*

Now there was a sinful woman in the city who learned that [Jesus] was at table in the house of the Pharisee. Bringing an alabaster flask of ointment, she stood behind him at his feet weeping and began to bathe his feet with her tears. Then she wiped them with her hair, kissed them, and anointed them with the ointment. . . . [Jesus] said to her, "Your sins are forgiven." The others at table said to themselves, "Who is this who even forgives sins?" But he said to the woman, "Your faith has saved you; go in peace."

Reflection

There was a man in my Catholic parish known as the whistler. During Mass, he would whistle the songs being sung by the congregation. The man was blind and whistling was his way of praying in song. He wasn't just a good whistler, he was amazing. He knew how much God loved him and that's all that mattered. That certainty freed him to bless the community just as he was. What we consider imperfections, God transforms into gift. In today's Gospel, an unnamed woman's burden of sin was lifted, and she blessed the feet of Jesus with her tears. Jesus transformed her brokenness and that became a blessing. What brokenness of mine can be transformed into a blessing?

Prayers *others may be added*

With faith in God's merciful love,
we pray:

℟. God our hope, hear and answer us.

- For a deeper awareness for one another's gifts and struggles, we pray: ℟.
- For all who seek a place of safety and welcome, we pray: ℟.
- For those whose hearts are hardened by fear, envy, or loss, we pray: ℟.
- For those who are broken in body or spirit, we pray: ℟.

Let us offer together the prayer
that Jesus taught us.

Our Father . . .

Loving God,
on you our every breath depends,
and at your touch we are made whole.
Free us from whatever keeps us from
blessing others
with the mercy you have given us.
Through Christ our Lord.
Amen.

✤ How great are the works of the Lord!

✤ Blessed the poor in spirit;
the Kingdom of heaven is theirs!

Psalm 34

page 370

Reading

Luke 8:1–3

Jesus journeyed from one town and village to another, preaching and proclaiming the good news of the Kingdom of God. Accompanying him were the Twelve and some women who had been cured of evil spirits and infirmities, Mary, called Magdalene, from whom seven demons had gone out, Joanna, the wife of Herod's steward Chuza, Susanna, and many others who provided for them out of their resources.

Reflection

Adventure travel is not for the weak. Just ask anyone who has tried to climb Mount Everest or rappel Victoria Falls in Costa Rica. The women Luke mentions in today's Gospel, Mary Magdalene, Joanna, and Susanna, were true adventure travelers. Bold and courageous, they abandoned the comforts of home and social norms to accompany Jesus, not knowing where the journey would take them. They followed Jesus from Galilee all the way to the cross and were among the first to witness his resurrection. Consider the women who have accompanied you in your life. How has their courage made a difference in your life? What is Jesus calling you to risk to accompany others?

Prayers

others may be added

Trusting that God hears our prayers, we bring our needs and petitions:

℟. God of all courage, hear us.

- For a greater understanding and appreciation for the diversity of gifts in the Church, we pray: ℟.
- For an end to practices of discrimination against women, we pray: ℟.
- For those bowed down by unemployment or financial stress, we pray: ℟.
- For those who seek healing for their addictions, we pray: ℟.

Let us offer together the prayer that Jesus taught us.

Our Father . . .

God of our ancestors,
from the beginning of time
you have called men and women
to teach, to preach, and to proclaim
your kingdom.
Give us the fortitude to follow Jesus
wherever that leads,
and help us to be fearless
in spreading the Good News.
Through Christ our Lord.
Amen.

✤ Blessed the poor in spirit;
the Kingdom of heaven is theirs!

Memorial of Sts. Andrew Kim Tae-gŏn, Priest, and Paul Chŏng Ha-sang, and Companions, Martyrs

Saturday, September 20, 2025

✚ Come with joy into the presence of the Lord.

Psalm 23

page 367

Reading

Luke 8:4–11

When a large crowd gathered, with people from one town after another journeying to Jesus, he spoke in a parable. "A sower went out to sow his seed. And as he sowed, some seed fell on the path and was trampled, and the birds of the sky ate it up. Some seed fell on rocky ground, and when it grew, it withered for lack of moisture. Some seed fell among thorns, and the thorns grew with it and choked it. And some seed fell on good soil, and when it grew, it produced fruit a hundredfold." After saying this, he called out, "Whoever has ears to hear ought to hear."

Then his disciples asked him what the meaning of this parable might be. He answered, "Knowledge of the mysteries of the Kingdom of God has been granted to you; but to the rest, they are made known through parables so that *they may look but not see, and hear but not understand*.

"This is the meaning of the parable. The seed is the word of God."

Reflection

Trying to grow plants in Georgia's red clay is tough. The soil is hard and dense when dry and can become waterlogged when there is abundant rainfall, preventing plants from taking root. The only way to get anything to grow is to add organic matter such as compost or manure. Material made of plants that are dead or dying is rich in nutrients, making it easy for new life to sprout. The soil in the human heart of which Jesus speaks also requires death and dying. When we die to selfishness, pride, and our own egotistical needs, we become more supple and yielding. Then the Word of God can immerse itself, take root, and bear fruit.

Prayers

others may be added

Believing that God will provide for our needs, let us pray with faithful hearts:

℟. God of all knowledge, hear us.

- For those who suffer persecution or misunderstanding, we pray: ℟.
- For renewed efforts to promote clean water and healthy soil, we pray: ℟.
- For favorable weather and abundant crops, we pray: ℟.
- For peace to the aging and those who face diminishment of health, we pray: ℟.

Let us offer together the prayer that Jesus taught us.

Our Father . . .

God of abundance,
you help us to see
that new life comes only from death.
Calm our fears
and in the midst of our pain
let us know your presence.
Through Christ our Lord.
Amen.

✚ Come with joy into the presence of the Lord.

✚ Graciously raise [us] up, O Lord.

Psalm 46

page 372

Reading

Luke 16:10–13

Jesus said to his disciples: "The person who is trustworthy in very small matters is also trustworthy in great ones; and the person who is dishonest in very small matters is also dishonest in great ones. If, therefore, you are not trustworthy with dishonest wealth, who will trust you with true wealth? If you are not trustworthy with what belongs to another, who will give you what is yours? No servant can serve two masters. He will either hate one and love the other, or be devoted to one and despise the other. You cannot serve both God and mammon."

Reflection

"What's in your wallet?" is a memorable marketing slogan designed to promote a credit card from Capital One Bank. "What's in your wallet?" is an interesting question and a clever way to ponder whether one is satisfied with its contents. Today's Gospel takes this question further and prompts us to examine our perspective on wealth. Jesus' parable encourages us to be trustworthy, just, creative, and intentional in managing our resources not for selfish gain, but for building up the kingdom of God. It calls us to recognize that everything we have, including what we've earned, is a gift from God. We are temporary stewards, called to use God's resources with generous care that impacts this life and the one to come.

Prayers

others may be added

With trust in God's generosity,
we bring forth our needs:

℟. God of all truth, hear us.

- For the voices in our lives that call us to justice, charity, simplicity and compassion, we pray: ℟.
- For wisdom in using natural resources, for the good of the earth and the poor, we pray: ℟.
- For families that face economic hardship or financial burden, we pray: ℟.
- For those without means for medical care, we pray: ℟.

Let us offer together the prayer
that Jesus taught us.

Our Father . . .

Eternal God,
in your Son Jesus
you have shown us the example
of a faithful servant.
Help us to recognize
that everything we have comes
from you,
that we may tend well the gifts your
love has made.
Through Christ our Lord.
Amen.

✚ Graciously raise [us] up, O Lord.

Monday, September 22, 2025

✤ The Lord has done marvels for us.

Psalm 47

page 372

Reading

Luke 8:16–18

Jesus said to the crowd: "No one who lights a lamp conceals it with a vessel or sets it under a bed; rather, he places it on a lampstand so that those who enter may see the light. For there is nothing hidden that will not become visible, and nothing secret that will not be known and come to light. Take care, then, how you hear. To anyone who has, more will be given, and from the one who has not, even what he seems to have will be taken away."

Reflection

Jesus uses the image of a lamp to speak about light in today's Gospel. In the Church, we use a paschal candle, which is lit at crucial moments in the life of a believer. The paschal candle is the preeminent symbol of the risen Christ. The paschal candle is also called the Easter candle because a new one is lit for the first time at the Easter Vigil, illuminating the procession into the sanctuary on the Church's holiest night. After it is incensed, it stands near the ambo where it remains throughout the Easter season. During the rest of the year, it is located in the baptistery and is lit at every baptism and every funeral. Each time it is lit, wax melts, and the candle becomes shorter as it spends itself for life's most profound moments. We who received the light of Christ at our baptism are also called to spend ourselves, sharing our light with one another.

Prayers

others may be added

Let us ask the Holy Spirit to enlighten our hearts and minds as we pray:

℟. Light of God, hear us.

- For the grace to be honest with ourselves and patient with one another, we pray: ℟.
- For those who live in the shadow of war or violence, we pray: ℟.
- For those mired in the darkness of fear and despair, we pray: ℟.
- For the protection of youth from the lure of drugs and alcohol, we pray: ℟.

Let us offer together the prayer that Jesus taught us.

Our Father . . .

Lord our God,
you sent your Son Jesus as the light
to guide our pathway.
Illumine our hearts to hear your word,
that we may be generous in sharing
the light of your love with all those
we meet.
Through Christ our Lord.
Amen.

✤ The Lord has done marvels for us.

✤ Let us go rejoicing to the house of the Lord.

Psalm 122

page 387

Reading

Luke 8:19–21

The mother of Jesus and his brothers came to him but were unable to join him because of the crowd. He was told, "Your mother and your brothers are standing outside and they wish to see you." He said to them in reply, "My mother and my brothers are those who hear the word of God and act on it."

Reflection

As a single parent, my mother leaned on her faith for strength. A devout Catholic, she made the church a second home. At the time of her death, she was still living in the town where she was born and raised in western Pennsylvania. I was living in Maryland and my brother was living in the Middle East. During the homily, the priest spoke to my brother and me, saying "As long as you stay close to the Body of Christ, you will always have mother, father, sister and brother." He was right. No matter where my brother and I have lived, the community of believers has been our family. They are the people who have heard and acted on the word of God, embracing us as their own.

Prayers

others may be added

God longs for us and so with confidence in his mercy, we pray:

℟. **Merciful God, hear us.**

- For all who have nurtured our faith and taught us to love, we pray: ℟.
- For justice on our streets, we pray: ℟.
- For those whom society neglects and avoids, we pray: ℟.
- For the hospitalized and the bedridden and all who are unable to join their faith communities, we pray: ℟.

Let us offer together the prayer that Jesus taught us.

Our Father . . .

God in our midst,
day in and day out
you invite the human community
to hear your Word and to act on it.
May we, who follow your Son Jesus,
the Incarnate Word,
speak your word
where it is needed most.
Through Christ our Lord.
Amen.

✤ Let us go rejoicing to the house of the Lord.

Wednesday, September 24, 2025

✠ Blessed be God, who lives for ever.

Psalm 62

page 374

Reading

Luke 9:1–6

Jesus summoned the Twelve and gave them power and authority over all demons and to cure diseases, and he sent them to proclaim the Kingdom of God and to heal the sick. He said to them, "Take nothing for the journey, neither walking stick, nor sack, nor food, nor money, and let no one take a second tunic. Whatever house you enter, stay there and leave from there. And as for those who do not welcome you, when you leave that town, shake the dust from your feet in testimony against them." Then they set out and went from village to village proclaiming the good news and curing diseases everywhere.

Reflection

The Aboriginal Australians, whose livelihood depended on hunting and gathering, had a saying, "If you can't carry it, you don't need it." The Aboriginals had to rely only on what their arms could carry, trusting that those things would be enough to sustain them. So often we carry more than we need. There is always one more thing to buy, one more activity in which to participate, one more "yes" to something we have neither time for nor interest in. There is also the emotional baggage we carry—the hurts that we can't let go of, the vengefulness we harbor, and the grief that prevents us from moving on. Today's Gospel reminds us that our journey of faith is simple. We don't need much to proclaim the kingdom of God, only a willing spirit and a complete reliance on God.

Prayers

others may be added

To God who calls us into being, let us offer our prayers for the whole human family:

℟. **Lord hear our prayer.**

- For the grace to let go of our accumulated possessions and our empty desires, we pray: ℟.
- For safe shelter for those who are displaced from their home, we pray: ℟.
- For the grace to simplify our living for the preservation of the environment and for future generations, we pray: ℟.
- For the healing of those who suffer trauma or painful memories, we pray: ℟.

Let us offer together the prayer that Jesus taught us.

Our Father . . .

O God, source of life,
in your Son Jesus
you have shown us the path of life.
Free us from everything that holds
us bound.
Renew our imagination that we may
move unencumbered
in new places toward you and
your kingdom of joy.
Through Christ our Lord.
Amen.

✠ Blessed be God, who lives for ever.

✤ The Lord takes delight in his people.

Psalm 63
page 375

Reading
Haggai 1:5–8

Now thus says the Lord of hosts: / Consider your ways! / You have sown much, but have brought in little; / you have eaten, but have not been satisfied; / You have drunk, but have not been exhilarated; / have clothed yourselves, but not been warmed; / And whoever earned wages / earned them for a bag with holes in it. / Thus says the LORD of hosts: / Consider your ways! / Go up into the hill country; / bring timber, and build the house / That I may take pleasure in it / and receive my glory, says the LORD.

Reflection

There are far fewer Catholic parishes in the United States now compared to the number of churches in the 1970s and 80s. Most of the churches that have been closed were built to serve immigrant populations arriving from Europe in the late nineteenth and early twentieth centuries. For migrants, these churches were more than mere buildings. They offered stability, identity, and a place to belong at a time when the future was uncertain. The prophet Haggai knew the importance of the temple to the people of Israel who had just returned from a devastating exile. Despite objections from some members of the community, Haggai encouraged the people to resume the reconstruction of the temple that was destroyed by the Babylonians. He believed a new temple would signal a renewal of Jewish life. Today is a good day to reflect on the churches that have been home to us, on the sacred moments shared there, on the ways that these spaces have formed our identity as the people of God.

Prayers
others may be added

Believing that God hears our prayers, we call out our needs:

℟. Lord of hosts, hear us.

- For reconciliation within our families, churches, and communities, we pray: ℟.
- For leaders in the Catholic Church, Catholic schools, and charitable organizations , we pray: ℟.
- For immigrants, refugees, and those who live on the margins of society, we pray: ℟.
- For the unemployed and those who feel discouraged or overwhelmed, we pray: ℟.

Let us offer together the prayer that Jesus taught us.

Our Father . . .

Generous God,
you transcend space and time
so that every age can call you Lord
and Savior.
Look with mercy this day
on the communities we love and serve,
and on the people we name and
hold dear
in the silence of our hearts.
Through Christ our Lord.
Amen.

✤ The Lord takes delight in his people.

Weekday

Friday, September 26, 2025

✤ Hope in God.

Psalm 67 *page 375*

page 375

Reading *Luke 9:18–22*

Once when Jesus was praying in solitude, and the disciples were with him, he asked them, "Who do the crowds say that I am?" They said in reply, "John the Baptist; others, Elijah; still others, 'One of the ancient prophets has arisen.'" Then he said to them, "But who do you say that I am?" Peter said in reply, "The Christ of God."

He rebuked them and directed them not to tell this to anyone. He said, "The Son of Man must suffer greatly and be rejected by the elders, the chief priests, and the scribes, and be killed and on the third day be raised."

Reflection

Just when the disciples think they have Jesus all figured out, he trumps their assumptions. When Peter declares Jesus as "the Christ of God," Jesus reveals the fate that awaits him. The disciples were expecting a Messianic ruler whose might would ultimately topple the Romans, not a man whose future included rejection and execution. Like the disciples, we too put God in a box, fitting God into our agenda instead of the other way around. But God is much larger than our boxes. Our God is a God who would have us love our enemies, rather than take revenge. Our God is the God who leaves the ninety-nine to look for the one, and who would rather hang out with the poor ones, the prostitute, and the outcast. When we draw near to the crosses in our own lives, we are better able to answer that question posed by Jesus, "Who do you say that I am?"

Prayers *others may be added*

With one voice, we bring our prayers before God:

℟. O God, hear us.

- For the desire to seek a greater understanding of our faith, we pray: ℟.
- For the protection of pregnant women and newborns , we pray: ℟.
- For an end to the death penalty and for the healing of all victims of violence, we pray: ℟.
- For all who bear the cross of illness and grief, we pray: ℟.

Let us offer together the prayer that Jesus taught us.

Our Father . . .

Faithful God,
to your sons and daughters
you give futures and possibilities
beyond what we could ever imagine.
Come in our trembling and doubt;
embrace us in your compassion
that we might be your truth-tellers,
proclaiming your wondrous love.
Through Christ our Lord.
Amen.

✤ Hope in God.

✤ O Lord, you have been our refuge.

Psalm 84

page 378

Reading

Zechariah 2:14–15a

Sing and rejoice, O daughter Zion! / See, I am coming to dwell among you, says the LORD. / Many nations shall join themselves to the LORD on that day, / and they shall be his people and he will dwell among you.

Reflection

Zechariah's visions anticipate that God's promises are about to be fulfilled for the people of Israel. According to the vision in today's reading, Jerusalem will be rebuilt and will become a beacon to the nations. Zechariah foresees a new era for the holy city, when walls that once defended the city against enemy attack will no longer be needed. God's presence will be protection enough and all people of good will are welcome within its walls. This idea is echoed in "Mending Wall", a poem by Robert Frost, about a wall that divides two neighbors. In this poem, something that remains unnamed continues to crumble part of the wall, prompting the two to reexamine its purpose. Today is a good day to ask the Holy Spirit to break down the walls that divide us from a deeper relationship with God and with one another.

Prayers others

may be added

United in faith, we bring our needs before God:

℟. **God of love, hear us.**

- For a deeper understanding of those who have different perspectives and experiences, we pray: ℟.
- For the grace to overcome the fears that keep us from helping people in their their need, we pray: ℟.
- For an end to racial stereotyping and the healing of all that gives birth to violence, we pray: ℟.
- For those who are bullied, harassed, or ridiculed, we pray: ℟.
- For all who will pass through soup kitchens and shelters this day, we pray ℟.

Let us offer together the prayer that Jesus taught us.

Our Father . . .

God of the lowly,
in Jesus your Son you welcomed those
who were poor.
Through your servant St. Vincent
de Paul you embraced the poor ones.
Give us a spirit of poverty,
that the walls that divide us may
crumble and fall.
Open our arms wide,
that we may welcome, embrace
and serve
those in need of your tender care.
Through Christ our Lord.
Amen.

✤ O Lord, you have been our refuge.

Sunday, September 28, 2025

✚ [We] give glory to your name
[O Lord.]

Psalm 85 *page 379*

Reading *Luke 16:24–31*

[The rich man] cried out, “Father Abraham, have pity on me. Send Lazarus to dip the tip of his finger in water and cool my tongue, for I am suffering torment in these flames.” Abraham replied, “My child, remember that you received what was good during your lifetime while Lazarus likewise received what was bad; but now he is comforted here, whereas you are tormented. Moreover, between us and you a great chasm is established to prevent anyone from crossing who might wish to go from our side to yours or from your side to ours.” He said, “Then I beg you, father, send him to my father’s house, for I have five brothers, so that he may warn them, lest they too come to this place of torment.” But Abraham replied, “They have Moses and the prophets. Let them listen to them.” He said, “Oh no, father Abraham, but if someone from the dead goes to them, they will repent.” Then Abraham said, “If they will not listen to Moses and the prophets, neither will they be persuaded if someone should rise from the dead.”

Reflection

In this story, which is unique to Luke’s Gospel, we find an unusual detail. One of the characters in the parable actually has a name. *Lazarus*, the Greek form of the Hebrew name, *Eleazar*, means “God is my help.” The rich man, on the other hand, remains unnamed. He finds his sole source of identity in his wealth. In life, he remains on the secure side of the door, so wrapped up in riches that he fails to notice the poor man at his doorstep. That indifference results in eternal punishment while Lazarus dwells in immortal comfort beside Abraham. May this Gospel challenge us to see the poor and suffering at our door, to choose empathy over apathy, and to serve out of love.

Prayers *others may be added*

With confidence in God’s mercy,
we pour out our needs:

℟. Forgiving God, hear us.

✦ For freedom from indifference toward those who are poor, we pray: ℟.

✦ For hospitality toward the migrant, the beggar, and all those in need, we pray: ℟.

✦ For those whose lives are demeaned by society, we pray: ℟.

✦ For those without jobs, food, or a safe place to rest, we pray ℟.

Let us offer together the prayer
that Jesus taught us.

Our Father . . .

O God,
open our eyes to witness the suffering
in our midst,
that our treatment of those in need
may always reflect the Gospel.
Through Christ our Lord.
Amen.

✚ [We] give glory to your name
[O Lord.]

✚ The Lord will build up Zion again,
and appear in all his glory.

Psalm 91
page 379

Reading
Daniel 7:9–10, 13–14

Thrones were set up / and the Ancient One took his throne. / His clothing was bright as snow, / and the hair on his head as white as wool; / his throne was flames of fire, / with wheels of burning fire. / A surging stream of fire / flowed out from where he sat; / Thousands upon thousands were ministering to him, / and myriads upon myriads attended him. / The court was convened and the books were opened.

As the visions during the night continued, I saw: / One like a son of man coming, / on the clouds of heaven; / when he reached the Ancient One / and was presented before him, / He received dominion, glory, and kingship; / nations and peoples of every language serve him. / His dominion is an everlasting dominion / that shall not be taken away, / his kingship shall not be destroyed.

Reflection

Days after I arrived in Italy for a sabbatical, my cousin in New York with whom I was close, passed away. I was overcome with grief and guilt at not being able to be present for his funeral. A young man I barely knew reached out to me with compassion and consolation. He was my angel during this time of grieving. And believe it or not, his name is Gabriel! Angels emerge throughout the Bible, usually to relay a message from God. Catholic tradition says that each believer has a guardian angel to protect and guide them. As we celebrate the feast of the archangels, may we give thanks for those persons who show up when we need them the most. They are our angels in disguise.

Prayers
others may be added

With all the saints and the angels, we celebrate the goodness of God as we pray:

℟. **God of heaven and earth, hear us.**

- For those who await a message of hope or a word of compassion, we pray: ℟.
- For all who bear the privilege and the burden of leadership, we pray: ℟.
- For the protection of the innocent and especially for children who are exploited, we pray: ℟.
- For those who experience a diminishment of mind, body, or mobility, we pray ℟.

Let us offer together the prayer
that Jesus taught us.

Our Father . . .

Gracious Lord,
fill our hearts with gratitude
and longing,
that one day we may join the angels
and archangels
to praise you in eternal glory.
Who live and reign for ever and ever.
Amen.

✚ The Lord will build up Zion again,
and appear in all his glory.

Memorial of St. Jerome,
Priest and Doctor of the Church

Tuesday, September 30, 2025

✚ Let my prayer come before you, O God.

Psalm 95

page 380

Reading

Zechariah 8:20–23

Thus says the LORD of hosts: / There shall yet come peoples, / the inhabitants of many cities; / and the inhabitants of one city shall approach those of another, / and say, "Come! let us go to implore the favor of the LORD"; / and, "I too will go to seek the LORD." / Many peoples and strong nations shall come / to seek the LORD of hosts in Jerusalem / and to implore the favor of the LORD. / Thus says the LORD of hosts: / In those days ten men of every nationality, / speaking different tongues, shall take hold, / yes, take hold of every Jew by the edge of his garment and say, / "Let us go with you, for we have heard that God is with you."

Reflection

The prophet Zechariah offers a foretaste of the future relationship between God and the chosen people. He indicates that this covenant relationship is not only meant for a small group, but for all. He sees a day when people from many nations and tongues will come to Jerusalem. They will seek the Lord by grasping the garments of believers, saying, "Take us with you, we have heard that God is with you." This is a reminder to us of the importance of giving witness to God's presence in our daily lives, so that seekers may tug on our sleeves saying, "Take us with you, we have heard that God is with you."

Prayers

others may be added

With joy in God's steadfast love,
we give voice to our needs:

℟. Lord of hosts, hear us.

- For readers, catechists, teachers, and preachers, and for all who proclaim the Good News, we pray: ℟.
- For deliverance from the grip of prejudice and fear, we pray: ℟.
- For inquirers, catechumens, candidates, and neophytes, we pray: ℟.
- For those who are long-suffering or who feel alone in their pain, we pray:℟.

Let us offer together the prayer
that Jesus taught us.

Our Father . . .

God of creation,
you call people from many nations
and tongues to be your own.
Move us beyond ourselves
and open wide our arms
to receive those who seek you with
sincere hearts.
May we witness your love to
the powerful and the poor,
the sick and the dying,
and all who await your word of hope.
Through Christ our Lord.
Amen.

✚ Let my prayer come before you, O God.

✤ Let my tongue be silenced if I ever forget you.

Psalm 98 *page 381*

Reading *Luke 9:57–62*

As Jesus and his disciples were proceeding on their journey, someone said to him, "I will follow you wherever you go." Jesus answered him, "Foxes have dens and birds of the sky have nests, but the Son of Man has nowhere to rest his head." And to another he said, "Follow me." But he replied, "Lord, let me go first and bury my father." But he answered him, "Let the dead bury their dead. But you, go and proclaim the Kingdom of God." And another said, "I will follow you, Lord, but first let me say farewell to my family at home." Jesus answered him, "No one who sets a hand to the plow and looks to what was left behind is fit for the Kingdom of God."

Reflection

It would be easy to read today's Gospel and assume that Jesus is telling his followers they must neglect their earthly duties and relationships in order to follow him. This would be a great misreading of Jesus! Rather, Jesus exhorts us to get our priorities straight: proclaiming and striving for the Kingdom of God before all else. If other things in our life distract or prevent us from following Jesus wholeheartedly, we must put them behind us. Jesus must be first in our lives, for only he is our Lord and Savior.

Prayers *others may be added*

Longing for the kingdom, we pray:

℟. **Lord, hear our prayer.**

- That priests and bishops may lead as Jesus did, we pray: ℟.
- That politicians and judges may work for justice, we pray: ℟.
- That those who are sick and burdened may find respite, we pray: ℟.
- That the kingdom may grow in our local communities, we pray: ℟

Let us offer together the prayer
that Jesus taught us.

Our Father . . .

Lord God,
protect us from all distractions
and false saviors
so that we may come to rest
in the peace of your kingdom.
Through Christ our Lord.
Amen.

✤ Let my tongue be silenced if I ever forget you.

Thursday, October 2, 2025

✤ The precepts of the Lord give joy
to the heart.

Psalm 103 *page 382*

Reading *Matthew 18:1–5, 10*

The disciples approached Jesus and said, "Who is the greatest in the Kingdom of heaven?" He called a child over, placed it in their midst, and said, "Amen, I say to you, unless you turn and become like children, you will not enter the Kingdom of heaven. Whoever humbles himself like this child is the greatest in the Kingdom of heaven. And whoever receives one child such as this in my name receives me.

"See that you do not despise one of these little ones, for I say to you that their angels in heaven always look upon the face of my heavenly Father."

Reflection

In today's Gospel, Jesus exhorts us to be like little ones and have confidence in the protection given by our Guardian Angels. Do we really trust that God has sent his angels to walk with us? It can be hard to remember this day-to-day since we can't actually see our angels. But they are always with us, praying for us, and shielding us from evil. Take some time today to thank your guardian angel and pray that you may be guided by their prayers to live a life pleasing to God.

Prayers *others may be added*

With confidence in our heavenly Father, we pray:

℟. Lord, hear our prayer.

- That the Church may safeguard the little ones entrusted to her care, we pray: ℟.
- That world leaders may work for peace and justice for all, we pray: ℟.
- That those in harm's way may find safety, we pray: ℟.
- That our communities may protect the innocence of children, we pray: ℟

Let us offer together the prayer that Jesus taught us.

Our Father . . .

Heavenly Father,
you have entrusted us to the care
of the angels.
Grant that under their protection
we may be kept safe from all harm
and guided toward holiness.
Through Christ our Lord.
Amen.

✤ The precepts of the Lord give joy
to the heart.

✤ For the glory of your name, O Lord, deliver us.

Psalm 115 *page 385*

Reading *Baruch 1:15–22*

During the Babylonian captivity, the exiles prayed: "Justice is with the Lord, our God; and we today are flushed with shame, we men of Judah and citizens of Jerusalem, that we, with our kings and rulers and priests and prophets, and with our ancestors, have sinned in the Lord's sight and disobeyed him. We have neither heeded the voice of the Lord, our God, nor followed the precepts which the Lord set before us. From the time the Lord led our ancestors out of the land of Egypt until the present day, we have been disobedient to the Lord, our God, and only too ready to disregard his voice. And the evils and the curse that the Lord enjoined upon Moses, his servant, at the time he led our ancestors forth from the land of Egypt to give us the land flowing with milk and honey, cling to us even today. For we did not heed the voice of the Lord, our God, in all the words of the prophets whom he sent us, but each one of us went off after the devices of his own wicked heart, served other gods, and did evil in the sight of the Lord, our God."

Reflection

Today's reading can be difficult to hear. We don't like to be told that we have sinned. We like to cling to our illusions of perfection, or at least that we're "good enough." But the standard is Jesus himself, and we come up woefully short. Fortunately, we don't have to save ourselves. God, in his infinite compassion, sent Jesus to offer mercy and forgiveness, especially through the sacrament of reconciliation. How great a gift we have been given! If it's been a while since you've confessed your sins, consider finding some time in the next week to go to confession. The Father is waiting to forgive you!

Prayers *others may be added*

With faith that our God hears us,
we pray:

℟. **Lord of justice, hear our prayer.**

- For the Church, that she may grow in holiness, we pray: ℟.
- For the world, that all peoples may enjoy peace and prosperity, we pray: ℟.
- For those who suffer, that they may be comforted, we pray: ℟.
- For our community, that we may serve one another in love, we pray: ℟.

Let us offer together the prayer
that Jesus taught us.

Our Father . . .

Jesus, our Lord and Savior,
you have called us to be perfect as you are perfect.
Give us the grace and courage to know and do your will.
Who live and reign for ever and ever.
Amen.

✤ For the glory of your name, O Lord, deliver us.

✚ The Lord listens to the poor.

Psalm 121 *page 386*

Reading *Luke 10:17–24*

The seventy-two disciples returned rejoicing and said to Jesus, "Lord, even the demons are subject to us because of your name." Jesus said, "I have observed Satan fall like lightning from the sky. Behold, I have given you the power 'to tread upon serpents' and scorpions and upon the full force of the enemy and nothing will harm you. Nevertheless, do not rejoice because the spirits are subject to you, but rejoice because your names are written in heaven."

At that very moment he rejoiced in the Holy Spirit and said, "I give you praise, Father, Lord of heaven and earth, for although you have hidden these things from the wise and the learned you have revealed them to the childlike. Yes, Father, such has been your gracious will. All things have been handed over to me by my Father. No one knows who the Son is except the Father, and who the Father is except the Son and anyone to whom the Son wishes to reveal him."

Turning to the disciples in private he said, "Blessed are the eyes that see what you see. For I say to you, many prophets and kings desired to see what you see, but did not see it, and to hear what you hear, but did not hear it."

Reflection

Jesus exhorts his disciples to be humble, even when they have accomplished incredible things in his name and with the authority he bestowed on them. They are not to base their faith on the miracles they had seen or the power they wielded, but on the promise that they have a place in the kingdom of God. We, too, are to base faith on the promise given to us at our baptism: that through the death and resurrection of Jesus we can enjoy eternity with him. How great a promise, and how great a Savior who has made it!

Prayers *others may be added*

Trusting in the promises of our Father, we pray:

℟. Lord, hear our prayer.

- That parents may guide their children toward great faith, we pray: ℟.
- That the goods of the world may be shared with all, we pray: ℟.
- That the poor may be raised up and their needs provided for, we pray: ℟.
- That we may be kept safe from harmful weather, we pray: ℟.

Let us offer together the prayer
that Jesus taught us.

Our Father . . .

God of power and might,
who call us your children through
baptism,
help us to live lives of holiness
so that we may one day rest with you
in your kingdom.
Through Christ our Lord.
Amen.

✚ The Lord listens to the poor.

✤ You are the Lord of all.

Psalm 138 *page 388*

Reading *Luke 17:5–10*

The apostles said to the Lord, "Increase our faith." The Lord replied, "If you have faith the size of a mustard seed, you would say to this mulberry tree, 'Be uprooted and planted in the sea,' and it would obey you.

"Who among you would say to your servant who has just come in from plowing or tending sheep in the field, 'Come here immediately and take your place at table'? Would he not rather say to him, 'Prepare something for me to eat. Put on your apron and wait on me while I eat and drink. You may eat and drink when I am finished'? Is he grateful to that servant because he did what was commanded? So should it be with you. When you have done all you have been commanded, say, 'We are unprofitable servants; we have done what we were obliged to do.'"

Reflection

Asking for our faith to be strengthened and increased may be one of the most honest prayers we can make. It acknowledges that we are humble servants of the Lord, in need of his grace, and that we still have ways to go in our journey as his disciples. This type of honesty before the Lord is the beginning of wisdom and growth in faith. When we think we don't need the Lord we turn inward and try to be our own savior. Instead, pray to see yourself as you are and ask the Lord to increase your faith in him.

Prayers *others may be added*

Relying on the Lord, without whom we can do nothing, we pray:

℟. Lord, hear our prayer.

- For the Church, that all the faithful may grow in holiness, we pray: ℟.
- For the world, that God's justice and peace may guide us, we pray: ℟.
- For the sick, that they may know God's presence and healing, we pray: ℟.
- For our communities, that those who don't know Jesus may encounter him and believe, we pray: ℟.

Let us offer together the prayer
that Jesus taught us.

Our Father . . .

Living God,
our faith in you is a gift.
Grant that we may remain
your servants
and gain the reward you have promised
to those who believe in you.
Through Christ our Lord.
Amen.

✤ You are the Lord of all.

Monday, October 6, 2025

✚ You will rescue my life from the pit,
O Lord.

Psalm 72 *page 376*

Reading *Luke 10:29–37*

[The scholar of the law] said to Jesus, "And who is my neighbor?" Jesus replied, "A man fell victim to robbers as he went down from Jerusalem to Jericho. They stripped and beat him and went off leaving him half-dead. A priest happened to be going down that road, but when he saw him, he passed by on the opposite side. Likewise a Levite came to the place, and when he saw him, he passed by on the opposite side. But a Samaritan traveler who came upon him was moved with compassion at the sight. He approached the victim, poured oil and wine over his wounds and bandaged them. Then he lifted him up on his own animal, took him to an inn, and cared for him. The next day he took out two silver coins and gave them to the innkeeper with the instruction, 'Take care of him. If you spend more than what I have given you, I shall repay you on my way back.' Which of these three, in your opinion, was neighbor to the robbers' victim?" He answered, "The one who treated him with mercy." Jesus said to him, "Go and do likewise."

Reflection

Asking "Who is my neighbor?" makes a pivotal assumption: that some people are worthy of my concern and others are not. Jesus' answer would have surprised his listeners, for whom hatred of Samaritans ran deep: your neighbor is anyone in need. There are no conditions attached, such as shared faith or political beliefs. Christians are to call all people "neighbor." This doesn't mean we won't have disagreements with other people. But it does mean that, even in the midst of disagreements, we are to recognize the dignity of each person and treat them as beloved creations of our Father.

Prayers *others may be added*

Longing for the day when all people will see the Lord face-to-face, we pray:

℟. **Lord of love, hear us.**

- For our deacons, that they may serve others with the heart of Christ, we pray: ℟.
- For world leaders, that they may be guided by God's justice, we pray: ℟.
- For the homeless, that they may find shelter and true neighbors, we pray: ℟.
- For our communities, that we may be neighbors to one another, we pray: ℟.

Let us offer together the prayer
that Jesus taught us.

Our Father . . .

God who calls us to love one another,
grant that we may see one another
as neighbor
and open our hearts to serve with
humility and love
Through Christ our Lord.
Amen.

✚ You will rescue my life from the pit,
O Lord.

✚ Guide me, Lord.

Psalm 84

page 378

Reading

Jonah 3:1–10

The word of the LORD came to Jonah a second time: "Set out for the great city of Nineveh, and announce to it the message that I will tell you." So Jonah made ready and went to Nineveh, according to the LORD's bidding. Now Nineveh was an enormously large city; it took three days to go through it. Jonah began his journey through the city, and had gone but a single day's walk announcing, "Forty days more and Nineveh shall be destroyed," when the people of Nineveh believed God; they proclaimed a fast and all of them, great and small, put on sackcloth.

When the news reached the king of Nineveh, he rose from his throne, laid aside his robe, covered himself with sackcloth, and sat in the ashes. Then he had this proclaimed throughout Nineveh, by decree of the king and his nobles: "Neither man nor beast, neither cattle nor sheep, shall taste anything; they shall not eat, nor shall they drink water. Man and beast shall be covered with sackcloth and call loudly to God; every man shall turn from his evil way and from the violence he has in hand. Who knows, God may relent and forgive, and withhold his blazing wrath, so that we shall not perish." When God saw by their actions how they turned from their evil way, he repented of the evil that he had threatened to do to them; he did not carry it out.

Reflection

Jonah, having neglected to heed God's command (and having spent three days in the belly of a fish for his disobedience!) hears from the Lord a second time. God, in effect, gives Jonah a second chance. Throughout the stories of the Bible, God gives his people chance after chance, even when by all accounts he should abandon them to their sins. Our God is a God of second chances, going so far as to send his own Son to die on a cross for us. What marvelous love we have been shown by God, and how much we owe him in return!

Prayers

others may be added

Confident in God's love, we pray:

℟. **Lord, hear our prayer.**

- For our priests, that they may never tire of extending God's forgiveness to others, we pray: ℟.
- For leaders in business, that they may respect the rights and dignity of workers, we pray: ℟.
- For those without steady work, that they may find gainful employment, we pray: ℟.

Let us offer together the prayer
that Jesus taught us.

Our Father . . .

Eternal God,
who never tire of forgiving us,
lead us by your Word
to grow as disciples of your Son.
Who lives and reigns for ever and ever.
Amen.

✚ Guide me, Lord.

Wednesday, October 8, 2025

✤ Lord, you are merciful and gracious.

Psalm 34

page 370

Reading

Luke 11:1–4

Jesus was praying in a certain place, and when he had finished, one of his disciples said to him, "Lord, teach us to pray just as John taught his disciples." He said to them, "When you pray, say:

Father, hallowed be your name, / your Kingdom come. / Give us each day our daily bread / and forgive us our sins / for we ourselves forgive everyone in debt to us, / and do not subject us to the final test."

Reflection

Sometimes, we think that our prayers need to be big, elaborate, and exceedingly formal to be heard by God. In today's Gospel, Jesus teaches his disciples the "Our Father," an exceedingly simple and informal prayer, yet also the most beloved prayer of Christians. In just a few lines Jesus teaches us to praise God, to ask for what we need, and to seek forgiveness and protection from evil. This pattern of prayer should inform how we talk with God, confident that our Father hears us, loves us, and will always provide what we need to follow him.

Prayers

others may be added

With faith, we pray:

℟. **Lord, hear our prayer.**

- For our bishops, that they may be true shepherds of their flocks, we pray: ℟.
- For peace among all nations, that all may live without violence, we pray: ℟.
- For migrants and those searching for a home, that they may be welcomed, we pray: ℟.
- For our communities, that all may find their place, we pray: ℟.

Let us offer together the prayer
that Jesus taught us.

Our Father . . .

Lord Jesus,
you taught us to pray to God as our
loving Father.
Through your example give us a faith
that never waivers
and the courage to live as his sons
and daughters.
You who live and reign for ever
and ever.
Amen.

✤ Lord, you are merciful and gracious.

✤ Blessed be the Lord.

Psalm 141 *page 389*

Reading *Malachi 3:13–20b*

You have defied me in word, says the LORD, / yet you ask, "What have we spoken against you?" / You have said, "It is vain to serve God, / and what do we profit by keeping his command, / And going about in penitential dress / in awe of the LORD of hosts? / Rather must we call the proud blessed; / for indeed evildoers prosper, / and even tempt God with impunity." / Then they who fear the LORD spoke with one another, / and the LORD listened attentively; / And a record book was written before him / of those who fear the LORD and trust in his name. / And they shall be mine, says the LORD of hosts, / my own special possession, on the day I take action. / And I will have compassion on them, / as a man has compassion on his son who serves him. / Then you will again see the distinction / between the just and the wicked; /Between the one who serves God, / and the one who does not serve him. / For lo, the day is coming, blazing like an oven, / when all the proud and all evildoers will be stubble, / And the day that is coming will set them on fire, / leaving them neither root nor branch, / says the LORD of hosts. / But for you who fear my name, there will arise / the sun of justice with its healing rays.

Reflection

In Malachi's time, the Israelites had returned to Jerusalem after exile in Babylon but had failed to amend their way of life. Many withheld their offerings and sacrifices, divorced their spouses to marry idolators, and neglected God's Word. The prophet, in turn, relates how God's justice will come upon them unexpectedly to condemn the wicked but to bring healing and salvation to those who fear the Lord. We must never fail to walk with the Lord, for we do not know the day or the hour when the kingdom will be established.

Prayers *others may be added*

Longing for justice, we pray:

℟. Lord of justice, hear our prayer.

✦ That the Church may continue to proclaim the kingdom and teach God's word, we pray: ℟.

✦ That all may work for the justice that establishes true peace, we pray: ℟.

✦ That those who seek justice may be heard, we pray: ℟.

✦ That we may walk with the Lord in holiness, we pray: ℟.

Let us offer together the prayer
that Jesus taught us.

Our Father . . .

Lord God, author of justice,
help us to walk in your ways
and be found worthy of your kingdom.
Through Christ our Lord.
Amen.

✤ Blessed be the Lord.

Weekday

Friday, October 10, 2025

✤ The Lord will judge the world with justice.

Psalm 33

page 369

Reading

Luke 11:15–23

When Jesus had driven out a demon, some of the crowd said: "By the power of Beelzebul, the prince of demons, he drives out demons." Others, to test him, asked him for a sign from heaven. But he knew their thoughts and said to them, "Every kingdom divided against itself will be laid waste and house will fall against house. And if Satan is divided against himself, how will his kingdom stand? For you say that it is by Beelzebul that I drive out demons. If I, then, drive out demons by Beelzebul, by whom do your own people drive them out? Therefore they will be your judges. But if it is by the finger of God that I drive out demons, then the Kingdom of God has come upon you. When a strong man fully armed guards his palace, his possessions are safe. But when one stronger than he attacks and overcomes him, he takes away the armor on which he relied and distributes the spoils. Whoever is not with me is against me, and whoever does not gather with me scatters."

Reflection

In today's Gospel Jesus reveals the true meaning behind his miracles: they demonstrate that God's kingdom is at hand. Many missed this lesson, however, because they expected a political kingdom that would overthrow Israel's enemies. Instead, Jesus shows that the kingdom is present wherever he is: with the poor, the marginalized, the outcast, the sick, and the oppressed. This is why they are the first to hear the proclamation of the kingdom and feel its effects. When we humble ourselves and ask Jesus for healing, the kingdom comes to us, too.

Prayers

others may be added

In our lowliness, we pray:

℟. Lord, hear our prayer.

- For the Church, that she may welcome the outcast and the poor, we pray: ℟.
- For the world, that we may live in fellowship with one another, we pray: ℟.
- For those who seek healing, that they may know the loving care of Christ, we pray: ℟.
- For our families, that we may be Christ for one another, we pray: ℟.

Let us offer together the prayer that Jesus taught us.

Our Father . . .

Lord of all,
through your Son Jesus
the kingdom has been planted
in the world.
Grant that, through our efforts,
it may continue to grow
until all people are gathered in you.
Through Christ our Lord.
Amen.

✤ The Lord will judge the world with justice.

✤ Rejoice in the Lord, you just!

Psalm 139 *page 389*

Reading *Luke 11:27–28*

While Jesus was speaking, a woman from the crowd called out and said to him, "Blessed is the womb that carried you and the breasts at which you nursed." He replied, "Rather, blessed are those who hear the word of God and observe it."

Reflection

Jesus reminds us that it is not enough to hear the Word of God. Many have heard the Word but not allowed it to take root in their hearts and change their lives. We must do more than merely hear the Word; we must observe it as well. This means reflecting on the Word, taking it seriously, and putting it into practice. This takes time; few people experience a total conversion of heart and life in a day! But, through God's grace, we can develop the habit of reading, reflecting on and observing God's Word. Ask yourself: How will I observe the Word of God in my life today?

Prayers *others may be added*

Attentive to God's Word, we ask for help in observing it in our lives:

℟. **Loving God, hear our prayer.**

- For all the faithful, that we may grow in holiness, we pray: ℟.
- For those who have not yet responded to the Word, that God may touch their hearts, we pray: ℟.
- For those who suffer, that God's Word may comfort them, we pray: ℟.
- For those who share God's Word, that they may be rewarded as faithful servants, we pray: ℟.

Let us offer together the prayer
that Jesus taught us.

Our Father . . .

God who speaks,
we give you thanks for sharing yourself
through your Word.
Give us the grace to hear you clearly
and to follow you boldly
Through Christ our Lord.
Amen.

✤ Rejoice in the Lord, you just!

✤ With you is found forgiveness, /
O God of Israel.

Psalm 122

page 387

Reading

Luke 17:11–19

As Jesus continued his journey to Jerusalem, he traveled through Samaria and Galilee. As he was entering a village, ten lepers met him. They stood at a distance from him and raised their voices, saying, "Jesus, Master! Have pity on us!" And when he saw them, he said, "Go show yourselves to the priests." As they were going they were cleansed. And one of them, realizing he had been healed, returned, glorifying God in a loud voice; and he fell at the feet of Jesus and thanked him. He was a Samaritan. Jesus said in reply, "Ten were cleansed, were they not? Where are the other nine? Has none but this foreigner returned to give thanks to God?" Then he said to him, "Stand up and go; your faith has saved you."

Reflection

The Samaritan leper who returned to give thanks and glory to Jesus demonstrates the humility that characterizes a Christian. The other nine seem to have accepted their healing as a matter of course, as if they had somehow earned or deserved it. The Samaritan, on the other hand, recognizes that he is unworthy of the gift Jesus has given him. How often do we see God's gifts as something ordinary or earned? How often do we fail to give thanks for all the incredible gifts we have been given? This is not the attitude of a disciple. God gives us his gifts out of love, asking only that we love him in return.

Prayers

others may be added

With thanks for all we have been given, we pray:

℟. Giver of all gifts, hear our prayer.

- For the Church, that we may remember all that God has given us, we pray: ℟.
- For the world, that we may share freely what we have been given, we pray: ℟.
- For the poor and oppressed, that we may work for their good and the alleviation of suffering, we pray: ℟.
- For those who have yet to recognize the graciousness of God, that they may see the many gifts he offers, we pray: ℟.

Let us offer together the prayer that Jesus taught us.

Our Father . . .

Heavenly Father,
you give us everything we need,
even when we fail to give you
the thanks you are due.
Open our hearts
and help us to form hearts full
of gratitude
Through Christ our Lord.
Amen.

✤ With you is found forgiveness, /
O God of Israel.

✤ The Lord has made known
his salvation.

Psalm 98

page 381

Reading

Romans 1:1–7

Paul, a slave of Christ Jesus, called to be an Apostle and set apart for the Gospel of God, which he promised previously through his prophets in the holy Scriptures, the Gospel about his Son, descended from David according to the flesh, but established as Son of God in power according to the Spirit of holiness through resurrection from the dead, Jesus Christ our Lord. Through him we have received the grace of apostleship, to bring about the obedience of faith, for the sake of his name, among all the Gentiles, among whom are you also, who are called to belong to Jesus Christ; to all the beloved of God in Rome, called to be holy. Grace to you and peace from God our Father and the Lord Jesus Christ.

Reflection

The victory spoken of in today's psalm was accomplished by Jesus on the cross. He conquered sin, overcame death, and opened heaven for those who believe in him. This was not done in secret and is not meant just for a select few; the whole world is meant to hear of God's triumph so that they may follow him! All members of the Church are called to share this good news by the example of their lives and the explicit proclamation of Jesus. How will you proclaim Jesus today? How will the example of your life demonstrate his victory?

Prayers

others may be added

Mindful of God's victory, we pray:

℟. Lord, giver of grace, hear us.

- That all the faithful may become missionary disciples, we pray: ℟.
- That all people will be open to the Gospel, we pray: ℟.
- That the poor and marginalized may be gathered into communities of love, we pray: ℟.
- That God's justice may prevail, we pray: ℟.

Let us offer together the prayer
that Jesus taught us.

Our Father . . .

God of victory,
your right hand has triumphed
through the resurrection of your Son.
May we who follow him share in
his victory
and live forever in your kingdom.
Through Christ our Lord.
Amen.

✤ The Lord has made known
his salvation.

Tuesday, October 14, 2025

✤ The heavens proclaim the glory of God.

Psalm 27 *page 368*

Reading *Luke 11:37–41*

After Jesus had spoken, a Pharisee invited him to dine at his home. He entered and reclined at table to eat. The Pharisee was amazed to see that he did not observe the prescribed washing before the meal. The Lord said to him, "Oh you Pharisees! Although you cleanse the outside of the cup and the dish, inside you are filled with plunder and evil. You fools! Did not the maker of the outside also make the inside? But as to what is within, give alms, and behold, everything will be clean for you."

Reflection

In today's Gospel, Jesus accuses the Pharisees of paying attention to the rituals prescribed by the law while ignoring God's call to holiness and interior purity. Washing the cups and dishes, as it were, is fruitless if it is not accompanied by a corresponding conversion of heart. Just so today: following the minutiae of Church law and liturgical rubrics, while important, mean nothing if they don't lead us to love our neighbor, serve the poor, and strive for holiness. Ask God to open your heart and avoid the hypocrisy of Jesus' enemies.

Prayers *others may be added*

Longing to be made perfect, we pray:

℟. **Lord of all goodness,**
hear our prayer.

- For the pope and all Church leaders, we pray: ℟.
- For governmental leaders and civil servants, we pray: ℟.
- For those who suffer discrimination and violence, we pray: ℟.
- For all those we love, we pray: ℟.

Let us offer together the prayer
that Jesus taught us.

Our Father . . .

Lord Jesus Christ,
you call us to imitate you in holiness
and perfection.
Give us the grace to avoid sin
and to live a virtuous life.
Who live and reign for ever and ever.
Amen.

✤ The heavens proclaim the glory of God.

✥ Lord, you give back to everyone according to his works.

Psalm 30

page 369

Reading

Romans 2:1–11

You, O man, are without excuse, every one of you who passes judgment. For by the standard by which you judge another you condemn yourself, since you, the judge, do the very same things. We know that the judgment of God on those who do such things is true. Do you suppose, then, you who judge those who engage in such things and yet do them yourself, that you will escape the judgment of God? Or do you hold his priceless kindness, forbearance, and patience in low esteem, unaware that the kindness of God would lead you to repentance? By your stubbornness and impenitent heart, you are storing up wrath for yourself for the day of wrath and revelation of the just judgment of God, who will repay everyone according to his works, eternal life to those who seek glory, honor, and immortality through perseverance in good works, but wrath and fury to those who selfishly disobey the truth and obey wickedness. Yes, affliction and distress will come upon everyone who does evil, Jew first and then Greek. But there will be glory, honor, and peace for everyone who does good, Jew first and then Greek. There is no partiality with God.

Reflection

In today's reading, St. Paul condemns those who think that, because they are further along the path of holiness, they should be exempt from having their own sins examined, even as they condemn others for their sins. We are all sinners in need of the love and mercy of God! Not one of us can claim to be perfect. Therefore, Paul exhorts us to extend mercy and forgiveness to one another so that we may be treated in a similar man-ner when we are called to account for our lives. Who do you need to forgive in your life? What condemnations are you holding on to? Ask God to give you a merciful heart—for your sake.

Prayers

others may be added

Relying on God's mercy we offer
our prayers:

℟. **Lord, hear our prayer.**

- For those who teach the faith, that they may do so with love, we pray: ℟.
- For those locked in conflict, that they may work for peace, we pray: ℟.
- For those who have been harmed by God's ministers, that they may find healing, we pray: ℟.

Let us offer together the prayer
that Jesus taught us.

Our Father . . .

Lord of mercy,
grant that we may work for peace
and reconciliation
in our lives and in our world.
Through Christ our Lord.
Amen.

✥ Lord, you give back to everyone according to his works.

Thursday, October 16, 2025

✤ With the Lord there is mercy,
and fullness of redemption.

Psalm 51 *page 373*

Reading *Romans 3:21–30*

Brothers and sisters: Now the righteousness of God has been manifested apart from the law, though testified to by the law and the prophets, the righteousness of God through faith in Jesus Christ for all who believe. For there is no distinction; all have sinned and are deprived of the glory of God. They are justified freely by his grace through the redemption in Christ Jesus, whom God set forth as an expiation, through faith, by his Blood, to prove his righteousness because of the forgiveness of sins previously committed, through the forbearance of God—to prove his righteousness in the present time, that he might be righteous and justify the one who has faith in Jesus.

What occasion is there then for boasting? It is ruled out. On what principle, that of works? No, rather on the principle of faith. For we consider that a person is justified by faith apart from works of the law. Does God belong to Jews alone? Does he not belong to Gentiles, too? Yes, also to Gentiles, for God is one and will justify the circumcised on the basis of faith and the uncircumcised through faith.

Reflection

We are all in need of a savior. None of us can claim to be perfect; we all fall short of the holiness demanded by God. Thankfully, God sent his only Son, Jesus, to die and rise again so that we might not only be forgiven but be made daughters and sons of him and live in his grace. There is no other means by which we can be saved! We cannot earn it, we cannot win it, we cannot assume it based on any inherent trait or characteristic. Salvation is pure gift, offered to all in love. All that is asked of us is to love him in return and follow as his disciples.

Prayers *others may be added*

Giving thanks for the salvation
we have been offered, we pray:

℟. **Lord, hear our prayer.**

✦ For the baptized, that they may recognize the life they now share in Christ, we pray: ℟.

✦ For those searching for God, that they may see Christ in our lives, we pray: ℟.

✦ For the sick, that they may find healing and comfort in Christ, we pray: ℟.

✦ For our communities, that we may live in the peace of Christ, we pray: ℟.

Let us offer together the prayer
that Jesus taught us.

Our Father . . .

Gracious God,
through the paschal mystery
we have been gathered into
your Church.
Grant that we may remain faithful
to our baptism
and enjoy eternal life with you.
Through Christ our Lord.
Amen.

✤ With the Lord there is mercy,
and fullness of redemption.

✚ Turn to the Lord, in time of trouble.

Psalm 34

page 370

Reading

Luke 12:1–7

At that time: So many people were crowding together that they were trampling one another underfoot. Jesus began to speak, first to his disciples, "Beware of the leaven—that is, the hypocrisy—of the Pharisees.

"There is nothing concealed that will not be revealed, nor secret that will not be known. Therefore whatever you have said in the darkness will be heard in the light, and what you have whispered behind closed doors will be proclaimed on the housetops. I tell you, my friends, do not be afraid of those who kill the body but after that can do no more. I shall show you whom to fear. Be afraid of the one who after killing has the power to cast into Gehenna; yes, I tell you, be afraid of that one. Are not five sparrows sold for two small coins? Yet not one of them has escaped the notice of God. Even the hairs of your head have all been counted. Do not be afraid. You are worth more than many sparrows."

Reflection

Jesus warns his followers to avoid the hypocrisy of the Pharisees, who say one thing but do another, because nothing is hidden from God. Many of us try to appear holy by condemning the sins of others while hiding our own sins. Jesus reminds us that when the kingdom of God comes,all will be revealed when we stand before his judgement. Our actions should match the Gospel we preach. In this way we demonstrate the fidelity due to God and witness to the beauty of our faith.

Prayers

others may be added

Confident in God's judgement, we pray:

℟. Lord of all holiness, hear us.

- That we may follow Christ's teaching in all we do, we pray: ℟.
- That the world may witness the truth of our faith, we pray: ℟.
- That we may serve the poor and welcome the outcast, we pray: ℟.
- That we may see the face of Jesus in those we meet today, we pray: ℟.

Let us offer together the prayer
that Jesus taught us.

Our Father . . .

Mighty God,
preserve us from the hypocrisy
 of the Pharisees
so that, walking in your light,
we may live a pure and authentic faith.
Through Christ our Lord.
Amen.

✚ Turn to the Lord, in time of trouble.

✚ The Lord remembers his covenant for ever.

Psalm 23

page 367

Reading

Luke 10:1–9

The Lord Jesus appointed seventy-two disciples whom he sent ahead of him in pairs to every town and place he intended to visit. He said to them, "The harvest is abundant but the laborers are few; so ask the master of the harvest to send out laborers for his harvest. Go on your way; behold, I am sending you like lambs among wolves. Carry no money bag, no sack, no sandals; and greet no one along the way. Into whatever house you enter, first say, 'Peace to this household.' If a peaceful person lives there, your peace will rest on him; but if not, it will return to you. Stay in the same house and eat and drink what is offered to you, for the laborer deserves payment. Do not move about from one house to another. Whatever town you enter and they welcome you, eat what is set before you, cure the sick in it and say to them, 'The Kingdom of God is at hand for you.'"

Reflection

Jesus reminds us that the task of evangelization requires us to go out and invite others to encounter the risen Christ. St. Luke, whose feast we celebrate today, wrote his Gospel for this very purpose: to lead others to faith in Jesus. We can't assume evangelization will happen on its own, or that others will do it in our place. All the faithful are called to be missionary disciples and to share the Good News with those they meet. Look for opportunities today to share your faith with someone and ask the Lord to open their hearts to his love and mercy.

Prayers

others may be added

Offering our lives to the Lord, we pray:

℟. **Lord, hear our prayer.**

- For those discerning their vocation, we pray: ℟.
- For doctors, nurses, and others who use their skill to heal, we pray: ℟.
- For migrants and those displaced by violence and insecurity, we pray: ℟.
- For all those who will die today, we pray: ℟.

Let us offer together the prayer
that Jesus taught us.

Our Father . . .

Lord God,
through St. Luke,
your Gospel has been shared
throughout the world.
Make us eager laborers
in your vineyard.
Through Christ our Lord.
Amen.

✚ The Lord remembers his covenant for ever.

✤ In the shadow of your wings
protect me.

Psalm 46 *page 372*

Reading *Luke 18:1–8*

Jesus told his disciples a parable about the necessity for them to pray always without becoming weary. He said, "There was a judge in a certain town who neither feared God nor respected any human being. And a widow in that town used to come to him and say, 'Render a just decision for me against my adversary.' For a long time the judge was unwilling, but eventually he thought, 'While it is true that I neither fear God nor respect any human being, because this widow keeps bothering me I shall deliver a just decision for her lest she finally come and strike me.' " The Lord said, "Pay attention to what the dishonest judge says. Will not God then secure the rights of his chosen ones who call out to him day and night? Will he be slow to answer them? I tell you, he will see to it that justice is done for them speedily. But when the Son of Man comes, will he find faith on earth?"

Reflection

The parable relayedin today's Gospel encourages us to pray without ceasing. Even when our prayers seem to go unanswered, or when what we pray for appears to be out of reach, Jesus encourages us to persevere in prayer. If the judge in the parable can relent due to the persistence of the widow's pleas, how much more will God, who loves us more than we can fathom, answer our prayers? Jesus exhorts us to keep the faith, even in the face of adversity or the profound silence of God, so that when the time comes we will be ready to receive what our Father has prepared for us.

Prayers *others may be added*

Awaiting the good things of the Lord,
we pray:

℟. Lord, hear our prayer.

- For the Holy Father, our bishops, and all who lead the Church, we pray: ℟.
- For national and local leaders, we pray: ℟.
- For those imprisoned for unjust reasons, we pray: ℟.
- For our faith communities and those we serve, we pray: ℟.

Let us offer together the prayer
that Jesus taught us.

Our Father . . .

Lord of heaven and earth,
you never fail to hear our prayers.
Open our hearts and prepare us
to receive your gifts
in this life and the kingdom to come.
Through Christ our Lord.
Amen.

✤ In the shadow of your wings
protect me.

Monday, October 20, 2025

✤ Blessed be the Lord.

Psalm 47

page 372

Reading

Luke 12:13–21

Someone in the crowd said to Jesus, "Teacher, tell my brother to share the inheritance with me." He replied to him, "Friend, who appointed me as your judge and arbitrator?" Then he said to the crowd, "Take care to guard against all greed, for though one may be rich, one's life does not consist of possessions."

Then he told them a parable. "There was a rich man whose land produced a bountiful harvest. He asked himself, 'What shall I do, for I do not have space to store my harvest?' And he said, 'This is what I shall do: I shall tear down my barns and build larger ones. There I shall store all my grain and other goods and I shall say to myself, "Now as for you, you have so many good things stored up for many years, rest, eat, drink, be merry!"' But God said to him, 'You fool, this night your life will be demanded of you; and the things you have prepared, to whom will they belong?' Thus will it be for the one who stores up treasure for himself but is not rich in what matters to God."

Reflection

Today, Jesus returns to a favorite theme of Luke's Gospel: not putting store in treasure and things, but being concerned first for the salvation of our souls. Jesus recognizes the tendency to become overly enamored of our possessions, thinking that they can save us or bring us happiness. But our hearts only find rest in the Lord, and only Jesus can bring us salvation. Things are a poor substitute that leave us unfulfilled. What things are you overly attached to in your life? How can you set them aside to make room for Jesus?

Prayers

others may be added

With eyes fixed on the Lord, we pray:

℟. **Lord, hear our prayer.**

- That all the baptized may share their faith, we pray: ℟.
- That business leaders may put people before profits, we pray: ℟.
- That the resources of the world may be shared with those in need, we pray: ℟.
- That those we meet today may encounter Christ in us, we pray: ℟.

Let us offer together the prayer
that Jesus taught us.

Our Father . . .

Lord Jesus,
you are the Alpha and the Omega
and in you we find all that we need.
Rid us of our greed and avarice
so that we may rest in you.
Who live and reign for ever and ever.
Amen.

✤ Blessed be the Lord.

✠ Here I am, Lord; I come
to do your will.

Psalm 71 *page 376*

Reading *Luke 12:35–38*

Jesus said to his disciples: "Gird your loins and light your lamps and be like servants who await their master's return from a wedding, ready to open immediately when he comes and knocks. Blessed are those servants whom the master finds vigilant on his arrival. Amen, I say to you, he will gird himself, have them recline at table, and proceed to wait on them. And should he come in the second or third watch and find them prepared in this way, blessed are those servants."

Reflection

In today's Gospel, Jesus admonishes us to be vigilant and prepared for the Day of the Lord, for we do not know the day or the hour it will come. The second and third watches would have been late in the night and the very early morning, when we would be tempted to give in to sleep. But woe to us if we are sleeping and unprepared when Jesus comes to us! Jesus' disciples will be awake and prepared to greet him with joy, not rubbing the sleep from their eyes and asking for a cup of coffee! Being watchful means not waiting until the last second. Reconcile with your enemies. Give to the poor. Ready your heart. Be prepared.

Prayers *others may be added*

With vigilant hearts, we pray:

℟. **Lord of light, hear us.**

- That Church leaders may help us prepare for Jesus, we pray: ℟.
- That world leaders may work for justice, we pray: ℟.
- That all workers may be paid a fair wage, we pray: ℟.
- That our communities may be places of hope, we pray: ℟.

Let us offer together the prayer
that Jesus taught us.

Our Father . . .

Compassionate God,
even though we falter
you still reach out to us in love.
Give us the strength
to prepare for the coming of your Son
and the grace to remain faithful to him.
Who lives and reigns for ever and ever.
Amen.

✠ Here I am, Lord; I come
to do your will.

Wednesday, October 22, 2025

✚ Our help is in the name of the Lord.

Psalm 62 *page 374*

Reading *Romans 6:12–18*

Brothers and sisters: Sin must not reign over your mortal bodies so that you obey their desires. And do not present the parts of your bodies to sin as weapons for wickedness, but present yourselves to God as raised from the dead to life and the parts of your bodies to God as weapons for righteousness. For sin is not to have any power over you, since you are not under the law but under grace.

What then? Shall we sin because we are not under the law but under grace? Of course not! Do you not know that if you present yourselves to someone as obedient slaves, you are slaves of the one you obey, either of sin, which leads to death, or of obedience, which leads to righteousness? But thanks be to God that, although you were once slaves of sin, you have become obedient from the heart to the pattern of teaching to which you were entrusted. Freed from sin, you have become slaves of righteousness.

Reflection

St. Paul offers a thoughtful reflection today on the nature of Christian freedom. For disciples, freedom isn't the ability to choose whatever we want and do whatever we choose. That isn't freedom, but slavery to our passions and disordered desires. True freedom is freedom from sin and death. Jesus won this freedom for us on the cross. At the same time, freedom is freedom for the sake of the Gospel: to preach the Good News, care for the poor, and work for a more just and peaceful world. This is what it means to be a slave to righteousness: to live in true freedom by following Christ and his commandments.

Prayers *others may be added*

Offering ourselves freely to our Lord, we pray:

℟. Lord of grace, hear us.

- That the Church may demonstrate the freedom we have in Christ, we pray: ℟.
- That all countries may be places of freedom and peace, we pray: ℟.
- That victims of human trafficking may be rescued and healed, we pray: ℟.
- That all people may come to know the freedom offered by Christ, we pray: ℟.

Let us offer together the prayer
that Jesus taught us.

Our Father . . .

Lord God,
you set the Israelites free
from the bonds of slavery
and sent your Son to rescue us from sin.
Grant that we may live in your freedom
and share it with the world.
Through Christ our Lord.
Amen.

✚ Our help is in the name of the Lord.

✤ Blessed are they who hope
in the Lord.

Psalm 63 *page 375*

Reading *Romans 6:19–23*

Brothers and sisters: I am speaking in human terms because of the weakness of your nature. For just as you presented the parts of your bodies as slaves to impurity and to lawlessness for lawlessness, so now present them as slaves to righteousness for sanctification. For when you were slaves of sin, you were free from righteousness. But what profit did you get then from the things of which you are now ashamed? For the end of those things is death. But now that you have been freed from sin and have become slaves of God, the benefit that you have leads to sanctification, and its end is eternal life. For the wages of sin is death, but the gift of God is eternal life in Christ Jesus our Lord.

Reflection

Why are we in need of rescuing? Because, through our sin, we have merited death and we do not have the ability to free ourselves from this death. Fortunately, out of his abundant goodness and love for us, God sent his Son, Jesus Christ, to bestow the gift of life on us again! We could not earn it; that is why salvation is a gift. We remember this great gift every time we celebrate the sacrament of reconciliation. When we confess our sins and experience God's forgiveness, we receive again the mercy he poured out on the cross. If you haven't been to confession in a while, God is waiting to offer you his forgiveness!

Prayers *others may be added*

Aware of God's mercy, we pray

℟. **Lord of forgiveness, hear us.**

✦ That the Church may continue to seek healing for the victims of abuse, we pray: ℟.

✦ That civic leaders may seek to recognize and atone for historic injustices, we pray: ℟.

✦ That those oppressed by habitual sin may know the freedom of God's mercy, we pray: ℟.

✦ That our parishes may be places of reconciliation and healing, we pray: ℟.

Let us offer together the prayer
that Jesus taught us.

Our Father . . .

Merciful God,
we give you thanks
for the gift of your love and grace.
Help us to be ministers of your mercy
so that all may come to know you.
Through Christ our Lord.
Amen.

✤ Blessed are they who hope
in the Lord.

Weekday

Friday, October 24, 2025

✤ Lord, teach me your statutes.

Psalm 67

page 375

Reading

Luke 12:54–59

Jesus said to the crowds, "When you see a cloud rising in the west you say immediately that it is going to rain—and so it does; and when you notice that the wind is blowing from the south you say that it is going to be hot—and so it is. You hypocrites! You know how to interpret the appearance of the earth and the sky; why do you not know how to interpret the present time?

"Why do you not judge for yourselves what is right? If you are to go with your opponent before a magistrate, make an effort to settle the matter on the way; otherwise your opponent will turn you over to the judge, and the judge hand you over to the constable, and the constable throw you into prison. I say to you, you will not be released until you have paid the last penny."

Reflection

Jesus again challenges his listeners for misplacing their priorities and failing to see the spiritual realities working around them. They know a lot about how to read the world but are unaware that the signs that the Messiah has come are right in front of their eyes! We too know a lot about technology, celebrities, and sports, but often fail to recognize Christ in the poor, the marginalized, and the downtrodden. Refocusing our vision through prayer, reading the Scriptures, and receiving the sacraments is the first step to seeing things rightly.

Prayers

others may be added

Longing for the kingdom, we pray:

℟. Lord, hear our prayer.

- That Church leaders may guide the faithful, we pray: ℟.
- That civic leaders may govern us justly, we pray: ℟.
- That those who are poor may have their needs met, we pray: ℟.
- That our communities may reflect the kingdom, we pray: ℟.

Let us offer together the prayer
that Jesus taught us.

Our Father . . .

Lord of heaven and earth,
grant us eyes that see the world
as you see it
and form our hearts and minds
so that we may keep our priorities
in line with your will.
Through Christ our Lord.
Amen.

✤ Lord, teach me your statutes.

✤ Lord, send out your spirit.

Psalm 84

page 378

Reading

Romans 8:2–11

For the law of the spirit of life in Christ Jesus has freed you from the law of sin and death. For what the law, weakened by the flesh, was powerless to do, this God has done: by sending his own Son in the likeness of sinful flesh and for the sake of sin, he condemned sin in the flesh, so that the righteous decree of the law might be fulfilled in us, who live not according to the flesh but according to the spirit. For those who live according to the flesh are concerned with the things of the flesh, but those who live according to the spirit with the things of the spirit. The concern of the flesh is death, but the concern of the spirit is life and peace. For the concern of the flesh is hostility toward God; it does not submit to the law of God, nor can it; and those who are in the flesh cannot please God. But you are not in the flesh; on the contrary, you are in the spirit, if only the Spirit of God dwells in you. Whoever does not have the Spirit of Christ does not belong to him. But if Christ is in you, although the body is dead because of sin, the spirit is alive because of righteousness. If the Spirit of the one who raised Jesus from the dead dwells in you, the one who raised Christ from the dead will give life to your mortal bodies also, through his Spirit that dwells in you.

Reflection

Through sin we merited death, but through Christ we receive the gift of life. We receive this gift in baptism: we die with Christ and rise to new life again with him. This new life is not our old life tainted by sin; rather, it is Christ who now lives in us, as St. Paul teaches today. Through our faith in him, Jesus lives in us so that, although our earthly bodies may die, his life continues and restores us to everlasting life. This is the promise we received at our baptism and that we renew every time with receive the Eucharist: Jesus lives in us so that we might live forever with him.

Prayers

others may be added

With gratitude for the life of Christ
in us, we pray:

℟. **Lord, hear our prayer.**

- That the Church may reflect the life of Christ in all believers, we pray: ℟.
- That world leaders may respect all life from conception until natural death, we pray: ℟.
- That those who mourn may find comfort in our prayers and care, we pray: ℟.

Let us offer together the prayer
that Jesus taught us.

Our Father . . .

Lord of life,
continue to pour out your grace
on the world
so that, empowered by the Holy Spirit,
your Church may be a sanctuary
of peace for all people.
Who live and reign for ever and ever.
Amen.

✤ Lord, send out your spirit.

Sunday, October 26, 2025

✚ Let the hearts that seek
the Lord rejoice.

Psalm 85

page 379

Reading

Luke 18:9–14

Jesus addressed this parable to those who were convinced of their own righteousness and despised everyone else. "Two people went up to the temple area to pray; one was a Pharisee and the other was a tax collector. The Pharisee took up his position and spoke this prayer to himself, 'O God, I thank you that I am not like the rest of humanity—greedy, dishonest, adulterous—or even like this tax collector. I fast twice a week, and I pay tithes on my whole income.' But the tax collector stood off at a distance and would not even raise his eyes to heaven but beat his breast and prayed, 'O God, be merciful to me a sinner.' I tell you, the latter went home justified, not the former; for whoever exalts himself will be humbled, and the one who humbles himself will be exalted."

Reflection

The difference between the one who exalts himself and the one who humbles himself is honesty. The tax collector in today's Gospel knows he is a sinner and rightfully acknowledges this before God, asking only for mercy. The Pharisee, on the other hand, is blinded by his status and importance. He cannot imagine that he would share anything with the tax collector—let alone that he too might be a poor sinner. Therefore, God cannot forgive him. Humility before God is the start of wisdom, which is why the tax collector walks away justified before the Lord.

Prayers

others may be added

In humility we bring our prayers
to the Lord:

℟. **Lord, hear the prayers
of your servants.**

- That Church leaders may serve with humility and honesty, we pray: ℟.
- That world leaders may work for the good of those who are poor and lowly, we pray: ℟.
- That all workers may be paid a fair wage for their labor, we pray: ℟.
- That we may never be blinded to the injustice in our communities, we pray: ℟.

Let us offer together the prayer
that Jesus taught us.

Our Father . . .

Lord of might,
you raise up the lowly and cast down
the haughty.
Make us aware of our weakness
and failures
so that we may bring them to you
in your mercy.
Who live and reign for ever and ever.
Amen.

✚ Let the hearts that seek
the Lord rejoice.

✤ Our God is the God of salvation.

Psalm 91 *page 379*

Reading *Romans 8:12–17*

Brothers and sisters, we are not debtors to the flesh, to live according to the flesh. For if you live according to the flesh, you will die, but if by the spirit you put to death the deeds of the body, you will live.

For those who are led by the Spirit of God are sons of God. For you did not receive a spirit of slavery to fall back into fear, but you received a spirit of adoption, through which we cry, "*Abba*, Father!" The Spirit himself bears witness with our spirit that we are children of God, and if children, then heirs, heirs of God and joint heirs with Christ, if only we suffer with him so that we may also be glorified with him.

Reflection

After his Ascension, Jesus did not leave us abandoned. He sent the Holy Spirit to be our guide and advocate. Thus, to be a disciple of Jesus is to be attentive to and led by the Spirit he sent. Each of us has been given charisms—gifts of the Holy Spirit—to be used on behalf of the Church and the poor. It takes time and discernment to discover our personal charisms, but when we cooperate with the Spirit we can do amazing things. Today, ask the Holy Spirit to show you what gifts you have been given and how you can use them in the world.

Prayers *others may be added*

Cooperating with the Holy Spirit,
we pray:

℟. **Lord, hear our prayer.**

- That the Spirit may guide all believers, we pray: ℟.
- That the Spirit may show us the way to peace and a more just society, we pray: ℟.
- That the Spirit may inspire us to care for those who are poor and outcast, we pray: ℟.
- That the Spirit may be evident in our preaching and service, we pray: ℟.

Let us offer together the prayer
that Jesus taught us.

Our Father . . .

Heavenly Father,
continue to pour out your Holy Spirit
on the Church founded by your Son
so that we may share our gifts
with everyone we meet.
Through Christ our Lord.
Amen.

✤ Our God is the God of salvation.

Tuesday, October 28, 2025

✤ The Lord has done marvels for us.

Psalm 95

page 380

Reading

Luke 6:12–16

Jesus went up to the mountain to pray, and he spent the night in prayer to God. When day came, he called his disciples to himself, and from them he chose Twelve, whom he also named Apostles: Simon, whom he named Peter, and his brother Andrew, James, John, Philip, Bartholomew, Matthew, Thomas, James the son of Alphaeus, Simon who was called a Zealot, and Judas the son of James, and Judas Iscariot, who became a traitor.

Reflection

Jesus is the model of prayer for Christians and today's Gospel shows just how integral prayer was to Jesus' earthly ministry. Before choosing his twelve apostles (including Sts. Simon and Jude, whose feast we celebrate today) Jesus went off to pray all night. He would not make the decision of whom to choose until he had spent time with his heavenly Father, entrusting the decision to him, and asking for strength for all that lay ahead. Like Jesus, we should regularly spend time in prayer, offering to the Lord all our concerns, doubts, joys, and sorrows.

Prayers

others may be added

Confident that God always hears us,
we pray.

℟. **Lord, hear our prayer.**

- That our bishops may serve with the same zeal and faith as the apostles, we pray: ℟.
- That missionaries may proclaim Jesus with joy and sincerity, we pray: ℟.
- That Catholic teachers and doctors may be inspired by Jesus in their work, we pray: ℟.
- That all believers may deepen their knowledge of the teaching of the apostles, we pray: ℟.

Let us offer together the prayer
that Jesus taught us.

Our Father . . .

Lord God,
we trust that you hear every prayer
offered by those who believe in you.
Hear our prayers and answer them
so that your will may be done
and the faith of your people may grow.
Through Christ our Lord.
Amen.

✤ The Lord has done marvels for us.

✤ My hope, O Lord, is in your mercy.

Psalm 98

page 381

Reading

Romans 8:26–30

Brothers and sisters: The Spirit comes to the aid of our weakness; for we do not know how to pray as we ought, but the Spirit himself intercedes with inexpressible groanings. And the one who searches hearts knows what is the intention of the Spirit, because he intercedes for the holy ones according to God's will.

We know that all things work for good for those who love God, who are called according to his purpose. For those he foreknew he also predestined to be conformed to the image of his Son, so that he might be the firstborn among many brothers. And those he predestined he also called; and those he called he also justified; and those he justified he also glorified.

Reflection

Jesus sent the Holy Spirit to be our advocate and guide after he had returned to his Father. Through the Spirit we continue to have access to our savior, for the Spirit makes up for what we are lacking in our human weakness. We should never fail to rely on the Spirit, especially when we are conscious of our sin. Even when we feel that we cannot pray, the desire to pray is itself a gift from the Spirit and pleasing to God. Ask the Spirit to give you the strength and desire to know God's will and to help you do it in your life.

Prayers

others may be added

With recourse to the Spirit, we pray:

℟. Lord, hear our prayer.

- That the Spirit may enliven the hearts of the faithful, we pray: ℟.
- That the Spirit of peace may permeate relations among all peoples,
  we pray: ℟.
- That those who do not know how to pray make be taught by the Spirit,
  we pray: ℟.
- That the gifts of the Spirit may serve those we meet today, we pray: ℟.

Let us offer together the prayer
that Jesus taught us.

Our Father . . .

Gracious Lord,
send your Spirit to teach us to pray
so that, growing closer to you,
we may know your will
and carry it out in the world.
Through Christ our Lord.
Amen.

✤ My hope, O Lord, is in your mercy.

Weekday

Thursday, October 30, 2025

✚ Save me, O Lord, in your mercy.

Psalm 103

page 382

Reading

Romans 8:31b–39

Brothers and sisters: If God is for us, who can be against us? He did not spare his own Son but handed him over for us all, how will he not also give us everything else along with him? Who will bring a charge against God's chosen ones? It is God who acquits us. Who will condemn? It is Christ Jesus who died, rather, was raised, who also is at the right hand of God, who indeed intercedes for us. What will separate us from the love of Christ? Will anguish, or distress, or persecution, or famine, or nakedness, or peril, or the sword? As it is written: *For your sake we are being slain all the day; we are looked upon as sheep to be slaughtered.* No, in all these things we conquer overwhelmingly through him who loved us. For I am convinced that neither death, nor life, nor angels, nor principalities, nor present things, nor future things, nor powers, nor height, nor depth, nor any other creature will be able to separate us from the love of God in Christ Jesus our Lord.

Reflection

St. Paul's questions evoke a courtroom setting. At the end of our lives we will be judged for how we have lived. Should we be afraid of being found guilty? Paul's answer is no, for God is our arbiter and judge. He who did not withhold his own Son but sent him to die and rise so that we can live with him is on our side. Nothing—not even our sins—can separate us from such a love. We can be assured that, as long as our faith endures, we have no need to fear of death and judgment, for the God who loves us will stand by our side

Prayers

others may be added

With confidence in our God we pray:

℟. Lord, hear our prayer.

- That the Church may continue to safeguard the faith given to us by Christ, we pray: ℟.
- That the resources of the world may be cared for and used for the good of all, we pray: ℟.
- That migrant workers may find steady work and a just wage, we pray: ℟.
- That our parishes may welcome those who have felt judged, we pray: ℟.

Let us offer together the prayer
that Jesus taught us.

Our Father . . .

Judge of all,
we trust that your love for us is true
and that you will not allow us to fall.
Be at our side through all of life's trials
and bring us, in the end,
to the kingdom you have prepared
for us.
Through Christ our Lord.
Amen.

✚ Save me, O Lord, in your mercy.

✤ Praise the Lord, Jerusalem.

Psalm 115

page 385

Reading

Luke 14:1–6

On a sabbath Jesus went to dine at the home of one of the leading Pharisees, and the people there were observing him carefully. In front of him there was a man suffering from dropsy. Jesus spoke to the scholars of the law and Pharisees in reply, asking, "Is it lawful to cure on the sabbath or not?" But they kept silent; so he took the man and, after he had healed him, dismissed him. Then he said to them, "Who among you, if your son or ox falls into a cistern, would not immediately pull him out on the sabbath day?" But they were unable to answer his question.

Reflection

Jesus' rebuke of the Pharisees is not meant to be a condemnation of the law itself, but to show those present that the law demands, first and foremost, that we love our neighbors. God desires that we live according to the love he has shown us. This isn't rote obedience, but a radical concern for those we meet in our everyday lives. The Pharisees lost sight of this, just as we so often do when we turn a blind eye to the poor, put our selfish desires before our family and friends, and put more stock in appearing to be holy than asking how we can love others better this day.

Prayers

others may be added

With love for our neighbor, we pray:

℟. Loving God, hear our prayer.

- That all believers may seek to be martyrs for charity, we pray: ℟.
- That world leaders seek to improve the lives of migrants and refugees, we pray: ℟.
- The those who live on the margins may be welcomed and loved, we pray: ℟.
- That we may be examples of Christ's love to those we meet today, we pray: ℟.

Let us offer together the prayer that Jesus taught us.

Our Father . . .

Loving Father,
through your Son you showed us
what it means to love our neighbors.
Give us hearts for others
and a faith that endures all things.
Through Christ our Lord.
Amen.

✤ Praise the Lord, Jerusalem.

✤ Let us all rejoice in the Lord, / as we celebrate the feast day in honor of all the Saints.

Psalm 27 *page 368*

Reading *Matthew 5:1–12a*

When Jesus saw the crowds, he went up the mountain, and after he had sat down, his disciples came to him. He began to teach them, saying: / "Blessed are the poor in spirit, / for theirs is the Kingdom of heaven. / Blessed are they who mourn, / for they will be comforted. / Blessed are the meek, / for they will inherit the land. / Blessed are they who hunger and thirst for righteousness, / for they will be satisfied. / Blessed are the merciful, / for they will be shown mercy. / Blessed are the clean of heart, / for they will see God. / Blessed are the peacemakers, / for they will be called children of God. / Blessed are they who are persecuted for the sake of righteousness, / for theirs is the Kingdom of heaven. / Blessed are you when they insult you and persecute you and utter every kind of evil against you falsely because of me. Rejoice and be glad, for your reward will be great in heaven."

Reflection

The powerful promises Jesus makes can get lost in the poetry of the Beatitudes. Think for a moment what it means to be comforted, satisfied, shown mercy, called children of God, to inherit, to see God. The first half of each Beatitude is a challenge to be sure. Each one could be the fruit of the slow steady work of a lifetime of prayer and practice. The second half, though, invites us to fall to our knees in gratitude. Who might we become, if we allow ourselves to be held so close to the heart of God that we know these things in our bones? Learning to accept this incredible love and mercy may just be the secret of the saints.

Prayers *others may be added*

Beloved, we are God's children now, and so we bring our prayers to God with confidence and trust.

℟. Loving God, hear our prayer.

- That we might imitate the saints in striving for heaven, we pray: ℟.
- That all those with power might use it toward the cause of peace, we pray: ℟.
- That those who mourn will be comforted and those who hunger will be satisfied, we pray: ℟.
- That our community will seek righteousness in word and action, we pray: ℟.

Let us offer together the prayer that Jesus taught us.

Our Father . . .

God of love and mercy,
incline your ear to your children
who long to see your face.
Hear and answer these prayers.
Draw us ever closer in your love
so that in word and action we might
always follow you.
Through Christ our Lord.
Amen.

✤ Let us all rejoice in the Lord, / as we celebrate the feast day in honor of all the Saints.

✠ Eternal rest grant unto them,
O Lord, / and let perpetual light
shine upon them.

Psalm 27

page 368

Reading

Luke 24:29–35

[The disciples] urged [Jesus], "Stay with us, for it is nearly evening and the day is almost over." So he went in to stay with them. And it happened that, while he was with them at table, he took bread, said the blessing, broke it, and gave it to them. With that their eyes were opened and they recognized him, but he vanished from their sight. Then they said to each other, "Were not our hearts burning within us while he spoke to us on the way and opened the Scriptures to us?" So they set out at once and returned to Jerusalem where they found gathered together the Eleven and those with them who were saying, "The Lord has truly been raised and has appeared to Simon!" Then the two recounted what had taken place on the way and how he was made known to them in the breaking of bread.

Reflection

When have you felt your heart "burning within you" at the presence of the Lord? Some of us receive that gift weekly or daily in the Eucharist, in the beauty of the world around us, or through the people who care for us. For others those experiences are rarer. On this All Souls' Day, think of the people who have gone before you who recognized Christ and lived with a heart burning with love for him. Ask them for their help so you might do the same.

Prayers

others may be added

Remembering God's faithful love
and mercy, we pray:

℟. **Lord, be with us, and hear our prayer.**

- Help us walk with you and recognize you in the breaking of the bread, we pray: ℟.
- Grant courage to those who lead to do right, we pray: ℟.
- Comfort those who are grieving a loss, we pray: ℟.
- Give us eyes to see and ears to hear all you would have us recognize, we pray: ℟.

Let us offer together the prayer
that Jesus taught us.

Our Father . . .

O God,
you are beyond time and time itself.
We encounter you
and all those we love and have loved
at your table of plenty.
Hear the cry of our hearts,
and answer us with your
loving presence.
Through Christ our Lord.
Amen.

✠ Eternal rest grant unto them,
O Lord, / and let perpetual light
shine upon them.

Weekday

Monday, November 3, 2025

✚ Lord, in your great love, answer me.

Psalm 91

page 379

Reading

Luke 14:12–14

On a sabbath Jesus went to dine at the home of one of the leading Pharisees. He said to the host who invited him, "When you hold a lunch or a dinner, do not invite your friends or your brothers or sisters or your relatives or your wealthy neighbors, in case they may invite you back and you have repayment. Rather, when you hold a banquet, invite the poor, the crippled, the lame, the blind; blessed indeed will you be because of their inability to repay you. For you will be repaid at the resurrection of the righteous."

Reflection

Picture the home of the "leading Pharisee" where Jesus has come to dine. Who might have been at the table that day with Jesus? Perhaps the wealthy, popular, and well connected. Were the host and his guests ready for Jesus' challenge? The Pharisees—like all those pursuing holiness—were eager to live righteous lives. In this context this passage (part of a larger banquet scene unique to Luke's account of the Gospel) instructs today's Christian on living a life of holiness. Give to those most in need. Give to those who cannot return the favor. Then you will find favor with God.

Prayers

others may be added

The Lord hears the poor and the afflicted and so we bring to him our needs:

℟. **Merciful God, hear us.**

- That all who seek holiness will do so with humility, we pray: ℟.
- That those most in need will be foremost in the minds of those with the power to help, we pray: ℟.
- That those who are afflicted will find support and hope, we pray: ℟.
- That this community will be attentive to the demands of mercy, we pray: ℟.

Let us offer together the prayer that Jesus taught us.

Our Father . . .

Lord Jesus,
you taught the Pharisees
and you teach us
how to live lives of holiness.
May we seek mercy, humility, kindness,
and generosity
so as to be one with you in your
kingdom forever.
Who live and reign for ever and ever.
Amen.

✚ Lord, in your great love, answer me.

✤ In you, O Lord, I have found
my peace.

Psalm 95

page 380

Reading

Romans 12:5–8

Brothers and sisters: We, though many, are one Body in Christ and individually parts of one another. Since we have gifts that differ according to the grace given to us, let us exercise them: if prophecy, in proportion to the faith; if ministry, in ministering; if one is a teacher, in teaching; if one exhorts, in exhortation; if one contributes, in generosity; if one is over others, with diligence; if one does acts of mercy, with cheerfulness.

Reflection

You have gifts. Use them! Devote yourself to prayer, goodness, compassion, and service! If we were looking for a motivational poster as Christians, this passage from Romans might just be it. Like a coach before the big game or the director before the big show, Paul's exhortation for the early Church to rededicate themselves to God is meant to energize and inspire. Let it be your inspiration today to use your gifts and live your faith.

Prayers

others may be added

Rejoicing with those who rejoice and weeping with those who weep, we bring our needs and the needs of our brothers and sisters before God:

℟. Receive our prayer, O God of love.

- That all the members of Christ's Body will hear the call to holiness and use their gifts to serve the Lord,
  we pray: ℟.
- That all who serve as elected leaders will do so in a spirit of service,
  we pray: ℟.
- That those on the margins will know the love of the Lord, we pray: ℟.
- That our community will be sincere in our love and hold onto what is good,
  we pray:

Let us offer together the prayer
that Jesus taught us.

Our Father . . .

O Lord,
you lift up the lowly
and invite all to your heavenly banquet.
Inspire us to use our gifts
to serve you and serve one another
in the love you call us to,
that we might grow ever closer to that
feast of unity.
Who live and reign for ever and ever.
Amen.

✤ In you, O Lord, I have found
my peace.

Wednesday, November 5, 2025

✚ The Lord is my light
and my salvation.

Psalm 98

page 381

Reading

Romans 13:8–10

Brothers and sisters: Owe nothing to anyone, except to love one another; for the one who loves another has fulfilled the law. The commandments, *You shall not commit adultery; you shall not kill; you shall not steal; you shall not covet*, and whatever other commandment there may be, are summed up in this saying, namely, *You shall love your neighbor as yourself.* Love does no evil to the neighbor; hence, love is the fulfillment of the law.

Reflection

"You shall love your neighbor as yourself." This teaching appears, in one form or another, in every world religion. Romans 18:9 is quoting Leviticus 19:18. Islam, Hinduism, and Buddhism each have their own version of loving others. Yet the human family cannot seem to come to terms with it. We continue—as individuals and as nations—to violate our neighbor's peace, safety, resources, and human dignity. Love is the fulfillment of God's law. And so let us seek to love one another as God has loved us.

Prayers

others may be added

With confidence and trust we bring to God our own needs and the needs of our neighbor, as we pray:

℟. **Hear us, O Lord.**

- For all disciples, that our actions on behalf of those in need will show the world the love of Christ, we pray: ℟.
- For leaders of nations, that they might consider their neighbors, we pray:
- For wealthy nations, that they prioritize the flourishing of those most in need, we pray: ℟.
- For our neighbors on the margins, for victims of war, violence, famine, and neglect, that the love of their human family might restore them, we pray: ℟.
- For our own community: that we might, through daily practice, come to love as Jesus loves, we pray: ℟.

Let us offer together the prayer
that Jesus taught us.

Our Father . . .

Heavenly Father,
you call us to reject what is evil
and embrace what is good.
Sharpen our vision
and strengthen our will.
Listen to our prayer
and help us to build your kingdom
of love here on earth.
Through Christ our Lord.

✚ The Lord is my light
and my salvation.

✤ The Lord is my light
and my salvation.

Psalm 103

page 382

Reading

Luke 15:3, 8–10

So Jesus addressed this parable to them. . . . "Or what woman having ten coins and losing one would not light a lamp and sweep the house, searching carefully until she finds it? And when she does find it, she calls together her friends and neighbors and says to them, 'Rejoice with me because I have found the coin that I lost.' In just the same way, I tell you, there will be rejoicing among the angels of God over one sinner who repents."

Reflection

An interesting element of the lost and found tales in the Gospel accounts is the invitation, "Rejoice with me." It's not simply that God is happy about redeeming lost souls, but each of us also gets an invitation to the party for these lost souls! The lost coin is a metaphor for lost souls. The seeker of the coin, the woman, is steadfast, patient, and thorough. But the seeker also wants us to join in the dancing once the search is over. God knows what we need, and asks us to forgive just as God forgives, with reckless abandon.

Prayers

others may be added

We bring our prayers to the one
who seeks us:

℟. O God of glory, hear our prayer.

- That the Church continue to seek for the lost, we pray: ℟.
- That leaders of nations will seek peace, we pray: ℟.
- That those struggling with addiction, housing, or mental illness will find support, shelter, and healing, we pray: ℟.
- That this community will answer the call to celebrate all those who are saved, we pray: ℟.

Let us offer together the prayer
that Jesus taught us.

Our Father . . .

O God,
you search us out when we're lost
and in trouble.
Hear us as we call out to you for help.
Help us to rejoice in the promise
of eternal salvation.
Through Christ our Lord.
Amen.

✤ The Lord is my light
and my salvation.

Friday, November 7, 2025

✠ The Lord is my light
and my salvation.

Psalm 115

page 385

Reading

Luke 16:1–8

Jesus said to his disciples, "A rich man had a steward who was reported to him for squandering his property. He summoned him and said, 'What is this I hear about you? Prepare a full account of your stewardship, because you can no longer be my steward.' The steward said to himself, 'What shall I do, now that my master is taking the position of steward away from me? I am not strong enough to dig and I am ashamed to beg. I know what I shall do so that, when I am removed from the stewardship, they may welcome me into their homes.' He called in his master's debtors one by one. To the first he said, 'How much do you owe my master?' He replied, 'One hundred measures of olive oil.' He said to him, 'Here is your promissory note. Sit down and quickly write one for fifty.' Then to another he said, 'And you, how much do you owe?' He replied, 'One hundred measures of wheat.' He said to him, 'Here is your promissory note; write one for eighty.' And the master commended that dishonest steward for acting prudently. For the children of this world are more prudent in dealing with their own generation than the children of light."

Reflection

The crafty steward is praised not for his dishonesty but for his cleverness. When faced with the prospect of losing his position he quickly comes up with a scheme to save himself. What if we used that same kind of creativity to overcome our spiritual challenges? If we don't have time to pray, how can we be clever in reclaiming our time? When we lose the desire to participate in our community of faith, how can we be crafty in reigniting it? The self-interested steward is resourceful. As people of faith we can still apply that kind of inventiveness—though for a different purpose—in the service of our beliefs

Prayers

others may be added

As children of the light we come to our Father with our needs and the needs of our world:

℟. Lord, hear your children.

- For the Church, that she will pursue holiness with diligence, we pray: ℟.
- For elected leaders, that they might use their position not for self-interest but for the common good, we pray: ℟.
- For the victims of unscrupulous practices, that they will find advocates and safety, we pray: ℟.
- That we might rededicate ourselves to God's purposes, we pray: ℟.

Let us offer together the prayer
that Jesus taught us.

Our Father . . .

O God,
you call us to live in your light.
Hear our prayer
and be our guide and guard.
Through Christ our Lord.
Amen.

✠ The Lord is my light
and my salvation.

✤ I will praise your name for ever, Lord.

Psalm 121 *page 386*

Reading *Luke 16:9–15*

Jesus said to his disciples: "I tell you, make friends for yourselves with dishonest wealth, so that when it fails, you will be welcomed into eternal dwellings. The person who is trustworthy in very small matters is also trustworthy in great ones; and the person who is dishonest in very small matters is also dishonest in great ones. If, therefore, you are not trustworthy with dishonest wealth, who will trust you with true wealth? If you are not trustworthy with what belongs to another, who will give you what is yours? No servant can serve two masters. He will either hate one and love the other, or be devoted to one and despise the other. You cannot serve God and mammon."

The Pharisees who loved money, heard all these things and sneered at him. And he said to them, "You justify yourselves in the sight of others, but God knows your hearts; for what is of human esteem is an abomination in the sight of God."

Reflection

No servant can serve two masters. How can we keep God at the head of our lives when we have so many material concerns? Today's reading does not ask us to shirk our duties in order to be good stewards of the resources we've been given. But we are being cautioned: handle with care and aways be conscious of money's ability to lead us into danger. Few of us can live without ever worrying about money, but when its pursuit comes before the concerns of others, that's when we have given precedence to the wrong master.

Prayers *others may be added*

We come to God with our needs
and concerns:

℟. Hear us, O God.

- That we might be trustworthy in all things, we pray: ℟.
- That leaders of nations will be good stewards of the resources entrusted them, we pray: ℟.
- That those most in need will find help and hope, we pray: ℟.
- That when our anxieties about the future overwhelm us, we may be given comfort, we pray: ℟.

Let us offer together the prayer
that Jesus taught us.

Our Father . . .

O God,
you know our hearts;
fill us with your goodness
and remove all in us that distracts us
from you.
Through Christ our Lord.
Amen.

✤ I will praise your name for ever, Lord.

Feast of the Dedication
of the Lateran Basilica
Sunday, November 9, 2025

✤ Behold God's dwelling with
the human race.

Psalm 122 *page 387*

Reading *John 2:13–22*

Since the Passover of the Jews was near, Jesus went up to Jerusalem. He found in the temple area those who sold oxen, sheep, and doves, as well as the money-changers seated there. He made a whip out of cords and drove them all out of the temple area, with the sheep and oxen, and spilled the coins of the money-changers and overturned their tables, and to those who sold doves he said, "Take these out of here, and stop making my Father's house a marketplace." His disciples recalled the words of Scripture, *Zeal for your house will consume me.* At this the Jews answered and said to him, "What sign can you show us for doing this?" Jesus answered and said to them, "Destroy this temple and in three days I will raise it up." The Jews said, "This temple has been under construction for forty-six years, and you will raise it up in three days?" But he was speaking about the temple of his Body. Therefore, when he was raised from the dead, his disciples remembered that he had said this, and they came to believe the Scripture and the word Jesus had spoken.

Reflection

When righteous anger overflows it can be uncomfortable, even scary. The protests in response to the killing of George Floyd shook the people of the United States and spread around the world. Some criticized the protests as unruly and disrespectful. The scene in today's reading seems to be about disrespect for the temple. Most commentators note that the cause of Jesus' rage is the money-changers taking advantage of temple's poorest visitors. We sometimes ask, "What would Jesus do?" about a particular situation. Here we see that in the face of injustice, outrage is sometimes the answer.

Prayers *others may be added*

God, your dwelling is a holy place
and yet you come to dwell even in us.
Aware of your indwelling presence,
we have the courage to bring to you
our needs:

**℟. O God who dwells among us,
hear our prayer.**

- That in word and action we will embody holiness, we pray: ℟.
- That governments will respect all holy places and protect people of every faith, we pray: ℟.
- That those persecuted for their faith will find safety, we pray: ℟.
- That we might be renewed in our faith, we pray: ℟.

Let us offer together the prayer
that Jesus taught us.

Our Father . . .

O God,
you are the master builder who
consecrates your house.
May we be your dwelling place,
a house of holiness and praise.
Through Christ our Lord.
Amen.

✤ Behold God's dwelling with
the human race.

✣ Guide me, Lord, along
the everlasting way.

Psalm 51

page 373

Reading

Luke 17:1–6

Jesus said to his disciples, "Things that cause sin will inevitably occur, but woe to the one through whom they occur. It would be better for him if a millstone were put around his neck and he be thrown into the sea than for him to cause one of these little ones to sin. Be on your guard! If your brother sins, rebuke him; and if he repents, forgive him. And if he wrongs you seven times in one day and returns to you seven times saying, 'I am sorry,' you should forgive him." And the Apostles said to the Lord, "Increase our faith." The Lord replied, "If you have faith the size of a mustard seed, you would say to this mulberry tree, 'Be uprooted and planted in the sea,' and it would obey you."

Reflection

Who have you had to forgive over and over? In our human foibles, we hurt each other, sometimes even intentionally. But God asks us to keep forgiving. This doesn't mean we have to be a doormat or allow others to abuse us! But it does mean that the mercy of God shines through us. "Forgive your brother even if he wrongs you seven times in one day." Even though this is meant as hyperbole in the Scripture, this can be our reality in family and community life. The mark of the Christian is to bear with one another.

Prayers

others may be added

Our faith might wax and wane but God is constant and so we bring our prayers before him:

℟. God of mercy, hear our prayer.

- That we might always ask the Lord to "increase our faith," we pray: ℟.
- That a spirit of reconciliation will inspire leaders of nations to seek peace, we pray: ℟.
- That all survivors of abuse find peace and safety, we pray: ℟.
- That we might always be an example of mercy and reconciliation, we pray: ℟.

Let us offer together the prayer that Jesus taught us.

Our Father . . .

O God,
our guide and guardian,
grant us the faith to follow you.
May we always forgive one another
and live with you in love.
Through Christ our Lord.
Amen.

✣ Guide me, Lord, along
the everlasting way.

✣ I will bless the Lord at all times.

Psalm 63

page 375

Reading

Wisdom 2:23—3:9

God formed man to be imperishable; / the image of his own nature he made them. But by the envy of the Devil, death entered the world, / and they who are in his possession experience it.

But the souls of the just are in the hand of God, / and no torment shall touch them. / They seemed, in the view of the foolish, to be dead; / and their passing away was thought an affliction / and their going forth from us, utter destruction. / But they are in peace. / For if before men, indeed, they be punished, / yet is their hope full of immortality; / Chastised a little, they shall be greatly blessed, / because God tried them / and found them worthy of himself. / As gold in the furnace, he proved them, / and as sacrificial offerings he took them to himself. / In the time of their visitation they shall shine, / and shall dart about as sparks through stubble; / They shall judge nations and rule over peoples, / and the Lord shall be their King forever. / Those who trust in him shall understand truth, / and the faithful shall abide with him in love: / Because grace and mercy are with his holy ones, / and his care is with his elect.

Reflection

When I was little, my family had an illustrated Bible which included horrific (if classic) images of the torments of hell. These images fascinated and terrified me. I surely wanted to avoid whatever the folks in those pictures had done to arrive in a place full of giant serpents and fire! I comforted myself with the idea that whatever they had done, it must have been really bad to land them there. In contrast today's reading—one that is often chosen for funeral liturgies—offers comfort and assurance. The role of fire is not sadistic torture but a means of refinement or purification—our "hope full of immortality." God made us to be imperishable, in God's image.

Prayers

others may be added

With trust in your great goodness,
we offer to God our prayers:

℟. **Abide with us in love, O Lord
and hear our prayer.**

- That those who trust in the Lord will understand truth, we pray: ℟.
- That wherever envy and death has entered the world, we might work to overcome it, we pray: ℟.
- That those who are dying, might be comforted, we pray: ℟.
- That we will grow in trust and faithfulness, we pray: ℟.

Let us offer together the prayer
that Jesus taught us.

Our Father . . .

O Lord, you shall be our King forever.
Hear our prayer
and grant us in your grace and mercy
that we might be your holy ones.
You who live and reign for ever
and ever.
Amen.

✣ I will bless the Lord at all times.

✚ Rise up, O God, bring judgment to the earth.

Psalm 27 *page 368*

Reading *Wisdom 6:1–11*

Hear, O kings, and understand; / learn, you magistrates of the earth's expanse! / Hearken, you who are in power over the multitude / and lord it over throngs of peoples! / Because authority was given you by the Lord / and sovereignty by the Most High, / who shall probe your works and scrutinize your counsels. / Because, though you were ministers of his kingdom, / you judged not rightly, / and did not keep the law, / nor walk according to the will of God, / Terribly and swiftly shall he come against you, / because judgment is stern for the exalted— / For the lowly may be pardoned out of mercy / but the mighty shall be mightily put to the test. / For the Lord of all shows no partiality, / nor does he fear greatness, / Because he himself made the great as well as the small, / and he provides for all alike; / but for those in power a rigorous scrutiny impends. / To you, therefore, O princes, are my words addressed / that you may learn wisdom and that you may not sin. / For those who keep the holy precepts hallowed shall be found holy, / and those learned in them will have ready a response. / Desire therefore my words; / long for them and you shall be instructed.

Reflection

In the *Spider Man* comics and movies, the oft-repeated adage of Peter Parker's (Spider Man's) Uncle Ben, "With great power comes great responsibility," seems to be an echo of the sentiment from this passage: "The mighty shall be mightily put to the test." We may not think of ourselves as mighty but if you are reading this page it's likely that you are among those privileged with the opportunity to learn about faith and so held to higher standard because of that lofty status. May we take seriously our responsibility to study God's ways and follow his precepts.

Prayers *others may be added*

Let us bring our needs to God who teaches us holy precepts:

℟. **Lord, hear our prayer and guide us to holiness.**

- That we might keep God's law and grow in faithfulness, we pray: ℟.
- That all who exercise power would do so in wisdom and be mindful of those most in need , we pray: ℟.
- That those who struggle to meet their basic needs will find help and hope, we pray: ℟.
- That the great and small in our own community might be one in the Lord, we pray: ℟.

Let us offer together the prayer that Jesus taught us.

Our Father . . .

Great teacher of goodness,
hear us now
and help us learn to keep your
holy precepts.
Through Christ our Lord.
Amen.

✚ Rise up, O God, bring judgment to the earth.

Memorial of St. Frances Xavier Cabrini, Virgin

Thursday, November 13, 2025

✤ Your word is for ever, O Lord.

Psalm 122

page 387

Reading

Luke 17:20–25

Asked by the Pharisees when the Kingdom of God would come, Jesus said in reply, "The coming of the Kingdom of God cannot be observed, and no one will announce, 'Look, here it is,' or, 'There it is.' For behold, the Kingdom of God is among you."

Then he said to his disciples, "The days will come when you will long to see one of the days of the Son of Man, but you will not see it. There will be those who will say to you, 'Look, there he is,' or 'Look, here he is.' Do not go off, do not run in pursuit. For just as lightning flashes and lights up the sky from one side to the other, so will the Son of Man be in his day. But first he must suffer greatly and be rejected by this generation."

Reflection

Every few years or so it seems there's some popular figure declaring that the end of the world is nigh. This is a distraction, Jesus tells us, "For behold, the Kingdom of God is among [us]." If the Kingdom of God is already here, is happening now, we must participate in it and perpetuate it. Not a "pie in the sky when you die" way, but the immediacy of the way we live right now. Let's not be misled or get caught up in fear, but instead live in the love that God's kingdom gives us.

Prayers

others may be added

The kingdom of God is at hand and so we bring our needs to him in love and trust:

℟. **Lord, hear our prayer.**

- That Church leaders might not lose heart, we pray: ℟.
- That world leaders will work for the common good., we pray: ℟.
- That those who feel lost or forgotten might find friendship and hope, we pray: ℟.
- That we will look for and work toward the coming of the kingdom of God, we pray: ℟.

Let us offer together the prayer that Jesus taught us.

Our Father . . .

O God of Wisdom
grant us sight to see your kingdom
before our eyes.
Grant us light to see the path before us,
a path that leads only to you.
Through Christ our Lord.
Amen.

✤ Your word is for ever, O Lord.

✠ The heavens proclaim
the glory of God.

Psalm 104

page 383

Reading

Wisdom 13:1–9

All men were by nature foolish who were in ignorance of God, / and who from the good things seen did not succeed in knowing him who is, / and from studying the works did not discern the artisan; / But either fire, or wind, or the swift air, / or the circuit of the stars, or the mighty water, / or the luminaries of heaven, the governors of the world, they considered gods. / Now if out of joy in their beauty they thought them gods, / let them know how far more excellent is the Lord than these; / for the original source of beauty fashioned them. / Or if they were struck by their might and energy, / let them from these things realize how much more powerful is he who made them. / For from the greatness and the beauty of created things / their original author, by analogy, is seen. / But yet, for these the blame is less; / For they indeed have gone astray perhaps, / though they seek God and wish to find him. / For they search busily among his works, but are distracted by what they see, because the things seen are fair. / But again, not even these are pardonable. / For if they so far succeeded in knowledge / that they could speculate about the world, / how did they not more quickly find its Lord?

Reflection

From the tiniest ant to the biggest mountain, from what we peek at under the microscope to what we peer at through the telescope, the universe is indeed full of wonders. These marvels should lead us to ask, "Who made this?" And more, they should foster in us a hunger to "discern the artisan," to seek out the Creator of these beautiful created things.

Prayers

others may be added

We recognize the handiwork of our Creator and in wonder and awe bring to him our needs:

℟. **Saving God, hear us.**

- Help us to see you in the world around us, we pray: ℟.
- Inspire us to protect and preserve the wonders of creation we pray: ℟.
- Strengthen our insight to recognize you in those who are poor, we pray: ℟.
- Allow us the wisdom to see and know you in one another, we pray: ℟.

Let us offer together the prayer
that Jesus taught us.

Our Father . . .

God of swift air and mighty water,
incline your ear to your people.
May our joy in your beauty inspire
us to worship.
Sharpen our sight so that we recognize
how far more excellent you are.
Through Christ our Lord.
Amen.

✠ The heavens proclaim
the glory of God.

Weekday

Saturday, November 15, 2025

✤ Remember the marvels
the Lord has done!

Psalm 105 *page 383*

Reading *Luke 18:1–8*

Jesus told his disciples a parable about the necessity for them to pray always without becoming weary. He said, "There was a judge in a certain town who neither feared God nor respected any human being. And a widow in that town used to come to him and say, 'Render a just decision for me against my adversary.' For a long time the judge was unwilling, but eventually he thought, 'While it is true that I neither fear God nor respect any human being, because this widow keeps bothering me I shall deliver a just decision for her lest she finally come and strike me.'" The Lord said, "Pay attention to what the dishonest judge says. Will not God then secure the rights of his chosen ones who call out to him day and night? Will he be slow to answer them? I tell you, he will see to it that justice is done for them speedily. But when the Son of Man comes, will he find faith on earth?"

Reflection

Does God get tired of our complaints? When we ask again and again for help with the same weakness or for a solution to a persistent problem does God get annoyed? It would seem not. Today's admonition to never give up is encouragement of the best kind. God will hear and answer us, Jesus tells us. God never tires of our whining, our frustration, our anger, and our need. Make a ruckus. Be in the habit of bringing your needs before the Lord like a cranky old widow. God will not be slow to answer.

Prayers *others may be added*

Our God sees to it that justice is done for all in need and so we bring their needs before God:

℟. Hear us, O Lord.

- For persistence in prayer, we pray: ℟.
- For a more just world, we pray: ℟.
- For those who are hungry, or lonely, or persecuted, we pray: ℟.
- For our local Church, we pray: ℟.

Let us offer together the prayer
that Jesus taught us.

Our Father . . .

Faithful Father,
you secure the rights
of your chosen ones.
Listen now,
hear us,
and help us.
Through Christ our Lord.
Amen.

✤ Remember the marvels
the Lord has done!

✤ Whatever you ask in prayer, /
believe that you will receive.

Psalm 122

page 387

Reading

Luke21:8–11

[Jesus said:] "See that you not be deceived, for many will come in my name, saying, 'I am he,' and 'The time has come.' Do not follow them! When you hear of wars and insurrections, do not be terrified; for such things must happen first, but it will not immediately be the end." Then he said to them, "Nation will rise against nation, and kingdom against kingdom. There will be powerful earthquakes, famines, and plagues from place to place; and awesome sights and mighty signs will come from the sky."

Reflection

These closing days of the Catholic liturgical year have us considering the end times. As our earth warms and tides rise, the apocalyptic readings can seem to be speaking to our present age. All the signs mentioned of the end of the world—earthquakes, famines plagues, war, insurrection—are already taking place. Jesus cautions us "do not be terrified." And we know—from Scripture and from our own observations of humanity—that trying to predict the end of the world is a loser's game. Instead, we are called to conduct ourselves so as to be ready for the Lord to return at any time.

Prayers

others may be added

We bring our prayers to God who comes to rule the earth with justice.

℟. God of justice, hear our prayer.

- That there be an end to division, we pray: ℟.
- That there be an end to war and all forms of violence, we pray: ℟.
- That all who hunger will be fed, we pray: ℟.
- That we might live as Jesus taught, we pray: ℟.

Let us offer together the prayer that Jesus taught us.

Our Father . . .

Arise, O Sun of Justice,
come to our aid.
Heal our divisions
and be our hope.
Who live and reign for ever and ever.
Amen.

✤ Whatever you ask in prayer, /
believe that you will receive.

Monday, November 17, 2025

✤ Give me life, O Lord.

Psalm 24

page 367

Reading

Luke 18:35–43

As Jesus approached Jericho a blind man was sitting by the roadside begging, and hearing a crowd going by, he inquired what was happening. They told him, "Jesus of Nazareth is passing by." He shouted, "Jesus, Son of David, have pity on me!" The people walking in front rebuked him, telling him to be silent, but he kept calling out all the more, "Son of David, have pity on me!" Then Jesus stopped and ordered that he be brought to him; and when he came near, Jesus asked him, "What do you want me to do for you?" He replied, "Lord, please let me see." Jesus told him, "Have sight; your faith has saved you." He immediately received his sight and followed him, giving glory to God. When they saw this, all the people gave praise to God.

Reflection

Like the older sibling hissing, "Behave!" to the little brother imping around when there are visitors, the crowd shushes the blind man as he cries out to Jesus. The man however, knows what he wants. He's not going to let social niceties get in the way. He asks, shouts, and calls out; and he does so more loudly after he is shushed! And Jesus delivers. Jesus even tells him that it's his faith that has saved him. May we all have that kind of confidence to ask for what we need from the Lord.

Prayers

others may be added

The Lord listens to our pleas and so with confidence we ask:

℟. O God, hear us.

- Inspire us to not grow weary in our pursuit of goodness, we pray: ℟.
- Grant wisdom to leaders of nations that they might build societies respectful of every faith, we pray: ℟.
- Heal all those who are suffering in body, mind, or spirit, we pray: ℟.
- Strengthen this community to walk with those in need, we pray: ℟.

Let us offer together the prayer that Jesus taught us.

Our Father . . .

Saving God,
listen to your people.
Grant us your mercy and healing
that we might serve
and give you glory.
Through Christ our Lord.
Amen.

✤ Give me life, O Lord.

✤ The Lord upholds my life.

Psalm 71 *page 376*

Reading *Luke 19:1–10*

At that time Jesus came to Jericho and intended to pass through the town. Now a man there named Zacchaeus, who was a chief tax collector and also a wealthy man, was seeking to see who Jesus was; but he could not see him because of the crowd, for he was short in stature. So he ran ahead and climbed a sycamore tree in order to see Jesus, who was about to pass that way. When he reached the place, Jesus looked up and said, "Zacchaeus, come down quickly, for today I must stay at your house." And he came down quickly and received him with joy. When they saw this, they began to grumble, saying, "He has gone to stay at the house of a sinner." But Zacchaeus stood there and said to the Lord, "Behold, half of my possessions, Lord, I shall give to the poor, and if I have extorted anything from anyone I shall repay it four times over." And Jesus said to him, "Today salvation has come to this house because this man too is a descendant of Abraham. For the Son of Man has come to seek and to save what was lost."

Reflection

The role of the crowd in the high drama story of Zacchaeus is first an impediment that drives our central character to comic lengths. Zacchaeus was desperate to see Jesus but can't see him over the crowd. Once the Lord sees him in the tree and calls him down, the crowd's role is to grumble against Jesus' mercy and forgiveness. In both cases, the crowd, perhaps unwittingly, attempts to come between Zacchaeus and Jesus. It's Zacchaeus' over-the-top responses to Jesus—climbing a tree in the first case and publicly repenting in the second—that gain him his reward. If we try to imitate the zeal of Zacchaeus more and imitate the crowd a little less, we might find ourselves a little closer to Jesus too.

Prayers *others may be added*

We seek the Lord who desires to save us and so we bring to God our prayers:

℟. Lord, hear our prayer.

- For the Church, that she might be a faithful example, we pray: ℟.
- For elected leaders, that they will serve honorably and work for the good of all their people, we pray: ℟.
- For those who find life burdensome, we pray: ℟.
- For the grace to be forgiving of one another, we pray: ℟.

Let us offer together the prayer
that Jesus taught us.

Our Father . . .

God of Mercy
you delight in seeking
and in saving the lost.
Hear us now
and help us home to you.
Through Christ our Lord.
Amen.

✤ The Lord upholds my life.

✚ Lord, when your glory appears,
my joy will be full.

Psalm 62

page 374

Reading

Luke 19:27

[Jesus said:] "'I tell you, to everyone who has, more will be given, but from the one who has not, even what he has will be taken away.'"

Reflection

This Gospel verse ends the parable of the ten pounds, a parable that Jesus told in response to the question about the imminence of the kingdom of God. The parable reveals to us that the ruler's request evoked many kinds of responses from the people who were subject to him. Some rejected the ruler, some served him the best they could, some met the ruler's wishes halfway, and some did the bare minimum. This diversity of responses to the ruler's commands illustrates the ways we respond to God's invitation to relationship. Sometimes we are good and faithful servants, sometimes we are halfway there, sometimes we give the bare minimum, and in some cases, we reject God's call outright. The kingdom of God is already at hand, but God's Spirit continues to inspire us to respond to the call of our heavenly ruler.

Prayers

others may be added

Striving to be good and faithful servants to build your kingdom, we pray:

℟. Lord, hear our prayer.

- For the Church, may we imitate those good and faithful servants who made a full profit of the ten pounds, using our own gifts and talents for the greater glory of God, we pray: ℟.
- For the courage to share our gifts, may we trust that those gifts and talents that make us unique are also for the great benefit of those around us, we pray: ℟.
- For forgiveness for the times we have rejected God's invitation to the fullness of life, may we turn away from anything that is sinful and stay faithful to the life-giving message of the Gospel, we pray: ℟.

Let us offer together the prayer that Jesus taught us.

Our Father . . .

O God,
you chose us to do your will
and follow your way.
Free us from fear
and grant our prayer.
Through Christ our Lord.
Amen.

✚ Lord, when your glory appears,
my joy will be full.

✤ The Lord is my light
and my salvation.

Psalm 63

page 375

Reading

Luke 19:41–44

As Jesus drew near Jerusalem, he saw the city and wept over it, saying, "If this day you only knew what makes for peace—but now it is hidden from your eyes. For the days are coming upon you when your enemies will raise a palisade against you; they will encircle you and hem you in on all sides. They will smash you to the ground and your children within you, and they will not leave one stone upon another within you because you did not recognize the time of your visitation."

Reflection

"If you want peace, work for justice," Pope Paul VI said. When Jesus wept for Jerusalem, did he know then that blood would continue to be shed there for the next thousands of years? Jerusalem, "if . . . you only knew what makes for peace." In the context of today's reading, not recognizing the Messiah is Jerusalem's failure. In the scope of human history, the failure of every people to recognize God present in their brothers and sisters is our universal failure. That every person might live in safety and dignity, free from fear and want, is a tall order, especially given the human addiction to greed and power. If you want peace, work for justice.

Prayers

others may be added

The peace of Christ dwells with us
and so we pray:

℟. **God of peace, hear our prayer.**

- May Church leaders always be a voice for peace and justice, we pray: ℟.
- May leaders of nations seek an end to hostility and pursue justice, we pray: ℟.
- That all victims of war, all displaced people, and every refugee, might find a place of safety and hope, we pray: ℟.
- That our efforts toward peace might bear lasting fruit, we pray:

Let us offer together the prayer
that Jesus taught us.

Our Father . . .

O God of justice,
hear our cries for peace
and strengthen us to seek your way
to peace.
Through Christ our Lord.
Amen.

✤ The Lord is my light
and my salvation.

Memorial of the Presentation
of the Blessed Virgin Mary
Friday, November 21, 2025

✚ We praise your glorious name,
O mighty God.

Psalm 67

page 375

Reading

Luke 19:45–48

Jesus entered the temple area and proceeded to drive out those who were selling things, saying to them, "It is written, *My house shall be a house of prayer, / but you have made it a den of thieves*." And every day he was teaching in the temple area. The chief priests, the scribes, and the leaders of the people, meanwhile, were seeking to put him to death, but they could find no way to accomplish their purpose because all the people were hanging on his words.

Reflection

Jesus' strongest criticisms throughout all the Gospel accounts are reserved for those who abuse their power. Hypocrisy—religious leaders who call for holiness but meanwhile behave in unscrupulous or self-serving ways—was just as much of a danger in Jesus' day as it is in our own. The wedge that hypocrisy drives between the faithful and their religion erodes trust, divides communities, and even destroys faith. Not every situation calls for the overturning of tables, but some injustices do indeed call for a riot. May God help us always to be outraged by injustice

Prayers

others may be added

God has given us holy places to gather and worship, and so with gratitude we bring to him our prayers:

℟. Lord, hear us.

✦ That both the buildings and the people that make up the Church will be held sacred, we pray: ℟.

✦ That those in authority safeguard all houses of worship, we pray: ℟.

✦ That all who face religious persecution or abuse will find help and hope, we pray: ℟.

✦ That we might foster respect and unity with all people of faith, we pray: ℟.

Let us offer together the prayer
that Jesus taught us.

Our Father . . .

God of goodness,
your holy places are holy
because we meet you there.
Hear our prayers, and
may every house of worship—from
the grandest cathedral to the chapel
of our heart—bring us closer to you.
Through Christ our Lord.
Amen.

✚ We praise your glorious name,
O mighty God.

✣ I will rejoice in your salvation,
O Lord.

Psalm 84

page 378

Reading

Luke 20:34–40

Jesus said to [the Sadducees,] "The children of this age marry and remarry; but those who are deemed worthy to attain to the coming age and to the resurrection of the dead neither marry nor are given in marriage. They can no longer die, for they are like angels; and they are the children of God because they are the ones who will rise. That the dead will rise even Moses made known in the passage about the bush, when he called 'Lord' the God of Abraham, the God of Isaac, and the God of Jacob; and he is not God of the dead, but of the living, for to him all are alive." Some of the scribes said in reply, "Teacher, you have answered well." And they no longer dared to ask him anything.

Reflection

As the liturgical year draws to a close, we read a sequence of passages from Luke, following Jesus on his journey to Jerusalem. He has entered the city in triumph and now, as he teaches in the temple area, his enemies seek to trap him with a question about the resurrection. With heavenly wisdom, Jesus responds to their objections—citing Moses, just as they did. God, he tells them, is the God of the living, yet he is also the God of Abraham, Isaac, and Jacob—and these ancestors must, therefore, be alive in God.

Prayers

others may be added

Our Lord is the God of the living and so we bring the needs of the world before him in confidence:

℟. Living God, hear us.

- For those who teach the doctrines of the Church, that they might do so with prudence, we pray: ℟.
- For leaders of nations, that they might seek to preserve and protect life, we pray: ℟.
- For all those grieving the loss of a loved one, we pray: ℟.
- For us, that we will seek to know and follow Christ in sincerity and love, we pray: ℟.

Let us offer together the prayer
that Jesus taught us.

Our Father . . .

God of the living,
guide us in right paths.
Hear our prayers
and grant them in your mercy.
Through Christ our Lord.
Amen.

✣ I will rejoice in your salvation,
O Lord.

Sunday, November 23, 2025

✤ To him belong glory and power
for ever and ever.

Psalm 85

page 379

Reading

1 Samuel 5:1–3

In those days, all the tribes of Israel came to David in Hebron and said: / "Here we are, your bone and your flesh. In days past, when Saul was our king, / it was you who led the Israelites out and brought them back. / And the LORD said to you, / 'You shall shepherd my people Israel / and shall be commander of Israel.'" / When all the elders of Israel came to David in Hebron, / King David made an agreement with them there before the LORD, / and they anointed him king of Israel.

Reflection

The Solemnity of Our Lord Jesus Christ, King of the Universe is one of the newest on the Church's calendar. It was instituted by Pope Pius XI in 1925. He hoped that this proclamation of Christ as King of the universe would serve as a corrective to the dangerous political ideas of his time—ideas that had led to one devastating world war and would soon bring on another. Jesus is a king like no other—a king who reigns from a cross, who has none of the trappings of earthly power but who, choosing to empty himself, leads us to paradise.

Prayers

others may be added

Trusting in the Lord's kindness and mercy we bring to him our prayers:

℟. God of David, hear us.

- For the Church, that she might be a force for healing in the world, we pray: ℟.
- For judges, legislators, and police officers, that they might carry out their duties with fairness and compassion, we pray: ℟.
- For all those facing death, we pray: ℟.
- For those facing difficulties, that they will find comfort in those around them, we pray:

Let us offer together the prayer
that Jesus taught us.

Our Father . . .

O Lord,
remember your mercy.
Show us your kindness
and grant that we might be with you
in paradise.
Through Christ our Lord.
Amen.

✤ To him belong glory and power
for ever and ever.

✤ Glory and praise for ever!

Psalm 91 *page 379*

Reading *Luke 21:1–4*

When Jesus looked up he saw some wealthy people putting their offerings into the treasury and he noticed a poor widow putting in two small coins. He said, "I tell you truly, this poor widow put in more than all the rest; for those others have all made offerings from their surplus wealth, but she, from her poverty, has offered her whole livelihood."

Reflection

More than one saint has recommended that while we may not all be able to perform great acts, we can all do small things with great love. God has a way of taking our little actions and building them into something beautiful. We do not need to be wealthy or powerful; we don't need to be a thought leader or a social media influencer to make a difference. We can offer what we do have—who we are, big or small—and it is enough.

Prayers *others may be added*

With praise and thanks for God's steadfast love we bring our needs and prayers.

℟. **Be with us Lord, and hear our prayer.**

- Encourage all those who teach the faith, we pray: ℟.
- Inspire those who are responsible for creating laws, we pray: ℟.
- Protect those who are widowed and orphaned, we pray: ℟.
- Awaken our desire to offer our whole lives to your service, we pray: ℟.

Let us offer together the prayer that Jesus taught us.

Our Father . . .

God of the mighty and the lowly,
You hear the prayers of all your people
Listen as we cry out to you.
Bless the work of our hands.
Through Christ our Lord.
Amen.

✤ Glory and praise for ever!

Tuesday, November 25, 2025

✤ Give glory and eternal praise
to [God].

Psalm 95 *page 380*

Reading *Luke 21:5–11*

While some people were speaking about how the temple was adorned with costly stones and votive offerings, Jesus said, "All that you see here—the days will come when there will not be left a stone upon another stone that will not be thrown down."

Then they asked him, "Teacher, when will this happen? And what sign will there be when all these things are about to happen?" He answered, "See that you not be deceived, for many will come in my name, saying, 'I am he,' and 'The time has come.' Do not follow them! When you hear of wars and insurrections, do not be terrified; for such things must happen first, but it will not immediately be the end." Then he said to them, "Nation will rise against nation, and kingdom against kingdom. There will be powerful earthquakes, famines, and plagues from place to place; and awesome sights and mighty signs will come from the sky."

Reflection

There are so many distractions that can lead us away from following Jesus. In today's reading, Jesus warns his disciples not to be misled. On the brink of the headlong sprint from Thanksgiving to Christmas—a season that can be emotionally, financially, and spiritually draining—we would do well to heed that warning. There is no gift or decorating scheme or party or exercise plan or credit card offer (or anything!) that can provide us with what Jesus gives. What we need is the love God has given us in Jesus.

Prayers *others may be added*

We offer our needs to God who listens to our pleas:

℟. O God, hear us.

- For all who exercise authority in the Church, that they will lead with wisdom and fidelity, we pray: ℟.
- For elected leaders, that they will govern with justice and peaceful efforts, we pray: ℟.
- For all those who fear death, that the knowledge of God's love and mercy will comfort them, we pray: ℟.
- For all Christians, that they might avoid false teachers and follow Jesus without fear, we pray: ℟.

Let us offer together the prayer
that Jesus taught us.

Our Father . . .

Eternal God,
your love made heaven and earth
and your might is tempered by mercy.
Hear our prayers,
calm our fears,
and call us ever deeper into your heart.
Through Christ our Lord.
Amen.

✤ Give glory and eternal praise
to [God].

✠ Give glory and eternal praise
to [God].

Psalm 98

page 381

Reading

Daniel 5:13–14, 16–17, 23–28

Then Daniel was brought into the presence of the king. The king asked him, "Are you the Daniel, the Jewish exile, whom my father, the king, brought from Judah? I have heard that the Spirit of God is in you, that you possess brilliant knowledge and extraordinary wisdom. I have heard that you can interpret dreams and solve difficulties; if you are able to read the writing and tell me what it means, you shall be clothed in purple, wear a gold collar about your neck, and be third in the government of the kingdom."

Daniel answered the king: "You may keep your gifts, or give your presents to someone else; but the writing I will read for you, O king, and tell you what it means. You have rebelled against the Lord of heaven. You had the vessels of his temple brought before you, so that you and your nobles, your wives and your entertainers, might drink wine from them; and you praised the gods of silver and gold, bronze and iron, wood and stone, that neither see nor hear nor have intelligence. But the God in whose hand is your life breath and the whole course of your life, you did not glorify. By him were the wrist and hand sent, and the writing set down."

Reflection

The handwriting is on the wall, literally. In fact, this story is where the expression originates. A king desecrates holy objects and a message of doom appears. The lesson is that we must honor God and keep holy the sacred. The arrogant are punished and Daniel's faithfulness to God is rewarded with special insight. It would be handy if every tyrant had a Daniel to interpret the handwriting on the wall. Would having a personal prophet change anyone's behavior? Doubtful. But there is appeal in the idea that those who wield their power might tremble in fear when they are faced with the consequences of their cruelty to others. May we have the courage of Daniel and speak truth in the face of powerful oppression.

Prayers

others may be added

With faith in God's goodness, we come before him with our prayers.

℟. **God of justice, save us.**

- For the strength to be the voice of truth, we pray: ℟.
- That tyrants might turn away from their cruelty, we pray: ℟.
- For refugees, asylum seekers, and all displaced people, we pray: ℟.

Let us offer together the prayer
that Jesus taught us.

Our Father . . .

God of all nations,
your justice is what we seek,
and your peace is what we long for.
Strengthen your people to do your will.
Through Christ our Lord.
Amen.

✠ Give glory and eternal praise
to [God].

Weekday

Thursday, November 27, 2025

✚ Give glory and eternal praise
to [God].

Psalm 103

page 382

Reading

Colossians 3:12–17

Brothers and sisters: Put on, as God's chosen ones, holy and beloved, heartfelt compassion, kindness, humility, gentleness, and patience, bearing with one another and forgiving one another, if one has a grievance against another; as the Lord has forgiven you, so must you also do. And over all these put on love, that is, the bond of perfection. And let the peace of Christ control your hearts, the peace into which you were also called in one Body. And be thankful. Let the word of Christ dwell in you richly, as in all wisdom you teach and admonish one another, singing psalms, hymns, and spiritual songs with gratitude in your hearts to God. And whatever you do, in word or in deed, do everything in the name of the Lord Jesus, giving thanks to God the Father through him.

Reflection

Old tensions can arise when families get together. Even when there's joy in coming together, bearing with the inevitable frustrations of holiday preparations can bring out the worst in us. Imagine dressing yourself in this holiday finery—compassion, gentleness, forgiveness, and kindness. Go about your day—yes, even with that long to-do list—doing each thing. If your responsibilities are light, what could you do to ease another person's burden? Generosity and gratitude are marks of the Christian and good tools for life!

Prayers

others may be added

God has blessed us abundantly and so with trust in his care for us, we pray:

℟. **Help us to love.**

- Where there is division Lord, we pray: ℟.
- Where there is no peace, we pray: ℟.
- When people go hungry Lord, we pray: ℟.
- When people are blind, we pray: ℟.

Let us offer together the prayer
that Jesus taught us.

Our Father . . .

O God,
you are love itself.
Bless us with the bond of perfection
that is your love.
May your peace fill our hearts
and may we be filled with gratitude
for all that you have given us.
Through Christ our Lord.
Amen.

✚ Give glory and eternal praise
to [God].

✣ Give glory and eternal praise
to [God].

Psalm 115 *page 385*

Reading *Luke 21:29–33*

Jesus told his disciples a parable. "Consider the fig tree and all the other trees. When their buds burst open, you see for yourselves and know that summer is now near; in the same way, when you see these things happening, know that the Kingdom of God is near. Amen, I say to you, this generation will not pass away until all these things have taken place. Heaven and earth will pass away, but my words will not pass away."

Reflection

How different would our lives be if we believed that the kingdom of God is near? If the kingdom is near would you love more? Would you be kinder? More generous? More radical? More concerned to be inclusive? To seek justice? It is human nature that the immediacy of something makes us more aware of its possibility. How can we be conscious of living the values of the kingdom of God? How might we live as if the kingdom will be fulfilled tomorrow? By paying attention to inbreaking of the kingdom, we help make it present in the here and now.

Prayers *others may be added*

The kingdom of God is near, in hope and trust we pray

℟. God of heaven and earth, hear us.

- For the Church, that she may see and respond to the signs of the times, we pray: ℟.
- For leaders of nations, that they will seek peace, we pray: ℟.
- For those who long for justice, we pray: ℟.
- For our communities of faith, that they might grow in unity, love, and faith, we pray: ℟.

Let us offer together the prayer
that Jesus taught us.

Our Father . . .

Lord Jesus Christ,
your kingdom is among us.
As we gather together in your name,
you are in our midst.
Teach us the kingship of humility
and service,
that we may bring forth your kingdom
here and now.
Who live and reign for ever and ever.
Amen.

✣ Give glory and eternal praise
to [God].

✚ Give glory and eternal praise
to [God].

Psalm 121

page 386

Reading

Luke 21:34–36

Jesus said to his disciples: "Beware that your hearts do not become drowsy from carousing and drunkenness and the anxieties of daily life, and that day catch you by surprise like a trap. For that day will assault everyone who lives on the face of the earth. Be vigilant at all times and pray that you have the strength to escape the tribulations that are imminent and to stand before the Son of Man."

Reflection

Modern life can become a series of numbing events. Between our reckless busyness, the unending cycle of bad news, and the many opportunities we have to disappear into our devices and distractions, it is the easiest thing to "become drowsy." Maintaining a vigilant attitude toward our faith and of how we are called to live as believers can be a real challenge. What strengthens or aids you in your efforts to remain vigilant? Prayer? Study? Participation in the sacraments? A community of faithful friends or believers? What's one thing you could do or change to help you be attentive to Jesus?

Prayers

others may be added

Attentive to the Lord, we offer to him the needs of our world:

℟. **O God, hear us.**

- For those who help others grow in faith, we pray: ℟.
- For peace in our homes, our nation, and around the world, we pray: ℟.
- For those suffering from severe weather and the impacts of climate change, we pray: ℟.
- For increased awareness of God's call, we pray: ℟.

Let us offer together the prayer
that Jesus taught us.

Our Γather . . .

God of all seasons
you call us to stay awake
to the present moment,
even as we long for the coming
of your kingdom.
Be with us now, and hear us.
In your mercy, lead us to you.
Through Christ our Lord.
Amen.

✚ Give glory and eternal praise
to [God].

Psalter

Psalm 13

2 How long, O LORD? Will you forget me forever?
How long will you hide your face from me?
3 How long must I bear grief in my soul,
have sorrow in my heart all day long?
How long shall my enemy prevail over me?

4 Look, and answer me, O LORD my God!
Give light to my eyes lest I fall asleep in death;
5 lest my enemy say, "I have prevailed over him";
lest my foes rejoice when they see me fall.

6 As for me, I trust in your merciful love.
Let my heart rejoice in your salvation.
I will sing to the LORD who has been bountiful with me.

Psalm 22

2 My God, my God, why have you forsaken me?
Why are you far from saving me,
so far from my words of anguish?
3 O my God, I call by day and you do not answer;
I call by night and I find no reprieve.

13 Many bulls have surrounded me,
fierce bulls of Bashan close me in.
14 Against me they open wide their mouths,
like a lion, rending and roaring.

16 Parched as burnt clay is my throat,
my tongue cleaves fast to my jaws.
You lay me in the dust of death.
17 For dogs have surrounded me;
a band of the wicked besets me.

They tear holes in my hands and my feet;
18 I can count every one of my bones.
They stare at me and gloat.
19 They divide my clothing among them,
they cast lots for my robe.

20 But you, O Lord, do not stay afar off;
my strength, make haste to help me!
21 Rescue my soul from the sword,
my life from the grip of the dog.
22 Save my life from the jaws of the lion,
my poor soul from the horns of wild bulls.

31 And my soul shall live for him, my descendants serve him.
They shall tell of the Lord to generations yet to come,
32 declare his saving justice to peoples yet unborn:
"These are the things the Lord has done."

Psalm 23

1 The LORD is my shepherd;
there is nothing I shall want.
2 Fresh and green are the pastures
where he gives me repose.
Near restful waters he leads me;
3 he revives my soul.

He guides me along the right path,
for the sake of his name.
4 Though I should walk in the valley of the shadow of death,
no evil would I fear, for you are with me.
Your crook and your staff will give me comfort.

5 You have prepared a table before me
in the sight of my foes.
My head you have anointed with oil;
my cup is overflowing.

6 Surely goodness and mercy shall follow me
all the days of my life.

In the LORD's own house shall I dwell
for length of days unending.

Psalm 24

The LORD's is the earth and its fullness,
the world, and those who dwell in it.
2 It is he who set it on the seas;
on the rivers he made it firm.

3 Who shall climb the mountain of the LORD?
Who shall stand in his holy place?
4 The clean of hands and pure of heart,
whose soul is not set on vain things,
who has not sworn deceitful words.

5 Blessings from the LORD shall he receive,
and right reward from the God who saves him.
6 Such are the people who seek him,
who seek the face of the God of Jacob.

Psalm 27

The LORD is my light and my salvation;
whom shall I fear?
The LORD is the stronghold of my life;
whom should I dread?

2 When those who do evil draw near
to devour my flesh,
it is they, my enemies and foes,
who stumble and fall.

3 Though an army encamp against me,
my heart would not fear.
Though war break out against me,
even then would I trust.

4 There is one thing I ask of the LORD,
only this do I seek:
to live in the house of the LORD
all the days of my life,
to gaze on the beauty of the LORD,
to inquire at his temple.

5 For there he keeps me safe in his shelter
in the day of evil.
He hides me under cover of his tent;
he sets me high upon a rock.

6 And now my head shall be raised
above my foes who surround me,
and I shall offer within his tent
sacrifices full of exultation.
I will sing and make music for the LORD.
7 O LORD, hear my voice when I call;
have mercy and answer me.
8 Of you my heart has spoken,
"Seek his face."

It is your face, O LORD, that I seek;
9 hide not your face from me.
Dismiss not your servant in anger;
you have been my help.

Do not abandon or forsake me,
O God, my Savior!
10 Though father and mother forsake me,
the LORD will receive me.

11 Instruct me, LORD, in your way;
on an even path lead me
because of my enemies.

12 Do not leave me to the will of my foes,
for false witnesses rise up against me,
and they breathe out violence.

13 I believe I shall see the LORD's goodness
in the land of the living.
14 Wait for the LORD; be strong;
be stouthearted, and wait for the LORD!

Psalm 30

2 I will extol you, LORD, for you have raised me up,
and have not let my enemies rejoice over me.

3 O LORD my God, I cried to you for help,
and you have healed me.
4 O LORD, you have lifted up my soul from Sheol,
restored me to life from those who sink into the pit.

5 Sing psalms to the LORD, you faithful ones;
give thanks to his holy name.
6 His anger lasts a moment; his favor all through life.
At night come tears, but dawn brings joy.

11 Hear, O LORD, and have mercy on me;
be my helper, O LORD.
12 You have changed my mourning into dancing,
removed my sackcloth and girded me with joy.
13 So let my soul sings psalms to you, and not be silent.
O LORD my God, I will thank you forever.

Psalm 33

1 Ring out your joy to the LORD, O you just;
for praise is fitting for the upright.
2 Give thanks to the LORD upon the harp;
with a ten-stringed lute sing him songs.
3 O sing him a song that is new;
play skillfully, with shouts of joy.

4 For the word of the LORD is upright,
and all his works to be trusted.
5 The LORD loves justice and right,
and his merciful love fills the earth.

20 Our soul is waiting for the LORD.
He is our help and our shield.
21 In him do our hearts find joy.
We trust in his holy name.

22 May your merciful love be upon us,
as we hope in you, O LORD.

Psalm 34

2 I will bless the LORD at all times,
praise of him is always in my mouth.
3 In the LORD my soul shall make its boast;
the humble shall hear and be glad.

4 Glorify the LORD with me;
together let us praise his name.
5 I sought the LORD, and he answered me;
from all my terrors he set me free.

6 Look toward him and be radiant;
let your faces not be abashed.
7 This lowly one called; the LORD heard,
and rescued him from all his distress.

8 The angel of the LORD is encamped
around those who fear him, to rescue them.
9 Taste and see that the LORD is good.
Blessed the man who seeks refuge in him.

10 Fear the LORD, you his holy ones.
They lack nothing, those who fear him.
11 The rich suffer want and go hungry,
but those who seek the LORD lack no blessing.

12 Come, children, and hear me,
that I may teach you the fear of the LORD.
13 Who is it that desires life
and longs to see prosperous days?

14 Guard your tongue from evil,
and your lips from speaking deceit.
15 Turn aside from evil and do good.
Seek after peace, and pursue it.

16 The LORD turns his eyes to the just one,
and his ears are open to his cry.
17 The LORD turns his face against the wicked
to cut off their remembrance from the earth.

18 When the just one cries out, the LORD hears,
and rescues him in all his distress.
19 The LORD is close to the brokenhearted;
those whose spirit is crushed he will save.

20 Many are the trials of the just one,
but from them all the LORD will rescue him.
21 He will keep guard over all his bones;
not one of his bones shall be broken.

22 Evil brings death to the wicked;
those who hate the just one are doomed.
23 The LORD ransoms the souls of his servants.
All who trust in him shall not be condemned.

Psalm 42

2 Like the deer that yearns
for running streams,
so my soul is yearning
for you, my God.

3 My soul is thirsting for God,
the living God;
when can I enter and appear
before the face of God?

4 My tears have become my bread,
by day, by night,
as they say to me all the day long,
"Where is your God?"

5 These things will I remember
as I pour out my soul:
for I would go to the place
of your wondrous tent,
all the way to the house of God,
amid cries of gladness and thanksgiving,
the throng keeping joyful festival.

6 Why are you cast down, my soul;
why groan within me?
Hope in God; I will praise him yet again,
my saving presence and my God.

9 By day the LORD decrees his loving mercy;
by night his song is with me,
a prayer to the God of my life.

10 I will say to God, my rock,
"Why have you forgotten me?
Why do I go mourning
oppressed by the foe?"

12 Why are you cast down, my soul;
why groan within me?
Hope in God; I will praise him yet again,
my saving presence and my God.

Psalm 46

2 God is for us a refuge and strength,
an ever-present help in time of distress:
3 so we shall not fear though the earth should rock,
though the mountains quake to the heart of the sea;
4 even though its waters rage and foam,
even though the mountains be shaken by its tumult.

The LORD of hosts is with us:
the God of Jacob is our stronghold.

5 The waters of a river give joy to God's city,
the holy place, the abode of the Most High.
6 God is in her midst, she cannot be shaken;
God will help her at the dawning of the day.
7 Nations are in tumult, kingdoms are shaken:
he lifts his voice, the earth melts away.

8 The LORD of hosts is with us:
the God of Jacob is our stronghold.

9 Come and behold the works of the LORD,
the awesome deeds he has done on the earth.
10 He puts an end to wars over all the earth;
the bow he breaks, the spear he snaps,
the shields he burns with fire:
11 "Be still and know that I am God,
exalted over nations, exalted over earth!"

12 The LORD of hosts is with us:
the God of Jacob is our stronghold.

Psalm 47

2 All peoples, clap your hands.
Cry to God with shouts of joy!
3 For the LORD, the Most High, is awesome,
the great king over all the earth.

4 He humbles peoples under us
and nations under our feet.
5 Our heritage he chose for us,
the pride of Jacob whom he loves.

6 God has gone up with shouts of joy.
The LORD goes up with trumpet blast.
7 Sing praise for God; sing praise!
Sing praise to our king; sing praise!

8 For God is king of all the earth.
Sing praise with a hymn.
9 God is reigning over nations.
God sits upon his holy throne.

Psalm 51

3 Have mercy on me, O God,
according to your merciful love;
according to your great compassion,
blot out my transgressions.
4 Wash me completely from my iniquity,
and cleanse me from my sin.

5 My transgressions, truly I know them;
my sin is always before me.
6a Against you, you alone, have I sinned;
what is evil in your sight I have done.

9 Cleanse me with hyssop, and I shall be pure;
wash me, and I shall be whiter than snow.

10 Let me hear rejoicing and gladness,
that the bones you have crushed may exult.
11 Turn away your face from my sins,
and blot out all my guilt.

12 Create a pure heart for me, O God;
renew a steadfast spirit within me.
13 Do not cast me away from your presence;
take not your holy spirit from me.

14 Restore in me the joy of your salvation;
sustain in me a willing spirit.

17 O Lord, open my lips
and my mouth shall proclaim your praise.

19 My sacrifice to God, a broken spirit:
a broken and humbled heart,
you will not spurn, O God.

Psalm 62

2 In God alone is my soul at rest;
my salvation comes from him.
3 He alone is my rock, my salvation,
my fortress; I shall not greatly falter.

4 How long will you all attack one man
to break him down,
as though he were a tottering wall,
or a tumbling fence?

5 Their plan is only to bring down someone of prominence;
they take pleasure in lies.
With their mouth they utter blessing,
but in their heart they curse.

6 In God alone be at rest, my soul,
for my hope is from him.
7 He alone is my rock, my salvation,
my fortress; never shall I falter.

8 In God is my salvation and glory,
my rock of strength;
in God is my refuge.
9 Trust him at all times, O people.
Pour out your hearts before him,
for God is our refuge.

11 Do not put your trust in oppression,
nor vain hopes on plunder.
Even if riches increase,
set not your heart on them.

12 For God has said only one thing;
only two have I heard:
that to God alone belongs power,
13 and to you, Lord, merciful love;
and that you repay each one
according to his deeds.

Psalm 63

2 O God, you are my God; at dawn I seek you;
for you my soul is thirsting.
For you my flesh is pining,
like a dry, weary land without water.
3 I have come before you in the sanctuary,
to behold your strength and your glory.

4 Your loving mercy is better than life;
my lips will speak your praise.
5 I will bless you all my life;
in your name I will lift up my hands.
6 My soul shall be filled as with a banquet;
with joyful lips, my mouth shall praise you.

8 For you have been my strength;
in the shadow of your wings I rejoice.
9 My soul clings fast to you;
your right hand upholds me.

Psalm 67

2 May God be gracious and bless us
and let his face shed its light upon us.
3 So will your ways be known upon earth
and all nations learn your salvation.

4 Let the peoples praise you, O God;
let all the peoples praise you.

5 Let the nations be glad and shout for joy;
with uprightness you rule the peoples,
you guide the nations on earth.

6 Let the peoples praise you, O God;
let all the peoples praise you.

7 The earth has yielded its fruit
for God, our God, has blessed us.
8 May God still give us his blessing
that all the ends of the earth may revere him.

Psalm 71

1 In you, O Lord, I take refuge;
let me never be put to shame.
2 In your uprightness, rescue me, free me;
incline your ear to me and save me.

3 Be my rock, my constant refuge,
a mighty stronghold to save me,
for you are my rock, my stronghold.
4a My God, free me from the hand of the wicked.

5 It is you, O Lord, who are my hope,
my trust, O Lord, from my youth.
6 On you I have leaned from my birth;
from my mother's womb, you have drawn me forth.
At all times I give you praise.

15 My mouth will tell of your justice,
and all the day long of your salvation,
though I can never tell it all.

17 O God, you have taught me from my youth,
and I proclaim your wonders still.

Psalm 72

O God, give your judgment to the king,
to a king's son your justice,
2 that he may judge your people in justice,
and your poor in right judgment.

3 May the mountains bring forth peace for the people,
and the hills bear peace in uprightness.
4 May he defend the poor of the people,
and save the children of the needy,
and crush the oppressor.

5 He shall endure like the sun and the moon
through all generations.
6 He shall descend like rain on the meadow,
like showers that water the earth.
7 In his days justice shall flourish,
and great peace till the moon is no more.

8 He shall rule from sea to sea,
from the River to the bounds of the earth.
9 Let the desert dwellers fall before him,
and his enemies lick the dust.

12 For he shall rescue the needy when they cry,
the poor who have no one to help.
13 He will have pity on the weak and the needy,
and save the lives of the needy.
14 From oppression and violence he redeems their life;
to him their blood is dear.

15 Long may he live, and the gold of Sheba be given him.
They shall pray for him without ceasing,
and bless him all the day.

17 May his name endure forever,
his name continue like the sun.
Every tribe shall be blest in him,
all nations shall call him blessed.

Psalm 80

2 O shepherd of Israel, hear us,
you who lead Joseph like a flock:
enthroned on the cherubim, shine forth
3 upon Ephraim, Benjamin, Manasseh.
Rouse up your might and come to save us.

4 Bring us back, O God;
let your face shine forth, and we shall be saved.

9 You brought a vine out of Egypt;
you drove out the nations and planted it.
10 Before it you cleared the ground;
it took root and filled the land.

18 May your hand be on the man at your right hand,
the son of man you have confirmed as your own.
19 And we shall never forsake you again;
give us life that we may call upon your name.

20 Bring us back, O LORD God of hosts;
let your face shine forth, and we shall be saved.

Psalm 84

2 How lovely is your dwelling place,
O LORD of hosts.
3 My soul is longing and yearning
for the courts of the LORD.
My heart and my flesh cry out
to the living God.

4 Even the sparrow finds a home,
and the swallow a nest for herself
in which she sets her young, at your altars,
O LORD of hosts, my king and my God.

5 Blessed are they who dwell in your house,
forever singing your praise.
6 Blessed the people whose strength is in you,
whose heart is set on pilgrim ways.

7 As they go through the Baca Valley,
they make it a place of springs;
the autumn rain covers it with pools.
8 They walk with ever-growing strength;
the God of gods will appear in Zion.

9 O LORD God of hosts, hear my prayer;
give ear, O God of Jacob.
10 Turn your eyes, O God, our shield;
look on the face of your anointed.

11 One day within your courts
is better than a thousand elsewhere.
The threshold of the house of my God
I prefer to the dwellings of the wicked.

12 For the LORD God is a sun, a shield;
the LORD will give us his favor and glory.
He will not withhold any good
to those who walk without blame.

13 O LORD of hosts, how blessed
is the man who trusts in you!

Psalm 85

8 Show us, O LORD, your mercy,
and grant us your salvation.

10 His salvation is near for those who fear him,
and his glory will dwell in our land.

11 Mercy and faithfulness have met;
justice and peace have kissed.
12 Faithfulness shall spring from the earth,
and justice look down from heaven.

13 Also the LORD will bestow his bounty,
and our earth shall yield its increase.
14 Righteousness will march before him,
and guide his steps on the way.

Psalm 91

1 He who dwells in the shelter of the Most High,
and abides in the shade of the Almighty,
2 says to the LORD, "My refuge,
my stronghold, my God in whom I trust!"

3a He will free you from the snare of the fowler;
4bc and under his wings you will find refuge.
His faithfulness is buckler and shield.

5 You will not fear the terror of the night,
nor the arrow that flies by day,
6 nor the plague that prowls in the darkness,
nor the scourge that lays waste at noon.

9 For you, O LORD, are my refuge.
You have made the Most High your dwelling.

10 Upon you no evil shall fall,
no plague approach your tent.
11 For you has he commanded his angels
to keep you in all your ways.

12 They shall bear you upon their hands,
lest you strike your foot against a stone.

15 When he calls on me, I will answer him;
I will be with him in distress;
I will deliver him, and give him glory.

Psalm 95

1 Come, let us ring out our joy to the LORD;
hail the rock who saves us.
2 Let us come into his presence, giving thanks;
let us hail him with a song of praise.

3 A mighty God is the LORD,
a great king above all gods.
4 In his hand are the depths of the earth;
the heights of the mountains are his.
5 To him belongs the sea, for he made it,
and the dry land that he shaped by his hand.

6 O come; let us bow and bend low.
Let us kneel before the LORD who made us,
7 for he is our God, and we the people,
the people of his pasture, the flock of his hand.

O that today you would listen to his voice!
8 "Harden not your hearts as at Meribah,
as on that day at Massah in the desert
9 when your forebears put me to the test;
when they tried me, though they saw my work.

10 For forty years I abhorred that generation,
and I said, 'Their heart goes astray;
this people does not know my ways.'
11 Then I took an oath in my anger,
'Never shall they enter my rest.'"

Psalm 96

1 O sing a new song to the LORD;
sing to the LORD, all the earth.
2 O sing to the LORD; bless his name.

Proclaim his salvation day by day.
3 Tell among the nations his glory,
and his wonders among all the peoples.

4 For the LORD is great and highly to be praised,
to be feared above all gods.

6 In his presence are majesty and splendor,
strength and honor in his holy place

7 Ascribe to the LORD, you families of peoples,
ascribe to the LORD glory and power;
8a ascribe to the LORD the glory of his name.

11 Let the heavens rejoice and earth be glad;
let the sea and all within it thunder praise.
12 Let the field and all it bears exult.

Then will all the trees of the wood shout for joy
13 at the presence of the LORD, for he comes,
he comes to judge the earth.
He will judge the world with justice,
and the peoples with faithfulness.

Psalm 97

1 The LORD is king, let earth rejoice;
let the many islands be glad.

8 Zion hears and is glad;
the daughters of Judah rejoice
because of your judgments, O LORD.

9 For you indeed are the LORD,
most high above all the earth,
exalted far above all gods.

11 Light shines forth for the just one,
and joy for the upright of heart.
12 Rejoice in the LORD, all you just;
to the memory of his holiness give thanks.

Psalm 98

1 O sing a new song to the LORD,
for he has worked wonders.
His right hand and his holy arm
have brought salvation.

2 The LORD has made known his salvation,
has shown his deliverance to the nations.
3ab He has remembered his merciful love
and his truth for the house of Israel.

4 Shout to the LORD, all the earth;
break forth into joyous song,
and sing out your praise.

5a Sing psalms to the LORD with the harp.
6 With trumpets and the sound of the horn,
raise a shout before the King, the LORD.

7 Let the sea and all within it thunder;
the world, and those who dwell in it.
8 Let the rivers clap their hands,
and the hills ring out their joy
9ab at the presence of the LORD, for he comes,
he comes to judge the earth.

Psalm 100

Cry out with joy to the LORD, all the earth.
2 Serve the LORD with gladness.
Come before him, singing for joy.

3 Know that he, the LORD, is God.
He made us; we belong to him.
We are his people, the sheep of his flock.

4 Enter his gates with thanksgiving
and his courts with songs of praise.
Give thanks to him, and bless his name.

5 Indeed, how good is the LORD,
eternal his merciful love.
He is faithful from age to age.

Psalm 103

Bless the LORD, O my soul,
and all within me, his holy name.
2 Bless the LORD, O my soul,
and never forget all his benefits.

3 It is the LORD who forgives all your sins,
who heals every one of your ills,
4 who redeems your life from the grave,
who crowns you with mercy and compassion,
5 who fills your life with good things,
renewing your youth like an eagle's.

6 The LORD does deeds of justice,
gives full justice to all who are oppressed.
7 He made known his ways to Moses,
and his deeds to the children of Israel.

8 The LORD is compassionate and gracious,
slow to anger and rich in mercy.
9 He will not always find fault;
nor persist in his anger forever.
10 He does not treat us according to our sins,
nor repay us according to our faults.

21 Bless the LORD, all his hosts,
his servants, who do his will.
22 Bless the LORD, all his works,
in every place where he rules.
Bless the LORD, O my soul!

Psalm 104

1 Bless the LORD, O my soul!
O LORD my God, how great you are,
clothed in majesty and honor,
2a wrapped in light as with a robe!

5 You set the earth on its foundation,
immovable from age to age.
6 You wrapped it with the depths like a cloak;
the waters stood higher than the mountains.

10 You make springs gush forth in the valleys;
they flow in between the hills.
12 There the birds of heaven build their nests;
from the branches they sing their song.

24 How many are your works, O LORD!
In wisdom you have made them all.
The earth is full of your creatures.

35c Bless the LORD, O my soul.

Psalm 105

1 Give thanks to the LORD; proclaim his name.
Make known his deeds among the peoples.

2 O sing to him, sing his praise;
tell all his wonderful works!
3 Glory in his holy name;
let the hearts that seek the LORD rejoice.

4 Turn to the LORD and his strength;
constantly seek his face.
5 Remember the wonders he has done,
his marvels and his words of judgment.

8 He remembers his covenant forever:
the promise he ordained for a thousand generations,
9 the covenant he made with Abraham,
the oath he swore to Isaac.

Psalm 111

1bc I will praise the LORD with all my heart,
in the meeting of the just and the assembly.
2 Great are the works of the LORD,
to be pondered by all who delight in them.

3 Majestic and glorious his work;
his justice stands firm forever.
4 He has given us a memorial of his wonders.
The LORD is gracious and merciful.

5 He gives food to those who fear him;
keeps his covenant ever in mind.
6 His mighty works he has shown to his people
by giving them the heritage of nations.

7 His handiwork is justice and truth;
his precepts are all of them sure,
8 standing firm forever and ever,
wrought in uprightness and truth.

9 He has sent redemption to his people,
and established his covenant forever.
Holy his name, to be feared.

10 The fear of the LORD is the beginning of wisdom;
understanding marks all who attain it.
His praise endures forever!

Psalm 115

1 Not to us, O LORD, not to us,
but to your name give the glory,
for your merciful love and fidelity.
2 Why should the nations say:
"Where is their God?"

3 But our God is in the heavens;
he does whatever he wills.
4 Their idols are silver and gold,
the work of human hands.

5 They have mouths but they cannot speak;
they have eyes but they cannot see.
6 They have ears but they cannot hear;
they have nostrils but they cannot smell.

7 They have hands but they cannot feel;
they have feet but they cannot walk.
They make no sound from their throats.
8 Their makers will come to be like them,
as will all who trust in them.

9 House of Israel, trust in the LORD;
he is their help and their shield.
10 House of Aaron, trust in the LORD;
he is their help and their shield.
11 Those who fear the LORD, trust in the LORD;
he is their help and their shield.

12 The LORD remembers us, and he will bless us;
he will bless the house of Israel.
He will bless the house of Aaron.

13 He will bless those who fear the LORD,
the little no less than the great.
14 To you may the LORD grant increase,
to you and all your children.

15 May you be blest by the LORD,
the maker of heaven and earth.
16 The heavens, the heavens belong to the LORD,
but to the children of Adam, he has given the earth.

17 The dead shall not praise the LORD,
nor those who go down into silence.
18 But we who live bless the LORD
both now and forevermore.
Alleluia!

Psalm 118

1 Give praise to the LORD, for he is good;
his mercy endures forever.

2 Let the house of Israel say,
"His mercy endures forever."
3 Let the house of Aaron say,
"His mercy endures forever."
4 Let those who fear the LORD say,
"His mercy endures forever."

5 I called to the LORD in my distress;
the LORD has answered and freed me.

19 Open to me the gates of righteousness:
I will enter and thank the LORD.

22 The stone that the builders rejected
has become the cornerstone.
23 By the LORD has this been done,
a marvel in our eyes.
24 This is the day the LORD has made;
let us rejoice in it and be glad.

25 We beseech you, O LORD, grant salvation;
we beseech you, O LORD, grant success.

28a You are my God, I praise you.
29 Give praise to the LORD, for he is good;
his mercy endures forever.

Psalm 121

I lift up my eyes to the mountains;
from where shall come my help?
2 My help shall come from the LORD,
who made heaven and earth.

3 He will keep your foot from stumbling.
Your guard will never slumber.
4 No, he sleeps not nor slumbers,
Israel's guard.

5 The LORD your guard, the LORD your shade
at your right hand.
6 By day the sun shall not smite you,
nor the moon in the night.

7 The LORD will guard you from evil;
he will guard your soul.
8 The LORD will guard your going and coming,
both now and forever.

Psalm 122

I rejoiced when they said to me,
"Let us go to the house of the LORD."
2 And now our feet are standing
within your gates, O Jerusalem.

3 Jerusalem is built as a city
bonded as one together.
4 It is there that the tribes go up,
the tribes of the LORD,
as it is decreed for Israel,
to give thanks to the name of the LORD.

5 There were set the thrones for judgment,
the thrones of the house of David.
6 For the peace of Jerusalem pray,
"May they prosper, those who love you."
7 May peace abide in your walls,
and security be in your towers.

8 For the sake of my family and friends,
let me say, "Peace upon you."
9 For the sake of the house of the LORD, our God,
I will seek good things for you.

Psalm 126

1 When the LORD brought back the exiles of Zion,
we thought we were dreaming.
2 Then was our mouth filled with laughter;
on our tongues, songs of joy.

Then they said among the nations,
"What great deeds the LORD worked for them!"
3 What great deeds the LORD worked for us!
Indeed, we were glad.

4 Bring back our exiles, O LORD,
as streams in the Negeb.
5 Those who are sowing in tears
will sing when they reap.

6 They go out, they go out, full of tears,
bearing seed for the sowing;
they come back, they come back with a song,
bearing their sheaves.

Psalm 130

Out of the depths I cry to you, O LORD;
2 Lord, hear my voice!
O let your ears be attentive
to the sound of my pleadings.

3 If you, O LORD, should mark iniquities,
Lord, who could stand?
4 But with you is found forgiveness,
that you may be revered.

5 I long for you, O LORD,
my soul longs for his word.
6 My soul awaits the LORD
more than watchmen for daybreak.

More than watchmen for daybreak,
7 let Israel hope for the LORD.
For with the LORD there is mercy,
in him is plentiful redemption.
8 It is he who will redeem Israel
from all its iniquities.

Psalm 138

I thank you, LORD, with all my heart;
you have heard the words of my mouth.
In the presence of the angels I praise you.
2 I bow down toward your holy temple.

I give thanks to your name
for your merciful love and your faithfulness.
For you have exalted over all
your name and your promise.
3 On the day I called, you answered me;
you increased the strength of my soul.

4 All earth's kings shall thank you, O LORD,
when they hear the words of your mouth.
5 They shall sing of the ways of the LORD,
"How great is the glory of the LORD!"

6 The LORD is high, yet he looks on the lowly,
and the haughty he knows from afar.
7 You give me life though I walk amid affliction;
you stretch out your hand against the anger of my foes.

With your right hand you save me;
8 the LORD will accomplish this for me.
O LORD, your merciful love is eternal;
discard not the work of your hands.

Psalm 139

1 O LORD, you search me and you know me.
2 You yourself know my resting and my rising;
you discern my thoughts from afar.
3 You mark when I walk or lie down;
you know all my ways through and through.

4 Before ever a word is on my tongue,
you know it, O LORD, through and through.

13 For it was you who formed my inmost being,
knit me together in my mother's womb.
14 I thank you who wonderfully made me;
how wonderful are your works,
which my soul knows well!

23 O search me, God, and know my heart.
O test me, and know my thoughts.
24 See that my path is not wicked,
and lead me in the way everlasting.

Psalm 141

I have called to you, LORD; O hasten to help me!
Hear my voice when I cry to you.
2 Let my prayer be as incense before you,
the raising of my hands like an evening oblation.

3 Set, O LORD, a guard on my mouth;
keep watch at the door of my lips!
4 Do not turn my heart to things that are evil,
to wicked deeds with those who are sinners.

Never allow me to share in their feasting.
5 If the upright strike me it is kindness;
but let the oil of the wicked not anoint my head.
Let my prayer be ever against their malice.

6 If they fall into the merciless hands of their judges,
they will grasp how kind are my words.
7 As clods of earth plowed up on the ground,
so their bones were strewn at the mouth of Sheol.

8 To you my eyes are turned, O LORD, my Lord.
In you I take refuge; spare my soul!
9 From the trap they have laid for me, keep me safe;
keep me from the snares of those who do evil.

10 Let the wicked together fall into their traps,
while I pursue my way unharmed.

Psalm 148

1b Praise the LORD from the heavens;
praise him in the heights.
2 Praise him, all his angels;
praise him, all his hosts.

3 Praise him, sun and moon;
praise him, all shining stars.
4 Praise him, highest heavens,
and the waters above the heavens.

5 Let them praise the name of the LORD.
He commanded: they were created.
6 He established them forever and ever,
gave a law which shall not pass away.

7 Praise the LORD from the earth,
sea creatures and all ocean depths,
8 fire and hail, snow and mist,
stormy winds that fulfill his command;

9 mountains and all hills,
fruit trees and all cedars,
10 beasts, both wild and tame,
creeping things and birds on the wing;

11 kings of the earth and all peoples,
princes and all judges of the earth,
12 young men and maidens as well,
the old and the young together.

13 Let them praise the name of the LORD,
for his name alone is exalted,
his splendor above heaven and earth.

14 He exalts the strength of his people.
He is the praise of all his faithful,
the praise of the children of Israel,
of the people to whom he is close.